MUSIC AND SENTIMENT

CHARLES ROSEN
MUSIC AND SENTIMENT

YALE UNIVERSITY PRESS
NEW HAVEN AND LONDON

Published with assistance from the Annie Burr Lewis Fund

For information about this and other Yale University Press publications please contact:
U.S. Office: sales.press@yale.edu   yalebooks.com
Europe Office: sales@yaleup.co.uk   www.yalebooks.co.uk

Set in Arno Pro by IDSUK (DataConnection) Ltd
Printed in the United States of America

Library of Congress Cataloging-in-Publication Data

Rosen, Charles, 1927-
  Music and sentiment / Charles Rosen.
    p. cm.
  Includes index.
  ISBN 978-0-300-12640-2
1. Music—Philosophy and aesthetics. 2. Music—History and criticism. I. Title.
  ML3845.R69 2010
  781'.11–dc22

                                                                    2010016214

ISBN 978-0-300-12640-2

A catalogue record for this book is available from the British Library.

10 9 8 7 6 5 4 3 2 1

For Kristina Muxfeldt

Contents

Preface

T HIS book was written from the conviction that understanding music does not come from memorizing an esoteric
code. Many aspects of music, of course, benefit from a long
study, but grasping its emotional or dramatic meaning is
either immediate or requires only becoming familiar with it.
Understanding music in the most basic sense simply means
enjoying it when you hear it. It is true that with music that is
unfamiliar and seems alien at first hearing, this requires a
few repeated experiences of it and, indeed, a certain amount
of good will to risk new sensations. It is, nevertheless, rare
that specialized knowledge is required for the spontaneous
enjoyment that is the reason for the existence of music.
However, specialized study can bring rewards by allowing
us to comprehend why we take pleasure in hearing what we
appreciate best, and can enlighten us on the way music acts
upon us to provide delight.

These chapters began as the William T. Patten Lectures at
the University of Indiana at Bloomington in the year 2002.

I enjoyed my brief stay there very much, as it is one of the most impressive centers of the study of music, with an astonishing range of activity.

I have been less concerned with identifying the sentiments represented by the music than with the radical changes in the methods of representation throughout two centuries, as these changes reveal important aspects of the history of style. In addition, seeing how the sentiment is represented is more important to our comprehension of the music than putting a name tag on its meaning. In fact, the significance of the music's sense is best clarified when we know the different ways that it could be revealed.

I am deeply indebted to Robert Marshall, emeritus professor of Brandeis University, for sharing his wisdom on the subject. I owe special thanks to Professor Kristina Muxfeldt of the University of Indiana at Bloomington for all her generous aid and friendship. I would never have written any book after my university thesis without the stimulus and help of Professor Henri Zerner of Harvard University. I owe a great debt to Malcolm Gerratt at Yale University Press, and am very grateful to the press for all its encouragement and patience.

Prologue

IN Shakespeare's *The Merchant of Venice,* act V, scene 1, we find this exchange between the two young lovers:

JESSICA I am never merry when I hear sweet music

LORENZO The reason is, your spirits are attentive

The opening of the finale of Beethoven's 'Emperor' Concerto provides a splendid example of the kind of theme that is the inspiration for this book. A completely unified theme that hangs together beautifully, it nevertheless portrays vividly a series of contrasting sentiments in a succession that amounts to a small narrative:

This is not always perfectly realized in performance, due to an error in the tempo marking that has taken almost two centuries to correct. The correct tempo is not simply *Allegro*, as most editions have it, but *Allegro, ma non troppo*. The slightly slower tempo is necessary to make clear the radical contrast between the rhythmically complex, heavily pedalled *fortissimo* fanfare of the first two bars and the simple German dance rhythm (*Teutscher* or *Allemande*) of bars 3 and 4, now soft and certainly intended to be performed with a lilting *grazioso*. After these four bars are repeated, a third sentiment is introduced with the indication of *espressivo* still within the soft dynamics of bars 3 and 4 – in Beethoven, as in most of his contemporaries, *espressivo* generally implied a slight slack ening or freedom of tempo. This *espressivo* lasts for two bars and leads directly into a new and different affective atmos phere, a more boisterous version of the simple German dance rhythm. The *espressivo* quickly returns: and since it is now marked *crescendo*, I assume that an initial return to the dynamic of *piano* is intended at first, but the new indication of *crescendo* reduces the contrast with the previous bars made by the first appearance of the *espressivo* phrase. The orchestra at last takes over the theme, and reduces the contrast between bars 1 to 2 and 3 to 4, playing the whole theme *forte* with much more agitated inner voices. The graceful lilt of bars 3 and 4 is now assimilated to the decisive energy of bars 1 and 2. All the expressive details of the piano's fourteen bars are reduced to a uniform *forte*. This overriding of the affective contrasts and oppositions within the theme is an essential trait of the style of the period.

It is intriguing that such a theme that combines different sentiments with strong contrast does not exist in music before the last decades of the eighteenth century. And it largely ceases to exist after the death of Beethoven. It is then replaced by a different and entirely new kind of complexity in the illustration of sentiment, while a still more novel method of representation appears at the end of the nineteenth century. The following pages examine how the change in representing sentiment in music was developed, and what it could mean for the conception of music – its style and its function.

In order to make the subject manageable, I shall treat mainly the initial presentation of a theme, as any extensive account of the way the meanings of motifs change in the course of a work would carry us too far afield, although on a few occasions I shall have to mention these developments briefly.

I

Fixing the Meaning of Complex Signs

DEALING with the representation of sentiment in music, I shall not often attempt to put a name to the sentiment, so readers who expect to find out what they are supposed to feel when they listen to a given piece of music will be inevitably disappointed. Happily, however, it is mostly quite obvious. That is: some music is sad and some is jolly. Sometimes it is ferocious or funereal and sometimes tender – and there is little difficulty in deciding what sentiment is being represented (but somewhat later we shall discuss the rare occasion and the odd reason for a mistake to be made in our response). The frivolity of naming the sentiments arises largely from the fact – as Mendelssohn once famously observed – that music is much more precise in these matters than language. The communication of information is one of the most important of the many different functions of language, but not of music (you cannot, for example, by purely musical means, ask your listeners to meet you tomorrow at Grand Central Station at 4 o'clock).

However, language must seek out poetic methods even to approach at a distance the subtlety and emotional resonance of music.

The power of music to illustrate sentiment and to awaken emotion in the auditors has been recognized and asserted for centuries, indeed for millennia. In his copy of the 1588 edition of his *Essais*, Montaigne added the following anecdote:

> Pythagoras, being in the company of young men, and sensing that, excited by the festivity, they were plotting to violate a respectable house, ordered the band to play in a different mode, and by a heavy, severe and spondaic music [that is, a poetic rhythm in which each single syllable is accented], cast a spell quite sweetly over their ardor and put it to sleep.
> *(Pythagoras, estant en compagnie de jeunes hommes, lesquels il sentit complotter, eschauffez de la feste, d'aller violer une maison pudique, commanda à la menstrière de changer de ton, et, par une musique poisante, severe, et spondaïque, enchanta tout doucement leur ardeur, et l'endormit.)*

We cannot, however, expect music to be always so effective for crowd control.

Shakespeare even asserts improbably (*The Merchant of Venice*, V, 1) that the sound of a trumpet will calm agitated wild colts. There is, indeed, a long tradition acknowledging the emotional power of music. We should remember, nevertheless, that directly experiencing a sentiment in life is very different from experiencing that sentiment represented by a work of music, as our admiration for the art of the representation will have a distancing effect. Listening to the 'Lacrymosa' of the Verdi Requiem, we enjoy our grief.

When the represented sentiment or affect – to use the old word – is evident, of course, I shall not deliberately avoid naming it, but in any case the identification of the sentiment is not my essential purpose. What will concern us here is the nature of the representation – whether the sentiment is unified or combined with other opposing sentiments, whether the force of the representation is steady and unchanging, and whether it increases or diminishes in intensity as the motif proceeds, and whether this increase is rapid or gradual. It will also be relevant to consider the way that a specific motif representing one sentiment is transformed into the representation of another, and to become aware of the methods of transformation. Naming the sentiments evoked is problematic not only because the evocation clearly defined by the music may be only coarsely and doubtfully translatable into language but also because the representation of sentiment, as the history of music proceeds, often becomes more unstable and dynamic, and, in addition, a motif may carry a different affective meaning depending upon its position in the musical form. In the simplest case, a motif repeated does not have exactly the same meaning the second time, and this will even slightly alter the significance of the first appearance in the listener's memory.

At the heart of the discussion is the radical change in the means of representation of sentiment throughout history. To take one example, the power of Wagner's music in the representation of erotic passion has been observed (with admiration or horror) from the first appearance of *Tristan*, but given the example of the duets of Guglielmo and Dorabella in *Così fan tutte* and of Don Giovanni and Zerlina in *Don Giovanni*, a lover of Mozart is not disposed to believe that Mozart did not do equally well. Nevertheless, as powerful as it may be, a love duet by Mozart can only last a few minutes, and drawing it out for three-quarters of an hour was beyond the musical techniques available to him. Of course, Mozart's eroticism is rather different from Wagner's, if no less salacious. It might be reasonably claimed, I suppose, that an erotic sentiment evoked so succinctly and economically is not the same as one that can build up over a long stretch of time, but this, while undoubtedly true, only goes to show the superficiality of trying to deal with the subject simply by putting a name to the emotion illustrated.

In opera, of course, a sentiment is given an identity tag by the libretto, but it is a fallacy of opera criticism to consider the literary text as primary and the music as an illustration or enhancement of the text. By the end of the eighteenth century, after the radical development of operatic style, the more interesting musical theorists, like Wilhelm Heinse, would claim that the music was primary and the words illustrated the music. However, a more sensible approach assumes music and text as an indissoluble whole that must be understood together in a reciprocal relationship. The text is primary only in the sense that it was written first – and sometimes not even that was true, as composers often demanded words for previously composed vocal lines, and also ordered exactly the kind of text that they needed for the music they had in mind. With pure instrumental music, believing that the naming of the sentiment portrayed is an adequate account of the significance of the music only transfers to the instrumental field the difficulties and ambiguities of operatic criticism.

In eighteenth-century music, with which we shall begin our discussion, it must be understood from the outset that affective meaning is created by the relation of consonance and dissonance: these terms do not indicate pleasant and unpleasant musical noises, but are part of the grammar of eighteenth-century tonality. A dissonance is not an ugly sound (some dissonances will seem exquisitely beautiful to any listener) but an interval or chord that must be resolved into a consonance – the basic consonance being the chord of the tonic triad, whose most important intervals are the octave and the fifth (slightly less fundamental are the third and its inversion the sixth, also components of the triad), because they must be present or at least implicit in the last chord of a piece of tonal music of the eighteenth century. Dissonance establishes an increase in tension, and consonance a release. Strictly viewed, everything in a tonal piece is more or less dissonant except for the tonic triad with which the work must end.

It is important for dissonance to be conceived not only harmonically (or vertically) but also melodically (or horizontally). A proper tonal melody in the 1700s outlines the tonic triad and establishes its key (Mozart's great *A Musical Joke* has an example in the slow movement of an opening theme that fails to do this, and he obviously considered this to be comically and delightfully inept). The notes of a melody are dissonant and consonant in relation to each other successively, both to the basic triad implied by each phrase and to the tonic chord established at the opening; and every phrase is consonant or dissonant in relation to any subsidiary tonal centre implied by each section of the work in which it occurs. Every well-formed tonal melody establishes its own underlying harmonic structure (that is how Bach could write sonatas for solo violin and Chopin the monophonic finale of the Sonata in B flat minor). The different degrees of tension are the initial basis for the expression of sentiment of any kind.

The minor and major modes provide an interesting large-scale example of this relation of dissonance and consonance, since the minor mode was for a long time considered a form of dissonance. This is, in fact, a paradox of eighteenth-century tonality (sometimes called 'triadic tonality' as it is based on a central triad and not merely the single bass note that gives the key its name), because a modulation in the sharp or dominant direction was immediately perceptible as more dissonant (and therefore an increase in tension) than a modulation in the flat or subdominant direction. This is due to the fact that the tonic is the dominant of the subdominant: this is why the first part of a fugue by Bach, or by anyone else before 1750, generally emphasizes the dominant harmonies, reserving the subdominant for the second half of the piece, and why the exposition of a sonata from 1750 to 1800 goes always to the dominant, and never to the subdominant (unless the composer was incompetent – I have found only one example of this incompetence, from an aristocratic pupil of Haydn), and the subdominant is reserved for later in the work, either the development, or, even more often and traditionally, the recapitulation – or, at times in Beethoven, the coda. The minor mode, however, was essentially a subdominant or flat colouring (as one can perceive visually at once, since going from C major to C minor entails adding three flats to the key signature).

This paradox ceased to exist after Beethoven's death, as the opposition between sharp and flat, or dominant and subdominant directions,[1] no longer had much meaning for composers in the nineteenth century, and was submerged in the increased chromaticism of the style and the reliance on mediant relationships. We may even conclude that eighteenth-century tonality was actually more complex than nineteenth-century, as harmonic dissonance was defined more strictly and elaborately. Both were more complex than the neo-tonal music of recent decades, in which any conception of dissonance between harmonic areas has disappeared. The tonal aspect largely consists of an understandable delight in using perfect triads, and all large-scale

---

[1]An eighteenth-century theorist like Koch discusses it in his account of first-movement form, but no nineteenth-century discussion of sonata form mentions it, as far as I know. Of composers, only Brahms retained some understanding of it.

richness of expressive tension has been drained away, the rich subtlety of eighteenth-century tonality now only a distant memory.

At the heart of any discussion of the representation of sentiment in music is the question: 'How did the eighteenth-century listener learn to comprehend this complex system?' The answer is certainly not by studying the theory of music. The system was learned the way children learn language, by listening to their parents and to their older siblings and friends, not by studying grammar and syntax. It is true that a comprehension of how literary style works may benefit from a study of rhetoric, but there is a very high level of understanding our literary culture that can be attained without discussing metaphor, simile, oxymoron or syzygy, and so forth, and we can be deeply affected by our reading without any of that, in much the same way that the average listener can be deeply moved by Mozart's representation of sentiment without being able to explain how he does it. I make this very obvious point as the basis for another conclusion. Any explanation of how a composer can move his listeners that relies upon their having previously learnt some kind of special code is bound to be inadequate or simply wrong.

✦ ✦ ✦ ✦ ✦

Unfortunately, most discussions of musical sentiment that I have ever seen seek to establish such a code, a symbolic system, even a relatively esoteric one with which listeners in the past were supposed to become acquainted. Indeed, in learning a language we are expected to learn to recognize the traditional meanings of a great many words. However, the trouble is that music is essentially a poor system of communication, precisely because it has a rather weak and ill-defined vocabulary, although a very rich and powerful grammar and syntax. The poverty of the musical vocabulary was already appreciated as long ago as 1751, when Denis Diderot, in an appendix to his *Letter on the Deaf and Dumb*, discussed the nature of music as a symbolic language ('hieroglyphic' is his term) and its employment in the inspiration of emotion:

In music, the pleasure of sensation depends on a particular disposition not only of the ear but of the entire nervous system.... In addition, music has a greater need to find in us these favourable dispositions of the organs than painting or poetry Its hieroglyph is so light and so fleeting, it is so easy to lose it or to misinterpret it, that the most beautiful movement of a symphony would have little effect if the infallible and subtle pleasure of sensation pure and simple were not infinitely above that of an often ambiguous expression.... How does it happen then that of the three arts that imitate Nature, the one whose expression is the most arbitrary and the least precise speaks the most powerfully to the soul?

(*En musique, le plaisir de la sensation dépend d'une disposition particulière non seulement de l'oreille, mais de tout le système des nerfs.... Au reste, la musique a plus besoin de trouver en nous ces favorables dispositions d'organes, que ni la peinture, ni la poésie. Son hieroglyphe est si léger et si fugitif, il est si facile de le perdre ou de le mésinterpréter, que le plus beau morceau de symphonie ne feroit pas un grand effet si le plaisir infaillible et subtil de la sensation pure et simple n'étoit infiniment audessus de celui d'une expression souvent équivoque. . . . Comment se fait-il donc que des trois arts imitateurs de la Nature, celui dont l'expression est la plus arbitraire et la moins précise parle le plus fortement à l'âme?)*

The weakness of the individual elements of music as bearers of meaning, their ambiguity and imprecision – the motifs, the harmonies, easy to misinterpret when taken out of context – is well asserted here. It implies the absolute importance of context for determining meaning. For this reason, Diderot's 'sensation pure and simple' is too naive: what is perceived in listening is not merely noise, but relationships, regularity of beat, *rubato*, symmetry, repetition, dissonance and release, and so on – and we take pleasure in all this just as a lover of poetry, without naming the devices, takes pleasure in rhyme, assonance and sound play – and this ends by giving us access to the meaning. What we perceive, consciously or unconsciously, is pattern, an ordering of sound; that is why some contemporaries of Diderot (and of Haydn) would claim that music and dance are the oldest forms of language – and gardening is older than agriculture (!) – the will to create order being the condition for the foundation of language or of culture and society.

It is by underestimating the ambiguity of the musical vocabulary and exaggerating its precision that investigations of music and sentiment most often founder. The best-known of these is Deryck Cooke's *The Language of Music*. It is not that Cooke is mistaken about the affective significance of the examples of tonal music he discusses, but that then – unfortunately or fortunately – everyone else, learned or unlearned, is generally right, too. I do not want this populist statement to be misunderstood: of course there are many aspects of music that can be best appreciated only with training, the contrapuntal learning in Bach fugues and canons, the ability of Haydn to play with the conventions of form of his time to create a series of shocks, some humorous, some dramatic, or the way that Beethoven in writing variations will often not decorate the theme but radically transform it by stripping it down to its essential tonal skeleton. To be sure, even some of this knowledge might, in fact, be arrived at merely by intensive listening and not solely by professional training. Nevertheless, what needs no study at all but just an easily acquired reasonable familiarity with the style is the perception of whether a piece of music is sad, grave, majestic, jokey, passionate, stormy, lyrical, cajoling, tranquil, disquieting, or menacing. In the movies, we know without being told whether the music is describing the innocent heroine being strapped to the railroad tracks or the villain tying her down.

Cooke thought he could explain the provoking of senti-ment in the listener by the existence of a traditional repertory of motifs, the contour of each motif basically determining the affective significance. For example, melodies in the minor mode starting on the fifth degree and descending stepwise to the leading-tone were indicators of grief for him, and he quoted the *Adagio ma non troppo* from the finale of Beethoven's Sonata in A flat major op. 110:

We may confirm, if need be, that this is indeed a portrayal of grief, since Beethoven labels it *Arioso dolente*. Unfortunately, Beethoven's scherzo of this very sonata has a principal theme in the minor mode as well that also descends from the fifth degree stepwise to the leading-tone:

And this is far from grief-stricken but is jolly and folksy, and perhaps a touch sinister or satirical owing to the diminished sevenths in bar 3.

Where does the distinction lie? In the very different rhythmic and harmonic configuration of the descending steps of the theme in the two movements, as well as the tempo and the accompaniment. In the *Arioso dolente*, the second note, the D flat, is sustained as a dissonance against the tonic harmony and resolved into the C flat; the next degree, the B flat, is also dissonant to the repeated harmony and resolved more rapidly and urgently upward to the C flat, increasing the tension. The final step is the placement of the tonic note itself, the A flat, but now this, too, is rendered dissonant by the change of harmony to the dominant in the bass, and the dissonance is sustained longer until the proper resolution. In sum, except for the first note of the theme, the E flat, every note on a strong beat is dissonant and satisfactorily resolved into a consonance. The atmosphere of grief is rendered not by the succession of pitches of the theme but by the interaction of the stepwise descent with the harmony, by the heavy pulsating bass like agitated heartbeats, and by the way the rhythm is varied into a hesitant *rubato* that becomes gradually more intense. The harmony acts like gravity on the melody: it pulls the D flat towards the C flat, forces the A flat down to the G.

Essential to the tradition is the way that the notes of this melody are arranged rhythmically by the composer to imply and create dissonances against each other. The D flat is dissonant to the C flat, the B flat to the C flat, and the A flat to the G; the gradual massing of dissonance endows this opening phrase with an intense expressive charge. Each of the dissonant notes is essentially an *appoggiatura*, which is the simplest bearer of tonal pathos from Sebastian Bach to Verdi, as we can see from Leonora's scena in the last act of *Il trovatore*, which displays the standard operatic rendition of sobbing:

In Beethoven's scherzo of op. 110, on the other hand, the strong beats of the first, second and fourth bars are all consonant; the third bar, although it has a dissonant diminished seventh harmony, is not sustained until its resolution into the dominant of the fourth bar, but is an energetically repeated chord which adds energy but avoids pathos. The particular motif used in these two movements by Beethoven may have been used by others for pathos, certainly by Mozart at the opening of the finale of the Viola Quintet in G minor, a movement that, if sensitively played, may easily elicit tears from the listeners:

Nevertheless, as Beethoven demonstrates, this series of pitches may be given a very different affective significance.

In short, the succession of pitches of the motif of the Adagio may indeed be used, as Cooke observes, to signify grief, but it can also be employed to mean more or less whatever else a composer chooses to do with it.

Liszt, in his Sonata for piano, can make any one of his motifs sound successively diabolical, amorous, religioso, majestic, transcendent, or what you will; Wagner and Richard Strauss can do the same with their leitmotifs. This should be enough to demonstrate the futility of a project that attempts to find a prearranged melodic code for affective meaning, but the prejudice persists that composers like Mozart or Beethoven, less chromatic than Liszt or Wagner, were somehow shackled by, or blessed with, a limited repertory of prefabricated motifs.

In much of the speculation, there is a confusion caused by one composer imitating another to accomplish a similar task. Let us take one famous example: in *Les Huguenots* by Meyerbeer, when the soprano unwillingly admits her love, the tenor replies ecstatically to the accompaniment of an excited tremolo in the strings and a vibrant solo cello, a musical effect that quickly became famous. In Verdi's *Un ballo in maschera*, too, the soprano admits that she loves the tenor King of Sweden (or Governor of Massachusetts, depending on which version of the libretto is being staged), and the impressive tremolo starts immediately, together with a melody for the solo cello and tenor. This does not mean that a string tremolo with a solo cello has become a traditional and identifiable symbol of the inadvertent admission of adulterous passion. It is a tribute paid by Verdi to the success of his predecessor, and it was a device that he knew he could use effectively and differently.

We should avoid an all-too-common error in musical research of confusing imitation with quotation. The first is only homage, and need not carry with it the significance of the earlier work, as it does not require us to recognize the model; the second, however, is a reference and we are expected to identify from where the quotation has been lifted. Imitation never requires recognition for understanding: on the contrary, what is imitated was evidently effective, and the imitation must be similarly effective without the listeners' awareness of the model. No previous knowledge is required for appreciation.

Statistics and a pile-up of examples will never be able to establish a tradition for the meaning of a simple eighteenth-century motif. All such motifs (particularly those used for opening a piece, but even subsidiary themes as well) must somehow define a tonic triad. The permutation of the twelve notes of the chromatic scale may provide a huge number of different tunes, but the three notes of the tonic triad will only give a much more modest result, and that is why so many melodies of tonal music necessarily resemble each other in their basic structure, as this structure must be convincingly perceptible in order to provide a proper tonal basis for any work. (This is what makes the popular activity of exposing the fact that composer X borrowed a tune from composer Y or Z so easy, and yet so tiresome and meaningless: every tonal motif automatically resembles hundreds of others.)

The contrast between the affective meanings of the opening phrases of Beethoven's Adagio and Scherzo of op. 110 is so great, although the initial motifs are basically identical in content, that we may easily understand how Diderot could write about the ease of misinterpreting the elements of music, even if, as I have said, misunderstanding of the emotional character of a work is actually very rare. It does occasionally occur, however, and we may glance very briefly at the topic as the causes are not complex. For example, in his 1919 biography of Mozart, Hermann Abert made something of a scandal that Schumann seemed to see in Mozart's late G minor Symphony a work only of grace and charm, where today's amateurs of Mozart find passion, despair, and even radical violence (the last certainly at the opening of the development section of the finale). Nevertheless, Schumann surely appreciated the craft of Mozart, but for him the equipoise and the serenity of the technique were of no help to his own activity as a composer or journalist, and must have seemed old-fashioned and even antipathetic as he waged his polemical campaign to make a new kind of music possible. Similarly, when Sebastian Bach came into fashion at the end of the eighteenth century, many experienced music-lovers, like Reichardt, the editor of the most influential musical review, the *Allgemeine musikalische Zeitung,* found Bach only a wonderful craftsman in counterpoint, insisting he had no feeling for sentiment and knew nothing of the human heart. A simple familiarity with Bach's work gradually made the next generation aware of its affective power, just as a closer attention to Mozart has restored to us a sense of his dramatic force. A reviewer (on a Boston paper, I think) once gave a favourable review to a short book I had written on Schoenberg, but was astonished that I thought Schoenberg's music so expressive, as the reviewer found no emotion in Schoenberg at all; this seemed peculiar to those of us who may occasionally find his music uncomfortable because of an exaggerated emotional character that borders on hysteria.

I bring this up here because there is sometimes a misunderstanding about why we enjoy certain styles of music, a belief that we relish above all the character of the sentiment, the emotional aura of the music. Yet, around 1810, when Beethoven was still very controversial, many were horrified by their first contact with his music and Goethe's friend and Mendelssohn's teacher, Georg Zelter, even described the taste for it as something like sexual perversion. After later hearings, as Zelter admitted, the majority of music lovers generally became fanatical devotees of his work. It was not because they enjoyed or approved of the sentiments that they were won over to the style, but the other way round. When they got used to the style, and felt at home with it, they were finally able to enter its emotional world.

The history of the reputation of Johann Sebastian Bach may also help us to understand an important aspect of the emotional power of music. The distinction made at first between the technical mastery of counterpoint and the power to awaken sentiment in the listener was not a distinction that stood up to examination as the experience of Bach's music grew. By 1814, E. T. A. Hoffmann would write:

There are moments – above all when I have been reading in the works of the great Sebastian Bach – in which the numerical relations, yes, the mystical rules of counterpoint, awake an inner terror.

(Es gibt Augenblicke – vorzüglich, wenn ich viel in des grossen Sebastian Bachs Werken gelesen – in denen mir die musikalischen Zahlenverhältnisse, ja die mystischen Regeln des Kontrapunkts ein inneres Grauen erwecken.)

This terror is a form of delight, a physical response to musical relations. It is not a sentiment to which one normally gives a name if one is analysing a response to the experience of music. Nevertheless, admiration of technical virtuosity, either of composition or of performance, is not simply an intellectual reaction but an emotion felt bodily. It took some decades for a familiarity and understanding of Bach's technical mastery to become so widespread that the pathos and the drama of his music were appreciated. A partial grasp, even if unconscious or only partly conscious, of technical ingenuity is a precondition for the comprehension of the affective significance of music.

✦ ✦ ✦ ✦ ✦

Early in the eighteenth century, there were collections of motifs (defined by rhythms as well as simply by pitches) – above all, that of Thomas Matheson of 1739 – that were thought helpful for the rendering of different sentiments. I am not sure if this so-called *Affektenlehre* really proved useful for many composers, but by the second half of the century, the ambiguity – or, to put it differently, the malleability – of motifs rather than any possibility of even attempting to fix a stable meaning became essential to the latest developments of musical style. Professor Daniel Heartz, however, in a lecture that I heard many years ago in San Francisco, wished to claim that a descending bass chromatic fourth in the minor mode, like the one in the Crucifixus of Bach's Mass in B minor, was a symbol of death throughout the eighteenth century, and produced a variety of examples of a descending chromatic fourth, many of them an *ostinato* bass, to illustrate his thesis. All these fourths, however, began without exception on the tonic and went to the dominant. The trouble is, there is no possibility of writing an *ostinato* bass in the eighteenth century that does anything else. So there is nothing particularly significant about the interval of a fourth, or indeed about the procedure of going from tonic to dominant, as almost all music at that time was expected to do. If a short phrase did not have a bass that went down a fourth from tonic to dominant, then it could not be repeated several times to make an *ostinato*, or the result would have been a monstrosity for the eighteenth-century ear. The only possible variant is an *ostinato* like Bach's Passacaglia that goes immediately up a fifth to the dominant and then back to the tonic, but the *ostinato* in the Crucifixus is more succinct and economical although not essentially different. It was a useful formula for writing serious music with an *ostinato* and survived for a long time:

Chaconne. J.S. Bach

TEMA. Beethoven, Variations in C minor
Allegretto.

Allegro. Schubert, Sonata in C minor

The last example puts the chromatic descent into the tenor, C, B flat, A natural, A flat, G, and Schubert may have been thinking here of the rhythm of the Beethoven Variations, but the motif was enough of a cliché that he could have found it elsewhere. None of these examples have specifically funerary implications, but of course they all sound serious. Liszt used the formula in his variations on *Weinen, Klagen*, and this does betray the odour of mortality, but the formula lingers on as late as the chaconne-style finale to the Symphony no. 4 by Brahms, although the chromatic descent in the bass is varied here by not being restricted to the bass but parcelled out to the other voices:

While the formula was a commonplace device for serious music in the minor mode, it is extravagant to believe that a chromatic descent from tonic to dominant had the same fixed symbolic meaning in all cases: it was a useful and even, at times indispensable, tonal procedure. The bass of the main theme of Chopin's 'Revolutionary' Étude op. 10 no. 12 in C minor chromatically descends a fourth from C to G: of course, revolutionaries often kill people, but there is nothing lugubrious or funereal about this piece. Heartz was naturally right about the affective character of several of the pieces he adduced. But in the end his thesis amounts only to a simple claim that slow chromatic music in the minor mode with a repeating bass is very sad or at the very least grave and serious, and that may be musicology, but it is not news.[2]

Other approaches to affective meaning in music that do not rely upon a code centred on single and simple parameters are far more fruitful, notably the wide-ranging semantic studies of Eero Tarasti, as well as Marta Grabocz's observations on the use of affective elements in constructing narrative in music, and Robert Hatten's cogent essays on the gestural aspects of tonal music. These serve as musical analysis. However, my own purpose here is more narrowly

---

[2] A more substantial proposal on a related subject is by Ellen Rosand, 'The descending Tetrachord: an Emblem of Lament', in *The Musical Quarterly*, vol. 65, no. 3, July 1979, pp. 346–59, who examines a series of vocal works from Monteverdi to Cavalli, all on texts of lamentation and using a descending *ostinato* bass. Rosand has identified and analysed an important and interesting set of works. In one small respect, however, considerations similar to those in the case of Heartz apply. The 'tetrachord' (or fourth from the tonic down to the dominant) is not a defining characteristic of these pieces, since once the composers had decided on an *ostinato* bass, they had no option other than outlining the tetrachord. On the other hand, the descending bass seems, indeed, to be the defining procedure of the genre presented, and Rosand remarks, in fact, on the freedom with which the bass was sometimes treated, occasionally rising rather than falling, although, of course, the latent presence of the tetrachord structure is inevitable throughout the examples, because that was part of the basic musical language of the time.

historical, to display the radical changes in the methods of representation of sentiment imposed on composers by changes of style over two centuries.

✦ ✦ ✦ ✦ ✦

The opening bars of Beethoven's Concerto no. 4 in G major have some exceptionally odd qualities that can show us why no isolated element of tonal music can ever give us a satisfactory approach to the expressive character of any work or of any phrase in which it may be found:

In one sense, this is an extreme example, as no harmonic dissonance is to be found here in the harmony until the last eighth note of the fourth bar, but the expressive effect of harmonic dissonance is created continually throughout the second, third and fourth bars entirely by means of rhythm, melody and phrasing. At the opening of the second bar the basic and central consonance of the tonic chord in root position appears strangely to be literally resolved into the dominant: this chord, also a perfect triad in root position, is resolved in turn back into the tonic. On the first beats of bar 3, this chord resolves by phrasing into the A minor chord of the second degree. After two bars of nothing but consonances of tonic and dominant, this has at once the effect of a dissonance, although it, too, is a triad in root position. The feeling of expressive dissonance that troubles a calm surface is increased by another new element: the dynamic, the *sforzando*; but another disturbing detail that augments the intensity is that the two-note slur of the phrasing would by tradition imply an accent on the first note and a decrescendo to the second, yet it is the second chord with the accent and the legato that imposes a feeling of effort (detach the chord on the first beat, and see how much less expressive it is, or retain the legato but remove the *sforzando* and observe how the warmth has gone out of the phrase). With the opening of the fifth bar, melody, harmony and rhythm all come together for the first time for an expressive dissonance that is resolved into the very short perfect triad of the dominant. To determine the affective character of this opening phrase by harmony alone or by melodic contour is impossible. Texture and rhythm play their part. The extreme simplicity of the harmony of the first two bars combines with the rhythmic agitation that acts to force the sense of dissonance and resolution onto the successive notes of the melody. The appoggiatura-like dissonance of the opening of the fifth bar introduces the conventional expression of a traditional half-cadence to round off the opening phrase, and the short last note gives us two beats of empty silence that will enhance the shock of the remote B major entrance chord of the orchestra. Although we cannot speak of any real contrast of sentiment with the entrance of the orchestra, the radical change of sonority and texture from solo to tutti is an essential characteristic of the style of the age.

Briefly to anticipate one of the topics that will concern us later: it is evident that the affective character of this phrase changes as it proceeds, beginning with the end of the second bar, where the doubling in the bass of the B in the melodic voice brings a new weight to the texture, and bars three and four continue to develop a more intense lyricism. Nevertheless, there is no contrast and no opposition except for the radical change of texture from solo to tutti: the affective development is gradual although complex, and it is completely integrated. The complexity of character within a single phrase was still something new in music of the early nineteenth century.

✦ ✦ ✦ ✦ ✦

In short, as we have seen, an insistence on providing a fixed meaning for single musical elements arises from a confusion between music and language – after all, music is often said to be a language, and seems to make sense just like language, so why should it not have an identifiable vocabulary, too? or it arises from a confusion between music and painting, another art that is supposed to imitate Nature and is also said to be a language.

Like music, painting does not possess all the functions and capacities of a spoken tongue, although Medieval and Renaissance painting did develop an elaborate symbolic or iconographic vocabulary. We can recognize the saints, St Peter by his keys or his being crucified upside down, St Catherine by her wheel, St Laurence by his grill, and Justice has her scales and a sword. Signs like these identifying objects in the world are present in music as well: bird song from Couperin to Beethoven, Liszt and Respighi transport us to the countryside, so do drone basses like bag-pipes, as in Beethoven's 'Pastoral' Sonata op. 28:

and, in the same work a few bars later (11 to 16), the yodel forms in the right hand give us the peasants in a Tyrolean landscape, as do the glockenspiel figures in *Die Zauberflöte*:

Soft horn calls heard as if from a distance in a forest may indicate Romantic nostalgia in Beethoven and Schubert, and louder horn calls can signify cuckoldry, as in *The Marriage of Figaro* and in *Falstaff* – but certainly not all horn fanfares, only those accompanied by a text that alludes to an unfaithful wife. Martial music naturally brings a military sense with it, modal chant and choral texture have ecclesiastical atmosphere in Beethoven quartets and in Chopin nocturnes, and drum rolls illustrate Hugo Wolf's drummer boy of the Eichendorff Lieder.

All these effects, however, are the picturesque, onomatopoetic elements of characteristic music, but abstract music continuously delineates sentiment with its everyday neutral elements, simple melodic turns of phrase, and motifs that appear everywhere and all the time. To attach a fixed affective meaning to these elements is an enterprise doomed to failure, as they change their significance at every turn in response to harmony, texture and rhythm. Harmonic significance is equally fluid, shifting from piece to piece, from phrase to phrase, and even from one end of a phrase to the other. After centuries of Romantic Italian opera, and many decades of sound movies and musical scores for silent films, perhaps a tremolo on a diminished seventh chord will signify approaching villainy to many listeners, but this is no help for understanding the music of most composers, not even that of Liszt, who tended to abuse this particular device.

Theories of painting that attach overly specific affective meanings to certain colours and to different arabesque forms have been similarly shattered when applied. Such theories when advanced by artists like Wassily Kandinsky, Paul Klee or Vincent van Gogh may perhaps be a guide to what they believed their paintings meant, although not to painting in general, and not even to whether the individual painter succeeded in conveying his meaning to the public.

As far as symbolic interpretation goes, painting has the advantage over music that some shapes have a clearly erotic appearance, except that, unless the artist can find a way to release that significance, it will not have any more effect than looking at a Rorschach test (there is, indeed, an old joke about the patient given a Rorschach test who asked the doctor afterwards if he could borrow the dirty pictures to show his wife). In music, too, composers can display the erotic potential of certain rhythmic and melodic figures, but it generally works only when accompanying a sufficiently explicit text.

One further proposal to ascribe meaning to a commonplace neutral element of tonal music has to be mentioned because it is met with frequently, but it is the least convincing of all. That is the ascription of affective meaning to certain keys or tonalities. This goes back all the way to the eighteenth century. Whatever small merit the theory had was acknowledged by Donald Francis Tovey, who swept most of the speculation aside masterfully, and I do not propose to redo his work here.

The main value of the speculation on the character of keys does not relate convincingly to the tradition of music in general or even to the music of a specific period, but lies in its calling attention to the very personal way that individual composers treated certain tonalities. Beethoven clearly had a special C minor style (and his example inspired later composers like Brahms to try something approaching it), and Mozart had his D minor style, and personal ways of treating other keys, like A major and B flat, but the practice of Mozart and Beethoven was not always systematic. Occasionally it was even confusing: Beethoven once declared that A flat was a 'barbarous' key, yet he wrote two of his most lyrical piano sonatas in it, op. 26 and op. 110, and the A flat major minuet in the Piano Trio op. 70 no. 2 in E flat major is one of his most exquisitely lovely works; Schubert even plagiarized what he perceived as some particularly Schubertian details from it. Perhaps Beethoven may have felt it to be a challenge to write lyrically in what he thought a barbarous key, but in the end we are not going to find out very much about the affective character of a work by considering its key: just listening to it will be equally if not more enabling.

Much speculation about the character of keys in the eighteenth century has been enhanced or muddied (depending on how you look at it) by questions of the tuning of keyboard instruments at that time. However Beethoven's pianos were tuned, he clearly thought in equal temperament, writing F double sharp and G natural at the same bar in different hands in the Sonata for Piano op. 78. Even when writing for string quartet, he would notate G flat in one instrument and F sharp simultaneously in another, although he knew perfectly well that string quartets did not play in equal temperament.

It has been suggested that J. S. Bach would determine the key of his piece in order to adapt its character to keyboard tunings then in use, but this idea has awkward consequences. Since he transposed a C minor fugue to C sharp minor for the second book of the *Well-Tempered Klavier*, either he was using equal temperament (not impossible at that time), or else he did not care how the piece sounded (no Werckmeister tuning will make C sharp minor sound as normal as C minor), or, alternatively, perhaps he may even have enjoyed hearing a complex chromatic piece in a tuning that was weird and ill-adapted to it. The transposition of the French Overture for publication from a basic C minor to an exotic B minor is even more puzzling (first of all he was forced to renounce the effective low bass note at a couple of the central dominant half-cadences of the dances, as his harpsichord had no low F sharp). Robert Marshall has suggested to me that, since the French Overture was published in the same volume with just the F major Italian Concerto, Bach wished the extreme tritone contrast of B minor and F major to emphasize and embody the contrast of styles; Hans Bischoff, on the other hand, believed that the change was made because with the six partitas of the first book of the *Klavierübung* and the Italian Concerto, Bach now had pieces in the keys of A, B, C, D, E, F and G, but nothing in H, the German letter for B natural (B being B flat). Both explanations seem plausible to me, and in line with Bach's symbolic and encyclopaedic cast of mind. I believe them both, and they are not incompatible. In any case, we cannot fix the character of his works by simply focusing on the keys, and although on occasion the key may have had some influence, this could be overridden.

II

Pre-Classical Sentiment

⟨~⟩

Every student (or at least every graduate student in musicology) knows that the aesthetic of the Unity of Sentiment governed the music of the early eighteenth century, and even continued to exert its influence with a few important figures as late as Carl Philipp Emanuel Bach towards the end of the century. Like most generalizations about the history of music, however, this one needs a few cavils or nuances. There is at least one kind of piece where the Unity of Sentiment had no sway in what is called the High Baroque, that is the period from 1680 to 1750. The works that escape the unity are those that seek to give the impression of improvisation, like a toccata or fantasy, and these may freely combine different affects, often in fragmentary form. Formally constructed pieces, however, were subject to the requirement of a single affect. A reigning aesthetic system commonly has no power over works that are considered to be outside the respectable canon, or that are somehow experimental in nature.[3] In formal structures, the unity of sentiment was ideally suited to the contemporary taste in rhythm and texture. With few exceptions in J. S. Bach's music, for example, a formal piece was a rhythmic continuum with an unstoppable drive to the final cadence, with few or no salient articulations to impede the drive, although it was varied with slight expressive oscillations of intensity – alterations in the thickness of sonority, changes in the dissonance content of the harmony, surface phenomena often wonderfully inventive that avoid the monotony threatened by a unchanging regularity. When, on a rare occasion, a strong articulation does occur, it has the power to shock. The most astonishing example is in the finale of the Brandenburg Concerto no. 4 in G major, where the orchestra pulls back three times without warning, breaking an otherwise unruffled pattern:

[3]Heinrich Wölfflin remarks somewhere that painters like Leonardo da Vinci and Albrecht Dürer knew that shadows are not really black but coloured, but they painted them as black because that was the tradition, though only in oil painting. On the other hand, in Dürer's watercolours, an experimental and less formal medium, the shadows are coloured.

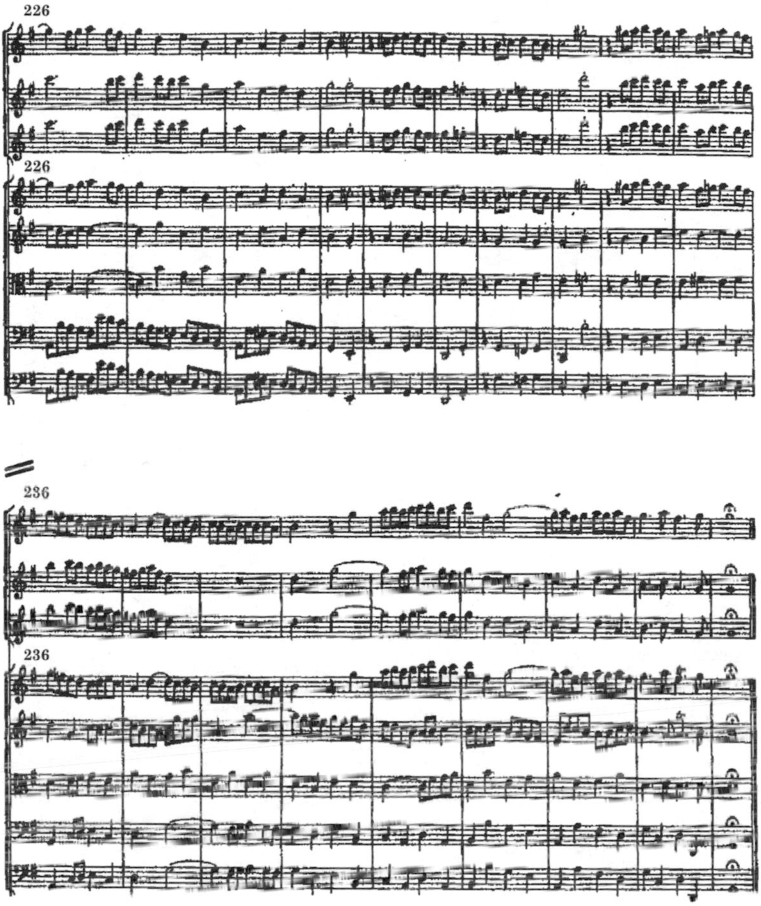
226
226
236
236

And the chorale prelude *Allein Gott in der Höh sei Her* offers an extraordinary interruption of texture:

This, however, is intended both to astonish and to reflect the text of the chorale. It is true that Handel's work presents more rhythmic discontinuities than Bach's, and has more in common with later developments, but then he was stylistically a somewhat more progressive composer than Bach, since so much of his music, unlike Bach's, was composed for public performance in an important urban and international venue. The final chorus of the late oratorio *Theodora* is a sarabande remarkably similar in character to a work that Handel cannot possibly have known, the final sarabande of the *St Matthew Passion*:

However, the Bach remains basically unchanged affectively throughout except for nuances of intensity, while Handel has one remarkable alteration of rhythmic texture in the middle:

Handel also ends with a short orchestral postlude that dies dramatically away with great pathos.

The Unity of Sentiment did not entail a monotonous representation of the affective content but allowed for subtle inflections. A brief look at one short piece will show us what could be accomplished and its limits: I offer it as a simple reminder of all the various aspects of music that contribute to affective meaning even with nothing more than keyboard sonority, aspects that remain valid for another two centuries, even when new procedures to represent sentiment were added to musical style. I have chosen an allemande of Bach, from the keyboard Partita no. 1 in B flat major, because when there was a return to early eighteenth-century technique after 1825, the rapidly mounting fame of Bach that was already manifest in the 1780s made him the most important influence and model for early nineteenth-century musicians, far more than any other composer of his time (Handel had lost some of his prestige, Vivaldi was long forgotten for many decades, and an interest in Domenico Scarlatti grew only slowly for some time to come). However, the return to many aspects of Baroque technique in the early nineteenth century was a major stylistic development.

The allemande is not displayed here as an average or typical work, but its oddity is useful to show the range of expression then possible, the subtle variety of inflections of sentiment contained within a well-defined framework:

Allemande

The rhythm is a steady and unrelenting sixteenth-note continuum. The opening bars are level with only the slightest increase of intensity as the top line rises step by step from F to B flat and the outer voices successively outline at each bar a fifth, a sixth, and then an expressive major seventh and octave; but the expressive accents added at the end of the fourth bar by the voice-leading (as if adding a new voice) prepare a much more expressive arabesque in the next bar, with a break in the sixteenth-note motion, the gap filled by the change of harmony in the bass. While the sixteenth-note movement continues unimpeded, a new and more sustained rhythm appears in the soprano (bar 12), and we may be tempted to use standard sonata form terminology and call it a 'second theme at the dominant': it is certainly an anticipation of later stylistic developments, but there is no trace of the articulation of the move to the dominant that would characterize the sonata. What was to become the standard reference to the dominant of the dominant preceding the new theme is missing here, although Bach, in fact, alludes to it in the second bar of the new theme (the half-cadence of V7 of V to V (the G major triad to a C major harmony). In other words, the basis of the classical system is already in place, but not the classical articulation, as everything here is accomplished seamlessly with all details enveloped by an unceasing forward movement. The sixteenth-note perpetual motion is transferred without a break from the soprano to the bass. Turning to the minor mode with a chromatic bass and then back to the major for the cadence adds still new intensity. At the end of the first part, the division of the sixteenth-note continuum into two voices announces the imminence of the cadence by doubling the accent of the rhythm with a new sonority that adds weight but does not interrupt the process. Unity of sentiment here is enforced by unity of motion, but it is constantly inflected by slight changes of intensity in the harmony and the texture and by tactful increases in the dissonance content of the arabesque line.

In the second section we can see the seed of future stylistic change even more clearly. The second half begins as if it will repeat the pattern of the first, going from dominant to tonic, but the pattern is radically rewritten in a new order. The firm settling into the relative minor (here G minor) will later become a commonplace of sonata development sections. The 'second theme' at the dominant returns very quickly, although not at the tonic, but in C minor (bar 27). This kind of reference in the last third of a work to the subdominant area (E flat major, the relative major of C minor) was standard practice in tonal music throughout the eighteenth century and held sway until the end of Beethoven's career. Replaying this theme in the subdominant area of the minor supertonic has the double function of a resolving recapitulation and of an increase of expressive intensity, strikingly emphasized here by the low register, mounting soon to the higher octave. Although accompanied by no break in the continuous motion, the undulations of expressive intensity are extraordinary. They are, however, never exaggerated, never set dramatically in relief. Changes of intensity can be sustained at a long range in this style without ostentation. It is true that few composers could do it as smoothly and powerfully as Bach. It is also true that the variations are so significant that we might like to claim that the sentiment has altered as the work proceeds, but there is no place where we can draw a line to differentiate one affect from another. We may retain the idea of unity of sentiment, provided that we understand that the basic sentiment is presented in an ever-changing chiaroscuro. Above all, the nuances of intensity and the harmonic structure, although never dramatically articulated, make up an implicit dramatic scenario, and are a prophecy of the developments to come a half century later – establishing a firm tonal basis, contrast, increasing excitement and pathos, and eventual resolution.

The technique of representing an affect in this allemande does not essentially differ from that used in Bach's most complex constructions, like the opening number of the *St Matthew Passion*, for example. The same undulations of intensity within a relentless rhythm are there, and the power that controls an unbroken movement without monotony to the final cadence. One apparent exception to the Unity of Sentiment can be seen in this opening chorus of the Passion with the superimposition of a chorale tune over the main body of the chorus, a procedure parallel to the double fugue, with two motifs of contrasting character. The technique demands that both motifs be eventually sounded together if not at once, and the basic affect that determines the unity is the combination of the two motifs. Nevertheless, it is only in the simulated improvisation of the toccatas and fantasies that any real successive variety of sentiment is to be found. When composers learned to integrate the fantastic contrasts of Baroque improvisation within a complex and formal structure, the Unity of Sentiment lost out to a new art of dynamic contrast.

III

Contradictory Sentiments

❦

From 1770, dramatic articulation became essential to musical style. The chief influence was clearly operatic, since Italian opera was the most prestigious genre. It is interesting, however, that pure instrumental music, which eventually sought to capture some of the prestige of opera, was at first much more innovative in finding new ways to articulate musical form than opera, which remained relatively conservative for a long time – it was also more difficult to flout accepted usage in a form that was so expensive to produce. The most striking examples of dramatic articulation are found first in the symphony and the string quartet, and even in the more modest (at least for a while) form of the piano sonata.

The unruffled (or only slightly ruffled) continuity of the High Baroque was no longer in fashion. The first half of a binary form like the sonata was no longer simply rounded off by a half or full cadence in the dominant like the first half of a binary dance form of the early eighteenth century. In the centre of the first half of the movement, the arrival at the dominant now became an event: sometimes a preceding half cadence on the dominant of the dominant set it off; often rhythm was disrupted; a new theme could be introduced. Even when, as in a number of cases in Haydn's symphonies, no new theme was used and there was greater continuity, the dominant was still more firmly established and the new key area was set in relief by a more active and eccentric rhythmic texture. The first thing we used to learn from music appreciation courses as children was that sonata forms have contrasting themes, the first masculine and the second feminine – this theory even works pretty well for the most part, although in Mozart's Piano Sonata in B flat major K. 333, for example, the main theme of the second group seems more decisive and masculine than the first theme to me, and so it does in Beethoven's Sonata in A flat major op. 110 – but the sex of themes is not perhaps a rewarding subject, so we will leave it and the subject of contrasting themes as well.

What is more fruitful here is the subject of the built-in contrast, the theme or motif that itself represents opposing sentiments, as if it were a miniature mirror image of the larger form. Such themes are infrequent but not rare, and they repay consideration, as they give us a sharp focus on the way the representation of sentiment functioned in the style of a few decades. Let us take a famous example, the opening theme of Mozart's 'Jupiter' Symphony:

The representation of sentiment in music has become a new art: a sentiment is not something static but a character in an action, in an *agon*. Instrumental music takes on a new dimension.

Mozart's counterstatement of the theme of the 'Jupiter' a few bars later reveals something further about the innovation:

Both halves of the original motif are still there, but the opposition has disappeared, they have been united by the flute obbligato, a process as important as the original contrast.

I should not like seriously to propose an analogy with Hegelian logic (invented only a couple of decades after Mozart's death), with its succession of thesis, antithesis and synthesis, but I was once taken to task by a musicologist I admire for not mentioning Kant's aesthetics in *The Classical Style*, so I mention Hegel here just to play safe. In any case, the presentation of an opposition and its resolution is fundamental to a good deal of dramatic form, if not actually to all, and certainly basic to the theatre during Mozart's era. The instrumental style of late eighteenth-century German music developed some of the dramatic effect of opera, making it more concentrated and more efficient, and the new power was given back to opera by Mozart.

Mozart's late Sonata for Piano in D major K. 576 employs exactly the same device as the 'Jupiter' Symphony, beginning with a theme with two opposing motifs: a peremptory hunting horn-call and a light and graceful answer of a half cadence, and repeating the theme at the supertonic minor with the same opposition:

As in the 'Jupiter' Symphony, the theme is repeated at once, and in this counterstatement an obbligato is added in the soprano that unites the two motifs and removes the opposition of sentiment. Following this synthesis is a display of conventional brilliant passagework that closes this opening paragraph. Both the brilliance and the conventionality are essential to the conception, and the increased intensity that they impose both contributes to the articulation of the form and is responsible for the clarity.

The opposition of sentiment within a single phrase is equally evident but more radical in Mozart's great Viola Quintet in C major. At first, in these opening five-bar phrases, the opposition between the dynamic cello and the expressive violin motifs is radical. The greater breadth will not permit a simple synthesis, but in a later statement Mozart compresses the five bars to four, so the two motifs are now partly superimposed and overlap, and become much more of a single if more ambiguous affect. Later in the work, the opposition is further resolved by reducing the five-bar to four-bar phrasing, and the two contrasting motifs now overlap and are combined. In the immediate counterstatement, beginning in bar 21, a synthesis is already initiated, when the powerful opening motif is transferred from cello to violin with the more lyrical ornament of the violin now in the bass:

Simple opposition was not the only way of combining sentiments within a single theme; much more complex essays were
possible. The main theme of Mozart's 'Prague' Symphony is
exceptionally rich in its combination of different affects:

The nervous palpitation of the opening violin rhythm on the tonic is superimposed over an expressive motif in parallel thirds, but the sustained repetition of the tonic note is quickly transformed into a much more energetic motif, and leads without interruption into a military fanfare in the horns over which is played a slightly more expressive but absolutely conventional cadential phrase (this motif is, in fact, identical with the motif that removed the antithesis in the counter-statement of the 'Jupiter' Symphony quoted above). A few bars later, in a second playing of the principal theme (bars 45 to 50), an obbligato in the oboe removes most of the contrast to be found in bars 2 to 4 of the initial theme.

Sometimes the conventional and brilliant cadential material can be incorporated into the main theme itself, changing the affective character in mid-exposition. The principal theme of the Allegro in the first movement of Mozart's Viola Quintet in D major does just that:

This theme is masterly in solving the problem of shifting to a rhythm of triplets, difficult to achieve convincingly (Brahms was not always completely successful at this, but I think he was temperamentally gratified by an awkward effect). Mozart does it beautifully here by the emphatic and grand off-beat accent on the unexpected chord of V7 of IV, the surprise of which amply justifies a new rhythm and a new kind of sentiment. The sudden brilliance is an integral part of a single motif, not an addition as in the D major Sonata K. 576 above.

We have here, however, a very different process from the examples we have been considering; the affective change does not contrast with the opening, the relation is not antithetical – the new affect, although of a strikingly different nature, grows directly out of the initial motif. The sudden surge of energy is a response to the series of accented dissonances, four dominant seventh chords, three V7 of F minor, one V7 of G major. The sudden dashing movement of triplets provides a justified relief of the pent up energy generated by the dissonant harmony and repeated off-beat accents. Since there is no contrasting opposition, there is no need to resolve the relation as we found in the 'Jupiter' Symphony and the Sonata K. 576.

A similar incorporation of new brilliance is exhibited by the opening theme of Haydn's Quartet in C major op. 33 no.3 (sometimes called 'The Bird'):

Here an initial repeating accompaniment figure (but in the treble, which gives it the importance of a motif) is covered by the almost minimal motif of a single note that is repeated faster with an *acciaccatura* in bar 3, and receives greater ornamental emphasis in bar 4. The material could not be simpler, but the change of affect is striking with the more vigorous and brilliant motif that concludes bar 4, continues into the next bar and is repeated at the lower octave, ending in bar 6, followed by two beats of silence. I spell out these obvious details only to set in relief the complex rhythmical development of such simple material. (It is faintly possible that Mozart unconsciously remembered details of this opening when he was writing the Viola Quintet in C major (quoted above), but this speculation is not worth carrying further, as an intentional allusion or quotation makes no sense, and in any case Mozart learned a great deal from the whole sets of Haydn's op. 20 and op. 33, his knowledge lasting him throughout his career as a composer of quartets.)

Haydn's dramatic contrasts of affect are rarely the juxtapositions of different character within a single theme that we can frequently find in Mozart (and they are by no means Mozart's normal procedure, but reveal an important aspect of his style). Haydn, however, was the master of a technique for creating a dramatic contrast with the use of a single theme, a technique that became even more important with other composers after Haydn's career was over: this was the double presentation of a theme in two different realizations with opposed affective significance. One spectacular example is the opening of his Piano Trio in E major (Hob. XV:28). This is particularly inventive, as Haydn has discovered here how to make the piano sound *pizzicato* (astonishingly, the pizzicato accompaniment of the violin and cello is not actually necessary for that effect in this place as the piano alone produces the *pizzicato* sonority), and the immediately following restatement of the theme by the piano gives an unprecedented radical change of atmosphere with its new passionately lyrical ornamentation and chromatic passing tones:

Of course, dynamic contrast and echo effects were possible many years before the last decades of the eighteenth century when Haydn wrote his great trios, and so, certainly, was the addition of expressive ornamentation, but nothing like the astonishing and dramatic juxtaposition of two ways of playing a theme could have been realized before this time.

It is important for the concept of this opening that the expressive transformation should follow immediately the original format, the personal and lyrical reinterpretation directly after the more neutral (in spite of the eccentric tone colour) but publicly decisive announcement of the theme. A second and equally radical transformation will appear in the development section (bar 44), and the grandiose and triumphant effect in the distant tonality of A flat major here depends partly on the exquisite initial contrast exhibited at the opening of the work with no change of key:

One of Haydn's last piano sonatas, in C major (Hob. XVI:50), employs similar procedures. The main theme is announced softly and delicately, and replayed immediately with violence and panache:

The reappearance in the bass register of the opening theme in the development section with a mysterious pedal effect in a remote key is a follow-up to this initial page:

And so is the return of theme in the tonic with an entirely new and lovely pedalled sonority in the highest register:

It is clear that at this time any theme can be given whatever emotional significance the composer chooses if he knows how to go about it.

The technique may be more complex, as we can observe at the opening of another sonata of Haydn of the same late period, perhaps the best-known of all his piano works, that in E flat major, Hob. XVI:52:

This combines Haydn's technique of rethinking the sonority and the dynamics of a theme in the first three bars with Mozart's preferred extension of the initial motif with a new and articulated contrasting motif, except that Haydn's extension is derived, typically for his aesthetic, from the initial motif, although the articulation of contrast is as great as in the examples we gave from Mozart. Just as we find in Mozart occasionally, the presentation of the theme ends with a conventional flourish of virtuosity; the contrast of this flourish with the main body of the phrase is more disconcerting and surprising than in Mozart, who normally preferred smoother integration.

In Mozart, contrast of sentiment within a single theme can be extraordinarily delicate and subtle. The most masterly example is found in the first of the six string quartets dedicated to Haydn, the Quartet in G major K. 387. The opening theme (bars 1 to 4) appears completely unified, but owes its richly expressive character to a hidden and symmetrical contrast of sentiments, at first opposed and then resolved when the phrase is repeated with new counterpoint in bars 11 to 16:

We begin with an alternating opposition of *forte* (bars 1 and 3) and *piano* (bars 2 and 4). There is also a parallel and related alternation of diatonic and chromatic harmony: bars 1 and 3 are diatonic, and although very different, are rounded off with the same melodic cadence, while bars 2 and 4 are heavily chromatic in both melody and harmony. Unfortunately, in many performances of this work very little contrast between the indications of *forte* and *piano* is carried out, and the change from *forte* to *piano* is often accomplished by a diminuendo. This goes contrary to Mozart's conception, as can be seen from the fourth bar, where the first violin finishes the diatonic motif still *forte* for an eighth note, before beginning the contrasting *piano* of the chromatic motif, while the other three instruments are already playing softly. (The slurs that indicate Mozart's phrasing also emphasize the separation of dynamic contrast, as the slur in the fourth bar for the first violin demonstrates that the *piano* should coincide with the beginning of the chromatic motif on the second note of the bar in the middle of a beat.)

The opposition of diatonic *forte* and chromatic *piano* accounts for the psychological complexity of this opening, and it is magnified as the exposition of the theme proceeds. Bars 5 and 6 couple a conventional diatonic cadence to a more expressive chromatic extension in bars 7 to 10. Then, in a remarkable development, the opening phrase reappears heavily rewritten, and the diatonic and chromatic harmonic opposition is removed as the two kinds of harmony and motif now interlock. Even the dynamic contrast is altered. The melody now begins in the second violin (bar 11), and the original second bar (now bar 12) is no longer *piano* but remains *forte*. The original bars 1 and 2, in fact, are now played together in a superimposed counterpoint, as the first violin plays the diatonic first bar while the second violin plays the chromatic second bar, combining the two harmonic characters. The original dynamic and harmonic alternation created an exceptionally complex affective character to this opening theme, and it gains even greater affective power as the opposition is resolved and the two sides are polyphonically combined. The subtlety of this page was new in music, not indeed for its contrapuntal mastery, but for a variety of affective nuances beyond the capacity of any other composer at that time, even Haydn. All the nuances are easily perceptible, as fleeting moments of firmness are followed by hesitation, touches of melancholy, and suggestions of greater urgency – but trying to put verbal names to the multiplicity of affective changes would be absurd, and would only serve to obscure the graceful clarity in spite of the complexity. We may take this page written in 1782, the first of a new series of quartets, as a manifesto of a new style for the representation of sentiment. We know that Mozart worked hard at these quartets, as he was taking up the form again after some years. They make for a stylistic revolution in quartet writing as great as Haydn's opus 20 and then again his opus 33.

I suspect that the opening theme of Haydn's Quartet in B flat major op. 64 no. 3, eight years later in 1790, is indebted to this page of Mozart, at least unconsciously:

The alternation of dynamics with a diatonic *forte* followed by a slightly more chromatic *piano* enforces a different affective character on each appearance of the short motif, or on each member of the phrase. As in Mozart, the modulation to the dominant makes for a more complex dynamic structure and alters the nature of the sentiment conveyed by the motif, making it more unified (bars 23–27):

This is not as subtle as Mozart, but its simplicity has a remarkable and eccentric dramatic energy typical of Haydn.

Another model for the combination of different sentiments is Haydn's 'Lark' Quartet:

The light, detached sonority of the first eight bars will turn out to be an accompaniment, but they are displayed as a principal theme and never entirely lose that character, while the conception realizes a double sentiment of scherzando and passionate lyricism that is both serious and not without humour. The effect is as thrilling as it amuses.

IV

The C Minor Style

❦

I do not want to imply any profound or symbolic meaning to the key of C in the late eighteenth century. But C is basic for technical reasons, both because it is made up of all the white keys on the keyboard, notated without sharps or flats, and the lowest note on the cello is C, and therefore a possible open-string sonority for a lot of string writing. D is equally basic because of the way the major string instruments were tuned (that is why so many operas and symphonies of the time are in D major). C minor is also significant since the horn, the most important brass instrument of the time, was most often the E flat horn, making C minor an easy key.

In any case, a tradition of dramatic C minor works developed in the late eighteenth century, many of which exhibit initial material of opposing sentiments. It is with these works that we can see the advantage for composers of displacing contrast from the large structure into the initial material itself, juxtaposing drama and pathos – the drama centred on an authoritative tonic harmony, while the pathos often emphasized the sixth degree, A flat, either in a fully realized or virtual implied harmony of a dominant ninth chord. The most impressive early piano sonata of Haydn is in C minor, but his C minor work more influential for the composers who followed him is the Symphony no. 78 of 1782. The opening presents elaborate oppositions both of dynamics and motivic material within the first eight bars, and promptly reworks the exposition into a texture removing almost all the antithetical aspect and creating a more unified presentation:

In bars 9 to 15 the opposition of *forte* and *pianissimo* has disappeared, and even much of the contrast of motifs and of harmony in bars 1 to 8 has gone with all the material woven tightly together.

We can see the sophistication in the depiction of senti-ment that Haydn developed in the 1780s if we compare this with the surprisingly similar but much simpler and more naive opening of the C minor Symphony, a decade earlier, no. 52, of 1771–2:

Here dynamic contrast is reserved for a second playing of the theme. By 1782, Haydn had learned how to exploit at once the emotional potential of his motifs.

Mozart, who almost certainly knew Symphony no. 78, and probably no. 52 as well, produced a grand C minor work in symphonic style for piano solo, the Sonata K. 457 of 1784. The kinship with the Haydn symphony is evident, as there is an attempt to reproduce orchestral sonority on the piano, and the contrast of a firm tonic harmony with the pathos of a diminished ninth:

Conforming to the instinctive feeling for stylistic resolution we have already observed, the counterstatement of the opening theme reduces the affective opposition of the first appearance for greater unity:

The C minor Fantasy K. 475 that Mozart published as an introduction to this sonata similarly begins with dynamic contrasts that gradually develop a more unified aspect.

Dramatic opposition was certainly inspired by Allegros in the minor mode. In an earlier sonata in the minor mode, the great A minor K. 310, Mozart already exhibited a contrast of dynamics and material in a less laconic form than the one he had learnt from Haydn:

This follows a commanding military rhythm with a more operatic pathos starting with the up-beat in bar 5 to bar 6. The second playing of the theme does not eliminate the contrast but develops the pathos directly out of the initial motif with no melodic break for the new sentiment.

The opening of Mozart's Concerto in C minor K. 491 is even closer to the model provided by Haydn. Once again the motif is in unison octaves, and a decidedly new and more expressive character is combined with the opening string motif by the subtle but emphatic reappearance of the sixth degree, A flat, that initiates the sustained descending chromatic line as the wind instruments enter:

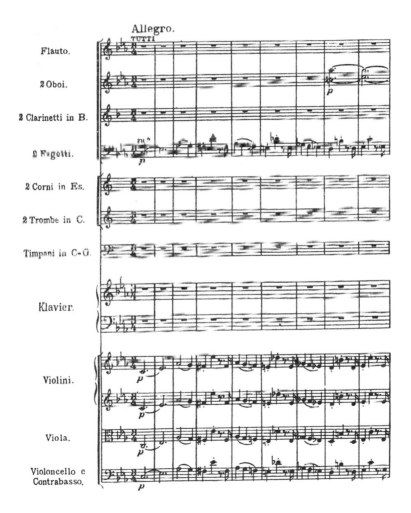

In 1790, Haydn returned to the C minor style, although not in a first movement but with the finale of the 'Emperor' Quartet op. 76 no. 3. The opening loud chords that we find often enough in works by Haydn as an introduction to set the key are not, however, introductory. When they reappear in bars 5 and 6 and then 12 and 13, we realize that they are an integral part of the main theme:

Finale: Presto

The technique has become more inventive. As usual, the dynamic contrast is muffled in the replaying of the theme from bar 12, and the opposition of two kinds of material is lessened by superimposing a triplet motion over both. Above all, those crashing chords not only open the theme but close it as well. Drama and pathos are brought closer together, as the diminished seventh which typically introduces the pathos of the softer third bar is already incorporated into the tonic-based *forte* chords of the opening.

A year after this quartet, Symphony no. 95 presents a new version of the C minor style:

The first nine bars have a dramatic opposition of sentiment, articulated by a separation of four and a half beats of silence. In the counterstatement that begins at once, Haydn gradually transforms the second bar of the staccato *forte* initial motif into the soft, expressive and eventual legato atmosphere of the second and more pathetic sentiment. The two-note motif of the second bar is twice repeated, no longer *forte*, and then quietly and expressively *legato* initiates the half cadence.

Haydn's final version of the C minor style is the 'The Representation of Chaos', which opens *The Creation*. In spite of the need to avoid traditional form in order to portray chaos, it exhibits all the elements of the tradition we have been examining. The opening phrase has a motif with a radical opposition of affects succeeded by an immediate reconciliation of the opposition:

The first affect is the most laconic, a single powerful tonic note unharmonized, realized by the full orchestra, and dramatically held for a long *diminuendo*. Contrasting sentiment and pathos follow immediately with the tradi-

tional A flat, played in a soft *crescendo* by the second
violin while the first violin moves chromatically to the A
flat an octave above. The contrast between the extremely
loud tonic note and the quiet A flat is reduced at once, as
the *forte* returns now incorporating the A flat in what
amounts to a varied but traditional counterstatement of
the first four bars

Beethoven's exploitation of the C minor style (as in the
Pathétique Sonata and the Fifth Symphony) is too well
known to explore at length here except for a few observations on the way he developed it from his predecessors. The
first solo exposition of the main theme of the Piano
Concerto no. 3 reveals how much he owed, and how he
personally altered, the tradition:

As in Mozart's sonata and Haydn's symphonies, the initial tonic section of the theme is in unison octaves and *forte*. Harmonization is introduced only for the pathos of the second phrase, now *piano*. From the following bar 122 on, the motivic material of the first opening phrase and the harmonic aspect of the second are now combined and developed under a more enveloping expressive arabesque. We have witnessed this technique before, but not with such passion. The adherence to tradition and the ostentatious increase in power are both evident; that is why there is no answer to the foolish question that so often comes up as to whether Beethoven is classical or romantic. It is difficult to say whether Beethoven's dependence on the style he learned when young was more or less impressive than his transformation of that tradition throughout his life.

Other examples of Beethoven's C minor style, like the Piano Sonata op. 10 no. 1, also continue the tradition by beginning with an emphatic tonic chord followed by a diminished-seventh harmony with an A flat. His final example of the style makes the most concentrated and efficient use of the procedure, at the opening of the Allegro of the last piano sonata, op. 111. The material is announced once again unharmonized, with multiple affective values, and with the traditional emphasis first given to the tonic note and then to the sixth degree:

The motif alters its character twice at the very beginning – a stern *forte*, then a lingeringly expressive *portamento*, and finally an excited agitation. At the recapitulation, further aspects of tone colour give still different versions of the laconic motif:

One of the most salient characteristics of Beethoven's last style is its economy.

V

Beethoven's Expansion

~~~~~~~~

It is evident that the rendition of sentiment in Beethoven's work has a greater range and is on a more heroic scale than was found in music before him. Paradoxically, however, although this aspect of his compositional practice becomes more inventive and original as his career progresses, he also draws closer in some ways to the stylistic principles and procedures of his great predecessors. Restricting ourselves largely to the subject we have taken, the use of basic material with built-in affective variety or even an articulated opposition, we find that Beethoven comes back to the technique of dramatic opposition followed by a reduction of the antithetical character, bridging the gap between the opposing forces, as if they constituted a structural dissonance that needed resolution.

Although the presentation of initial material in a work by Beethoven largely retains the eighteenth-century stability or the articulated contrast and its later resolution, keeping extravagant crescendos of intensity for the centre of the form, we find dramatic increase of intensity in a very few sonata expositions, which do not affect the presentation of the principal theme but only the transition to the dominant. One of the most remarkable examples of this is found very early in Beethoven's career in the Sonata in A major op. 2. no. 2, bars 50 to 78:

This displaces the excitement usually left for the central development section to the transition from opening theme to second group, although the initial display of the thematic material still relies on the classical opposition of *forte* and *piano* for its excitement. Nevertheless, the rising bass that would become such a spectacular phenomenon in the 'Appassionata' already makes its presence felt here, and is a major expansion of the classical aesthetic. It is, however, surely derived from Haydn's practice of beginning a fragmentary development of the opening material as early as the transition to the dominant in the exposition.

As with Mozart, initial thematic material in Beethoven that lacks unity of sentiment is the exception rather than the rule, but the rare examples make it easier to study the change in his conception over the years. A relatively early work, the Sonata for Piano in F major op. 10 no. 2, opens with a striking multiplicity of different motifs:

First, there is a Haydnesque motif of two soft *staccato* peremptory tonic chords that set the key and the tempo and wake up the auditors. This is followed by a tiny scherzando answer, which serves to announce a different character to the movement, and the two motifs are repeated to exhibit the harmony of the dominant. A long tenderly lyrical arabesque takes over with a full sustained legato, and with a smooth and rich accompaniment of thick chords that stay within the treble range, confirming the lyrical tone and emphasizing the new expressive mood. The affective gap is bridged only slightly by the way that the ornaments at the end of the new legato line slightly recall the second scherzando motif. In this work Beethoven does not feel that the disparate material needs resolution.

In the sonatas of 1803, particularly the 'Tempest' in D minor op. 31 no. 2, the disparity is so great that energetic measures were needed to resolve the structural dissonance. The principal disparity is the extraordinary difference of tempi: a brief Largo *pianissimo* and a fermata, followed by an Allegro of three bars imitating orchestral string writing, *piano* and *crescendo*, and ending in an Adagio half-cadence:

A dozen bars later, the *pianissimo* Largo motif returns *forte* at the Allegro tempo, removing at least some of the disparity and restoring unity. The two motifs are so different that one might question the justice of treating them as a single phrase, but as an opening motif, neither has any intelligible meaning standing alone. The opening phrase of a tonal work of 1803 must establish the key. We have, one must admit, lost some of the sensitivity that any eighteenth-century musician or music-lover had to this question. The opening Largo arpeggio as a first inversion chord does, in fact, imply that it is a dominant (it would oddly have more of the character of a tonic A major chord if the soprano stopped at the dominant E of the line A C♯E without going on to the final A). A tonality at that time could only be established by setting the dominant in relief as well as a tonic, and generally needs at least to suggest the subdominant as well,[4] which is done by the Allegro motif, so that the two motifs make a single entity at the beginning. (The Largo motif can only be separated later by the fragmentation typical of a development section technique, and then recom-posed in a new sequence.) When the Largo motif returns at the Allegro tempo in the bass soon after the opening (bar 21), a new completion must be added to replace the second motif:

[4] A loss of this sense after 1850 or so has allowed even a great and almost infal-lible critic like Hermann Abert in his biography of Mozart to claim that in the introduction to Mozart's famous 'Dissonance' Quartet in C major K. 465, the tonality is unclear, but C major is firmly established at once, as bars 1 and 2 exhibit the tonic, bar 2 the dominant, and bars 4 to 7 the subdominant, and the rest of the introduction exhibits only the tonic minor and the dominant. All other harmonies are clearly subsidiary effects of the voice-leading. At no point in the introduction is any other key than C possible. The voice-leading even unequivocally signifies that the minor mode will be resolved into the major.

The tension between the two different tempi is so great, however, that further action is needed at the recapitulation. The Largo motif is now followed by a new continuation, a recitative in operatic style still at the Largo tempo, and still *pianissimo* with a mysterious pedal effect throughout, marked *con espressione e semplice*:

For the rest of the movement, the Largo motif no longer returns at the Allegro tempo.

The opening material of the next sonata, op. 31 no. 3 in E flat major, is extraordinarily sophisticated in its polysemous character, a triumph of Beethoven's new style:

Six bars of an eccentric and passionate motif, with an increasingly urgent chromatic rise, *ritardando* and *crescendo* leading to a fermata, are followed by a comically witty deflation with a sudden conventional full cadence. This confirms the tonality, although there has never been any real doubt concerning it, as only E flat makes sense (A flat would be absurdly incompetent with the F added to the initial chord, and D flat is only a very remote possibility, contradicted very soon by the A natural in the bass). The combination of urbane but eccentric passion with the banal but graceful deflation was an elaborate irony difficult to attain in pure instrumental music, although Mozart achieved a similar irony by the use of extremely conventional phrases in *The Marriage of Figaro* when Susanna surprisingly comes out of the closet (where Cherubino had been hiding) to the strain of the most innocent and simple minuet.

An initial resolution of the clash of sentiments in the sonata comes a few bars later when the initial motif translated into descending fifths and sixths is used to create its own cadence:

However, the most exquisite resolution is reserved for the end of the exposition, where a graceful descending sixth that recalls the opening motif is closed by a cadence as conventional as the end of the first phrase but with an expressive simplicity that makes no affective contrast to the previous bars, and so preserves the lyrical tone:

Later in his career Beethoven was able to invent basic material with an interior opposition, creating complexes of affective significance that achieved a psychological unity by a concentration on very small motivic cells that retain their identity while changing their affective meaning. The Sonata in E minor op. 90, published in 1815, begins with an affective opposition, with a formal technique already familiar to us from Mozart and Haydn:

A commanding and peremptory two bars of *forte* and a detached sonority contrast with a softer, more lingering two bars; and this four-bar pattern is repeated in a rising sequence. A larger and more radical contrast of texture then follows (bars 9 to 16). A sustained and eloquently expressive line, with a gradual *diminuendo* and *ritardando*, takes over from the last note of the previous phrase and descends, ending on a half cadence, a B major dominant fermata. The sharp contrast of this lyrical descent with the nervous and dramatically mounting first phrase is not left without a reconciliation.

The whole musical paragraph closes with eight more bars, beginning with the rhythm of the initial cell of the first phrase. However, while the dramatic rhythmic cell of the opening phrase is recalled, the texture is no longer the detached sonorities but the sustained *cantabile* of bars 9 to 16, made, indeed, even more intensely expressive by the extraordinary octave displacement with which the original rhythmic cell, now rewritten, swoops twice down the interval of a fourteenth to a low F sharp from a high E, uniting the highest and lowest registers. The opposed textures, first detached and then *legato*, of the first two phrases are partially resolved or over-ridden by combining the sustained legato texture with the original rhythmic cell of the opening, and the *forte* and *piano* opposition of dynamics which originally separated the melodic cells is also tempered and unified by the new sustained line. In short, all the articulated oppositions of the style that Beethoven inherited are realized now with an organization that is much more tightly knit and subtly unified. Starting with two opposed phrases, a rise and a descent, and then combining high and low registers together in a more intense expression, has the effect of a narrative form. It has a plot.

One final example from Beethoven foreshadows developments that were to become of major importance after his death, the opening of the 'Hammerklavier' Sonata in B flat major op. 106:

This begins with a radical example of an opposition of sentiment, but, almost a trademark of Beethoven's style, using
the same material for the two extremes. The interval of a
third, B flat to D, is triumphantly displayed *fortissimo* and
displaced to the leap of a seventeenth (and then at once to a
twenty-fourth and thirty-first, using most of the octave Ds
available to two hands, combining the highest and lowest
registers), and the process is repeated for the interval B flat
to F. To the D and F respectively are added an E flat and G,
acting as dissonances like *appoggiature*. In bars 5 to 8, the
process is reworked in a more intimately expressive *piano*,
the original intervals no longer heard as leaps but going
stepwise from the B flat to the D and E flat, and then to the

F and G, and closing with a half cadence. The high register disappears, and the upper part of the low is only gradually and unobtrusively introduced, concentrating on the middle register, most suitable on the piano for its *cantabile* sonority.

What was revolutionary is the lengthy third phrase that begins in bar 9 (in fact, few slurs in musical notation of that time are as long as the seven-bar slur in the left hand), starting from the melodic pattern of bars 5 to 8, the sonority; and the character of the second phrase returns little by little back to the affective world of the first with an extraordinary crescendo of intensity. It is true that the end of the process in bar 18 is not marked *fortissimo* but only *forte*, with each strong beat having an extra *sforzando*, and this effectively equals the sonority of the first bars. The scale of the resolution of the initial contrast may be unprecedented, but the scale of that contrast is also unprecedented for the opening of a keyboard work, and I have not encountered any earlier orchestral work that opens with so elaborate a violent opposition. Even in Beethoven's Symphony no. 5, the dynamic contrast seems to me less ambitious.

Most original, however, is the continuity. Gradual increases of intensity on the scale of bars 9 to 18 (with the *poco a poco crescendo* and the grand *legato* descent from treble to the lowest bass) had previously been restricted to the central developments of works or to the codas, but do not appear in the presentation of defining material in an exposition. It is true that Beethoven had already invented beginnings of slightly increasing intensity, like the 'Waldstein' Sonata or the Quartet in F major op. 59 no. 1, but never before on this scale. Any increases of intensity in the opening material had generally been accomplished by him before, as they had been by his predecessors, with a clearly articulated move to a higher level as in the sudden *forte* in the 'Appassionata' Sonata after twelve bars of *pianissimo*.

It is, in fact, in the development section of the 'Appassionata' that Beethoven carried the process of a continuous rise of intensity further than it had ever been taken by any composer, in a seventeen-bar climax where the bass rises four octaves and a *sempre più forte* to a *fortissimo* that lasts for eleven bars at the end of the development section. But not until the opening of the 'Hammerklavier' had he tried to accomplish an equally continuous transition in an exposition from a delicate sonority in the high register of the keyboard to the biggest sound of which the instrument was capable. And this was in a work that, in spite of all its evident innovations, incorporates important aspects of the piano sonatas that he had written two decades before, like op. 10 no. 3, aspects which had ceased to inspire him in piano music for all those years, like a long and elaborate Largo slow movement in sonata form and a four-movement structure with a minuet or scherzo. Among all the innovations, however, the huge crescendo of intensity in an initial presentation of opening material is one that had an important future.

Both the kinship of op. 106 with the early works of Beethoven and the radical innovation it also embodied can be easily seen if we compare the presentation of the main theme with the opening bars of his first mature Sonata, op. 2 no. 1:

As in the 'Hammerklavier', we start with a two-bar motif, outlining a third immediately repeated slightly higher to form the initial four-bar phrase. The next phrase, adapting the motif and enlarging it to a fifth, is a unified four-bar phrase, very similar to bars 5 to 8 of op. 106. This articulation of 2 + 2 bars preceding a 4-bar unit is a common pattern of the time, on which E. T. Cone wrote many years ago. One should add, however, that both op. 2 no. 1 and op. 106 achieve the four bars 5 to 8 by first reducing the two-bar motifs to one-bar fragments leading to a two-bar half-cadence, which increases the rhythmic excitement, before unifying and resolving the phrase.

What Beethoven in op. 106 adds to the standard pattern of op. 2 no. 1 is yet another common pattern from the eighteenth century, the opposition of dynamics and texture we have been considering, an opposition, however, on a grand scale unheard before. With the third phrase he then transforms the texture and dynamics and even the range of the second phrase gradually back into the affective world of the first. We can see here the dependence of late Beethoven on the old techniques he had learnt as a child and the tremendous expansion of that tradition he was able to accomplish.

VI

Romantic Intensity

A̲FTER Beethoven's death, themes with an interior opposition of sentiment almost cease to exist. The return to something like the late Baroque unity of sentiment was not simply a modish fashion but came from a profound change in sensibility. Just as Romantic poets wanted to realize, not the underlying logic of experience, but its continuity – not a series of independent events, but the metamorphosis of one state of sensibility into another – so the precise and dramatic articulation of late eighteenth-century musical style, with each important structural point marked by emphatic changes of texture, half or full cadences, and significant pauses, became not merely old-fashioned but even antipathetic for the most progressive musicians. The short slurs that marked the phrasing of Mozart and Haydn and the slightly longer ones typical of Beethoven gave way in Chopin to immensely long slurs, sometimes going over pages. Typically, a Chopin phrase slur does not end with the last note of the phrase but with the first note of the next phrase.

The exceptional cases of initial thematic material with
internal opposition that we find are, like Liszt's *Harmonies
poétiques et religieuses* (above all, the original version of 1834),
free forms, quasi-improvisations, making a case similar to the
variety of affects that can exist in a Bach toccata or fantasy. A
more interesting apparent exception is the Scherzo no. 2 in B
flat minor of Chopin:

However, we are dealing here with a very different and larger
scale of time than we have found in previous composers, as
each bar of this scherzo is like a single beat. And we must
consider here not only each bar as a beat, but even every set

of four bars as a slow beat superimposed. The opening four bars are not an independent motif but simply an upbeat, an initial part of the dramatic power that follows, and an after-beat as well leading to the next appearance. They offer not so much a contrast to the motif that follows as simply an essential introductory element. The whole passage must exceptionally be performed with metronomic precision, or the rhythmic notation at bar 22 makes no sense.

The originality of the composers of the 1830s in the delineation of sentiment was not a simple return to Baroque unity but a new conception of intensity that altered the nature itself of the sentiments. The changes of intensity in the initial presentation of material in early and late eighteenth-century music were nuances and oscillations held within fairly narrow limits (indeed, the instruments of the time would not have been capable of really violent dynamic contrasts). In the second half of the eighteenth century, large-scale increases of intensity were generally reserved for the later sections of the work when the material could be freely developed, fragmented and reworked: in particular, the preparation of a grand return could be the occasion for building up a feeling of excitement. Still later, the operas of Rossini provided wonderfully useful examples of a rousing final *stretto*, but it was the composers that arrived after he had ceased to write operas that were able to incorporate some of this mounting excitement within the basic material itself that opened a work.

Schumann's Lied from the Heine *Liederkreis*, 'Ich wandelte unter den Baümen', gives us an increase of tension so sudden that we might speak of a change of sentiment, but this would be misleading as there is no sense of contrast or opposition whatever. The continuity is absolute, and we can only experience an accelerated transformation of a single sentiment as it proceeds:

The character of the melodic line of bars 9 and 10 is in no way different from bars 5 to 8, but the more expressive harmony starting in bar 9 creates and forces the passion of bar 11. We have both an affective unity and a dramatic change within the character of the sentiment that goes far beyond the affective nuances of Baroque style. What adds to the intensity, indeed, is the fact that the voice does not resolve at the end of the phrase or even finish the phrase, which needs to be taken down to the A sharp of the harmony of the dominant, but only suspends its line, leaving the piano to provide the necessary rounding off of a half cadence. The radical postponement of resolution is a characteristic not only of many large forms at this time but even of the initial material that fixes the emotional setting of the individual work.

Once we have acquired an appreciation of the musical language of Mozart or Beethoven, we ought to become unwilling to say that the music of Chopin, Liszt or Wagner is more dramatic or more passionate, but we must recognize a difference of scale. And it is important to understand that it is not simply that Wagner's music is louder and longer, that Liszt's is louder, flashier with more notes in both treble and bass, or that Chopin's is more richly chromatic – it is, in fact, difficult to be more chromatic than Mozart when he puts his mind to it, as at the opening of the development section of the Piano Concerto in B flat K. 595. Nevertheless, certain aspects of the musical style from 1830 to 1850 acquire a density that transforms the affective power of music.

This density comes in many different ways. The openings of three nocturnes of Chopin will demonstrate that variety. His first published Nocturne of 1832 immediately displays the opening motif twice, the second time with expressive and extravagant decoration:

The ornament comes from Italian opera, and is even more extravagant six bars later, but the early appearance of such richness of detail is astonishing. Not that such extravagance was foreign to the operatic tradition even of the eighteenth century, but there is no reason to believe that it was ever introduced at the opening of an aria, at the initial presentation of the material. It was reserved for later appearances of the melodies (even here the initial motif is played simply at first, as a kind of acknowledgment of tradition), and Chopin did not discover this outlandish effect in the nocturnes of John Field, where he first came upon the genre.

A year later, 1833, the Nocturne op. 15 no. 1 in F major reveals a more subtle kind of density in the opening bars.

The first two bars are innocent pastoral with a lovely rich sonority with the tenor doubling the soprano. The increase of tension is remarkable. In bar 3, the doubling diverges into counterpoint, creating an immediate and poignant dissonance of a minor ninth on the second beat. In the fourth bar, both tenor and bass develop important independent lines that thicken the harmony, which moves not to the dominant of C major, but to the dominant of A minor emphasized by the *ritenuto* – and then rapidly resolves – or, rather dissolves – into the dominant of F major, set in relief by a sudden *piano* and *dolcissimo*, a dynamic that has the effect of a negative reflection of an accent. This chromatic complexity at the opening of a main theme was relatively new in music: even Mozart's famous introduction to the 'Dissonance' Quartet (K. 465), so often mistakenly described as tonally ambiguous, is actually more conventional, exhibiting first a half cadence on the dominant, and then one on the subdominant,[5] and Beethoven's ambiguous opening of the Sonata in E flat major, op. 31 no. 3, moves quickly to the tonic. Even the elaborate passing harmonies of the 'Waldstein' Sonata's principal theme clearly articulate successively the simple tonic, dominant, subdominant, and dominant again. There is no ambiguity about Chopin's opening, of course, but the harmonic inflections below the surface invest the theme with an unbroken crescendo of intensity. What is also new is the density of dissonance, placed to give life to the rhythm: the most powerful dissonances put the weight in bars 2 to 6 on the second beat, and shift to the third beat in bars 7 and 8 to make the cadence effective.

[5]See the footnote above, page 91. Introductions are granted a luxurious improvisatory freedom denied to principal themes.

In the next set of nocturnes, published three years later in 1836, the unremitting magnification of intensity within a theme of Chopin can be found at its most accomplished in the D flat major op. 27 no. 2, with a new sophistication that coordinates rhythm, chromaticism, range of melody, and polyphony:

The range of the melody gradually expands from an octave in the first bars to more than two octaves, the rhythm is more agitated, the intervals outlined more dissonant (as in the climactic rapid descent from the high G flat to C), the harmony ever more chromatic. The accompaniment is a fluid and agitated image of the principal voice, constantly producing displaced hidden octaves doubling with it, and magnifies the density of sonority. All this is done with no feeling of contrast or opposition, a unity that results in a continuously growing passion, accomplished most strikingly by the way the A natural in bar 5 is held for a full bar before being released into the expected resolution, apparently making a five-bar phrase in place of the expected four. Resolving the A natural more quickly and conventionally would have lowered the tension, but the delay increases it and makes the following three bars more urgent. This triggers the more troubled and complex rhythmic motion of bars 7 to 9 that returns us to an orthodox eight-bar pattern.

Liszt's technique of expanding the built-in passion of the material itself is less subtle but more spectacular and more insistent. An impressive magnification of intensity is displayed by (1) the introductory theme and (2) the principal theme of Liszt's 'Funérailles' from the *Harmonies poétiques et religieuses*:

(1) Introductory theme

(2) Principal theme

Every detail of the introductory theme is calculated for an increase of tension with almost no respite. The direction is always upward until the very end, and the dynamics an almost unbroken crescendo. In the main theme, the harmonies become ever more distant from the tonic. In bar 54, the sudden drop to a soft *piano*, far from lowering the tension actually increases it for an effect of lugubrious despair. Liszt's method is derived from opera, and used simply with powerful effect. The introduction is an extended dominant minor ninth chord projected over two dozen bars. Like Chopin, Liszt could find models in contemporary Italian opera for melodies in which, after a few bars, the passion bursts out of the initial frame.

The greatest beneficiary of this new aesthetic of continuously rising tension will be Richard Wagner. The notorious prelude to *Das Rheingold* is a piece where nothing happens over a single chord for minutes on end, except for a tremendous increase in tension. The ultimate production of an unbroken growing tension carried to the limit, however, is surely the prelude of *Tristan und Isolde*, where it is sustained beyond what anyone would have thought possible and often inspires conductors to take the slowest possible tempo in order to see to what extraordinary length the effect may be stretched. It is doubtful that the unity of sentiment can be taken any further. As the prelude proceeds, new motivic material is introduced, but so similar in character to the original that it is not perceived as an addition but only as an extension of the opening bars. This concern for an increase of tension even within the basic material itself of the work is an essential part of the new aesthetic called Romanticism that tries to postpone resolution to a point as close to the end of a movement as possible, in contrast to the late eighteenth-century sonata aesthetic that most often situates the climax and initial resolution three-quarters of the way through a work, just preceding and including the moment that initiates the recapitulation.

In a few rare cases, we might say that a continuous increase of tension could be achieved negatively and paradoxically, in the long opening section of Chopin's F major Ballade no. 2, for example, by a refusal to employ any of the traditional means of adding tension, with an almost completely static surface, no crescendo and no change of register, restricting everything to the smallest range in the centre of the piano and with minimal nuances of rhythm (Chopin even struck out at publication almost all of the very few indications of phrasing in the manuscript, replacing them with an amazingly long slur, as if to block any attempt to ruffle the surface and to discourage any obvious form of articulation). The music even starts as if it has been going on for some time and shrinks gradually at the end to the continuous playing of only one note, A natural. Any overt attempt to introduce much expression or drama to these pages ends up by defeating both. The tiny oscillations of harmonic and melodic intensity make their effect only when executed with the utmost simplicity, but this is a *tour de force* of composition. A somewhat similar effect is achieved by Schumann in the 'Mondnacht' of the Eichendorff *Liederkreis* with the repetition of a single phrase, but here the static surface is broken at last by the passion of the penultimate verse. Nevertheless, once again we cannot speak of contrast or opposition since the integration is so complete, and the repetition and the static surface impel and imply the arrival of greater force.

The complement to the extensive display of static material is found in those rare works that start at a pitch of tension so great that any increase is unthinkable. The opening of Schumann's Phantasie in C major op. 17 is the most famous of these, starting at a level of tension that makes only a descent into exhaustion possible, a process that is repeated over and over again throughout the first movement (justifying the title 'Ruins' originally given to the movement), the resolving arrival of the tonic chord of C major in root position withheld until the last page.

The first piece of the *Kreisleriana* by Schumann also starts at the upper limit of intensity:

The phrasing of the first edition, printed here, makes the agitation more telling by indicating with a two-note slur that the right hand should give a slight accent to the strong beats, and this allows us to hear that the left hand is always off the beat until the last bar. The brutal and detached V–I cadence at the very end is astonishingly laconic – almost too much so, in fact, particularly if the two chords are played as dryly as they are notated; a short staccato resolution restricted to the highest register of a thick passage that has covered almost the whole piano keyboard is a calculated eccentricity, leaving an overhang in the ear of unresolved deep sonorities.

The late eighteenth century's clearly articulated delineation of sentiment that made possible a dramatic scenario of opposing sentiments was old-fashioned by the 1830s and was largely replaced by a greater unity, with the dramatic effect conceived not through contrast and opposition, but essentially by an increase of intensity. The variety of means to accomplish this was significant: the tension could be magnified through rhythm, harmony, range, dynamics, dissonance, texture, and any or all of these combined, or even by static iteration that implied the imminence of action.

The missing figure in this discussion has been Schubert, master of the evocation of sentiment, who belonged to both worlds. The sustaining of a single sentiment for extraordinary length through subtle inflections was the signal character of his art in his last years (above all, in the songs), but the classical technique of opposition was not absent from his works, although, with some important exceptions, less tightly and economically realized than in the work of his predecessors. A study of Schubert in these matters would demand too great an extension, but we must at least consider one example that shows his command of both traditions, the return of the principal theme from the slow movement of the great final Piano Sonata in B flat major:

Here the tension builds through reiteration, through the gradual crescendo. An insistent accompaniment and the steady rise in pitch create the drama with unbroken continuity. However, there is an extraordinary event, the simultaneous shift from C sharp minor to C major and from *forte* to *pianissimo*, the negative accent of a sudden drop in dynamics, and this, though harmonically revolutionary, is the classical effect of articulated opposition, the radical transformation of emotion within a theme by contrast and opposition.

VII

Obsessions

INITIAL material of contrasting character has largely disappeared by the latter half of the nineteenth century, and opening themes with astonishing surges of intensity become rare as well. Most composers, from Verdi to Tchaikovsky and Brahms, are principally concerned with inventing material that evenly sustains a significant level of interest and excitement. There are often effective increases of urgency as their themes develop, but rarely the initial sudden, dramatic and even exaggerated surges of intensity that we find in the composers of the 1830s and '40s.

It was, however, a goal of Brahms's career to revive and master the techniques and procedures of composers from Haydn to Schubert (although his knowledge of, and his profit from, earlier composers like Couperin and Bach were profound, and the influence of Chopin on his work equally powerful). He could, when he wanted, reproduce the classical device of an initial theme with interior affective opposition, and does so in at least one notable example modelled on the

opening of Beethoven's Piano Concerto no. 4 in G major
(the Beethoven is quoted and discussed above, pages 28–30).
In the Beethoven concerto a five-bar phrase of quietly expressive character ends with a simple half cadence on the dominant D major, and is followed by a remote harmony, B major,
the dominant of the submediant, initiating a second phrase
equally quiet and expressive but with a radical change of
sonority, as the first phrase is for the solo piano, the second
for the orchestra, which continues and finishes the theme.
This is the pattern followed by Brahms at the opening of the
Violin Concerto op. 77, but in a remarkably innovative form:

He enhances the procedure and renders it more sophisticated, making the harmonic change at the beginning of the second phrase much more radical than the Beethoven by moving directly to the flattened leading tone, the chord of C major. Disdaining a facile opposition of solo and tutti, he achieves the contrasting change of sonority by different means, opening instead with unharmonized unison octaves in only the low strings and the horns with a mostly steady quarter-note rhythm, and creating the new texture and sonority for the second phrase by an oboe solo and a richer, more agitated accompaniment in all the strings. The affective character does not change markedly between the two phrases, but, although Brahms damps down the opposition of sonority made by Beethoven's contrast of solo and tutti, the new texture in Brahms is so surprisingly different that it is hard to say whether this should be considered a contrast of sentiment or an increase of intensity. In both Beethoven's and Brahms's versions, we do not have a marked change of sentiment, but a new perspective on the original one.

What is a harbinger of the future in Brahms is the way the effect is created largely by tone colour. The violin concerto was published in 1878, and a generation later, tone colour with Debussy, Skryabin and Richard Strauss will have won for itself a role in composition as important and preponderant as pitch and rhythm. We do not often think of Brahms for his mastery of tone colour, but this was often at the heart of his conceptions. We can see this most clearly if we compare the initial statement (1) of the main theme of the Sonata in F major for cello and piano with the return of the tonic and the main theme (2) at the end of the development, bar 112:

This is a remarkable demonstration of how the same basic melodic motif can be used to produce spectacularly different sentiments by changes of rhythm and texture.

The increasing importance of tone colour for the delineation of sentiment can be illustrated by another work of Brahms, the Intermezzo in B minor op. 119 no. 1, about which Brahms himself wrote, in a letter to Clara Schumann, that to extract the full melancholy of all the dissonances, it was not enough to play Adagio, but that 'every note must be played *ritardando*':

His direction may be hyperbolic, but it makes sense for the harmonic structure of the theme, which creates eleventh chords by piling on an obsessive series of thirds in a descending arpeggio and then adding one more on top (the penultimate harmony of the piece is a thirteenth chord at last). The acoustics of the piano work naturally with a slight delay, and every successive descending third reactivates the overtones of the held notes above it but requires a fraction of a second for the strings of the upper notes to respond audibly. The sonority builds up gradually during the execution of each arpeggiated harmony, often requiring at least an infinitesimal *ritardando* to exploit the increase in vibrancy, to make it perceptible and allow us to savour it. (This demands, of course, that the pianist listen carefully to each sound he or she produces, and the necessary *rubato* adds an expressive touch, all the better for the style of this work.)

The crisis of tonality in the late nineteenth and early twentieth century explains why tone colour began to take over some of the importance of pitch in fixing musical meaning. There was a change of the tonal system throughout the nineteenth century, as it became less precise and more diffuse, through a rich and complex chromaticism. In eighteenth-century music each chord and each note has a measurable harmonic distance from the tonic on the circle of fifths, and functions as if it were moving away from, or towards, resolution. This gives each phrase of a work a precise tonal significance that allows the listener to feel the precise degree of harmonic tension, and we can generally tell if a passage is distant from the tonic in a sharp (or dominant) direction or in the flat (or subdominant) area, which changes its affective meaning. The richer mediant relations that dominate the nineteenth century made a new range of affects possible but reduced the simple precision of harmonic meaning that was more easily audible to earlier listeners. By the end of the century, the diffusion of possible large-scale harmonic meaning in works by composers as different as Reger and Fauré could seem almost anarchic. A proposal to get rid of tonality was made by Debussy, who never, of course, went quite that far, but the dissatisfaction with the old-fashioned harmonic system can already be felt in his music as he went some way to supplant the role of pitch by tone colour.

The consequences for the representation of sentiment were serious. The most radical development can be clearly observed in Richard Strauss's *Salome* of 1905. One detail stands out with shocking clarity. When the soldiers descend into the cistern to cut off the head of the Baptist, the double basses play a short high note, with the pitch made not by pressing the string against the fingerboard but by pinching the string between thumb and index finger to 'produce a sound like a woman's repressed groan or moan', over and over again at short intervals that accelerate, an exceptionally irritating sound. When Strauss was asked what that meant, he replied that it represented the impatience of Salome to have the head. In the traditional meaning of the representation of sentiment, however, the effect does not actually *represent* anything at all. That is, it is not a sound-image of impatience for the listener, but rather provokes the sentiment of impatience by irritation – that is, it causes impatience by manipulating the listeners' sensibility.

The technique can be compared to the contemporary development of the style of late nineteenth-century French fiction, called the *style artiste*, best shown in the novels of Edmond and Jules Goncourt, who claimed that they did not want simply to describe something for their readers, but to hammer it into their heads. Traditional representation (a metaphorical process of resemblance of form) was replaced by acting directly on the nerves of reader or listener, and similarly in symbolist literature description was replaced by suggestion. Stimulating the nervous systems of the readers would force their imaginations to cooperate in the creation of the work and its significance, and so increase the power of the art.

The increase of affective power is undeniable in *Salome*, and the technique is well adapted to the morbidity of the subject. (Strauss was not alone in this. Other composers of the time found different methods of working on the nerves. In Puccini's *Tosca*, for example, after the scenes of torture, the murder of Scarpia is made more horrifying by having his death set to a stately and respectable old-fashioned Baroque dance, the dramatic pathos magnified by the ironic tone.) The last few minutes of *Salome* are perhaps the most extravagantly affective of the opera. The musical picture of the sexual excitement of Salome kissing the head and her triumphant orgasm are enforced by a continuous, absolutely unchanging soft trill in the high woodwinds, harmonically independent of the climactic melody, insistently creating unremitting dissonances throughout for several minutes. This trill acts subliminally on the nerves of the public like a friction throughout the scene.

The chromatic saturation of the musical language after Schubert made it very difficult for any composer musically to represent a simple emotion like innocent, uncomplicated happiness. Purely diatonic material tended to appear as picturesque or ethnographically characteristic music, such as we find in the mazurkas of Chopin (the rare purely rustic ones), the jolly folk styles (Germanic for Schumann, Norwegian for Grieg), or Liszt's Swiss landscapes from the *Années de pèlerinage*. The only recourse that Strauss had to convey innocent youthful happiness at the end of *Der Rosenkavalier*, when his lovers, fifteen and sixteen years old, go off together, is a pastiche of Mozart:

Strauss must surely have expected us to recognize the duet of Papageno and Pamina from *Die Zauberflöte*, 'Könnte jeder brave Mann solche Glöckchen finden', from the first act finale:

For *Der Rosenkavalier* he studied Mozart's score to absorb the proper Viennese atmosphere into his Bavarian style.

In the first act, the irruption into the aristocratic bedroom of the Marschallin's crude country cousin, Baron Ochs, brings another Mozartian pastiche, this time slightly less obvious:

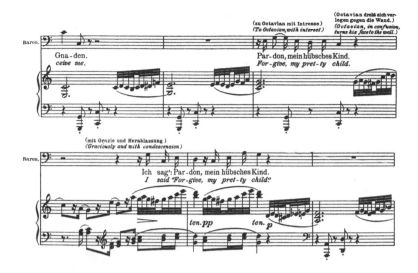

In neither case has Strauss even bothered to change the key of his model, here the Trial by Fire and Water from the second act finale of *Die Zauberflöte*:

Pastiche of an antique style in the eighteenth and nine-teenth centuries had largely been confined to the evocation of religious atmosphere in opera, liturgical works, and nocturnes, although Brahms also developed a medieval-sounding troubadour style for episodes in chamber music with an effect of Olde-Tyme Chivalrye.

It is, indeed, with the music of Brahms that nostalgia for the style of the past invades the musical world ('How wonderful it was to be a composer at the time of Mozart when it was easy to write music!' he is said to have remarked), a nostalgia that is most effective when the pastiche is unconvincingly authentic – in other words, when the style of the past is conveyed with enough added anachronistic modern detail to let us sense how far distant and alien the past is. At its greatest, that is the principle of Debussy's Image, *Hommage à Rameau*, which is, astonishingly and paradoxically, his most Wagnerian work for piano, in which the old-fashioned sarabande rhythm is transformed by memories of *Parsifal*,[6] both in the rhythmic construction of the central section with its waves of growing intensity and the sweep of the climaxes. It even starts like the opening of *Parsifal* with a long unhar-monized, unaccompanied melody followed by a chorale cadence.

---

[6]Debussy used to give lectures on *Parsifal* with illustrations at the piano. He lamented that he had trouble keeping Klingsor out of *Pelléas et Mélisande*, but the leitmotif of Klingsor is prominently quoted unaccompanied during Mélisande's death scene – perhaps that was Debussy's way of exorcising the old wizard.

Stravinsky's neo-classicism also emphasizes its distance from the past. In the Sonata for Piano, for example, almost every tonic note of the opening melody is harmonized by a dominant, every melodic note implying the dominant by a tonic chord. The composer himself claimed that he used classical formulas and phrases the way he previously used folk melodies; in both cases they were treated as exotic and picturesque material, and he subverted the original musical systems to which they belonged and turned them into something instantly recognizable as Stravinsky, as Picasso did with the borrowed forms of Ingres.

Before Stravinsky's neoclassical work, however, he had already developed a shock technique, more austere and less lush than the one Strauss had created in *Salome*. The most powerful affective creation of early Stravinsky is surely the second scene of *Petrushka*, where the unexpected explosion of off-beat accents and the desperate reiteration of small detail convey the frustrated rage of the puppet hero. Stravinsky has often been quoted as claiming that music has no affective significance (a statement provoked by the irrelevant romantic phrasing and *rubati* used by conductors of his work), but the deliberate austerity of the *Symphonies of Wind Instruments* is nevertheless itself an impressive emotion, physically experienced with delight by any listener who has learned to listen sympathetically. In both *Le sacre du printemps* and *Les noces* the disruption of the bodily expectations of rhythm and accent are essential parts of the tradition of the sentiment of the twentieth century. Composers have always played with surprise at least since the madrigals of Luca Marenzio, but the modernist style of the past century has gone further than any other in frustrating our unconscious physical expectations of systematic regularity. Haydn and other composers of the past still startle us physically even when we know the surprise is coming, but the density of the attacks on our bodily reliance on regular rhythm and harmonic resolution was greater in the twentieth century than at any time before.

After the poetic evocation of the Spring night at the opening of *Le sacre du printemps*, the staggered off-beat accents of the barbaric dance that follows still jolt our sensibilities. The effect became integral to the music of the twentieth century. The beginning of Debussy's first Étude 'in the style of Mister Czerny' exhibits the profound influence of Stravinsky's brutality with a similar effect of shock through rhythm, dissonance and dynamics combined:

The repeated A flat in the right hand is a deliberately alien element, and the following opposition of white and black keys was foreshadowed by Stravinsky's clash of C major and F sharp major triads in *Petrushka*.

The pervading chromaticism and the more easygoing use of dissonance made it more difficult for composers to achieve an effective contrast of sentiment by simply opposing major and minor modes or contrasting diatonic and chromatic harmony. They often had recourse to the device of an obsessive use of one kind of chord for a long passage, or section – or even for a whole piece. The technique may derive from the innovations of Chopin's Études. Using one interval for an entire piece gives it a marked and characteristic sonority with an easily identifiable affective character: thirds and sixths, for example, are more melting than octaves and fifths to an ear trained in tonality. Chopin's Black Key Étude is not actually very pentatonic, as the left-hand harmony uses a lot of white keys, but nevertheless it has an individual harmonic character.

The use of a single chord and its transpositions for a phrase or a long stretch in piano music by later composers does not have Chopin's excuse of exercising the pianist's hand, but it effectively produces an individual and characteristic sonority with an individual atmosphere. Debussy developed the technique with great mastery. Almost every chord in the opening phrase of 'Et la lune descend sur le temple qui fut' (*Images*, Book II) has a fourth plus a second, and when the fourth disappears the second continues to function, making dissonances of delicate clarity:

The sentiment is enforced more by the sonority than by the melodic contour, and later pages continue to exploit the fourths and seconds that define the character of the piece. In the final page we encounter these two intervals everywhere, arpeggiated at the end and outlining the fourths and seconds in slow detached notes:

A prelude of Debussy that would seem to define a sentiment similar to the above *Image* obsessively uses a chord with
a sonority so different, although equally soft, that it exposes
the futility of verbal description of musical sentiment. It may
be difficult to put a label to this sentiment, but we do not need
to name it to recognize and appreciate it. The title of the
prelude, 'La terrasse des audiences du clair de lune' ('The
reception terrace by moonlight'), is no real help in understanding Debussy's intention at the moment of composing, as
it comes from a newspaper account of travel in India that

Debussy read about this time. In any case, giving a name to sentiments is often not illuminating, as I remarked at the opening of this study. (It is obvious, for example, that the similar slow movements of Beethoven's op. 10. no. 3 and op. 106 both represent grief and despair, and both are a Largo in 6/8, but the emotion is so different in the two cases that characterizing it amounts simply to giving a detailed description of a performance of each.)

Like the *Image* we have just been considering, the prelude represents a meditative calm with the remnants of distantly recalled turbulence:

However, the texture here, much thicker and more chromatic than the fourths and seconds of the *Image*, has a different and more troubling impact. The basic repeated chord is a dominant seventh in first inversion (the least harsh position,[7] a dominant seventh of an E major triad with G sharp as the bass note), which appears at the end of the first phrase, followed by a single transposition and an arabesque that outlines dominant seventh chords with roots on G natural and C sharp. Then there is a series of more transpositions of the chord, some with octave doublings, making eight-note chords. After a return of the arabesque, seven pure triads thickly doubled in the highest register radically change the affective character as if clearing the air. The disappearance of the dominant seventh dissonance combined with the new high register is like a change of mode. The style and the sentiment depend on a concentration on one kind of sonority

---

[7]The acoustic quality of the intervals defined in terms of their relation to the bass note gives the character of the chord. The first or root position of the dominant seventh emphasizes the fifth and the seventh, with the fifth giving stability and the seventh brilliance; the second position gives the more mellifluous sixth between the bass and soprano the greatest prominence; the third position is the most dissonant as it sets a fourth in relief between the bass and alto.

repeated in various transpositions. The climax concentrates on the different inversions of the still omnipresent dominant seventh:

The technique becomes even more obsessive with Ravel, and dominates his three Lisztian tone poems, *Gaspard de la nuit,* the greatest of his works for piano. The first piece, a sound image of a nymph, *Undine,* opens with the shimmering of light on water represented by a complex trill with a perfect triad and an added flat sixth degree (C sharp triad plus an A natural); this sonority with slight alterations – the sixth degree sharpened, the triad diminished, and so on – governs a large part of the piece:

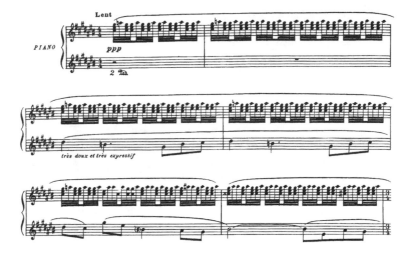

At the end the nymph clearly dives into the water with a huge splash, and the initial chord descends in four transpositions, and returns arpeggiated after indicating a circular motion G♯ F♯ C♯ D♯ repeated many times more and more slowly, a natural representation of the larger and larger circles formed in the water after the splash and finally recalling the melancholy sound of the initial harmony:

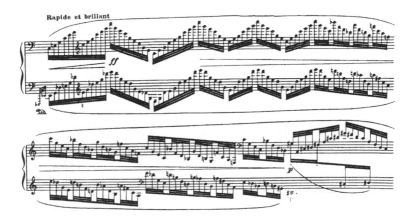

136

A very high proportion of all the harmonies on this page and throughout the piece exhibit transposed versions of the same chord, a perfect triad with a single added dissonance of a minor second.

The second piece, *Le gibet* ('The Gallows'), is the most obsessive of all our examples, as the B flat above middle C tolls softly and absolutely inexorably for a good five minutes in a slightly asymmetrical but unchanging rhythm from beginning to end:

By 1900, the eighteenth-century harmonic system of triadic tonality, or the more chromatic version of tonality of the nineteenth century, could no longer inspire a coherent and original representation of an individual and distinctive sentiment that would set a piece off except by seeking an idiosyncratic element of tone colour, a single note (not the tonic), or a special interval, or an interesting chord that at times almost replaces the tonic as a stable unifying device. The technique transforms harmony into a medium of texture and of tone colour.

The situation in the twentieth century became more acute when, with atonality, serialism and the dodecaphonic system, the contrast of the major and minor modes no longer seemed available for expression. Every change of style implies a loss as well as a gain, like the loss of the refined, precise nuances of the eighteenth century with the coming of the fatter and weightier style after 1830 (as Brahms, quoted above, sensed when he deplored how much more difficult music was after Mozart). By 1920 the loss was felt perhaps most poignantly by Alban Berg in the opera *Wozzeck*, and in his first serial work, the Chamber Concerto for Piano, Violin and Winds. He dealt with it in both works by methods that closely resemble Debussy's way of attaining an idiosyncratic unity of tone colour. In *Wozzeck*, the musical climax surrounding the murder is conceived as three obsessive inventions: invention on a note, B, invention on a six-note chord, and finally an invention on a tonality, D minor. The recourse to obsession is significant, but it was important to affirm the effect of resolution by an explosion of all the tensions of the opera.

For the Chamber Concerto, the method was similar but more subtle. In the first movement, a set of variations for piano and winds, Berg finds a way to give an individual cast to each variation. There are different ways of arriving at all twelve notes of the chromatic scale by the repeated transposition of simple chords without playing any note twice. These are

1) three diminished seventh chords:

2) four augmented triads:

3) the two forms of the whole tone scale:

Employing one set of these transposed chords gives both a totally chromatic non-tonal basis and an individual harmonic character as well, and Berg uses each set in a different variation, creating an identifiably unique expressive sound for each. The harmonies they provide serve as a chromatically saturated neutral background for the basic twelve-tone series of the whole work. These two solutions of the opera and the chamber concerto are singular experiments, one-offs, not to be tried again if one wishes to retain some pretence to originality.

The second half of the twentieth century still seems chaotic in retrospect with all of the competing ideologies: neo-tonal classicism, neo-tonal romanticism, orthodox dodecaphonic style, Darmstadt serialism, minimalism, neoclassicism, and so on. If serious music survives in something like its present form, in a decade or two we may have some idea of which fraction of these competing dogmatisms will remain seductive and coherent. A representation of sentiment is not equally efficient in all of these rival trends, but is present in all.

We require a certain humility, however, to remind ourselves that the power of music on our sensibilities depends much less on composition than on execution. In the 1820s, the poet Giacomo Leopardi remarked:

> The miracles of music, its natural power over our emotions, the pleasure that it naturally arouses, its ability to awaken enthusiasm and imagination and so on, consist and lie properly in the sound or in the voice, to the extent that the sound or the voice is pleasing, and in the

harmony of sounds and of the voices, to the extent that the mixture of sounds and voices is naturally pleasing to the ear, and not in the melody; and that consequently the principle of music and of its effects does not belong to the theory of the beautiful proper more than that which belongs to the consideration of smells, tastes, and simple colours, and so on. . . . Considering these observations, it is not surprising that savages and even animals have taken such delight in our music.

To this identification of the art of music with the arts of cooking and mixing perfumes, implying that it caters to the basest and least intellectual human instincts, Leopardi adds persuasively that a beautiful melody badly sung gives little pleasure and that a wretched melody perfectly performed by an instrument or by a very agreeable voice creates great pleasure. This would imply that a good deal of the foregoing account of the way composers move us and create such a rich variety of sentiments is less relevant to the experience of the average concertgoer than we might like to believe. However, we can cheer ourselves up by reflecting that the greater and the more profound our experience of music becomes, the more we expect the performers to create more than just a pleasing sound, but to move us by illuminating and setting in relief what is most significant in the musical score.

Index

Page numbers in bold type indicate music examples

Piano Trio in E major (Hob.
XV:28) 60, **61–2**
String Quartets 60, 68
op. 33 no. 3 ('The Bird') **59**–60
op. 64 no. 3 **68–9**
op. 64 no. 5 ('The Lark') **70**–1
op. 76 no. 3 ('Emperor') **78–9**
Symphonies
no. 52 in C minor **74**–5
no. 78 in C minor **73**–5
no. 95 in C minor 79, **80**–**1**
Heartz, Daniel 24, 27
Hegel, Georg Wilhelm Friedrich 52
Heinse, Wilhelm 8
Hoffmann, E. T. A. (Ernst Theodor
Amadeus) 22–3
Ingres, Jean-Auguste-Dominique 128
Kandinsky, Wassily 33
Kant, Immanuel 52
Klee, Paul 33
Leopardi, Giacomo 140–1
Liszt, Franz 19, 31, 33, 104,
108–11, 135
Années de pèlerinage 124
Harmonies poétiques et religieuses
101, **108–10**, 111
Piano Sonata 19
Variations on *Weinen, Klagen,
Sorgen, Zagen* 25
Marenzio, Luca 129
Matheson, Thomas 23
Mendelssohn, Felix 5, 22
Meyerbeer, Giacomo (*Les
Huguenots*) 19
de Montaigne, Michel (*Essais*) 6
Monteverdi, Claudio 27n.
Mozart, Wolfgang Amadeus 8, 10,
12, 19, 21, 34–5, 52–60,
65–70, 75, 89, 94, 100, 104,
124–5, 127, 138

Così fan tutte 8
Don Giovanni 8
Fantasy in C minor K. 475 76
Ein musikalischer Spass (*Musical
Joke*) 10
Le Nozze di Figaro 32, 93
Piano Concertos
K. 491 in C minor **77–8**
K. 595 in B♭ major 104
Piano Sonatas
K. 310 in A minor **76**
K. 333 in B♭ major 50
K. 457 in C minor **75**–6, 84
K. 576 in D major **53**–4, 59
String Quartets 60, 65, 68
K. 387 in G major **65–6**, 67
K. 465 in C major
('Dissonance') 91n., 106
String Quintets
K. 515 in C major 54, **55–6**,
60
K. 516 in G minor 18
K. 593 in D major **58–9**
Symphonies
no. 38 in D major ('Prague')
56–7, 58
no. 40 in G minor 21
no. 41 in C major ('Jupiter')
50–4, **51–2**, 57, 59
Die Zauberflöte 31–32, 124,
125–6
Picasso, Pablo 128
Puccini, Giacomo (*Tosca*) 123
Pythagoras 6
Ravel, Maurice (*Gaspard de la nuit*)
135–8
'Ondine' 135, **136–7**
'Le gibet' **137**–8
Reger, Max 122
Respighi, Ottorino 31

Canadian Mathematical Society
Société mathématique du Canada

Editors-in-Chief
Rédacteurs-en-chef
Jonathan M. Borwein
Peter Borwein

Springer
New York
Berlin
Heidelberg
Barcelona
Hong Kong
London
Milan
Paris
Singapore
Tokyo

CMS Books in Mathematics
Ouvrages de mathématiques de la SMC

George M. Phillips

Two Millennia of Mathematics

From Archimedes to Gauss

Springer

George M. Phillips
Mathematical Institute
University of St. Andrews
St. Andrews KY16 9SS
Scotland

Editors-in-Chief
Rédacteurs-en-chef
Jonathan M. Borwein
Peter Borwein
Centre for Experimental and Constructive Mathematics
Department of Mathematics and Statistics
Simon Fraser University
Burnaby, British Columbia V5A 1S6
Canada

Mathematics Subject Classification (2000): 00A05, 01A05

Library of Congress Cataloging-in-Publication Data
Phillips, G.M. (George McArtney)
    Two millennia of mathematics : from Archimedes to Gauss / George M. Phillips.
       p. cm. — (CMS books in mathematics ; 6)
    Includes bibliographical references and index.
    ISBN 0-387-95022-2 (alk. paper)
       1. Mathematics—Miscellanea.   2. Mathematics—History.   I. Title.   II. Series.
QA99 .P48 2000
510—dc21   00-023807

Printed on acid-free paper.

Production managed by Timothy Taylor; manufacturing supervised by Erica Bresler.
Photocomposed copy prepared from the author's LATEX files.
Printed and bound by Hamilton Printing Co., Rensselaer, NY.
Printed in the United States of America.

9 8 7 6 5 4 3 2 1

ISBN 0-387-95022-2   SPIN 10762921

Springer-Verlag   New York Berlin Heidelberg
A member of BertelsmannSpringer Science+Business Media GmbH

Preface

This book is intended for those who love mathematics, including undergraduate students of mathematics, more experienced students, and the vast number of *amateurs*, in the literal sense of those who do something for the love of it. I hope it will also be a useful source of material for those who teach mathematics. It is a collection of loosely connected topics in areas of mathematics that particularly interest me, ranging over the two millennia from the work of Archimedes, who died in the year 212 BC, to the *Werke* of Gauss, who was born in 1777, although there are some references outside this period. In view of its title, I must emphasize that this book is certainly not pretending to be a comprehensive history of the mathematics of this period, or even a complete account of the topics discussed. However, every chapter is written with the history of its topic in mind. It is fascinating, for example, to follow how both Napier and Briggs constructed their logarithms before many of the most relevant mathematical ideas had been discovered. Do I really mean "discovered"? There is an old question, "Is mathematics *created* or *discovered*?" Sometimes it seems a shame not to use the word "create" in praise of the first mathematician to write down some outstanding result. Yet the inner harmony that sings out from the best of mathematics seems to demand the word "discover." Patterns emerge that are sometimes reinterpreted later in a new context. For example, the relation

$$(a^2 + b^2)(c^2 + d^2) = (ac - bd)^2 + (ad + bc)^2,$$

showing that the product of two numbers that are the sums of two squares is itself the sum of two squares, was known long before it was reinterpreted as a property of complex numbers. It is equivalent to the fact that the modulus of the product of two complex numbers is equal to the product of their moduli. Other examples of the inner harmony of mathematics occur again and again when generalizations of known results lead to exciting new developments.

There is one matter that troubles me, on which I must make my peace with the reader. I need to get at you before you find that I have cited my own name as author or coauthor of 11 out of the 55 items in the Bibliography at the end of this book. You might infer from this either that I must be a mathematician of monumental importance or that I *believe* I am. Neither of these statements is true. As a measure of my worth as a mathematician, I would not merit even one citation if the Bibliography contained 10,000 items. (Alas, the number 10,000 could be increased, but let us not dwell on that.) However, this is *one* mathematician's account (mine!) of *some* of the mathematics that has given him much pleasure. Thus references to some of the work in which I have shared demonstrates the depth of my interest and commitment to my subject, and I hope that doesn't sound pompous. I think it may surprise most readers to know that many interesting and exciting results in mathematics, although usually not the most original and substantial, have been obtained (discovered!) by ordinary mortals, and not only by towering geniuses such as Archimedes and Gauss, Newton and Euler, Fermat and the hundreds of other well-known names. This gives us a feel for the scale and the grandeur of mathematics, and allows us to admire all the more its greatest explorers and discoverers. It is only by asking questions ourselves and by making our own little discoveries that we gain a real understanding of our subject. We should certainly not be disappointed if we later find that some well-known mathematician found "our" result before us, but should be proud of finding it independently and of being in such exalted company. One of the most impressive facts about mathematics is that it talks about absolute truths, which are not dependent on opinion or fashion. Any theorem that was proved two thousand years ago, or at any time in the past, is still true today.

No two persons' tastes are exactly the same, and perhaps no one else could or would have made the same selection of material as I have here. I was extremely fortunate to begin my mathematical career with a master's degree in number theory at the University of Aberdeen, under the supervision of E. M. Wright, who is best known for his long-lived text *An Introduction to the Theory of Numbers*, written jointly with the eminent mathematician G. H. Hardy. I then switched to approximation theory and numerical analysis, while never losing my love for number theory, and the topics discussed in this book reflect these interests. I have had the good fortune to collaborate in mathematical research with several very able mathematicians, valued friends from whom I have learned a great deal while sharing the excitement of research and the joys of our discoveries. Although the results that most mathematical researchers obtain, including mine, are of minuscule importance compared to the mathematics of greatest significance, their discoveries give enormous pleasure to the researchers involved.

I have often been asked, "How can one do research in mathematics? Surely it is all known already!" If this is your opinion of mathematics, this book may influence you towards a different view, that mathematics was not brought down from Mount Sinai on stone tablets by some mathematical Moses, all ready-made and complete. It is the result of the work of a very large number of persons over thousands of years, work that is still continuing vigorously to the present day, and with no end in sight. A rather smaller number of individuals, including Archimedes and Gauss, have made such disproportionately large individual contributions that they stand out from the crowd.

The year 2000 marks the 250th anniversary of the death of J. S. Bach. By a happy chance I read today an article in *The Guardian* (December 17, 1999) by the distinguished pianist András Schiff, who writes, "A musician's life without Bach is like an actor's life without Shakespeare." There is an essential difference between Bach and Shakespeare, on the one hand, and Gauss, a figure of comparable standing in mathematics, on the other. For the music of Bach and the literature of Shakespeare bear the individual stamp of their creators. And although Bach, Shakespeare, and Gauss have all greatly influenced the development, at least in Europe, of music, literature, and mathematics, respectively, the work of Gauss does not retain his individual identity, as does the work of Bach or Shakespeare, being rather like a major tributary that discharges its waters modestly and anonymously into the great river of mathematics. While we cannot imagine anyone but Bach creating his *Mass in D Minor* or his *Cello Suites*, or anyone but Shakespeare writing *King Lear* or the *Sonnets*, we must concede that *all* the achievements of the equally mighty Gauss would, sooner or later, have been *discovered* by someone else. This is the price that even a prince of mathematics, as Gauss has been described, must pay for the eternal worth of mathematics, as encapsulated in the striking quotation of G. H. Hardy at the beginning of Chapter 1.

Mathematics has an inherent charm and beauty that cannot be diminished by anything I write. In these pages I can pursue my craft of seeking to express sometimes difficult ideas as simply as I can. But only *you* can find mathematics *interesting*. As Samuel Johnson said, "Sir, I have found you an argument; but I am not obliged to find you an understanding." I find this a most comforting thought.

The reader should be warned that this author likes to use the word "we." This is not the royal "we" but the mathematical "we," which is used to emphasize that author and reader are in this together, sometimes up to our necks. And on the many occasions when I write words such as "We can easily see," I hope there are not too many times when you respond with "Speak for yourself!"

If you are like me, you will probably wish to browse through this book, omitting much of the detailed discussion at a first reading. But then I hope some of the detail will seize your attention and imagination, or some of the Problems at the end of each section will tempt you to reach for pencil and paper to pursue your own mathematical research. Whatever your mathematical experience has been to date, I hope you will enjoy reading this book even half as much as I have enjoyed writing it. And I hope you learn much while reading it, as I indeed have from writing it.

George M. Phillips
Crail, Scotland

Acknowledgments

Thanks to the wonders of LaTeX, an author of a mathematics text can produce a book that is at least excellent in its appearance. Therefore, I am extremely grateful not only to the creators of LaTeX but also to those friends and colleagues who have helped this not so old dog learn some new tricks. Two publications have been constantly on my desk, *Starting LaTeX*, by C. D. Kemp and A. W. Kemp, published by the Mathematical Institute, University of St Andrews, and *Learning LaTeX*, by David F. Griffiths and Desmond J. Higham, published by SIAM. I am further indebted to David Kemp for ad hoc personal tutorials on LaTeX, and to other St Andrews colleagues John Howie and Michael Wolfe for sharing their know-how on this topic. It is also a pleasure to record my thanks to John O'Connor for his guidance on using the symbolic mathematics program Maple, which I used to pursue those calculations in the book that require many decimal places of accuracy. My colleagues John O'Connor and Edmund Robertson are the creators of the celebrated website on the History of Mathematics, which I have found very helpful in preparing this text.

I am also very grateful to my friend and coauthor Halil Oruç for his help in producing the diagrams, and to Tricia Heggie for her cheerful and unstinting technical assistance.

My mathematical debts are, of course, considerably greater than those already recorded above. In the Preface I have mentioned my fortunate beginnings in Aberdeen, and it is appropriate to give thanks for the goodness of my early teachers there, notably Miss Margaret Cassie, Mr John Flett, and Professor H. S. A. Potter. In my first lecturing appointment, at the University of Southampton, I was equally fortunate to meet Peter Taylor, my long-time friend and coauthor from whom I learned much about numerical analysis.

Several persons have kindly read all or part of the manuscript, and their comments and suggestions have been very helpful to me. My thanks thus go to my good friends Cleonice Bracciali in Brazil, Dorothy Foster and Peter Taylor in Scotland, Herta Freitag and Charles J. A. Halberg in the U.S.A., and Zeynep Koçak and Halil Oruç in Turkey. Of course, any errors that remain are my sole responsibility. In addition to those already mentioned I would like to acknowledge the encouragement and friendship, over the years, of Bruce Chalmers, Ward Cheney, Philip Davis, Frank Deutsch, and Ted Rivlin in the U.S.A.; Peter Lancaster, A. Sharma, Bruce Shawyer, and Sankatha Singh in Canada; A. Sri Ranga and Dimitar Dimitrov in Brazil; Colin Campbell, Tim Goodman, and Ron Mitchell in Scotland; Gracinda Gomes in Portugal; Wolfgang Dahmen in Germany; Zdeněk Kosina and Jaroslav Nadrchal in the Czech Republic; Blagovest Sendov in Bulgaria; Didi Stancu in Romania; Lev Brutman in Israel; Kamal Mirnia in Iran; B. H. Ong, H. B. Said, W.-S. Tang, and Daud Yahaya in Malaysia; Lee Seng Luan in Singapore; Feng Shun-xi, Hou Guo-rong, L. C. Hsu, Shen Zuhe, You Zhao-yong, Huang Chang-bin, and Xiong Xi-wen in China; and David Elliott in Australia. I must also thank Lee Seng Luan for introducing me to the wonderful book of Piet Hein, *Grooks*, published by Narayana Press, and in particular to the "Grook" that I have quoted at the beginning of Chapter 4. This was often mentioned as we worked together, since it so cleverly sums up the tantalizing nature of mathematical research.

Mathematics has been very kind to me, allowing me to travel widely and meet many interesting people. I learned at first hand what my dear parents knew without ever leaving their native land, that we are all the *same* in the things that matter most. I have felt at home in all the countries I have visited. It pleases me very much that this book appears in a Canadian Mathematical Society series, because my mathematical travels began with a visit to Canada. It was on one of my later visits to Canada that I met the editors, Peter and Jon Borwein. I am grateful to them for their support for this project. Their constructive and kind comments encouraged me to add some further material that, I believe, has had a most beneficial influence on the final form of this book.

I wish to acknowledge the fine work of those members of the staff of Springer, New York who have been involved with the production of this book. There are perhaps only two persons who will ever scrutinize every letter and punctuation mark in this book, the author and the copyeditor. Therefore, I am particularly grateful to the copyeditor, David Kramer, who has carried out this most exacting task with admirable precision.

George M. Phillips
Crail, Scotland

Contents

1

From Archimedes to Gauss

Archimedes will be remembered when Aeschylus is forgotten because languages die and mathematical ideas do not.

G. H. Hardy

This opening chapter is about certain arithmetical processes that involve *means*, such as $\frac{1}{2}(a + b)$ and $\sqrt{ab}$, the arithmetic and geometric means of a and b. At the end of the eighteenth century, Gauss computed an elliptic integral by an inspired "double mean" process, consisting of the repeated evaluation of the arithmetic and geometric means of two given positive numbers. Strangely, the calculations performed by Archimedes some two thousand years earlier for estimating π can also be viewed (although not at that time) as a double mean process, and the same procedure can also be used to compute the logarithm of a given number. With the magic of mathematical time travel, we will see how Archimedes could have gained fifteen more decimal digits of accuracy in his estimation of π if he had known of techniques for speeding up convergence. We also give a brief summary of other methods used to estimate π since the time of Archimedes. These include several methods based on inverse tangent formulas, which were used over a period of about 300 years, and some relatively more recent methods based on more sophisticated ideas pioneered by Ramanujan in the early part of the twentieth century.

1.1   Archimedes and Pi

In the very long line of Greek mathematicians from Thales of Miletus and Pythagoras of Samos in the sixth century BC to Pappus of Alexandria in the fourth century AD, Archimedes of Syracuse (287-212 BC) is the undisputed leading figure. His pre-eminence is the more remarkable when we consider that this dazzling millennium of mathematics contains so many illustrious names, including Anaxagoras, Zeno, Hippocrates, Theodorus, Eudoxus, Euclid, Eratosthenes, Apollonius, Hipparchus, Heron, Menelaus, Ptolemy, Diophantus, and Proclus.

Although his main claim to fame is as a mathematician, Archimedes is also known for his many discoveries and inventions in physics and engineering, which include his invention of the water screw, still used in Egypt until recently for irrigation, draining marshy land and pumping out water from the bilges of ships, and his invention of various devices used in defending Syracuse when it was besieged by the Romans, including powerful catapults, the burning mirror, and systems of pulleys. It was his pride in what he could lift with the aid of pulleys and levers that provoked his glorious hyperbole, "Give me a place to stand and I will move the earth." This saying of Archimedes is even more grandly laconic in Greek, in the eight-word almost monosyllabic sentence "δος μοι που στω καὶ κινω τὴν γην." (See Heath [27].) There is also his much-recounted discovery of the hydrostatic principle that a body immersed in a fluid is subject to an upthrust equal to the weight of fluid displaced by the body. This discovery is said to have inspired his famous cry "Eureka" (I have found it).

Before discussing briefly the work covered in his book *Measurement of the Circle*, we mention a few of the other significant contributions that Archimedes made to mathematics. He computed the area of a segment of a parabola, employing a most ingenious argument involving the construction of an infinite number of inscribed triangles that "exhausted" the area of the parabolic segment. This is a most beautiful piece of mathematics, in which he showed that the area of the parabolic segment is $\frac{4}{3}$ the area of a triangle of the same base and altitude. He computed the area of an ellipse by essentially "squashing" a circle. He found the volume and surface area of a sphere. Archimedes gave instructions that his tombstone should have displayed on it a diagram consisting of a sphere with a circumscribing cylinder. C. H. Edwards (see [13]) writes how Cicero, while serving as quaestor in Sicily, had Archimedes' tombstone restored. Edwards amusingly adds, *"The Romans had so little interest in pure mathematics that this action by Cicero was probably the greatest single contribution of any Roman to the history of mathematics."* Archimedes discussed properties of a spiral curve defined as follows: The distance from a fixed point O of any point P on the spiral is proportional to the angle between OP and a fixed line through O. This is called the *Archimedean spiral.* In his evaluation of areas involving the spiral he anticipated methods of the calculus that were not developed until the seventeenth century AD. He also found the volumes of various solids of revolution, obtained by rotating a curve about a fixed straight line.

The following three propositions are contained in Archimedes' book *Measurement of the Circle*.

1. The area of a circle is equal to that of a right-angled triangle where the sides including the right angle are respectively equal to the radius and the circumference of the circle.

2. The ratio of the area of a circle to that of a square with side equal to the circle's diameter is close to 11:14. (This is equivalent to saying that π is close to the fraction $\frac{22}{7}$.)

3. The circumference of a circle is less than $3\frac{1}{7}$ times its diameter but more than $3\frac{10}{71}$ times the diameter. Archimedes obtained these inequalities by considering the circle with radius unity and estimating the perimeters of inscribed and circumscribed regular polygons of ninety-six sides.

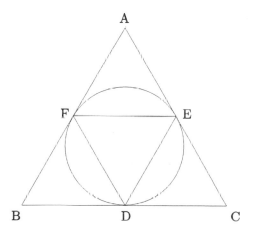

FIGURE 1.1. Circle with inscribed and circumscribed regular polygons with 3 sides (equilateral triangles).

We define π as the ratio of the *perimeter* of a given circle to its diameter. Let us begin with a circle of radius 1. Its perimeter is thus 2π, which is equivalent to saying that, in radian measure, the angle corresponding to one complete revolution is 2π. Let p_n and P_n denote, respectively, half of the perimeters of the inscribed and circumscribed regular polygons with n sides. Recall that a regular polygon is one whose sides and angles are all equal; for example, the regular polygon with 4 sides is the square. Archimedes argued that

$$p_n < \pi < P_n.$$

With $n = 3$ (see Figure 1.1) we find that $DE = \sqrt{3}$ and hence

$$p_3 = \frac{1}{2} \cdot 3\sqrt{3} < \pi < 3\sqrt{3} = P_3.$$

With $n = 4$ and $n = 6$ we obtain

$$p_4 = 2\sqrt{2} < \pi < 4 = P_4$$

and

$$p_6 = 3 < \pi < 2\sqrt{3} = P_6,$$

respectively.

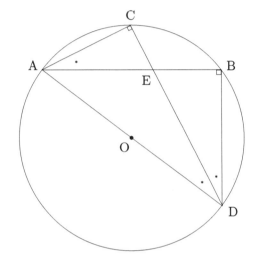

FIGURE 1.2. Archimedes used a diagram like this to show how p_{2n} is related to p_n.

Archimedes deduced how p_{2n} is related to p_n, and also how P_{2n} is related to P_n. To obtain the first of these relations, let us use Figure 1.2, where AB and AC denote one of the sides of the inscribed regular n-gons and regular $2n$-gons, respectively, so that C is the midpoint of the arc ACB. Also, AD is a diameter of the unit circle, so that $AO = 1$, and E is the point of intersection of AB and DC. As a consequence of the "angle at the centre" theorem (see Problem 2.5.1) the angles ACD and ABD are both right angles, and the three marked angles CAE, CDA, and BDE are all equal, the latter two being subtended by two arcs of equal length. We deduce that the three triangles CAE, CDA, and BDE are all *similar*, meaning that they have the same angles, and so their corresponding sides bear the same ratio to each other. Therefore,

$$\frac{DA}{CD} = \frac{AE}{CA} \quad \text{and} \quad \frac{BD}{CD} = \frac{EB}{AC}.$$

Thus

$$\frac{DA + BD}{CD} = \frac{AE + EB}{AC} = \frac{AB}{AC},$$

which yields, with the aid of Pythagoras's theorem,

$$\frac{2 + \sqrt{4 - AB^2}}{\sqrt{4 - AC^2}} = \frac{AB}{AC}, \tag{1.1}$$

since $DA = 2$. If we now cross multiply in (1.1) and square both sides, we may combine the terms in AC^2 to give

$$AC^2 = \frac{AB^2}{2 + \sqrt{4 - AB^2}}. \tag{1.2}$$

Since

$$p_n = \frac{1}{2}\, n \cdot AB \qquad \text{and} \qquad p_{2n} = \frac{1}{2}\, 2n \cdot AC,$$

we deduce from (1.2) that

$$p_{2n}^2 = \frac{2p_n^2}{1 + \sqrt{1 - p_n^2/n^2}}. \tag{1.3}$$

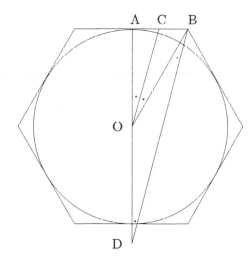

FIGURE 1.3. This diagram is used to show how P_{2n} is related to P_n.

We now turn to Figure 1.3 to derive Archimedes' relation connecting the circumscribed regular polygons. This is more easily obtained than the relation we have just found for the inscribed polygons. In Figure 1.3, which illustrates the case where $n = 6$, AB denotes *half* the length of one side of the circumscribing regular n-gon and AC half the length of one side of

n	p_n	P_n
6	3.0000	3.4642
12	3.1058	3.2154
24	3.1326	3.1597
48	3.1393	3.1461
96	3.1410	3.1428

TABLE 1.1. Lower and upper bounds for π derived by following Archimedes' method of computing half the perimeters of the inscribed and circumscribed regular polygons with 6, 12, 24, 48, and 96 sides.

the circumscribing regular $2n$-gon. The point D is located where the line through B parallel to CO meets the extension of the radius AO. From this construction it is clear that the four marked angles AOC, COB, OBD, and ODB are all equal to $\pi/(2n)$ and that the triangles OAC and DAB are similar. We note also that $OB = OD$, since the angles OBD and ODB are equal. It follows from the similar triangles that

$$\frac{AC}{OA} = \frac{AB}{DA}.$$

Since $OA = 1$ and $OB = OD$, we obtain

$$AC = \frac{AB}{1 + OD} = \frac{AB}{1 + OB}.$$

Thus we have

$$AC = \frac{AB}{1 + \sqrt{1 + AB^2}}. \tag{1.4}$$

On replacing AC and AB by $P_{2n}/(2n)$ and P_n/n, respectively, we find that

$$P_{2n} = \frac{2P_n}{1 + \sqrt{1 + P_n^2/n^2}}. \tag{1.5}$$

Archimedes began with inscribed and circumscribed regular hexagons, with $p_6 = 3$ and $P_6 = 2\sqrt{3}$. He first needed to compute a sufficiently accurate value of $\sqrt{3}$, and he found that

$$1.73202 < \frac{265}{153} < \sqrt{3} < \frac{1351}{780} < 1.73206, \tag{1.6}$$

where we have inserted the two decimal numbers, not used by Archimedes, to let us more easily admire his accuracy. (We note in passing that $x = 265$ and $y = 153$ satisfy the equation $x^2 - 3y^2 = -2$, while $x = 1351$ and $y = 780$ satisfy the equation $x^2 - 3y^2 = 1$. Moreover, we are drawn to suppose that Archimedes had some familiarity with continued fractions, since his lower and upper bounds are convergents to the simple continued fraction for $\sqrt{3}$. See Problem 4.4.15.) Archimedes used each of his formulas (1.3) and (1.5) four times (see Table 1.1) to derive his famous inequalities

$$3.1408 < 3\tfrac{10}{71} < p_{96} < \pi < P_{96} < 3\tfrac{1}{7} < 3.1429, \tag{1.7}$$

where again we have inserted the two decimal numbers to see the accuracy of his bounds. With a sure mastery of his art of calculation, he rounded *down* his values for p_n and rounded *up* his values for P_n so that he obtained *guaranteed* lower and upper bounds for π. Thus the accuracy in (1.7) is of the order of one millimetre in measuring the perimeter of a circle whose diameter is one metre. Although this may not seem so very accurate, Archimedes could, in principle, have estimated π to any accuracy, and Knorr (see [30]) argues that he did indeed obtain a more accurate approximation than that given by (1.7).

Problem 1.1.1 Verify the values of p_n and P_n given above for $n = 3, 4$, and 6.

Problem 1.1.2 Show that p_6 and P_4 are the only values of p_n and P_n that are integers.

Problem 1.1.3 Show that the four marked angles in Figure 1.3 are all equal to $\pi/(2n)$.

Problem 1.1.4 If $\theta = \frac{\pi}{10}$, verify that $\sin 2\theta = \cos 3\theta$ and deduce from the identities

$$\sin 2\theta = 2 \sin \theta \cos \theta \quad \text{and} \quad \cos 3\theta = 4 \cos^3 \theta - 3 \cos \theta$$

that $x = \sin \theta$ satisfies the quadratic equation $4x^2 + 2x - 1 = 0$. Hence show that $\sin \frac{\pi}{10} = \frac{1}{4}(\sqrt{5} - 1)$ and that half the perimeter of the inscribed regular polygon with 10 sides (a *decagon*) of the unit circle is

$$p_{10} = \frac{5}{2}(\sqrt{5} - 1).$$

Problem 1.1.5 Write $p_n = n \sin \theta$ and $P_n = n \tan \theta$ (see the beginning of Section 1.2), where $\theta = \pi/n$, and so verify formulas (1.3) and (1.5) for p_{2n} and P_{2n}.

Problem 1.1.6 Verify that

$$P_n = \frac{p_n}{\sqrt{1 - p_n^2/n^2}}.$$

Problem 1.1.7 Verify that

$$x^4(1-x)^4 = (1 + x^2)(4 - 4x^2 + 5x^4 - 4x^5 + x^6) - 4$$

and hence show that

$$\int_0^1 \frac{x^4(1-x)^4}{1+x^2}\,dx = \frac{22}{7} - \pi,$$

thus justifying Archimedes' inequality $\frac{22}{7} > \pi$. This result, which is both amusing and amazing, was obtained by D. P. Dalzell [12]. Following Dalzell, use the inequalities

$$\frac{1}{2}\int_0^1 x^4(1-x)^4 dx \leq \int_0^1 \frac{x^4(1-x)^4}{1+x^2}\,dx \leq \int_0^1 x^4(1-x)^4 dx$$

to show that

$$\frac{1979}{630} \leq \pi \leq \frac{3959}{1260}.$$

1.2 Variations on a Theme

Some of the material in this section appeared in [42], which is republished in the fine survey *Pi: A Source Book* [4]. We will see how a simple device called "extrapolation to the limit" can be used to adapt Archimedes' method to give much more accurate approximations to π.

In Figure 1.2, the length OA is 1 and the angle AOB is $2\pi/n$, and so $\frac{1}{2}AB = \sin(\pi/n)$. In Figure 1.3, which is concerned with P_n, the radius OA is 1 and angle AOB is π/n, and so $AB = \tan(\pi/n)$. Since p_n and P_n are n times these respective quantities, we have

$$p_n = n \sin\frac{\pi}{n} \quad \text{and} \quad P_n = n \tan\frac{\pi}{n}. \tag{1.8}$$

Let us now write $\theta = \pi/n$ and express the sum of p_n and P_n as

$$p_n + P_n = n \sin\theta\left(\frac{\cos\theta + 1}{\cos\theta}\right) = n\,\frac{2\sin\theta\,\cos^2\frac{1}{2}\theta}{\cos\theta},$$

on using the identity $\cos\theta = 2\cos^2\frac{1}{2}\theta - 1$. Next we find that

$$\frac{2p_n P_n}{p_n + P_n} = \frac{n\sin\theta}{\cos^2\frac{1}{2}\theta} = 2n\,\tan\frac{1}{2}\theta,$$

since $\sin\theta = 2\sin\frac{1}{2}\theta\cos\frac{1}{2}\theta$. This gives the interesting relation

$$P_{2n} = \frac{2p_n P_n}{p_n + P_n}. \tag{1.9}$$

Again using the above identity involving $\sin\theta$, we readily discover the equally fine relation

$$p_{2n} = \sqrt{p_n P_{2n}}. \tag{1.10}$$

Note that the expression on the right of (1.9) has the form

$$\frac{2ab}{a+b} = \frac{1}{\frac{1}{2}(1/a + 1/b)}.$$

This is the reciprocal of the arithmetic mean of the reciprocals of a and b, which is called the *harmonic mean* of a and b. Also, recall that $\sqrt{ab}$ is the *geometric mean* of a and b. Thus we see from (1.9) that P_{2n} is the harmonic mean of p_n and P_n, while from (1.10), p_{2n} is the geometric mean of p_n and P_{2n}. The "entwined" formulas (1.9) and (1.10) allow us to compute P_{2n} and p_{2n} from P_n and p_n with only one evaluation of a square root, whereas three square roots are required if we use Archimedes' formulas (1.3) and (1.5). Archimedes would surely have valued the entwined harmonic–geometric mean formulas.

In view of the trigonometrical expressions for p_n and P_n in (1.8), it is natural to make use of the series

$$\sin\theta = \theta - \frac{\theta^3}{3!} + \frac{\theta^5}{5!} - \frac{\theta^7}{7!} + \cdots \tag{1.11}$$

and

$$\tan\theta = \theta + \frac{1}{3}\theta^3 + \frac{2}{15}\theta^5 + \frac{17}{315}\theta^7 + \cdots . \tag{1.12}$$

Putting $\theta = \pi/n$ and multiplying these last two equations throughout by n, we see that

$$p_n - \pi = \frac{a_2}{n^2} + \frac{a_4}{n^4} + \frac{a_6}{n^6} + \cdots \tag{1.13}$$

and

$$P_n - \pi = \frac{b_2}{n^2} + \frac{b_4}{n^4} + \frac{b_6}{n^6} + \cdots , \tag{1.14}$$

where, for example,

$$a_2 = -\frac{\pi^3}{6n^2} \qquad \text{and} \qquad b_2 = \frac{\pi^3}{3n^2}.$$

Although we may not be so familiar with the coefficients b_j as we are with the a_j, it does not matter, for we do not need to know the values of either sequence of coefficients in what follows. We will now develop (1.13), the error series for p_n, and this analysis applies equally to the error series for P_n. First we replace n by $2n$ in (1.13) to obtain

$$p_{2n} - \pi = \frac{a_2}{(2n)^2} + \frac{a_4}{(2n)^4} + \frac{a_6}{(2n)^6} + \cdots . \tag{1.15}$$

We can now eliminate the term in $1/n^2$ between the error formulas for p_n and p_{2n}: we multiply (1.15) throughout by 4, subtract (1.13), and divide by 3 to derive

$$p_n^{(1)} - \pi = \frac{a_4^{(1)}}{n^4} + \frac{a_6^{(1)}}{n^6} + \cdots , \tag{1.16}$$

where we have written

$$p_n^{(1)} = \frac{4\,p_{2n} - p_n}{3}. \tag{1.17}$$

We said above that the actual values of the coefficients a_j do not concern us, and so we do not need to know the values of the coefficients $a_j^{(1)}$ in (1.16). Since the leading term of the error series for $p_n^{(1)}$ is $1/n^4$, we expect that for n large, $p_n^{(1)}$ will be a better approximation to π than either p_n or p_{2n}. For example, with $n = 6$ we can substitute the values of p_6 and p_{12} from Table 1.1 into (1.17) to give $p_6^{(1)} \approx 3.1411$, which is much closer to π than either p_6 or p_{12} and is more comparable in accuracy to p_{96}.

Given the above error series (1.16) for $p_n^{(1)}$, we can use the same trick and eliminate the term involving $1/n^4$. The leading term in the corresponding series for the error in $p_{2n}^{(1)}$, obtained by replacing n by $2n$ in (1.16), is $a_4^{(1)}/(2n)^4$. So we must multiply the error series for $p_{2n}^{(1)}$ by $2^4 = 16$, subtract the error series for $p_n^{(1)}$, and consequently divide by $16 - 1 = 15$ to obtain

$$p_n^{(2)} - \pi = \frac{a_6^{(2)}}{n^6} + \frac{a_8^{(2)}}{n^8} + \cdots, \tag{1.18}$$

where the $a_j^{(2)}$ are constants and

$$p_n^{(2)} = \frac{16\,p_{2n}^{(1)} - p_n^{(1)}}{15}. \tag{1.19}$$

It is now clear that we can keep on extrapolating in this way. Thus we define $p_n^{(k+1)}$ recursively in terms of $p_n^{(k)}$ and $p_{2n}^{(k)}$ by the relation

$$p_n^{(k+1)} = \frac{4^{k+1}\,p_{2n}^{(k)} - p_n^{(k)}}{4^{k+1} - 1}, \tag{1.20}$$

for $k = 1, 2, \ldots$, where the error in each $p_n^{(k)}$ has the form

$$p_n^{(k)} - \pi = \frac{a_{2(k+1)}^{(k)}}{n^{2(k+1)}} + \frac{a_{2(k+2)}^{(k)}}{n^{2(k+2)}} + \cdots. \tag{1.21}$$

This process is called repeated extrapolation to the limit, and it accelerates the convergence of any sequence whose error has a series like (1.13). Since the sequence P_n also has an error series of this form (see (1.14)), we can apply the same process to P_n, writing down (1.20) with P in place of p. Repeated extrapolation is also applicable to the trapezoidal integration rule, since if $T_n(f)$ denotes the composite trapezoidal rule, using n subintervals, for approximating to the integral of f over $[a, b]$, the error

$$T_n(f) - \int_a^b f(x)dx$$

n	p_n	$p_n^{(1)}$	$p_n^{(2)}$	$p_n^{(3)}$
3	2.59807621			
		3.13397460		
6	3.00000000		3.14158006	
		3.14110472		3.14159265
12	3.10582854		3.14159245	
		3.14156197		
24	3.13262861			

TABLE 1.2. Repeated extrapolation, based on the numbers p_3, p_6, p_{12}, and p_{24}.

can be expressed as a series like that on the right side of (1.13), provided that the integrand f is sufficiently differentiable. The process of repeated extrapolation in this case is called Romberg integration, after Werner Romberg (born 1909). See the fine survey by Claude Brezinski [9], or Phillips and Taylor [44].

Let us now look at a numerical example. Table 1.2 shows the result of repeated extrapolation on p_3, p_6, p_{12}, and p_{24}. The number in the last column is $p_3^{(3)}$, which gives π correct to 8 decimal places. We can do even better than this. Let us begin with $p_3 = 3\sqrt{3}/2$ and, following Archimedes, compute p_6, p_{12}, and so on, up to p_{96} and then repeatedly extrapolate. This would yield a table like Table 1.2, but with six numbers in the column headed p_n, five in the next column, and so on, reducing to one number in the last column, this number being $p_3^{(5)}$. Since we would need to give each number to about 20 digits, we will not display this table for reasons of space. However, to 20 decimal places we have

$$p_3^{(5)} \approx 3.14159\ 26535\ 89703\ 23765, \tag{1.22}$$

$$\pi \approx 3.14159\ 26535\ 89793\ 23846.$$

Thus $p_3^{(5)}$ is smaller than π by an amount less than one unit in the eighteenth decimal place. It seems almost like magic to conjure such amazing accuracy out of such unpromising initial material, consisting of six numbers approximating π, the closest being not quite correct to *three* decimal places. Of course, we need to begin with about 20 digits of accuracy in the values of p_n from which $p_3^{(5)}$ is derived.

As we have said, we can apply repeated acceleration in exactly the same way to the sequence P_n. We obtain

$$P_3^{(5)} \approx 3.14159\ 26535\ 51,$$

which, differing from π in the eleventh decimal place, is not nearly as accurate as $p_3^{(5)}$. Now it is true, as we have already remarked, that we do not need to know the coefficients in the error series for p_n and P_n in order to carry out the extrapolation process. But by examining these coefficients and those of the extrapolated series, we can easily explain why we obtain much better approximations to π by extrapolating the sequence (p_n) rather than the sequence (P_n). To emphasize that the following analysis applies to any series like those in (1.13) and (1.14), we begin with a general series of the form

$$s(n) = \frac{c_2}{n^2} + \frac{c_4}{n^4} + \frac{c_6}{n^6} + \cdots \tag{1.23}$$

and repeatedly extrapolate exactly as we did above, removing one by one the terms in $1/n^2$, $1/n^4$, and so on. We find that the coefficients of the powers $1/n^{2j}$ after one extrapolation are

$$c_{2j}^{(1)} = -\frac{\left(1 - 1/4^{j-1}\right)}{4 - 1} c_{2j}, \quad j \geq 2,$$

and after the second extrapolation we see that the coefficients of the powers $1/n^{2j}$ are

$$c_{2j}^{(2)} = \frac{\left(1 - 1/4^{j-1}\right)\left(1 - 1/4^{j-2}\right)}{(4 - 1)(4^2 - 1)} c_{2j}, \quad j \geq 3.$$

After k extrapolations the coefficients of powers $1/n^{2j}$ of the resulting series are

$$c_{2j}^{(k)} = (-1)^k \frac{\left(1 - 1/4^{j-1}\right)\left(1 - 1/4^{j-2}\right) \cdots \left(1 - 1/4^{j-k}\right)}{(4 - 1)(4^2 - 1) \cdots (4^k - 1)} c_{2j}, \quad j \geq k + 1.$$

If we write $q = \frac{1}{4}$, we can express this more neatly as

$$c_{2j}^{(k)} = (-1)^k q^{k(k+1)/2} \begin{bmatrix} j - 1 \\ k \end{bmatrix} c_{2j}, \quad j \geq k + 1, \tag{1.24}$$

where (see Section 3.4)

$$\begin{bmatrix} j - 1 \\ k \end{bmatrix} = \frac{[j - 1]!}{[k]! \, [j - 1 - k]!} = \frac{[j - 1][j - 2] \cdots [j - k]}{[1][2] \cdots [k]}.$$

This is called a q–binomial coefficient or a Gaussian polynomial, which is constructed from quantities of the form

$$[r] = \frac{1 - q^r}{1 - q}.$$

Note that $[1] = 1$ and that $[r] \to r$ as $q \to 1$. We refer to $[r]$ as a q-integer. Using this notation we can express $c_{2(k+1)}^{(k)}$, the first nonzero term in the series obtained by extrapolating the series (1.23) k times, in the form

$$c_{2(k+1)}^{(k)} = (-1)^k q^{k(k+1)/2} c_{2(k+1)} = \frac{(-1)^k}{2^{k(k+1)}} c_{2(k+1)}, \tag{1.25}$$

since $q = \frac{1}{4}$. Let us take a further look at (1.24) and write, as we did above,

$$\begin{bmatrix} j-1 \\ k \end{bmatrix} = \frac{[j-1][j-2]\cdots[j-k]}{[k]!}. \tag{1.26}$$

Since $0 < q < 1$ and, for $r > 1$,

$$[r] = 1 + q + q^2 + \cdots + q^{r-1} < \frac{1}{1-q}$$

and $[k]! \geq 1$ for all k, we may deduce from (1.26) that

$$0 < \begin{bmatrix} j-1 \\ k \end{bmatrix} < \frac{1}{(1-q)^{k-1}}$$

for all $j \geq k+1$. It thus follows from (1.24) that

$$\left| c_{2j}^{(k)} \right| \leq \frac{q^{k(k+1)/2}}{(1-q)^{k-1}} \, |c_{2j}| \tag{1.27}$$

for all $j \geq k+1$.

For the special case of the error series for $p_n - \pi$, the coefficient of $1/n^{2(k+1)}$ is

$$a_{2(k+1)} - (-1)^{k+1} \frac{\pi^{2k+3}}{(2k+3)!}.$$

After k repeated extrapolations we see from (1.25) that the coefficient of $1/n^{2(k+1)}$ in the series for $p_n^{(k)} - \pi$ is

$$a_{2(k+1)}^{(k)} = \frac{-1}{2^{k(k+1)}} \cdot \frac{\pi^{2k+3}}{(2k+3)!}.$$

In view of (1.27) the error series for $p_n^{(k)} - \pi$ is dominated by its first term, which we see is always negative, and

$$p_n^{(k)} - \pi \approx \frac{-1}{2^{k(k+1)}} \cdot \frac{\pi^{2k+3}}{(2k+3)!} \cdot \frac{1}{n^{2(k+1)}}. \tag{1.28}$$

The following theorem follows from the arguments given above.

Theorem 1.2.1 If for any positive integer n we carry out k repeated extrapolations on the numbers $p_n, p_{2n}, \ldots, p_{2^k \cdot n}$, where p_n is half the perimeter of the regular polygon with n sides inscribed in the unit circle, then the extrapolated values $p_n^{(k)}$ are all underestimates for π, as are the original numbers p_n. Further, $p_n^{(k)}$ tends to π monotonically in n and k, with an error given approximately by (1.28). ∎

Putting $n = 3$ and $k = 5$ in (1.28) we obtain

$$p_3^{(5)} - \pi \approx -0.817 \cdot 10^{-18},$$

which is in very close agreement with our earlier calculation (1.22). Turning to the error series for $P_n - \pi$, our analysis above shows why the results from repeated extrapolation on the P_n in no way match those obtained from the p_n. It is because the coefficients b_{2j}, derived from the series for $\tan\theta$, tend to zero much less rapidly than the coefficients a_{2j}, derived from the series for $\sin\theta$. This slower convergence also gives poorer accuracy in our error estimate. For the coefficient of θ^{13} in the series for $\tan\theta$ is $21844/6081075$, and this leads to the error estimate

$$P_3^{(5)} - \pi \approx -\frac{1}{4^{15}} \cdot \frac{\pi^{13}}{3^{12}} \cdot \frac{21844}{6081075} \approx -0.183 \cdot 10^{-10},$$

correctly showing that $P_3^{(5)}$ is too *small*, with an error in the eleventh decimal place. The magnitude of the error estimate is of the right order but is only about half the true value of the error. In this case the first term in the error series, which is all that we are using, significantly underestimates the sum of the whole series.

A little calculation using (1.28) shows that with $n = 3$, that is, extrapolating k times on the values $p_3, p_6, \ldots, p_{3 \cdot 2^k}$, we can estimate π to 100 decimal places by taking $k = 15$, and to 1000 decimal places by taking $k = 53$. Having mentioned evaluating π to a thousand decimal places, one must immediately say that by the end of the twentieth century π had been calculated to billions of decimal places, using much faster methods than those described above. We will have more to say on this presently.

In the two millennia and more since the time of Archimedes, there have been many approaches to the calculation of π. There were three famous unsolved problems from Greek mathematics, arising from unsuccessful attempts to carry out three particular geometrical constructions using the traditional tools of "ruler and compasses." The compasses are for drawing circles, and the ruler is simply a straightedge with no markings on it. The Greek geometers created a large number of constructions achievable with ruler and compasses, such as drawing a right angle, bisecting a given angle, drawing a circle that passes through the vertices of a given triangle, constructing a square having the area of a given triangle or other polygon, and so on. The famous three classical constructions that were never found are the following :

1. Duplication of the cube.

2. Trisection of any given angle.

3. Squaring the circle.

A *square* can easily be duplicated, that is, a square can be constructed having twice the area of a given square, and an angle can be bisected, so why cannot a cube be duplicated or an angle trisected? Likewise, a square can be constructed to match the area of a given polygon or even a sector of a parabola, so why cannot a square be constructed with the area of a given circle? The above three classical constructions teased mathematicians for more than two thousand years until they were eventually shown, one by one, to be impossible. The quest to square the circle led eventually to two important discoveries about π, first that π is irrational and then the much deeper result that π is *transcendental*, meaning that π is not a root of any equation of the form

$$a_0 + a_1 x + a_2 x^2 + \cdots + a_n x^n = 0,$$

where $a_0, a_1, \ldots, a_n$ are integers. Any number that *is* a root of such a polynomial equation is called *algebraic*, and it can be shown that beginning with a unit length (thinking of the radius of a circle), any length that can be constructed from it by ruler and compasses must be an algebraic number. The irrationality of π was first proved in 1767 by J. H. Lambert (1728–1777), and in 1882 C. L. F. Lindemann (1852–1939) showed that π is transcendental. Lindemann's result thus finally settled the question of the squaring of the circle.

After Archimedes the next noteworthy approximation for π is that due to Zŭ Chōngzhī (429–500), who obtained (see [36])

$$\pi \approx \frac{355}{113} \approx 3.1415929,$$

with an error in the seventh decimal place. It is not known how Zŭ Chōngzhī obtained this very accurate result, but it appears significant that this fraction is one of the convergents of the continued fraction to π. (See (4.75).) However, in 1913 S. Ramanujan (1887–1920) published (see [45]) a highly ingenious ruler and compasses construction in which, beginning with a circle of radius r, he created a square whose area is $\frac{355}{113} r^2$.

For about 300 years, most estimates for π depended on formulas involving the inverse tangent. If $x = \tan y$, we write the inverse function as $y = \tan^{-1} x$. In 1671 James Gregory (1638–75) obtained the series for the inverse tangent,

$$\tan^{-1} x = x - \frac{x^3}{3} + \frac{x^5}{5} - \frac{x^7}{7} + \cdots,$$

and this is valid for $-1 < x \le 1$. In particular, with $x = 1$, we obtain

$$\frac{\pi}{4} = 1 - \frac{1}{3} + \frac{1}{5} - \frac{1}{7} + \cdots.$$

Although this series converges very slowly, methods derived from the series for the inverse tangent were used to obtain approximations to π. One such formula,

$$\frac{\pi}{4} = 4\tan^{-1}\left(\frac{1}{5}\right) - \tan^{-1}\left(\frac{1}{239}\right), \qquad (1.29)$$

was used by John Machin (1680–1751) as early as 1706 to estimate π to one hundred decimal places.

Example 1.2.1 Let us use Machin's formula (1.29), taking the first 21 terms of the series for $\tan^{-1}(1/239)$ and the first 71 terms of the series for $\tan^{-1}(1/5)$, and multiply the resulting estimate of the right side of (1.29) by 4 to obtain an approximation, say a, for π. We find that

$$\pi - a \approx 0.12 \times 10^{-100}. \qquad \blacksquare$$

Following Machin, many mathematicians estimated π using variants of the above inverse tangent formula. In 1973, using a formula due to Gauss,

$$\pi = 48\tan^{-1}\left(\frac{1}{18}\right) + 32\tan^{-1}\left(\frac{1}{57}\right) - 20\tan^{-1}\left(\frac{1}{239}\right),$$

J. Guilloud and M. Bouyer found that the millionth decimal digit of π (counting 3 as the first digit) is 1. (See Borwein and Borwein [6], Blatner [5].)

The "pi calculating game" gained a new lease on life when the work of Ramanujan was eventually brought into play. For in 1914 Ramanujan published a most significant paper in which he used *modular equations* to obtain (see [46]) a large number of unusual approximations to π, for instance

$$\pi \approx \frac{12}{\sqrt{190}} \log\left((2\sqrt{2} + \sqrt{10})(3 + \sqrt{10})\right),$$

which is correct to 18 decimal places. In [46], which is brimming over with formulas, Ramanujan also described another ruler and compasses construction, which yields

$$\pi \approx \left(9^2 + \frac{19^2}{22}\right)^{1/4}.$$

This "curious approximation to π", as Ramanujan himself called it, is correct to 8 decimal places. However, this is a very humble formula to be in the same paper as

$$\frac{1}{\pi} = \frac{2\sqrt{2}}{99^2} \sum_{n=0}^{\infty} \frac{(4n)!}{(n!)^4} \frac{(1103 + 26390n)}{396^{4n}}. \qquad (1.30)$$

If we truncate this last formula after one, two, three, and four terms and take reciprocals, we obtain estimations that agree with π to 6, 15, 23, and 31 figures, respectively, after the decimal point, and with each additional term we obtain no fewer than 8 further decimal places of accuracy.

The calculation of π via (1.30) is effectively a first-order process, in which errors decrease by a constant factor. Even with such a very small factor of about 10^{-8} in this case, for even faster rates of convergence we need to use *higher-order* processes, such as those where the error is squared or cubed at each stage. (We have more to say on rates of convergence in Section 1.4.) Inspired by the work of Ramanujan, other authors have also used the theory of of modular equations, which is concerned with the transformation theory of elliptic integrals (see Section 1.4), to derive higher-order methods for estimating π. For example, Borwein and Borwein [8] give the following process, which converges *quartically* to $1/\pi$, meaning that the error at stage $n + 1$ behaves like a multiple of the *fourth* power of the error at stage n. With $y_0 = \sqrt{2} - 1$ and $\alpha_0 = 6 - 4\sqrt{2}$, we define the sequences (y_n) and (α_n) recursively from

$$y_{n+1} = \frac{1 - (1 - y_n^4)^{1/4}}{1 + (1 - y_n^4)^{1/4}}, \tag{1.31}$$

$$\alpha_{n+1} = (1 + y_{n+1})^4 \alpha_n - 2^{2n+3} y_{n+1}(1 + y_{n+1} + y_{n+1}^2). \tag{1.32}$$

Then the sequence (α_n) converges to $1/\pi$. Since $\alpha_0 \approx 0.343$ and $1/\pi \approx 0.318$, these two numbers agree only in the first place after the decimal point. However, we find from (1.31) and (1.32) that α_1, α_2, and α_3 respectively agree with $1/\pi$ to 9, 40, and 171 figures after the decimal point, in keeping with the stated quartic convergence, where we expect the number of correct figures to increase by something like a factor of four with each iteration. The sequence (α_n) defined in (1.32) satisfies the error bounds (see [8])

$$0 < \alpha_n - 1/\pi < 16 \cdot 4^n e^{-2 \cdot 4^n \pi},$$

so that a mere 15 iterations of (1.31) and (1.32) are needed to give more than a billion correct digits for $1/\pi$. (Borwein and Borwein's paper [8], together with the two papers of Ramanujan [45] and [46], are republished in [4].)

Problem 1.2.1 Let a_n and A_n denote the *areas* of the inscribed and circumscribed regular n-sided polygons of a unit circle. Show that

$$a_{2n} = \sqrt{a_n A_n} \quad \text{and} \quad A_{2n} = \frac{2a_{2n} A_n}{a_{2n} + A_n}.$$

Problem 1.2.2 From the data in Table 1.1, compute the corresponding members of a sequence (Q_n) defined by

$$Q_n = \frac{2p_n + P_n}{3}.$$

Explain why this new sequence gives better approximations to π than either of the two sequences from which it is derived.

Problem 1.2.3 Show that in carrying out the $(k+1)$th extrapolation on the series for $s(n)$ defined by (1.23), we need to multiply $c_{2j}^{(k)}$ by the factor

$$\frac{(4^{k+1}/4^j) - 1}{4^{k+1} - 1}.$$

Deduce that

$$c_{2j}^{(k+1)} = -q^{k+1}\frac{[j - k - 1]}{[k+1]}\, c_{2j}^{(k)}, \quad j \geq k + 2,$$

where $q = \frac{1}{4}$, and hence verify (1.24) by induction on k.

Problem 1.2.4 Put $\alpha = \beta$ in the identity

$$\tan(\alpha + \beta) = \frac{\tan\alpha + \tan\beta}{1 - \tan\alpha\tan\beta}$$

to show that if $\alpha = \tan^{-1}\frac{1}{5}$, then

$$\tan 2\alpha = \frac{5}{12} \quad \text{and} \quad \tan 4\alpha = \frac{120}{119}.$$

Deduce that $\tan(4\alpha + \beta) = 1$, where $\beta = -\tan^{-1}(1/239)$, and so verify the formula (1.29) used by Machin.

Problem 1.2.5 Verify that

$$\frac{\pi}{6} = \tan^{-1}\frac{1}{\sqrt{3}} = \frac{1}{\sqrt{3}}\left(1 - \frac{1}{3\cdot 3} + \frac{1}{3^2\cdot 5} - \frac{1}{3^3\cdot 7} + \cdots\right)$$

and show that using 10 terms of this series we obtain $\pi \approx 3.14159$.

1.3   Playing a Mean Game

Let us take a fresh look at the relations

$$P_{2n} = \frac{2p_n P_n}{p_n + P_n} \quad \text{and} \quad p_{2n} = \sqrt{p_n P_{2n}},$$

which we derived in the last section. To get away from the geometrical origins of the sequences (p_n) and (P_n), we will work instead with

$$a_{n+1} = \frac{2a_n b_n}{a_n + b_n} \quad \text{and} \quad b_{n+1} = \sqrt{a_{n+1}b_n}, \quad n \geq 0, \qquad (1.33)$$

where a_0 and b_0 are both positive. For convenience, we have increased the subscripts by one for the a's and b's, instead of doubling them as we did with the p's and P's. We will go on to show that such sequences (a_n) and (b_n), with initial values a_0 and b_0 satisfying $0 < b_0 < a_0$, share some of the properties of their special cases, the sequences (P_n) and (p_n). We obtain immediately from (1.33) that

$$a_{n+1} - a_n = \frac{a_n(b_n - a_n)}{a_n + b_n} \quad \text{and} \quad a_{n+1} - b_n = \frac{b_n(a_n - b_n)}{a_n + b_n}. \quad (1.34)$$

We also have

$$\frac{b_{n+1}}{a_{n+1}} = \sqrt{\frac{b_n}{a_{n+1}}} \quad \text{and} \quad \frac{b_{n+1}}{b_n} = \sqrt{\frac{a_{n+1}}{b_n}}, \quad (1.35)$$

and we can now state a property of the sequences (a_n) and (b_n).

Theorem 1.3.1 If for the sequences (a_n) and (b_n) defined by (1.33) we have $0 < b_0 < a_0$, then

$$0 < b_0 < b_1 < \cdots < b_n < a_n < \cdots < a_1 < a_0 \quad (1.36)$$

for all $n > 0$ and the sequences (a_n) and (b_n) converge to a common limit.

Proof. We may use induction on n to verify the inequalities (1.36). First, (1.36) holds for $n = 0$. Let us assume that it holds for some $n \geq 0$. Then, using (1.34) and (1.35), we can easily verify that it holds when n is replaced by $n + 1$. For we can deduce from the two equations in (1.34) that

$$a_{n+1} < a_n \quad \text{and} \quad b_n < a_{n+1},$$

so that $b_n < a_{n+1} < a_n$. Then we similarly show from (1.35) that $b_n < b_{n+1} < a_{n+1}$. Thus, by induction, (1.36) holds for all n. To pursue this proof we require the following well-known result concerning the convergence of sequences. A sequence (s_n) that is monotonic increasing and is bounded above converges to a limit. Also, a sequence that is monotonic *decreasing* and is bounded *below* has a limit. By monotonic increasing, we mean that $s_{n+1} \geq s_n$ for all n, and by bounded above we mean that there exists some constant M, say, such that $s_n \leq M$ for all n. (See, for example, Haggerty [23].) Thus the sequence (a_n) is monotonic decreasing and is bounded below, by b_0, and so has a limit, say α. Likewise, the sequence (b_n) is monotonic increasing and is bounded above, by a_0, and so has a limit, say β. Finally, (1.33) shows that $\alpha = \beta$, and this completes the proof. ∎

Having shown that for any positive values of a_0 and b_0 the two sequences a_n and b_n have a common limit, it would be nice to know the value of this limit. It is clear from (1.33) that if the starting values a_0 and b_0 lead to the limit α, the starting values λa_0 and λb_0 lead to the limit $\lambda \alpha$, for any positive λ. So we need concern ourselves only with the *ratio* b_0/a_0. We need to consider two cases, $a_0 > b_0$ and $a_0 < b_0$. (What happens when $a_0 = b_0$?)

When $a_0 > b_0 > 0$, following the special case concerning the sequences (P_n) and (p_n) defined in (1.8) above, let us write

$$a_0 = \lambda \tan \theta \qquad \text{and} \qquad b_0 = \lambda \sin \theta, \tag{1.37}$$

where λ is positive and $0 < \theta < \pi/2$. Thus

$$0 < \frac{b_0}{a_0} = \cos \theta < 1, \tag{1.38}$$

and to determine λ in terms of a_0 and b_0 only let us write

$$\frac{1}{1 - \sin^2 \theta} = 1 + \tan^2 \theta,$$

from which we have

$$\frac{1}{1 - b_0^2/\lambda^2} = 1 + \frac{a_0^2}{\lambda^2}.$$

On solving for λ, we obtain

$$\lambda = \frac{a_0 b_0}{(a_0^2 - b_0^2)^{1/2}}, \tag{1.39}$$

and it follows from (1.38) that

$$\theta = \cos^{-1}(b_0/a_0). \tag{1.40}$$

Let us now return to (1.33), put $n = 0$, and express a_0 and b_0 as in (1.37). We obtain, after a little manipulation,

$$a_1 = 2\lambda \tan \frac{1}{2}\theta \qquad \text{and} \qquad b_1 = 2\lambda \sin \frac{1}{2}\theta.$$

This shows that at each iteration we multiply by 2 and halve the angle of the tangent and sine, and an induction argument justifies our conclusion that

$$a_n = 2^n \lambda \tan(\theta/2^n) \qquad \text{and} \qquad b_n = 2^n \lambda \sin(\theta/2^n). \tag{1.41}$$

Since $\sin \theta$ and $\tan \theta$ both behave like θ for small θ (see (1.11) and (1.12)), it is clear from the latter equations that the sequences (a_n) and (b_n) converge to the common limit

$$\lambda \theta = \frac{a_0 b_0}{(a_0^2 - b_0^2)^{1/2}} \cos^{-1}(b_0/a_0). \tag{1.42}$$

The "Archimedes" case, if we begin with P_3 and p_3, corresponds to the choice $a_0 = 3\sqrt{3}$ and $b_0 = 3\sqrt{3}/2$, so that $\theta = \pi/3$ and $\lambda = 3$.

The sequences $(1/a_n)$ and $(1/b_n)$, where (a_n) and (b_n) are defined by (1.33), were studied by J. Schwab and C. W. Borchardt, and a different proof of their common limit, equivalent to (1.42) above, is given by I. J. Schoenberg (1903–90) in [49].

If a_0 is *smaller* than b_0 and we again use the relations (1.34) and (1.35), we see that the inequalities in (1.36) hold with the a's and b's interchanged. This time we find that the sequence (a_n) is increasing and (b_n) is decreasing, and the two sequences again converge to a common limit. To find this limit we cannot begin, as we did in the first case, by expressing b_0/a_0 as a cosine, since we cannot have $\cos\theta > 1$ for a real value of θ. However, we can use hyperbolic functions. Recall the definitions of the hyperbolic sine, cosine, and tangent in terms of the exponential function:

$$\sinh\theta = \frac{1}{2}\left(e^\theta - e^{-\theta}\right), \quad \cosh\theta = \frac{1}{2}\left(e^\theta + e^{-\theta}\right), \quad \tanh\theta = \frac{\sinh\theta}{\cosh\theta}.$$

Then we can proceed much as before, replacing trigonometrical relations (involving sine, cosine, or tangent) with the corresponding hyperbolic relations. Thus, for $0 < a_0 < b_0$, we write

$$\frac{b_0}{a_0} = \cosh\theta \quad \text{and} \quad \lambda = \frac{a_0 b_0}{\left(b_0^2 - a_0^2\right)^{1/2}}.$$

We see from its definition above that $\cosh\theta \geq 1$ for all real θ, which is appropriate for this case. We then find that we can write

$$a_0 = \lambda\tanh\theta \quad \text{and} \quad b_0 = \lambda\sinh\theta.$$

On working through (1.33) for $n = 0, 1, 2$, and so on, we find that

$$a_n = 2^n\lambda\tanh(\theta/2^n) \quad \text{and} \quad b_n = 2^n\lambda\sinh(\theta/2^n). \tag{1.43}$$

Note how the latter equations compare with (1.41). In this case, where $0 < a_0 < b_0$, we find that the two sequences converge to the common limit

$$\lambda\theta = \frac{a_0 b_0}{\left(b_0^2 - a_0^2\right)^{1/2}} \cosh^{-1}(b_0/a_0). \tag{1.44}$$

Since the hyperbolic cosine is defined in terms of the exponential function (see above), is not very surprising that the *inverse* hyperbolic cosine can be expressed as a (natural) logarithm. We have (see Problem 1.3.2)

$$\cosh^{-1}x = \log\left(x + \sqrt{x^2 - 1}\right), \quad x \geq 1. \tag{1.45}$$

Now let us define a_0 and b_0 in terms of a parameter t, by

$$a_0 = 2t \quad \text{and} \quad b_0 = t^2 + 1,$$

where $t > 1$, and note that $b_0 - a_0 = (t - 1)^2 > 0$. Then, with $x = b_0/a_0$, we find that

$$\sqrt{x^2 - 1} = \frac{t^2 - 1}{2t},$$

so that

$$\log(x + \sqrt{x^2 - 1}) = \log t.$$

We have therefore obtained the following result, which we present for its mathematical interest rather than as a recommended method of computing a logarithm.

Theorem 1.3.2 If we choose

$$a_0 = 2t \quad \text{and} \quad b_0 = t^2 + 1, \tag{1.46}$$

where $t > 1$, as initial values in the iterative process defined by (1.33), then the two sequences (a_n) and (b_n) both converge monotonically to the common limit

$$\frac{2t(t^2 + 1)}{t^2 - 1} \log t. \quad \blacksquare \tag{1.47}$$

Example 1.3.1 Let us choose $t = 2$ in (1.46), so that $a_0 = 4$ and $b_0 = 5$, and find a_{10} and b_{10} by using (1.33) 10 times. We obtain

$$a_{10} \approx 4.6209805 \quad \text{and} \quad b_{10} \approx 4.6209816,$$

and thus from (1.47) we obtain

$$0.6931470 < \log 2 < 0.6931473. \quad \blacksquare$$

In the process defined in Theorem 1.3.2 for finding $\log t$, the errors in a_n and b_n tend to zero like $1/4^n$. There is another algorithm, due to B. C. Carlson (see references [11], [49], and [51]), which also computes a logarithm. Given any initial values $a_0 > b_0 > 0$, Carlson's algorithm computes the sequences (a_n) and (b_n) from

$$a_{n+1} = \sqrt{\tfrac{1}{2} a_n(a_n + b_n)} \quad \text{and} \quad b_{n+1} = \sqrt{\tfrac{1}{2} b_n(a_n + b_n)}. \tag{1.48}$$

The two sequences converge (see Problem 1.3.4) to the common limit

$$L(a_0, b_0) = \sqrt{\frac{a_0^2 - b_0^2}{2 \log(a_0/b_0)}}. \tag{1.49}$$

For Carlson's algorithm, the errors tend to zero like $1/2^n$.

We can also explore what happens to the sequences (a_n) and (b_n), defined by (1.33), in the complex plane. In this case we can think of a_n and b_n as vectors in the Argand diagram. On making a sensible choice of the two complex-valued square roots in (1.33), choosing b_{n+1} as the vector that bisects the *smaller* angle between a_{n+1} and b_n, we find that the sequences (a_n) and (b_n) are monotonic in modulus and argument. (See [43].)

However, there is a much more substantial generalization of (1.33) than merely changing a_0 and b_0 from positive real values to complex values, which follows from our observation that a_{n+1} is the harmonic mean of a_n and b_n and b_{n+1} is the geometric mean of a_{n+1} and b_n. This suggests the following generalization, in which we begin with positive numbers a_0 and b_0 and define the iterative process

$$a_{n+1} = M(a_n, b_n) \quad \text{and} \quad b_{n+1} = M'(a_{n+1}, b_n), \tag{1.50}$$

where M and M' are arbitrary means. Since mathematicians are always looking for work, we can rejoice that the change from (1.33) to (1.50) creates an infinite number of algorithms! This generalization was proposed by Foster and Phillips [15], who describe (1.50) as an *Archimedean* double-mean process, to distinguish it from a Gaussian double-mean process, which we will consider in Section 1.4. They began by *defining* a class of means. We will repeat their definition here. Let $\Re^+$ denote the set of positive real numbers. Then we define a *mean* as a mapping from $\Re^+ \times \Re^+$ to $\Re^+$ that satisfies the three properties

$$a \leq b \quad \Rightarrow \quad a \leq M(a, b) \leq b, \tag{1.51}$$

$$M(a, b) = M(b, a), \tag{1.52}$$

$$a = M(a, b) \quad \Rightarrow \quad a = b. \tag{1.53}$$

The first property (1.51) is absolutely essential, that a mean of a and b lies between a and b. The second property (1.52) says that M is *symmetric* in a and b. Other definitions allow means that are not symmetric. We also remark that the property (1.51) implies that $M(a, a) = a$.

It is easily verified that the arithmetic, geometric, and harmonic means all satisfy the above definition. These three means also satisfy the property

$$M(\lambda a, \lambda b) = \lambda M(a, b) \tag{1.54}$$

for any positive value of λ. A mean that satisfies (1.54) is said to be *homogeneous*.

Example 1.3.2 The following observation allows us to generate an infinite number of means. Let h denote a continuous mapping from $\Re^+$ to $\Re^+$ that is also monotonic. This implies that the inverse function h^{-1} exists. Then M defined by

$$M(a, b) = h^{-1}\left(\frac{1}{2}(h(a) + h(b))\right) \tag{1.55}$$

is a mean, since it is easy to verify that it satisfies the three properties (1.52), (1.51), and (1.53). ∎

We now obtain a generalization of Theorem 1.3.1, when the harmonic and geometric means in (1.33) are replaced by any *continuous* means belonging to the set defined above.

Theorem 1.3.3 Given any positive numbers a_0 and b_0, let

$$a_{n+1} = M(a_n, b_n) \qquad \text{and} \qquad b_{n+1} = M'(a_{n+1}, b_n),$$

where M and M' are any continuous means satisfying the properties (1.51), (1.52), and (1.53), then the two sequences (a_n) and (b_n) converge monotonically to a common limit.

Proof. Let us consider the case where $a_0 \leq b_0$. We will show by induction that

$$a_n \leq a_{n+1} \leq b_{n+1} \leq b_n \tag{1.56}$$

for $n \geq 0$. First we have $a_0 \leq b_0$. Now let us assume that $a_n \leq b_n$ for some $n \geq 0$. Then from (1.50) and (1.51) we have

$$a_n \leq a_{n+1} \leq b_n \tag{1.57}$$

and also

$$a_{n+1} \leq b_{n+1} \leq b_n. \tag{1.58}$$

Then (1.56) follows from (1.57) and (1.58). We may deduce, as in the proof of Theorem 1.3.1, that the sequence (a_n), being an increasing sequence that is bounded above by b_0, must have a limit, say α. Similarly, (b_n), being a decreasing sequence that is bounded below by a_0, must have a limit, say β. By the continuity of M and M', as $a_n \to \alpha$ and $b_n \to \beta$ we obtain from (1.50) that

$$\alpha = M(\alpha, \beta) \qquad \text{and} \qquad \beta = M'(\alpha, \beta)$$

and by (1.53) each of these two relations implies that $\alpha = \beta$. The case where $a_0 > b_0$ may be proved similarly. ∎

We can pursue this double-mean process further to show that, remarkably, no matter which means we choose (provided that they are sufficiently *smooth*), the rate of convergence of the two sequences (a_n) and (b_n) is always the same. In general, if a sequence (s_n) converges to a limit s and

$$\lim_{n \to \infty} \frac{s_{n+1} - s}{s_n - s} = \kappa$$

where $\kappa \neq 0$, then we say that the rate of convergence is *linear* or that we have *first-order* convergence, and we say that the error $s_n - s$ tends to zero like κ^n. (In writing this, we assume that $s_n \neq s$ for all n.) We will show that if the sequences (a_n) and (b_n) defined recursively by (1.50) converge to the common limit α, then

$$\lim_{n \to \infty} \frac{a_{n+1} - \alpha}{a_n - \alpha} = \lim_{n \to \infty} \frac{b_{n+1} - \alpha}{b_n - \alpha} = \frac{1}{4},$$

so that we have first-order convergence in this case, with the errors $a_n - \alpha$ and $b_n - \alpha$ tending to zero like $1/4^n$. We need to assume, in addition to the continuity of M and M', that their partial derivatives up to those of second order are continuous. Then, writing M_x to denote the partial derivative of M with respect to its first variable, we have

$$M_x(\alpha, \alpha) = \lim_{\delta \to 0} \frac{M(\alpha + \delta, \alpha) - M(\alpha, \alpha)}{\delta}$$
$$= \lim_{\delta \to 0} \frac{M(\alpha, \alpha + \delta) - M(\alpha, \alpha)}{\delta},$$

on using (1.52), so that

$$M_x(\alpha, \alpha) = M_y(\alpha, \alpha). \tag{1.59}$$

We now write

$$\alpha + \delta = M(\alpha + \delta, \alpha + \delta)$$
$$= M(\alpha, \alpha) + \delta \, M_x(\alpha, \alpha) + \delta \, M_y(\alpha, \alpha) + O(\delta^2)$$
$$= \alpha + 2\delta \, M_x(\alpha, \alpha) + O(\delta^2),$$

where we have expanded M as a Taylor series in the two variables and used the properties $M(\alpha, \alpha) = \alpha$ and (1.59). Letting $\delta \to 0$, we deduce that

$$M_x(\alpha, \alpha) = M_y(\alpha, \alpha) = \frac{1}{2}, \tag{1.60}$$

and it is worth emphasizing that this holds for all means M with continuous second-order partial derivatives.

To determine the rate of convergence of the sequences (a_n) and (b_n) to the common limit α, let us write $a_n = \alpha + \delta_n$ and $b_n = \alpha + \epsilon_n$. Substituting these relations into (1.50) we have

$$\alpha + \delta_{n+1} = M(\alpha + \delta_n, \alpha + \epsilon_n) \qquad \text{and} \qquad \alpha + \epsilon_{n+1} = M'(\alpha + \delta_{n+1}, \alpha + \epsilon_n).$$

On expanding each of M and M' as a Taylor series in two variables, and using

$$M(\alpha, \alpha) = M'(\alpha, \alpha) = \alpha$$

and (1.60), we readily find that

$$\delta_{n+1} = \frac{1}{2}(\delta_n + \epsilon_n) + O\left(\delta_n^2 + \epsilon_n^2\right) \tag{1.61}$$

and

$$\epsilon_{n+1} = \frac{1}{4}(\delta_n + 3\epsilon_n) + O\left(\delta_n^2 + \epsilon_n^2\right). \tag{1.62}$$

Note that we need to make use of (1.61) in deriving (1.62). We now recall that (a_n) and (b_n) converge *monotonically* and suppose that $\delta_n > 0$ and

$\epsilon_n < 0$, with the sequences (δ_n) and (ϵ_n) both tending to zero. (The case where $\delta_n < 0$ and $\epsilon_n > 0$ may be treated in a similar way, and we can exclude the case where $\delta_n = \epsilon_n = 0$ for some value of n, since this entails that $a_m = b_m = \alpha$ for all $m \geq n$.) It follows immediately from (1.61) and (1.62) that

$$\frac{\epsilon_n - \epsilon_{n+1}}{\delta_n - \delta_{n+1}} = \frac{\frac{1}{4}(\epsilon_n - \delta_n) + O\left(\delta_n^2 + \epsilon_n^2\right)}{\frac{1}{2}(\delta_n - \epsilon_n) + O\left(\delta_n^2 + \epsilon_n^2\right)},$$

which is equivalent to saying that

$$\epsilon_n - \epsilon_{n+1} = -\frac{1}{2}(\delta_n - \delta_{n+1}) + (\delta_n - \delta_{n+1}) \cdot O\left(|\delta_n| + |\epsilon_n|\right).$$

If we now replace n by $n+1, n+2, \ldots, n+p-1$ and add, using the fact that δ_n and ϵ_n tend to zero monotonically, we obtain

$$\epsilon_n - \epsilon_{n+p} = -\frac{1}{2}(\delta_n - \delta_p) + (\delta_n - \delta_{n+p}) \cdot O\left(|\delta_n| + |\epsilon_n|\right).$$

The purpose of this last move is that we can now let $p \to \infty$ and so obtain

$$\epsilon_n = -\frac{1}{2}\delta_n + O\left(\delta_n^2 + \epsilon_n^2\right). \tag{1.63}$$

If we pause and reflect on how we got to this point on a journey that began with (1.8), we see that the relation (1.63) between δ_n and ϵ_n is a generalization of the fact that the coefficient of θ^3 in the series for $\sin\theta$ is minus one-half of the coefficient of θ^3 in the series for $\tan\theta$!

From (1.61), (1.62), and (1.63) we can deduce that

$$\delta_{n+1} = \frac{1}{4}\delta_n + O\left(\delta_n^2\right),$$

$$\epsilon_{n+1} = \frac{1}{4}\epsilon_n + O\left(\epsilon_n^2\right).$$

We have thus established the following result concerning the rate of convergence of the two sequences (a_n) and (b_n).

Theorem 1.3.4 Given any positive numbers a_0 and b_0, let the sequences (a_n) and (b_n) be generated by

$$a_{n+1} = M(a_n, b_n) \quad \text{and} \quad b_{n+1} = M'(a_{n+1}, b_n),$$

for $n \geq 0$, where M and M' are any means satisfying the properties (1.51), (1.52), and (1.53) and whose partial derivatives up to those of second order are continuous. Then the sequences both converge in a first-order manner to a common limit and the *errors* $a_n - \alpha$ and $b_n - \alpha$ both tend to zero like $1/4^n$. ∎

The relation (1.63) shows that

$$b_n - \alpha = -\frac{1}{2}(a_n - \alpha) + O\left(\delta_n^2 + \epsilon_n^2\right)$$

and thus, on multiplying throughout by $\frac{2}{3}$,

$$\frac{1}{3}(a_n + 2b_n) - \alpha = O\left(\delta_n^2 + \epsilon_n^2\right)$$

Thus the sequence (c_n), where $c_n = (a_n + 2b_n)/3$, converges to α faster than the sequences (a_n) and (b_n). (See also Problem 1.2.2.) In Foster and Phillips [15] it is proved that

$$\frac{c_{n+1} - \alpha}{c_n - \alpha} \to \frac{1}{16} \quad \text{as} \quad n \to \infty$$

unless $4M_{xx}(\alpha, \alpha) + M'_{xx}(\alpha, \alpha) = 0$.

In Foster and Phillips [16] there is a discussion of the special case of (1.50) where $M = M'$ and M is a mean of the form

$$M(a, b) = h^{-1}\left(\frac{1}{2}\left(h(a) + h(b)\right)\right),$$

where h is a continuous monotonic function. (See Example 1.3.2.) Then (1.50) becomes

$$h(a_{n+1}) = \frac{1}{2}(h(a_n) + h(b_n)), \tag{1.64}$$

$$h(b_{n+1}) = \frac{1}{2}(h(a_{n+1}) + h(b_n)), \tag{1.65}$$

We see that this is equivalent to replacing both M and M' by the arithmetic mean, for the above process converges to $h(\alpha)$, where α is the limit of the process

$$a_{n+1} = \tfrac{1}{2}(a_n + b_n),$$

$$b_{n+1} = \tfrac{1}{2}(a_{n+1} + b_n).$$

If we again write $a_n = \alpha + \delta_n$ and $b_n = \alpha + \epsilon_n$, we find that

$$\delta_{n+1} = \frac{1}{2}(\delta_n + \epsilon_n) \quad \text{and} \quad \epsilon_{n+1} = \frac{1}{4}(\delta_n + 3\epsilon_n),$$

and following through the analysis we pursued for the general case above, from (1.61) and (1.62) to (1.63), we obtain in this, the simplest, case,

$$\epsilon_n = -\frac{1}{2}\delta_n, \quad \delta_{n+1} = \frac{1}{4}\delta_n, \quad \text{and} \quad \epsilon_{n+1} = \frac{1}{4}\epsilon_n.$$

Since the latter equations hold for all n, we find that

$$a_0 - \alpha = \delta_0 = -2\epsilon_0 = -2(b_0 - \alpha),$$

from which we obtain

$$\alpha = \frac{1}{3}(a_0 + 2b_0).$$

Thus the sequences (a_n) and (b_n) defined by (1.64) and (1.65) converge to the common limit $h(a_0 + 2b_0)/3$.

Given two means M and M' and two positive numbers a_0 and b_0, it would be very nice to obtain a general method for determining the common limit α of the two sequences (a_n) and (b_n) generated by the Archimedean double-mean process (1.50). However, there does not appear to be any general approach to the solution of this problem. Let us write $\alpha = L(a_0, b_0)$ to denote this limit, where L depends, of course, on M and M'. If the two means are homogeneous, as in (1.54), then we may deduce from (1.50) that

$$L(\lambda a_0, \lambda b_0) = \lambda L(a_0, b_0).$$

In particular, we have

$$L(a_0, b_0) = b_0 \, L(a_0/b_0, 1),$$

with $b_0 > 0$. Thus, for homogeneous means, the limit L can be expressed essentially as a function of *one* variable. For example, for the process defined by

$$a_{n+1} = \frac{1}{2}(a_n + b_n) \qquad \text{and} \qquad \frac{1}{b_{n+1}} = \frac{1}{2}\left(\frac{1}{a_{n+1}} + \frac{1}{b_n}\right), \qquad (1.66)$$

Foster and Phillips [16] deduce from

$$L(a_0, b_0) = L(a_1, b_1)$$

that

$$L(1 + x, 1) = L\left(1 + \frac{1}{2}x, \frac{1 + \frac{1}{2}x}{1 + \frac{1}{4}x}\right) = \left(\frac{1 + \frac{1}{2}x}{1 + \frac{1}{4}x}\right) \cdot L\left(1 + \frac{1}{4}x, 1\right),$$

and thus

$$\left(1 + \frac{1}{4}x\right) \cdot L(1 + x, 1) = \left(1 + \frac{1}{2}x\right) \cdot L\left(1 + \frac{1}{4}x, 1\right). \qquad (1.67)$$

If we now write

$$L(1 + x, 1) = 1 + c_1 x + c_2 x^2 + \cdots,$$

it follows from (1.67) that

$$\left(1 + \frac{1}{4}x\right)(1 + c_1 x + c_2 x^2 + \cdots) = \left(1 + \frac{1}{2}x\right)\left(1 + c_1 \frac{x}{4} + c_2 \left(\frac{x}{4}\right)^2 + \cdots\right).$$

On comparing coefficients of x^m, we obtain

$$c_m + \frac{1}{4}c_{m-1} = \frac{c_m}{4^m} + \frac{1}{2} \cdot \frac{c_{m-1}}{4^{m-1}}$$

and hence

$$c_m = -\left(\frac{4^{m-1} - 2}{4^m - 1}\right)c_{m-1},$$

for $m \geq 1$, with $c_0 = 1$. We deduce that $c_1 = \frac{1}{3}$ and

$$c_m = (-1)^{m-1} \frac{(4^{m-1} - 2) \cdots (4 - 2)}{(4^m - 1) \cdots (4 - 1)} \tag{1.68}$$

for $m \geq 2$, so that

$$L(1 + x, 1) = 1 + \frac{1}{3}x - \frac{2}{45}x^2 + \frac{4}{405}x^3 - \cdots,$$

and this series is valid for $-1 < x < 4$. (We require that $1 + x > 0$ so that $L(1 + x, 1)$ is defined, and $|x| < 4$ ensures that the above series converges.) Another expression is derived for $L(1 + x, 1)$ in [16] that covers the case where $x \geq 4$.

Let us now generalize (1.66) to

$$a_{n+1} = \mu a_n + (1 - \mu)b_n \quad \text{and} \quad \frac{1}{b_{n+1}} = \frac{1 - \mu}{a_{n+1}} + \frac{\mu}{b_n}. \tag{1.69}$$

If we choose $\mu = \frac{1}{2}$ in (1.69), we recover (1.66). We will take $0 < \mu < 1$, and then (1.69) defines a_{n+1} as a mean of a_n and b_n, and b_{n+1} as a mean of a_{n+1} and b_n. Thus, given any two positive values for a_0 and b_0, this process converges to a common limit $L(a_0, b_0)$. Since these means are homogeneous, it suffices to take, say, $b_0 = 1$ and $a_0 = 1 + x$. We then obtain

$$a_1 = 1 + \mu x \quad \text{and} \quad b_1 = \frac{1 + \mu x}{1 + \mu^2 x},$$

and we can easily verify by induction that

$$a_n = \frac{(1 + \mu x) \cdots (1 + \mu^{2n-1} x)}{(1 + \mu^2 x) \cdots (1 + \mu^{2n-2} x)}$$

for $n \geq 2$ and

$$b_n = a_n / (1 + \mu^{2n} x)$$

for $n \geq 0$. Thus the common limit is

$$L(1+x,1) = \prod_{r=1}^{\infty} \left(\frac{1 + \mu^{2r-1}x}{1 + \mu^{2r}x} \right). \tag{1.70}$$

To obtain a series representation for L, let us write

$$L(1+x,1) = c_0 + c_1 x + c_2 x^2 + \cdots, \tag{1.71}$$

where obviously $c_0 = 1$. On replacing x by $\mu^2 x$ we see from (1.70) that

$$(1 + \mu x)\, L(1 + \mu^2 x, 1) = (1 + \mu^2 x)\, L(1 + x, 1),$$

which generalizes (1.67). Now we express $L(1 + \mu^2 x, 1)$ and $L(1 + x, 1)$ in their series form (1.71) and equate coefficients of x^j to give

$$\mu^{2j} c_j + \mu^{2j-1} c_{j-1} = c_j + \mu^2 c_{j-1},$$

so that

$$c_j = - \left(\frac{\mu^2 - \mu^{2j-1}}{1 - \mu^{2j}} \right) c_{j-1} \tag{1.72}$$

for $j \geq 1$. We obtain $c_1 = \mu/(1 + \mu)$, and for $j > 1$, we derive

$$c_j = (-1)^{j-1} \frac{\mu^{2j-1}}{1 + \mu} \cdot \frac{(1 - \mu)(1 - \mu^3) \cdots (1 - \mu^{2j-3})}{(1 - \mu^4)(1 - \mu^6) \cdots (1 - \mu^{2j})}, \tag{1.73}$$

which generalizes (1.68). Since $0 < \mu < 1$, it follows that

$$\lim_{j \to \infty} \left| \frac{c_{j+1} x}{c_j} \right| = \mu^2 |x|,$$

and we see from the ratio test that the series (1.71) converges for $|x| < 1/\mu^2$. If we transform the series (1.71) into a *continued fraction* (see Section 4.4), we obtain the following representation of L, which holds for all $x \geq -1$:

$$L(1+x,1) = 1 + \frac{\mu x}{1 + \mu +} \; \frac{\mu^2 x}{1 + \mu^2 +} \; \frac{\mu^3 x}{1 + \mu^3 +} \cdots. \tag{1.74}$$

In the above analysis, we have been concerned with values of μ strictly between 0 and 1. It is amusing to see what happens to this process if we allow μ to tend to 1 from below. As we will see, this is *not* the same as putting $\mu = 1$ in (1.69). In the limit as $\mu \to 1$ the continued fraction (1.74) gives

$$L(1+x,1) = 1 + \frac{x}{2+} \; \frac{x}{2+} \; \frac{x}{2+} \cdots,$$

and in view of the way this continued fraction repeats, we can see that

$$L(1+x,1) = 1 + \frac{x}{1 + L(1+x,1)}.$$

On solving this equation for $L(1+x, 1)$, which must be positive, we obtain

$$L(1 + x, 1) = (1 + x)^{1/2}. \tag{1.75}$$

Also, from (1.72) we have

$$\lim_{\mu \to 1} \frac{c_j}{c_{j-1}} = \lim_{\mu \to 1} \frac{\mu^2 - \mu^{2j-1}}{\mu^{2j} - 1}.$$

We may use L'Hôpital's rule and differentiate numerator and denominator with respect to μ to give

$$\lim_{\mu \to 1} \frac{c_j}{c_{j-1}} = \lim_{\mu \to 1} \frac{2\mu - (2j-1)\mu^{2j-2}}{2j\,\mu^{2j-1}} = \frac{3 - 2j}{2j}.$$

Thus as $\mu \to 1$ we have

$$\frac{c_j}{c_{j-1}} = \frac{3/2 - j}{j}$$

for $j \geq 1$. Hence

$$c_j = \begin{pmatrix} 1/2 \\ j \end{pmatrix},$$

a binomial coefficient, and (1.71) does indeed give the well-known series for $(1 + x)^{1/2}$

Problem 1.3.1 Show that for the sequences that are generated by the Archimedean double-mean process (1.33),

$$\frac{a_{n+1} - b_{n+1}}{a_n - b_n} - \frac{a_{n+1}b_n}{(a_{n+1} + b_{n+1})(a_n + b_n)}$$

and deduce that

$$\lim_{n \to \infty} \frac{a_{n+1} - b_{n+1}}{a_n - b_n} = \frac{1}{4}.$$

Problem 1.3.2 For any $x \geq 1$, the relation $y = \cosh^{-1} x$ defines the unique $y \geq 0$ such that

$$x = \cosh y = \frac{1}{2} \left(e^y + e^{-y} \right).$$

Deduce that e^y satisfies the quadratic equation $(e^y)^2 - 2xe^y + 1 = 0$ and show that this equation has the two roots

$$e^{y_1} = x + (x^2 - 1)^{1/2} \qquad \text{and} \qquad e^{y_2} = x - (x^2 - 1)^{1/2}.$$

Verify that $e^{y_1} e^{y_2} = 1$. Deduce that one root is greater than 1 and one is less than 1 and so we need to choose the *plus* sign, thus justifying (1.45), that

$$\cosh^{-1} x = \log \left(x + \sqrt{x^2 - 1} \right).$$

Problem 1.3.3 Show that if we choose

$$a_0 = \frac{t^2 - 1}{t^2 + 1} \quad \text{and} \quad b_0 = \frac{t^2 - 1}{2t},$$

where $t > 1$, as initial values in the iterative process defined by (1.33), then the two sequences (a_n) and (b_n) both converge monotonically to the common limit $\log t$.

Problem 1.3.4 For Carlson's sequences defined by (1.48) show that if $a_0 > b_0 > 0$, then

$$a_n > a_{n+1} > b_{n+1} > b_n > 0$$

for all $n \geq 0$, and deduce that the two sequences converge to a common limit, say α. Next write

$$\phi_n = \sqrt{\left(\frac{a_n^2 - b_n^2}{2\log(a_n/b_n)}\right)} \quad \text{and} \quad \theta_n = 1 - b_n/a_n,$$

and note that $\theta_n \to 0$ as $n \to \infty$. For all $n \geq 0$, show that

$$\phi_{n+1} = \phi_n$$

and

$$\phi_n^2 = a_n^2(1 - \theta_n/2) \cdot \frac{\theta_n}{-\log(1 - \theta_n)}.$$

By using the inequalities for the logarithm quoted in Problem 2.3.4, show that

$$\phi_n \to \alpha \quad \text{as} \quad n \to \infty$$

and hence show that the common limit α is given by (1.49).

Problem 1.3.5 Verify that $M(a, b)$ defined by (1.55) satisfies the three properties of a mean given by (1.51), (1.52), and (1.53).

Problem 1.3.6 Find a function h such that (1.55) reduces to $M(a, b) = \sqrt{ab}$.

Problem 1.3.7 Verify that

$$M_H(a, b) \leq M_G(a, b) \leq M_A(a, b)$$

for all $a, b > 0$, where M_H, M_G, and M_A denote respectively the harmonic, geometric, and arithmetic means.

Problem 1.3.8 Show that the arithmetic, geometric, and harmonic means and the Minkowski mean

$$\mu_p(a, b) = ((a^p + b^p)/2)^{1/p},$$

with $p \neq 0$, are all means of the form (1.55). Find the appropriate function h in each case.

Problem 1.3.9 Verify directly that (1.60) holds for the arithmetic, geometric, and harmonic means.

Problem 1.3.10 For any twice differentiable mean M satisfying (1.51), (1.52), and (1.53), show that

$$M_{xx}(\alpha, \alpha) = -M_{xy}(\alpha, \alpha) = M_{yy}(\alpha, \alpha).$$

Problem 1.3.11 Let us choose

$$a_0 = \lambda \tanh \theta \quad \text{and} \quad b_0 = \lambda \sinh \theta$$

as the initial values in the iterative process (1.33), with λ and θ positive. Show that $0 < a_0 < b_0$. Verify that a_n and b_n are given by (1.43) and that the two sequences (a_n) and (b_n) converge to the common limit given by (1.44).

1.4   Gauss and the AGM

In this section we will consider the double-mean process defined by the recurrence relations

$$a_{n+1} - M(a_n, b_n) \quad \text{and} \quad b_{n+1} - M'(a_n, b_n) \qquad (1.76)$$

for $n = 0, 1, \ldots$, where M and M' belong to the class of means defined in Section 1.3 and a_0 and b_0 are given positive numbers. We call (1.76) a *Gaussian* double-mean process. Note that the Gaussian process (1.76) and the similar Archimedean process (1.50) differ only in how b_{n+1} is defined, one as $M'(a_m, b_n)$ and the other as $M'(a_{n+1}, b_n)$. We saw that the Archimedean process converges linearly, or we say that the process converges in a first-order manner, and the errors $a_n - \alpha$ and $b_n - \alpha$ tend to zero like $1/4^n$, where α is the common limit of the two sequences (a_n) and (b_n). More generally, if a sequence (s_n) converges to a limit s in such a way that for some positive k the sequence (t_n) given by

$$t_n = \frac{s_{n+1} - s}{(s_n - s)^k}$$

exists and tends to a limit as $n \to \infty$, then we say that the sequence (s_n) converges in a kth-order manner. If $k = 2$, we may alternatively describe the rate of convergence as *quadratic*, and if $k = 3$, we say that we have *cubic* convergence. At the end of Section 1.2 we discussed a process with *quartic* convergence, corresponding to $k = 4$. We will see that the Gaussian process converges at least quadratically. D. H. Lehmer [33] showed that the double-mean process (1.76) converges quadratically for the cases where M and M' are means of the form

$$\mu_p(a, b) = ((a^p + b^p)/2)^{1/p} \qquad (1.77)$$

for $p \neq 0$ (the Minkowski means) or of the form

$$M_p(a, b) = \frac{a^p + b^p}{a^{p-1} + b^{p-1}},$$ (1.78)

in each case using two different values of p for M and M'. The arithmetic, geometric, and harmonic means can be recovered from (1.77) by taking $p = 1, 0$ (in the limit), and -1, respectively. The Lehmer means (1.78) also include the arithmetic, geometric, and harmonic means, which are obtained by choosing $p = 1, \frac{1}{2}$, and 0 (in the limit), respectively, in (1.78).

Foster and Phillips [15] showed that the quadratic convergence of (1.76) extends to *all* means that satisfy the three properties (1.51), (1.52), and (1.53) and whose third-order partial derivatives are continuous. First let us assume that M and M' are continuous means satisfying (1.51), (1.52), and (1.53). Then it follows immediately from (1.76) that

$$\min(a_n, b_n) \leq \min(a_{n+1}, b_{n+1}) \leq \max(a_{n+1}, b_{n+1}), \leq \max(a_n, b_n),$$

and an argument like that used in the proof of Theorem 1.3.3 shows that the two sequences $(\min(a_n, b_n))$ and $(\max(a_n, b_n))$ converge to a common limit, say α, and thus the sequences (a_n) and (b_n) also converge to α. Next, let us assume that M and M' have continuous third-order partial derivatives. We saw in (1.60) that all such means M and M' satisfy

$$M_x(\alpha, \alpha) = M_y(\alpha, \alpha) = \frac{1}{2},$$

and we can similarly show (see Problem 1.3.10) that, for their second-order derivatives, we have

$$M_{xx}(\alpha, \alpha) = -M_{xy}(\alpha, \alpha) = M_{yy}(\alpha, \alpha).$$

Then, as before, let us write $a_n = \alpha + \delta_n$ and $b_n = \alpha + \epsilon_n$. On substituting these relations into (1.76) and using Taylor series expansions in the two variables, we obtain

$$\delta_{n+1} = \frac{1}{2}(\delta_n + \epsilon_n) + \frac{1}{2}M_{xx}(\alpha, \alpha)(\delta_n - \epsilon_n)^2 + O\left(|\delta_n|^3 + |\epsilon_n|^3\right)$$ (1.79)

and

$$\epsilon_{n+1} = \frac{1}{2}(\delta_n + \epsilon_n) + \frac{1}{2}M'_{xx}(\alpha, \alpha)(\delta_n - \epsilon_n)^2 + O\left(|\delta_n|^3 + |\epsilon_n|^3\right).$$ (1.80)

On subtracting, we obtain

$$\delta_{n+1} - \epsilon_{n+1} = \frac{1}{2}\{M_{xx}(\alpha, \alpha) - M'_{xx}(\alpha, \alpha)\}(\delta_n - \epsilon_n)^2 + O\left(|\delta_n|^3 + |\epsilon_n|^3\right).$$

If $M_{xx}(\alpha, \alpha) \neq M'_{xx}(\alpha, \alpha)$, it is not hard to see that unless $a_n = b_n = \alpha$ for some $n \geq 0$, the sequences (δ_n) and (ϵ_n) eventually converge monotonically to zero, one from above zero and one from below. Then, using the same approach as we did in developing (1.61) and (1.62), we can show that

$$\delta_{n+1} = O\left(\delta_n^2\right) \qquad \text{and} \qquad \epsilon_{n+1} = O\left(\epsilon_n^2\right) \qquad \text{as} \qquad n \to \infty. \qquad (1.81)$$

The nature of the convergence is *quadratic*, as defined at the beginning of this section. We have thus shown the following result.

Theorem 1.4.1 Given any positive numbers a_0 and b_0, let the sequences (a_n) and (b_n) be generated by

$$a_{n+1} = M(a_n, b_n) \qquad \text{and} \qquad b_{n+1} = M'(a_n, b_n),$$

for $n \geq 0$, where M and M' are any means satisfying the properties (1.51), (1.52), and (1.53) and whose partial derivatives up to those of *third* order are continuous. Then the sequences both converge at least *quadratically* to a common limit ∎

With a more detailed argument (see [15]), we can refine (1.81) to give

$$\delta_{n+1} = \{M_{xx}(\alpha, \alpha) - M'_{xx}(\alpha, \alpha)\}\delta_n^2 + O\left(|\delta_n|^3\right) \qquad (1.82)$$

and

$$\epsilon_{n+1} = -\left[M_{xx}(\alpha, \alpha) - M'_{xx}(\alpha, \alpha)\right]\epsilon_n^2 + O\left(|\epsilon_n|^3\right) \qquad (1.83)$$

as $n \to \infty$. We remark in passing that the convergence would be even faster than quadratic if $M_{xx}(\alpha, \alpha) - M'_{xx}(\alpha, \alpha) = 0$.

We mentioned earlier that Carlson's process (1.48), which computes the logarithm (see (1.49)), converges linearly, and yet it appears to have the form of a *quadratically* convergent Gaussian-type process (1.76). The reason for this apparent contradiction is that the means used in Carlson's process are not *symmetric*, which is one of the properties required in Theorem 1.4.1.

We now turn to a special case of (1.76), defined by

$$a_{n+1} = \frac{1}{2}(a_n + b_n) \qquad \text{and} \qquad b_{n+1} = \sqrt{a_n b_n}. \qquad (1.84)$$

This is the arithmetic–geometric mean (AGM). Let $L(a_0, b_0)$ denote the common limit of the sequences (a_n) and (b_n) generated by the AGM process (1.84) for given positive initial values a_0 and b_0. John Todd [51] describes how C. F. Gauss (1777–1855) calculated $L(1, \sqrt{2})$ to very high accuracy as early as 1791, and in 1799 Gauss estimated the definite integral

$$\int_0^1 \frac{dt}{\sqrt{1 - t^4}},$$

also with great accuracy. He then observed (and this is almost unbelievable) that the *product* of his two calculations agreed to many decimal places with

n	δ_n	ϵ_n
0	-0.1981	0.2161
1	$0.8967 \cdot 10^{-2}$	$-0.8933 \cdot 10^{-2}$
2	$0.1671 \cdot 10^{-4}$	$-0.1671 \cdot 10^{-4}$
3	$0.5829 \cdot 10^{-10}$	$-0.5829 \cdot 10^{-10}$
4	$0.7088 \cdot 10^{-21}$	$-0.7088 \cdot 10^{-21}$

TABLE 1.3. The errors at each stage of the AGM process, beginning with $a_0 = 1$ and $b_0 = \sqrt{2}$.

$\frac{1}{2}\pi$. By December 1799 he had indeed *proved* that

$$\frac{1}{L(1, \sqrt{2})} = \frac{2}{\pi} \int_0^1 \frac{dt}{\sqrt{1 - t^4}}. \tag{1.85}$$

For the AGM process, the means used in (1.76) are $M(a, b) = \frac{1}{2}(a + b)$ and $M'(a, b) = \sqrt{ab}$, and we may readily verify that

$$M_{xx}(\alpha, \alpha) = 0 \qquad \text{and} \qquad M'_{xx}(\alpha, \alpha) = -\frac{1}{4\alpha}.$$

Then we see from (1.82) and (1.83) that the errors in the AGM process satisfy

$$\delta_{n+1} \approx \frac{1}{4\alpha}\delta_n^2 \qquad \text{and} \qquad \epsilon_{n+1} \approx -\frac{1}{4\alpha}\epsilon_n^2. \tag{1.86}$$

Example 1.4.1 To illustrate the AGM process, let us take $a_0 = \sqrt{2}$ and $b_0 = 1$. After four iterations we obtain

$$a_4 = 1.19814\ 02347\ 35592\ 20744\ 06 \cdots,$$
$$b_4 = 1.19814\ 02347\ 35592\ 20743\ 92 \cdots.$$

Table 1.3 shows the errors $\delta_n = a_n - \alpha$ and $\epsilon_n = b_n - \alpha$. Note the approximate squaring of the errors at each stage. With a little calculation we can also see how closely the errors agree with (1.86). Gauss [20] gave four numerical examples on the AGM, computing all his iterates to about 20 decimal places. In his first three examples, he chose $a_0 = 1$ and selected 0.2, 0.6 and 0.8 as the values of b_0. The initial values $a_0 = \sqrt{2}$ and $b_0 = 1$ used above in this Example are those chosen by Gauss in his "Exemplum 4." It is exciting and awe-inspiring to turn the pages of Gauss's writings, viewing the very source of so much significant mathematics, and all written in Latin. It now seems quite surprising that this one-time common language of Western Christianity also survived for so long as the common language of European scholarship. With the initial values $\sqrt{2}$ and 1, Gauss's fourth iterates appear in [20], in his notation, as

$$a'''' = 1, 19814\ 02347\ 35592\ 20744\ 1,$$
$$b'''' = 1, 19814\ 02347\ 35592\ 20743\ 9.$$

Note the commas used to denote the decimal point.   ■

Since the arithmetic and geometric means are homogeneous, so that both satisfy $M(\lambda a, \lambda b) = \lambda M(a, b)$, it follows that the common limit of the AGM process satisfies $L(\lambda a_0, \lambda b_0) = \lambda L(a_0, b_0)$. We also have

$$L(a_0, b_0) = L(a_1, b_1) = L(a_2, b_2) \tag{1.87}$$

and so on, and $L(a, b) = L(b, a)$. Then, following the treatment of the AGM in Borwein and Borwein [6], we let

$$t = \frac{2\sqrt{x}}{1 + x},$$

and using (1.87), we find that

$$L(1 \mid t, 1 - t) - L(1, \sqrt{1 - t^2}) = L(1, (1 - x)/(1 + x)) \tag{1.88}$$

and so derive the key identity

$$L(1 + t, 1 - t) = \frac{1}{1 + x} L(1 + x, 1 - x). \tag{1.89}$$

Now, if $L(1 + x, 1 - x) = F(x)$, we have

$$F(-x) = L(1 - x, 1 + x) = L(1 + x, 1 - x) = F(x),$$

so that $L(1 + x, 1 - x)$, and therefore its reciprocal, is an *even* function. Since also $L(1 + x, 1 - x) = 1$ when $x = 0$, we may write

$$\frac{1}{L(1 + x, 1 - x)} = 1 + c_1 x^2 + c_2 x^4 + c^3 x^6 + \cdots . \tag{1.90}$$

From the latter equation and (1.89) we obtain

$$(1+x)(1+c_1 x^2 + c_2 x^4 + \cdots) = 1 + c_1 \left(\frac{2\sqrt{x}}{1 + x}\right)^2 + c_2 \left(\frac{2\sqrt{x}}{1 + x}\right)^4 + \cdots . \tag{1.91}$$

On comparing the coefficients of x, x^2, and x^3 we find that $c_1 = \frac{1}{4}$, $c_2 = \frac{9}{64}$, and $c_3 = \frac{25}{256}$, which, as Gauss [20] observed, are the squares of

$$\frac{1}{2}, \quad \frac{1}{2} \cdot \frac{3}{4}, \quad \text{and} \quad \frac{1}{2} \cdot \frac{3}{4} \cdot \frac{5}{6},$$

respectively. The general coefficient is

$$c_j = \left(\frac{1}{2} \cdot \frac{3}{4} \cdots \frac{2j-1}{2j} \right)^2 = \left\{ \left(\begin{array}{c} 2j-1 \\ j \end{array} \right) / 2^{2j-1} \right\}^2. \tag{1.92}$$

We note from the binomial expansion that

$$\sum_{i=0}^{2j-1} \left(\begin{array}{c} 2j-1 \\ i \end{array} \right) = (1+1)^{2j-1} = 2^{2j-1},$$

and thus c_j is the square of a fraction; the numerator of this fraction is the largest coefficient in the expansion of $(1+x)^{2j-1}$, which occurs twice, and the denominator is the sum of all the coefficients in this expansion, which is 2^{2j-1}.

Now let us define

$$I_j = \frac{2}{\pi} \int_0^{\pi/2} \sin^j \theta \, d\theta, \tag{1.93}$$

and using the results of Problems 1.4.3 and 1.4.4, we may write

$$\frac{2}{\pi} \int_0^{\pi/2} \frac{d\theta}{\sqrt{1 - x^2 \sin^2 \theta}} = \sum_{j=0}^{\infty} (-1)^j \left(\begin{array}{c} -1/2 \\ j \end{array} \right) I_{2j} \, x^{2j} = \sum_{j=0}^{\infty} c_j x^{2j}, \tag{1.94}$$

where c_j is defined by (1.92). Subject to the verification of (1.92), a comparison of (1.94) and (1.90) yields

$$\frac{1}{L(1, \sqrt{1 - x^2})} = \frac{2}{\pi} \int_0^{\pi/2} \frac{d\theta}{\sqrt{1 - x^2 \sin^2 \theta}}, \tag{1.95}$$

since $L(1+x, 1-x) = L(1, \sqrt{1-x^2})$ from (1.88). The latter integral is called a *complete elliptic integral of the first kind*. On replacing $1 - x^2$ by x^2 in (1.95), we obtain the following result of Gauss.

Theorem 1.4.2 For $0 < x < 1$, the limit $L(1, x)$ of the AGM process with initial values $a_0 = 1$ and $b_0 = x$ satisfies

$$\frac{1}{L(1, x)} = \frac{2}{\pi} \int_0^{\pi/2} \frac{d\theta}{\sqrt{1 - (1 - x^2) \sin^2 \theta}}. \quad \blacksquare \tag{1.96}$$

Before proving this theorem, we note that the elliptic integral is a special case of the *hypergeometric series*,

$$F(a, b; c; x) = \sum_{n=0}^{\infty} \frac{(a)_n (b)_n}{(c)_n} \frac{x^n}{n!}, \tag{1.97}$$

where

$$(a)_0 = 1 \quad \text{and} \quad (a)_n = a(a+1) \cdots (a+n-1), \quad n \geq 1.$$

(We remark that some writers use $_2F_1(a, b; c; x)$ rather than $F(a, b; c; x)$ to emphasize that the hypergeometric series may be viewed as a special case of a more general class of functions. Given the clue that the 2 in $_2F_1(a, b; c; x)$ refers to $(a)_n$ and $(b)_n$ and the 1 refers to $(c)_n$, you should be able to guess the nature of this general class of functions.) The convergence of the hypergeometric series was rigorously examined by Gauss in 1812. (See Eves [14].) Then, as we may readily verify from (1.94), the elliptic integral can be expressed as

$$\int_0^{\pi/2} \frac{d\theta}{\sqrt{1 - x^2 \sin^2 \theta}} = \frac{\pi}{2} F\left(\frac{1}{2}, \frac{1}{2}; 1; x^2\right), \tag{1.98}$$

and so, using the relation (1.96), which we are about to justify, we can express this particular hypergeometric series in terms of the AGM as

$$F\left(\frac{1}{2}, \frac{1}{2}; 1; x\right) = \frac{1}{L(1, (1-x)^{1/2})}. \tag{1.99}$$

We now present a proof of Theorem 1.4.2 that is based directly on the relation

$$L(a, b) = L\left(\frac{1}{2}(a+b), \sqrt{ab}\right),$$

as in (1.87). We will show that

$$\frac{1}{L(a, b)} = \frac{2}{\pi} \int_0^{\pi/2} \frac{d\theta}{\sqrt{a^2 \cos^2 \theta + b^2 \sin^2 \theta}},$$

so that (1.96) is recovered by putting $a = 1$ and $b = x$. Let us make the change of variable $x = b \tan \theta$. Then

$$\cos^2 \theta = \frac{1}{1 + \tan^2 \theta} = \frac{b^2}{b^2 + x^2},$$

$$\sin^2 \theta = 1 - \cos^2 \theta = \frac{x^2}{b^2 + x^2},$$

and

$$dx = b \sec^2 \theta \, d\theta = \frac{1}{b}(b^2 + x^2)d\theta.$$

Since $0 \le \theta < \pi/2$ corresponds to $0 \le x < \infty$, we obtain

$$\frac{2}{\pi} \int_0^{\pi/2} \frac{d\theta}{\sqrt{a^2 \cos^2 \theta + b^2 \sin^2 \theta}} = \frac{1}{\pi} \int_{-\infty}^{\infty} \frac{dx}{\sqrt{(a^2 + x^2)(b^2 + x^2)}}. \tag{1.100}$$

The latter integrand is an even function of x, and it is convenient to take the integral over $(-\infty, \infty)$ rather than twice the integral over $(0, \infty)$.

We now replace a and b by a_0 and b_0, respectively, and make a second substitution, putting $t = \frac{1}{2}(x - a_0 b_0 / x)$. This gives

$$dt = \frac{1}{2}\left(1 + \frac{a_0 b_0}{x^2}\right) dx,$$

and with $a_1 = \frac{1}{2}(a_0 + b_0)$ and $b_1 = \sqrt{a_0 b_0}$, we see that

$$a_1^2 + t^2 = \frac{1}{4}\left(x + \frac{a_0^2}{x}\right)\left(x + \frac{b_0^2}{x}\right) \quad \text{and} \quad b_1^2 + t^2 = \frac{1}{4}\left(x + \frac{a_0 b_0}{x}\right)^2.$$

Thus we find that

$$\int \frac{dt}{\sqrt{(a_1^2 + t^2)(b_1^2 + t^2)}} = \int \frac{2dx}{\sqrt{(a_0^2 + x^2)(b_0^2 + x^2)}}.$$

Further, for this change of variable defined by $t = \frac{1}{2}(x - a_0 b_0 / x)$, we see that $a_1 = \sqrt{a_0 b_0} \le x < \infty$ corresponds to $0 \le t < \infty$ and $0 < x < a_1$ corresponds to $-\infty < t < 0$, and we have proved the following remarkable result.

Theorem 1.4.3 If a_1 and b_1 are respectively the arithmetic and geometric means of a_0 and b_0, then

$$\frac{1}{\pi}\int_{-\infty}^{\infty} \frac{dx}{\sqrt{(a_1^2 + x^2)(b_1^2 + x^2)}} = \frac{1}{\pi}\int_{-\infty}^{\infty} \frac{dx}{\sqrt{(a_0^2 + x^2)(b_0^2 + x^2)}}. \quad \blacksquare \quad (1.101)$$

Let us now write, using (1.100),

$$I(a, b) = \frac{1}{\pi}\int_{-\infty}^{\infty} \frac{dx}{\sqrt{(a^2 + x^2)(b^2 + x^2)}} = \frac{2}{\pi}\int_{0}^{\pi/2} \frac{d\theta}{\sqrt{a^2 \cos^2 \theta + b^2 \sin^2 \theta}}.$$

Since from Theorem 1.4.3 I is *invariant* under the AGM transformation, in which a and b are replaced by $\frac{1}{2}(a + b)$ and $\sqrt{ab}$, respectively, we have

$$I(a_0, b_0) = I(a_1, b_1) = I(a_2, b_2) = \cdots = \lim_{n \to \infty} I(a_n, b_n) = I(\alpha, \alpha),$$

say, where $\alpha = L(a_0, b_0)$, the limit of the AGM process applied to a_0 and b_0. We find immediately that

$$I(\alpha, \alpha) = \frac{1}{\alpha} = \frac{1}{L(a_0, b_0)},$$

and so

$$\frac{1}{L(a_0, b_0)} = \frac{2}{\pi}\int_{0}^{\pi/2} \frac{d\theta}{\sqrt{a_0^2 \cos^2 \theta + b_0^2 \sin^2 \theta}}, \quad (1.102)$$

proving Theorem 1.4.2 and so also justifying (1.92).

In this section we have discussed processes with linear or quadratic rates of convergence. The best-known process with quadratic convergence is that known as *Newton's method,* for approximating a root of an algebraic equation of the form $f(x) = 0$, where f is differentiable in the vicinity of the root. In Newton's method we choose a suitable initial estimate x_0 and compute a sequence (x_n) recursively from

$$x_{n+1} = x_n - \frac{f(x_n)}{f'(x_n)}. \tag{1.103}$$

If x_0 is sufficiently close to a simple root, the process converges quadratically. By suitably extending the notion of derivative, the process can be generalized, for example to find the solution of a system of nonlinear equations. One of the simplest applications of Newton's method is to replace $f(x)$ in (1.103) by $x^2 - a$, where $a > 0$, and consequently replace $f'(x)$ by $2x$. On simplifying (1.103) we obtain the process

$$x_{n+1} = \frac{1}{2}\left(x_n + \frac{a}{x_n}\right), \tag{1.104}$$

which converges quadratically to $\sqrt{a}$, for any choice of positive x_0. This famous process for computing a square root was known long before Newton's time, and is linked with the name of Heron of Alexandria in the first century AD. (See Eves [14].) If x_n is smaller than $\sqrt{a}$ in (1.104), the term a/x_n will be larger, and vice versa. Thus it seems sensible to take the arithmetic mean of these two quantities as the next iterate, as an approximation to their geometric mean, which we are seeking. However, this simple observation does nothing to explain the quadratic convergence of (1.104). (See Problem 1.4.8.) The reader may wish to try the process

$$x_{n+1} = \frac{1}{8x_n^3}\left(3(x_n^2 + a)^2 - 4a^2\right), \tag{1.105}$$

which converges cubically to $\sqrt{a}$. The reason that (1.105) is not as well known as the quadratically convergent process (1.104) is that it is not as efficient computationally, since each iteration requires significantly more work.

We conclude this chapter by mentioning a double-mean process obtained by Borwein and Borwein [7] that, like the AGM, computes a hypergeometric series. The process generates sequences (a_n) and (b_n) recursively from

$$a_{n+1} = \frac{1}{3}(a_n + 2b_n) \quad \text{and} \quad b_{n+1} = \sqrt[3]{\frac{1}{3}b_n(a_n^2 + a_nb_n + b_n^2)} \tag{1.106}$$

for $n = 0, 1, \ldots$, beginning with arbitrary positive numbers a_0 and b_0. Let us denote the limit of this process by $M(a_0, b_0)$. We note that the first mean in (1.106) is not symmetric, but that both means are homogeneous, so that $M(\lambda a_0, \lambda b_0) = \lambda M(a_0, b_0)$. This process converges cubically, and its limit satisfies the relation

$$F\left(\frac{1}{3}, \frac{2}{3}; 1; x\right) = \frac{1}{M(1, (1-x)^{1/3})}, \tag{1.107}$$

which makes a fine companion result for (1.99). Borwein and Borwein [7] define a more general double-mean process that includes the parameter $N > 1$,

$$a_{n+1} = \frac{a_n + (N-1)b_n}{N},$$

$$b_{n+1} = \left(\left(\frac{a_n + (N-1)b_n}{N}\right)^N - \left(\frac{a_n - b_n}{N}\right)^N\right)^{1/N}.$$

It is easily verified that we recover the second-order AGM process (1.84) and the third-order process (1.106) on taking 2 and 3, respectively, for the values of the parameter N in the above generalized process. It also follows from our discussion about (1.84) and (1.106) that with $a_0 = 1$ and $b_0 = x$, the process converges for $N = 2$ and 3 to the limit α_N, where

$$\frac{1}{\alpha_N} = F\left(\frac{1}{N}, 1 - \frac{1}{N}; 1; 1 - x^N\right).$$

Such a correspondence is not known for any other value of N.

Example 1.4.2 With $a_0 = 1$ and $b_0 = \frac{2}{3}$ in (1.106), the sequences (a_n) and (b_n) converge to the common limit α, where

$$\frac{1}{\alpha} = F\left(\frac{1}{3}, \frac{2}{3}; 1; \frac{19}{27}\right).$$

We find that a_4 and b_4 agree to 106 decimal places and that the errors in the first few elements of the two sequences are given by

$$a_1 - \alpha \approx 0.50 \times 10^{-3}, \quad b_1 - \alpha \approx -0.25 \times 10^{-3},$$
$$a_2 - \alpha \approx 0.59 \times 10^{-11}, \quad b_2 - \alpha \approx -0.30 \times 10^{-11},$$
$$a_3 - \alpha \approx 0.94 \times 10^{-35}, \quad b_3 - \alpha \approx -0.47 \times 10^{-35},$$

in keeping with the cubic convergence of this process. ∎

Problem 1.4.1 Show that if $0 < b_0 \leq a_0$, members of the sequences (a_n) and (b_n) generated by the AGM process (1.84) satisfy

$$b_n \leq b_{n+1} \leq a_{n+1} \leq a_n,$$

so that the sequence (b_n) is monotonic increasing and (a_n) is monotonic decreasing. Show also that

$$0 \le a_{n+1} - b_{n+1} = \frac{1}{2}\frac{(a_n - b_n)^2}{(\sqrt{a_n} + \sqrt{b_n})^2} \le \frac{1}{8b_0}(a_n - b_n)^2.$$

Problem 1.4.2 Show that members of the sequences (a_n) and (b_n) generated by the AGM process (1.84) satisfy

$$\frac{a_{n+1} - b_{n+1}}{a_{n+1} + b_{n+1}} = \left(\frac{\sqrt{a_n} - \sqrt{b_n}}{\sqrt{a_n} + \sqrt{b_n}}\right)^2 \le \left(\frac{a_n - b_n}{a_n + b_n}\right)^2$$

and deduce that

$$\lim_{n \to \infty} \frac{a_{n+1} - b_{n+1}}{(a_n - b_n)^2} \le \frac{1}{2L(a_0, b_0)}.$$

Problem 1.4.3 Use integration by parts to show that

$$\int \sin^{j-1}\theta \, \sin\theta \, d\theta - -\sin^{j-1}\theta \, \cos\theta + (j - 1)\int \sin^{j-2}\theta \, \cos^2\theta \, d\theta$$

and deduce that I_j defined by (1.93) satisfies the recurrence relation

$$I_j - (j - 1)(I_{j-2} - I_j)$$

for $j \ge 2$. Note that $I_0 = 1$ and show that

$$I_{2j} = \left(\frac{2j-1}{2j}\right)\left(\frac{2j-3}{2j-2}\right)\cdots\frac{1}{2} = \left(\frac{2j-1}{j}\right)/2^{2j-1}$$

for $j \ge 1$.

Problem 1.4.4 Show that

$$\binom{-1/2}{j} = (-1)^j \frac{1}{j!}\cdot\frac{1}{2}\cdot\frac{3}{2}\cdots\frac{2j-1}{2} = (-1)^j \binom{2j-1}{j}/2^{2j-1}$$

for $j \ge 1$.

Problem 1.4.5 By making the substitution $t = \sin\theta$, show that

$$\int_0^{\pi/2} \frac{d\theta}{\sqrt{1 - (1 - k^2)\sin^2\theta}} = \int_0^1 \frac{dt}{\sqrt{(1 - t^2)(1 - (1 - k^2)t^2)}}.$$

Problem 1.4.6 Deduce from (1.102) that

$$\frac{1}{L(1, \sqrt{2})} = \frac{2}{\pi}\int_0^{\pi/2} \frac{d\theta}{\sqrt{1 + \sin^2\theta}}$$

and hence, using the result in Problem 1.4.5 with $k = \sqrt{2}$, show that (1.85) holds.

Problem 1.4.7 Let us choose M and M' as the arithmetic and harmonic means in the Gaussian double-mean process (1.76). Show by induction that $a_{n+1}b_{n+1} = a_n b_n$, and deduce that the two sequences (a_n) and (b_n) converge quadratically to the common limit $\sqrt{a_0 b_0}$.

Problem 1.4.8 Show that the iterates generated by the square root process (1.104) satisfy

$$x_{n+1} - a^{1/2} = \frac{1}{2x_n}(x_n - a^{1/2})^2$$

and deduce that

$$\frac{x_{n+1} - a^{1/2}}{x_{n+1} + a^{1/2}} = \left(\frac{x_n - a^{1/2}}{x_n + a^{1/2}}\right)^2$$

and that (x_n) converges to $a^{1/2}$. Finally, show that

$$\lim_{n\to\infty} \frac{x_{n+1} - a^{1/2}}{(x_n - a^{1/2})^2} = \frac{1}{2a^{1/2}}.$$

Problem 1.4.9 Show that if we carry out the square root process (1.104) with $x_0 = 1$, the sequence (x_n) coincides with the sequence (a_n) of Problem 1.4.7 with $a_0 = a$ and $b_0 = 1$.

Problem 1.4.10 Show that if we define x_{n+1} to be the *harmonic* mean of x_n and a/x_n, instead of the arithmetic mean chosen in (1.104), we obtain a process that is equivalent to applying Newton's method (1.103) to the equation $x - a/x = 0$. Show also that the iterates of this "harmonic mean" process satisfy the relation

$$\frac{a^{1/2} - x_{n+1}}{a^{1/2} + x_{n+1}} = \left(\frac{a^{1/2} - x_n}{a^{1/2} + x_n}\right)^2.$$

Problem 1.4.11 Observe that the errors $a_n - \alpha$ and $b_n - \alpha$ in Example 1.4.2 appear to satisfy the relation

$$b_n - \alpha \approx -\frac{1}{2}(a_n - \alpha).$$

Explain why this should be so.

2
Logarithms

Population, when unchecked, increases in a geometrical ratio.
Subsistence only increases in an arithmetical ratio.

Thomas Robert Malthus

The first tables of logarithms appeared in the early part of the seventeenth century, the best known being due to John Napier and Henry Briggs. We will see something of the ingenuity that went into the creation of these tables in this precalculus era. A little later in the seventeenth century Gregory of St. Vincent cleverly deduced that the logarithm may be expressed as the area under a hyperbola. Following the development of the calculus, his result is seen to be obvious! As so often in the history of mathematics, a hard-won mathematical truth is subsequently viewed as "only" a special case of some grander truth. Yet such pioneering discoveries, including that of Gregory of St. Vincent, remain wonderful achievements.

2.1 Exponential Functions

First let us recall what we mean by writing a^m, when a is real and positive and m is a positive integer. For example, we write 2^5 to denote five 2's multiplied together, so that

$$2^5 = 2 \times 2 \times 2 \times 2 \times 2 = 32.$$

In the line above, we say that 2 is multiplied by itself five times. Thus if a is any positive real number, and m is any positive integer, a^m means a

multiplied by itself m times. From this definition, we can see that if m and n are any positive integers, then

$$a^m \cdot a^n = a^{m+n}, \tag{2.1}$$

since each side of (2.1) denotes the number a multiplied by itself $m + n$ times.

The function a^x is called an *exponential function*, and x is called the *exponent*. So far we have defined a^x only when x is a positive integer. We will show how, step by step, we can extend this definition to all real values of x. First we define a^x for *reciprocals* of positive integers. Let $a = y^n$, where y is a positive real number and n is a positive integer. Then a will be a positive real number, and we say that $y = a^{1/n}$. Note that this is a *definition* of what we mean by writing $a^{1/n}$, and it is worth expressing it in other words, as follows. Given a real value of $a > 0$, the number $a^{1/n}$ is the positive number y such that $a = y^n$. We know that this defines a unique value of y, since y^n is a continuous function of y that assumes all values between 0 and ∞ as y runs from 0 to ∞. Next we define

$$a^{m/n} = b^m, \qquad \text{where} \qquad b = a^{1/n},$$

and m and n are positive integers. Thus the definition of $a^{m/n}$ builds on the definitions of the exponential function for positive integers and for their reciprocals. At this stage we have defined a^x for all positive *rational* values of x.

If x is any positive rational number, we define

$$a^{-x} = 1/a^x,$$

which extends the definition of an exponential function to all rational values of x except for $x = 0$. If we put $n = 0$ in (2.1), which we showed was valid when m and n are positive integers, we would have

$$a^m \cdot a^0 = a^{m+0} = a^m,$$

and to make this equation hold we require that $a^0 = 1$.

Note that for any positive integer n,

$$a^{n+1} = a^n \cdot a.$$

If $a > 1$, then $a^{n+1} > a^n$, and so a^n is an increasing function of n. If $0 < a < 1$, we see that a^n is a decreasing function of n. The key property of the exponential function is exhibited by the identity

$$a^x \cdot a^y = a^{x+y}. \tag{2.2}$$

We observed above that this holds when x and y are positive integers or zero, and it is not difficult (see Problems 2.1.1 and 2.1.2) to show that (2.2) holds for all rational values of x and y.

Recall that an *irrational* number is a real number that is not of the form m/n, where m is an integer and n is a positive integer. How can we define a^x if x is irrational? For example, we require a definion of a^x when $x = \sqrt{2}$. The answer is to use the notion of continuity to "fill in the gaps" between the rational numbers. As we will now see, if we wish to extend the definition of a^x to irrational values of x so that a^x is *continuous* for all real x, then this is a sufficient constraint to determine uniquely the values of a^x for irrational values of x. We will show how to do this when $a > 1$. The case where $a < 1$ can be handled in a similar way, and when $a = 1$ we simply define $a^x = 1$ for all real x. Given any positive integer n, we can find *rational* numbers x_0 and x_1, whose values both depend on n and x, such that

$$x - \frac{1}{n} < x_0 < x < x_1 < x + \frac{1}{n}.$$

This is just saying that the irrational number x lies between the rational numbers x_0 on the left and x_1 on the right, and that each of these two rational numbers is within a distance $1/n$ of x. We choose a value for a^x that lies between a^{x_0} and a^{x_1}. Now we see from (2.2) that

$$a^{x_1} - a^{x_0} = a^{x_0}\left(a^{x_1-x_0} - 1\right), \tag{2.3}$$

and it follows from the way we have defined x_0 and x_1 that

$$0 < x_1 - x_0 < \frac{2}{n}. \tag{2.4}$$

Then, since $a > 1$, a^x is an increasing function of x, and it follows from (2.3) and (2.4) that

$$a^{x_1} - a^{x_0} < a^{x_0}\left(a^{2/n} - 1\right). \tag{2.5}$$

As we have seen, the rational numbers x_0 and x_1 depend on n, and as we increase n, the difference between a^{x_1} and a^{x_0} tends to zero. (See Problem 2.1.3.) This determines a unique value for a^x for an irrational value of x, and completes the derivation of a^x for all real values of x for the case where $a > 1$. A continuity argument like that used above shows that (2.2) holds for all real numbers x and y.

If a is greater than 1, its reciprocal $1/a$ is less than 1. Thus for $a > 1$ the exponential function a^x, where x assumes all real values, is an increasing function of x, and the "reciprocal" exponential function $(1/a)^x = a^{-x}$ is a decreasing function of x. (Note that this generalizes the similar results obtained above for the case where x is restricted to positive integer values.) So we can obtain the graph of $(1/a)^x$ by "reflecting" the graph of a^x in the y-axis, which is the effect of replacing x by $-x$. Thus, to study the graphs of a^x for all choices of $a > 0$, it suffices to consider only values of $a \geq 1$. Since when $a = 1$, a^x takes the constant value 1, we need consider only the

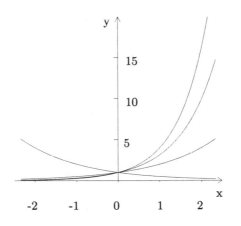

FIGURE 2.1. Graphs of the three increasing exponential functions $2^x, \pi^x$, and 4^x, and the decreasing exponential function 2^{-x}, for $-2 \leq x \leq 2$.

values $a > 1$. Now with $a > 1$ and $b > 1$, our above study of exponential functions tells us that there exists a unique real number λ such that $b = a^\lambda$. If $b < a$, then $0 < \lambda < 1$, and if $b \geq a$, then $\lambda \geq 1$. Thus, for any $b \neq a$, $b^x = a^{\lambda x}$, and the graph of the function b^x can be obtained from that of a^x by contracting the x-axis by a factor λ if $0 < \lambda < 1$ or stretching it by that factor if $\lambda > 1$. To sum up: we require the graph of only *one* exponential function a^x, for any positive $a \neq 1$. The graphs of *all* exponential functions can be derived from this one graph by contracting or stretching the x-axis by an appropriate factor λ followed, if necessary, by reflecting the graph in the y-axis. Figure 2.1 shows part of the graphs of $2^x, \pi^x, 4^x$, and 2^{-x}.

Problem 2.1.1 Let x be a positive integer and y a negative integer. Show that the identity (2.2) holds in this case. (Consider the two cases $x \geq |y|$ and $x < |y|$.)

Problem 2.1.2 Write $y_1 = a^{p_1/q_1}$, $y_2 = a^{p_2/q_2}$, where p_1, p_2 are integers and q_1, q_2 are positive integers. Show that

$$(y_1 y_2)^{q_1 q_2} = y_1^{q_1 q_2} \cdot y_2^{q_1 q_2} = a^{p_1 q_2 + p_2 q_1}$$

and hence show that (2.2) holds for $x_1 = p_1/q_1$ and $x_2 = p_2/q_2$.

Problem 2.1.3 For $a > 1$ show that $a^{1/n} > 1$ and that $(a^{1/n})$ is a decreasing sequence. Since the sequence $(a^{1/n})$ is decreasing and is bounded below by 1, it has a limit. Show that the limit is 1.

2.2   Logarithmic Functions

We have seen that for any fixed choice of $a > 0$,

$$y = a^x$$

is defined for all real values of x. To each value of x we have a unique value of y, so that y is indeed a function of x. But it is also true in this case that given any *positive* real value of y, there is a unique real value of x. This means that x is a function of y. It is called a *logarithmic function*, and to emphasize its dependence on the number a, we say that x is the logarithm of y to the *base a*. We write

$$x = \log_a y. \tag{2.6}$$

Whatever choice we make of the positive real number a, as x assumes all real values between $-\infty$ and ∞, the function $y = a^x$ takes all *positive* real values. Thus each logarithmic function $x = \log_a y$ is defined only for positive values of y. For any positive real a, the corresponding exponential and logarithmic functions $y = a^x$ and $x = \log_a y$ are said to be *inverse* functions of each other.

Given two real numbers x_1 and x_2, let us define

$$y_1 = a^{x_1} \quad \text{and} \quad y_2 = a^{x_2} \tag{2.7}$$

for some fixed choice of $a > 0$, and so we have

$$x_1 = \log_a y_1 \quad \text{and} \quad x_2 = \log_a y_2. \tag{2.8}$$

We find that

$$y_1 y_2 = a^{x_1} \cdot a^{x_2} = a^{x_1 + x_2},$$

on using (2.2). Since

$$y_1 y_2 = a^{x_1 + x_2}, \tag{2.9}$$

it follows from the definition of logarithm that

$$x_1 + x_2 = \log_a y_1 y_2,$$

and from (2.8) we obtain

$$\log_a y_1 + \log_a y_2 = \log_a y_1 y_2. \tag{2.10}$$

Equation (2.10) is the logarithmic function's raison d'être. Suppose we have a table of logarithms: each entry in the table consists of a positive number y with its logarithm $x = \log_a y$ alongside it. To multiply two such numbers y_1 and y_2 in the table, we look up their logarithms, x_1 and x_2, respectively, and *add* them (see (2.10)) to give the logarithm of $y_1 y_2$. Now we need only

Number	Logarithm to base 2
1	0
2	1
4	2
8	3
16	4
32	5

TABLE 2.1. Partial table of logarithms to base 2.

to look in the table to see which number has this as its logarithm, and we have found the product y_1y_2. This latter process, finding the number that has a given number as its logarithm, is called taking the *antilogarithm*. In practice, since the table cannot display the logarithms of *all* numbers, we usually have to settle for a number *near* to the required antilogarithm. Consider the partial table of logarithms to the base 2 given in Table 2.1. To multiply 4 by 8 we find from the table that $\log_2 4 = 2$ and $\log_2 8 = 3$. We now *add* 2 and 3 to give 5. Finally, we seek the number whose logarithm to base 2 is 5, that is, the antilogarithm of 5. From the table we find that the answer is 32. Thus $4 \times 8 = 32$. Of course, this is a very trivial example. Any logarithm table that is designed to be a practical aid to calculation has many more entries than this. Also, the number 2 is not a particularly suitable base, given that we usually express our numbers in the decimal scale. This is why 10 was favoured as a more practical base. For example, we see from (2.10) that

$$\log_{10} 3456 = \log_{10}(1000 \times 3.456) = 3 + \log_{10} 3.456,$$

since $\log_{10} 1000 = 3$ and

$$\log_{10} 0.03456 = \log_{10}(0.01 \times 3.456) = -2 + \log_{10} 3.456,$$

since $\log_{10} 0.01 = -2$. Thus we do not need to tabulate values of base 10 logarithms outside the range $[1, 10]$.

With the aid of a logarithm table, we can easily compute an nth root of a positive number c. Using logarithms to any base, we can show (see Problem 2.2.1) that

$$\log c^\lambda = \lambda \log c \tag{2.11}$$

for any positive real number c and any real number λ. In particular, for any positive integer n we have

$$\log c^{1/n} = \frac{1}{n} \log c,$$

and, taking logarithms again to avoid doing the division on the right, we obtain

$$\log \left(\log c^{1/n} \right) = \log \left(n^{-1} \log c \right) = \log \left(\log c \right) - \log n.$$

We thus compute $\log(\log c) - \log n$ and take its antilogarithm *twice* to give the value of $c^{1/n}$.

The use of logarithm tables as an aid to calculation decayed very rapidly (one might say *exponentially*) as they were swiftly supplanted, in the first instance, by pocket calculators. But the logarithmic *function* retains its longstanding important role as one of the "standard" mathematical functions, along with polynomials, rational functions, circular functions, exponential functions, and others.

For any positive real numbers a and b, we saw in the last section that if there exists a real number λ such that $a = b^\lambda$, then we have $\lambda = \log_b a$. Now, for a given positive number x, let us write

$$y = \log_a x \qquad \text{and} \qquad z = \log_b x,$$

so that

$$x = b^z = a^y = (b^\lambda)^y = b^{\lambda y}.$$

It follows that

$$z = \lambda y,$$

and hence we obtain

$$\log_b x = \log_b a \log_a x. \tag{2.12}$$

This shows that to convert the logarithm of x from base a to another base b we merely need to multiply by a factor whose value, $\log_b a$, depends only on a and b and not on x. If $1 < a < b$, then $0 < \log_b a < 1$, and if $1 < b < a$, we have $\log_b a > 1$.

Since the graphs of all logarithmic functions differ only by a multiplicative constant, they are all essentially the same, and it might seem that no particular base a should be especially preferred. Equivalently, we might suppose that there is no one exponential function a^x that is more desirable than any other. But it turns out that there *is* one particular choice of a that gives *the* exponential function, and that is the base for *the* logarithm. We can "discover" this particular value of a if we study the derivative of the function a^x. Let us recall that the derivative of a function f at a point x, denoted by $f'(x)$, is defined by the limit

$$f'(x) = \lim_{h \to 0} \frac{f(x+h) - f(x)}{h},$$

if it exists. Thus the derivative of a^x is

$$\frac{d}{dx} a^x = \lim_{h \to 0} \frac{a^{x+h} - a^x}{h}.$$

Using (2.2) we can write

$$a^{x+h} - a^x = a^x(a^h - 1)$$

and thus express the derivative of a^x as

$$\frac{d}{dx}a^x = a^x \lim_{h \to 0} \frac{a^h - 1}{h}. \tag{2.13}$$

This is a most interesting result. For, assuming that the last limit exists, it means that the derivative of a^x is simply a constant multiple of a^x. When we say "constant" here, we mean a number that does not depend on the variable x. For the factor

$$\lim_{h \to 0} \frac{a^h - 1}{h} \tag{2.14}$$

depends only on a. Now, given any value of $h = h_0 > 0$, let us repeatedly halve h_0, creating a sequence $h_n = h_0/2^n$, for $n = 0, 1, 2, \ldots$, and we note that $h_n \to 0$ as $n \to \infty$. Since $h_{n+1} = h_n/2$ we obtain

$$\frac{a^{h_n} - 1}{h_n} = \left(\frac{a^{h_{n+1}} - 1}{h_{n+1}}\right) \cdot \left(\frac{a^{h_{n+1}} + 1}{2}\right). \tag{2.15}$$

At this stage, we will assume that $a > 1$, and it is not difficult to adapt the argument that follows to deal with the case where $0 < a < 1$. (Note that the case $a = 1$ is trivial, the limit (2.14) being zero.) Since for $a > 1$ each quotient $(a^{h_n} - 1)/h_n$ is positive and

$$\left(\frac{a^{h_{n+1}} + 1}{2}\right) > 1,$$

it follows from (2.15) that the sequence (s_n), defined by

$$s_n = \frac{a^{h_n} - 1}{h_n}, \quad n = 0, 1, 2, \ldots,$$

is monotonic decreasing and is bounded below (by zero). Hence, using the well-known result concerning such sequences, which we have already employed in the proof of Theorem 1.3.1, we conclude that the sequence (s_n) has a limit. For $a = 10$ the sequence converges to the limit 2.302585, to 6 decimal places. Table 2.2 gives the approximate values of some members of this sequence, beginning with $h_0 = 1$ so that $h_n = 1/2^n$.

Having shown that the limit in (2.14) exists, for any choice of the positive real number a, let us write

$$L(a) = \lim_{h \to 0} \frac{a^h - 1}{h}, \tag{2.16}$$

since the value of the limit depends on a. Then for any positive real number λ we have

$$L(a^\lambda) = \lim_{h \to 0} \frac{a^{\lambda h} - 1}{h} = \lambda \lim_{h \to 0} \frac{a^{\lambda h} - 1}{\lambda h}. \tag{2.17}$$

n	$(a^{h_n} - 1)/h_n$
0	9
5	2.387451
10	2.305176
15	2.302666
20	2.302588
30	2.302585

TABLE 2.2. Values of $(a^{h_n} - 1)/h_n$ for $a = 10$ and $h_n = 1/2^n$.

If $h \to 0$, then $\lambda h \to 0$, and so

$$\lim_{h \to 0} \frac{a^{\lambda h} - 1}{\lambda h} = \lim_{h \to 0} \frac{a^h - 1}{h},$$

and it follows from (2.17) that

$$L(a^\lambda) = \lambda L(a), \tag{2.18}$$

for all positive real numbers a and λ. Although we have restricted λ to be positive in the derivation of (2.18), it is not difficult to show (see Problem 2.2.4) that (2.18) holds for *all* real values of λ. In particular, when $\lambda = -1$, we have $L(1/a) = -L(a)$. The equation (2.18) is reminiscent of our earlier equation (2.11). Indeed, the function $L(x)$ is a logarithmic function. Since for a fixed positive value of h the quotient $(a^h - 1)/h$ is an increasing function of a, it follows that $L(a)$ is also an increasing function of a. Table 2.3 gives some values of $L(a)$ to 4 decimal places. At least to within this accuracy it is clear that $L(2) + L(3) = L(6)$, as we expect of a logarithmic function. We also see from Table 2.3 that $L(3) > 1$, and it follows from (2.18) that

$$L(3^N) > N,$$

and so $L(a) \to \infty$ as $a \to \infty$. Thus, for $a > 1$, the values of $L(a)$ range from 0 to ∞. Since $L(1/a) = -L(a)$, we see that the values of $L(a)$ range from $-\infty$ to 0 for values of a between 0 and 1. From an inspection of Table 2.3 we infer the existence of one very special value of a, the value for which $L(a) = 1$. The run of the numbers in Table 2.3 suggests that this value of a lies between 2 and 3 and is rather nearer to 3. This is the famous number e, named after Leonhard Euler (1707–83). Its value is approximately 2.71828. From the above argument,

$$L(e) = \lim_{h \to 0} \frac{e^h - 1}{h} = 1,$$

and it follows from (2.13) that

$$\frac{d}{dx} e^x = e^x. \tag{2.19}$$

a	$L(a)$
1.0	0
1.5	0.405
2.0	0.693
2.5	0.916
3.0	1.099
3.5	1.253
4.0	1.386
4.5	1.504
5.0	1.609
5.5	1.705
6.0	1.792

TABLE 2.3. Some values of $L(a)$.

We have thus found a very special function that is unchanged under the operation of differentiation. The only other functions that have this property are multiples of e^x, and this includes the zero function as a trivial case. Suppose that it is possible, for x belonging to some suitable interval, to express e^x as an infinite series of the form

$$e^x = a_0 + a_1 x + a_2 x^2 + a_3 x^3 + \cdots , \qquad (2.20)$$

where the coefficients $a_0, a_1, a_2, a_3, \ldots$ are independent of the value of x. If we put $x = 0$, we see that we must choose $a_0 = 1$, since, as we saw earlier, all exponential functions a^x take the value 1 at $x = 0$. Let us also suppose that we obtain the correct value for the derivative of e^x by differentiating the series in (2.20) *term by term*. Then from this and (2.19) we deduce that

$$a_1 + 2a_2 x + 3a_3 x^2 + 4a_4 x^3 + \cdots = a_0 + a_1 x + a_2 x^2 + a_3 x^3 + \cdots .$$

If we equate the constant coefficients and the coefficients of x, and of x^2, and so on in the latter equation, we obtain

$$a_1 = a_0, \quad 2a_2 = a_1, \quad 3a_3 = a_2, \quad 4a_4 = a_3, \qquad (2.21)$$

and, in general, $na_n = a_{n-1}$. An inspection of this sequence shows that the value of a_1 depends on a_0, which we know to have the value 1, that of a_2 depends on a_1 and thus on a_0, and so on. We find, in turn, that

$$a_0 = a_1 = 1, \quad a_2 = \frac{1}{2!}, \quad a_3 = \frac{1}{3!}, \quad a_4 = \frac{1}{4!},$$

and so on. On substituting these values into (2.20), we obtain

$$e^x = 1 + \frac{x}{1!} + \frac{x^2}{2!} + \frac{x^3}{3!} + \cdots + \frac{x^n}{n!} + \cdots . \qquad (2.22)$$

In the second term on the right of (2.22) we have written 1!, which equals 1, for the sake of uniformity. (We could even replace the first term on the right of (2.22) by $x^0/0!$, where 0! is defined to be 1.) This series is valid for all real values of x, and indeed for all complex values. Putting $x = 1$ in (2.22) we obtain an infinite series for e itself:

$$e = 1 + \frac{1}{1!} + \frac{1}{2!} + \frac{1}{3!} + \cdots . \qquad (2.23)$$

The number e appears in many guises in mathematics. It may be defined as a limit,

$$e = \lim_{n \to \infty} \left(1 + \frac{1}{n}\right)^n, \qquad (2.24)$$

or as an infinite *continued fraction* (see Section 4.4),

$$e = 2 + \frac{1}{1+} \frac{1}{2+} \frac{1}{1+} \frac{1}{1+} \frac{1}{4+} \frac{1}{1+} \frac{1}{1+} \frac{1}{6+} \cdots . \qquad (2.25)$$

The limit (2.24) has a simple interpretation. Suppose that the very generous Bank A offers an investor 100% interest *per annum* on an investment, while Bank B offers 50% interest every half year. Which should the investor choose? An investment with Bank A appreciates by a factor 2 after one year. With Bank B, an investment appreciates by a factor 1.5 after 6 months, and by another factor 1.5 over the second 6-month period. So, after one year, an investment with Bank B will grow by a factor $1.5 \times 1.5 = 2.25$. So Bank B's interest rate is the more attractive. If there were a Bank C in which an investment grew by a factor $1 + \frac{1}{12}$ every *month* and a Bank D in which (in a non leap year) an investment grew by a factor $1 + \frac{1}{365}$ every *day*, then after one year, these investments would grow by the factors

$$\left(1 + \frac{1}{12}\right)^{12} \approx 2.613 \quad \text{and} \quad \left(1 + \frac{1}{365}\right)^{365} \approx 2.715,$$

respectively. The rate of growth of an investment in Bank D differs very little from that in the aptly named Bank E where the interest is added "continuously," and every year, an investment grows by the factor e.

To sum up the above account of exponential and logarithmic functions, we have seen that for each positive number a there corresponds an exponential function a^x and a logarithmic function to base a. Each of the two functions is the inverse of the other, in the sense that if $y = a^x$, then $x = \log_a y$. This means that if for any positive number a we begin with any real number x, evaluate a^x, and take its logarithm to base a, we recover the original number x, that is,

$$\log_a a^x = x.$$

Conversely, given any positive value of x, we also have

$$a^{\log_a x} = x.$$

Note that we have to begin with a *positive* value of x in the latter case because the logarithm is defined only for positive values of x. We also found that the value $a = e$ is rather special, since it leads to the exponential function e^x, whose derivative is itself. Given any other positive a, we can find a unique real value of λ such that $a = e^\lambda$, since the function e^x attains all positive real values as x goes from $-\infty$ to ∞. Then we can write

$$a^x = e^{\lambda x}.$$

From the definition of λ it follows that $\lambda = \log_e a$. We can use the "chain rule" (see below) to differentiate $e^{\lambda x}$, giving

$$\frac{d}{dx} a^x = \frac{d}{dx} e^{\lambda x} = \lambda e^{\lambda x} = \lambda a^x = (\log_e a) \cdot a^x.$$

Logarithms with base 10 were important in the past when logarithm tables were used as aids to calculation. But in mathematics, because of (2.19), the most important logarithmic function is that with base e. It is called the *natural logarithm*, a most appropriate name. In (2.12) we can substitute e for b to give

$$\log_e x = \log_e a \cdot \log_a x,$$

which gives

$$\log_a x = \frac{1}{\log_e a} \log_e x, \qquad (2.26)$$

so that every logarithmic function is simply a constant multiple of the natural logarithm. In everyday usage, we tend to drop the e from $\log_e x$ and simply write $\log x$ to denote the natural logarithm, although we sometimes write $\log x$ to denote a logarithm to any base. It should always be clear from the context whether we mean any base or base e. (Mathematicians have also to cope with the fact that some writers use $\ln x$ to denote the natural logarithm.)

We discussed the derivative of the exponential functions. What about the derivative of of $\log_e x$? (We will continue to include e for the present to avoid any ambiguity!) Let us recall the "function of a function" rule, or "chain" rule, for differentiation. If for some range of values of t and x, y is a function of x and x is a function of t, say

$$y = f(x) \qquad \text{and} \quad x = g(t),$$

then $y = f(g(t))$, that is, y is a function of t that is the *composition* of the two functions f and g. The chain rule for differentiation tells us that

$$\frac{dy}{dt} = \frac{dy}{dx} \cdot \frac{dx}{dt}.$$

For example, if $y = e^x$ and $x = t^2$, then $y = e^{t^2}$ and

$$\frac{dy}{dt} = e^x \cdot 2t = 2te^{t^2}.$$

So the derivative of e^{t^2} is $2te^{t^2}$, or, replacing t by x, the derivative of e^{x^2} is $2xe^{x^2}$.

An important application of the chain rule, which we need here, is to the case where $y = f(x)$ and an inverse function $x = g(y)$ exists for some range of values of x. In this case, we have $y = f(g(y))$, and the chain rule gives

$$1 = \frac{dy}{dy} = \frac{dy}{dx} \cdot \frac{dx}{dy},$$

from which we obtain the valuable result that

$$\frac{dx}{dy} = \frac{1}{\frac{dy}{dx}}. \tag{2.27}$$

In particular, for $y = \log_e x$ we have $x = e^y$, and we obtain from (2.27) that

$$\frac{dx}{dy} = e^y = \frac{1}{\frac{dy}{dx}} = \frac{1}{\frac{d}{dx} \log_e x},$$

and from $e^y = x$ we have

$$\frac{d}{dx} \log_e x = \frac{1}{x}. \tag{2.28}$$

Since $\log_e x$ is not defined for $x = 0$, we cannot express $\log_e x$ as a series of the form $a_0 + a_1 x + a_2 x^2 + a_3 x^3 + \cdots$, as we did for e^x. However, we can obtain a series for $\log_e(1 + x)$. For from the chain rule and (2.28), we have

$$\frac{d}{dx} \log_e(1 + x) = \frac{1}{1 + x}.$$

We can expand $1/(1 + x)$ as an infinite series,

$$\frac{1}{1 + x} = 1 - x + x^2 - x^3 + x^4 - x^5 + \cdots,$$

and this representation of $1/(1 + x)$ is valid for all those values of x for which the series converges, which is the interval $-1 < x < 1$. (When $x = -1$ the series is an endless sum of 1's, and when $x = 1$ we obtain a sum of alternating plus and minus 1's, both sums being meaningless.) Thus we have

$$\frac{d}{dx} \log_e(1 + x) = 1 - x + x^2 - x^3 + x^4 - x^5 + \cdots. \tag{2.29}$$

Now, what series has the series on the right of (2.29) as its derivative? Assuming that it is valid to differentiate such a series term by term, it must be a series of the form

$$c + x - \frac{x^2}{2} + \frac{x^3}{3} - \frac{x^4}{4} + \frac{x^5}{5} - \frac{x^6}{6} + \cdots,$$

where c is any constant, since the derivative of a constant is zero. This series has the value c when $x = 0$, and if we put $x = 0$ in $\log_e(1 + x)$ we obtain the value $\log_e 1 = 0$. So we need to choose $c = 0$, giving the series

$$\log_e(1 + x) = x - \frac{x^2}{2} + \frac{x^3}{3} - \frac{x^4}{4} + \frac{x^5}{5} - \frac{x^6}{6} + \cdots. \qquad (2.30)$$

The expansion (2.30) is valid for all values of x for which the series converges. It is convergent for $|x| < 1$ and is divergent for $|x| > 1$. What happens for $|x| = 1$? When $x = -1$, $\log_e(1 + x)$ is not defined, and the series is

$$-1 - \frac{1}{2} - \frac{1}{3} - \frac{1}{4} - \frac{1}{5} - \cdots,$$

the negative of the *harmonic series*, which diverges. (See Problem 2.2.5.) As x tends to -1 from above, that is, as x approaches -1 from the direction of 0, both $\log_e(1 + x)$ and the series in (2.30) tend to $-\infty$. On the other hand, for $x = 1$ the series is

$$1 - \frac{1}{2} + \frac{1}{3} - \frac{1}{4} + \frac{1}{5} + \cdots,$$

which converges. Thus we have the series for $\log_e 2$,

$$\log_e 2 = 1 - \frac{1}{2} + \frac{1}{3} - \frac{1}{4} + \frac{1}{5} + \cdots. \qquad (2.31)$$

(See Problems 2.2.6 and 2.2.7.) This series converges very slowly. For example, the sum of the first 10 terms of the series is approximately 0.646, to be compared with $\log_e 2 \approx 0.693$, and 500 terms give $\log_e 2$ only to three correct decimal digits.

Problem 2.2.1 For any positive real numbers a and c and any real number λ, write

$$\log_a c^\lambda = z,$$

so that $a^z = c^\lambda$. Deduce that $a^{z/\lambda} = c$ and hence

$$\log_a c^\lambda = \lambda \log_a c.$$

Problem 2.2.2 Let a and b be two positive real numbers. By interchanging a and b in (2.12), show that

$$\log_a b = 1/\log_b a.$$

Problem 2.2.3 Verify the statement made in the text that $0 < \log_a b < 1$ for $1 < b < a$ and that $\log_a b > 1$ for $1 < a < b$.

Problem 2.2.4 Deduce from (2.16) that for $a > 0$ and $\lambda > 0$,

$$L(a^{-\lambda}) = \lim_{h \to 0} \frac{a^{-\lambda h} - 1}{h} = \lim_{h \to 0} \frac{1 - a^{\lambda h}}{h a^{\lambda h}},$$

and hence show that $L(a^{-\lambda}) = -L(a^{\lambda})$ and that (2.18) holds for $a > 0$ and *all* real numbers λ.

Problem 2.2.5 For $n \geq 0$, let us write

$$s_n = 1 + \frac{1}{2} + \frac{1}{3} + \cdots + \frac{1}{2^n},$$

so that s_n is the the sum of the first 2^n terms of the harmonic series. Now write s_n as the sum of the following $n + 1$ terms:

$$s_n = s_0 + (s_1 - s_0) + (s_2 - s_1) + \cdots + (s_n - s_{n-1}).$$

The first term is $s_0 = 1$. Show that each of the remaining n terms is greater than or equal to $\frac{1}{2}$, for example,

$$s_3 - s_2 = \frac{1}{5} + \frac{1}{6} + \frac{1}{7} + \frac{1}{8} > \frac{1}{8} + \frac{1}{8} + \frac{1}{8} + \frac{1}{8} = \frac{4}{8} = \frac{1}{2}.$$

Deduce that $s_n \geq 1 + \frac{1}{2}n$, and so the series diverges.

Problem 2.2.6 Let S_n denote the sum of the first n terms of the series given in (2.31) for $\log_e 2$. By writing the series in the form

$$\left(1 - \frac{1}{2}\right) + \left(\frac{1}{3} - \frac{1}{4}\right) + \cdots$$

show that $\log_e 2 > S_{2n}$, and by writing the series as

$$1 - \left(\frac{1}{2} - \frac{1}{3}\right) - \left(\frac{1}{4} - \frac{1}{5}\right) - \cdots$$

show that $\log_e 2 < S_{2n-1}$, for any $n \geq 1$, so that $\log_e 2$ lies between any two consecutive partial sums of its series.

Problem 2.2.7 Consider a sequence $(S_n)_{n=1}^{\infty}$, where S_n is the sum of the first n terms of the alternating series

$$u_1 - u_2 + u_3 - u_4 + \cdots,$$

where $(u_n)_{n=1}^{\infty}$ is a sequence of positive numbers that tends monotonically to zero. (The above series for $\log_e 2$ has this property.) Show that

$$S_2 < S_4 < S_6 < \cdots < S_{2n} < S_{2n-1} < S_{2n-3} < \cdots < S_3 < S_1.$$

Deduce that the sequence with *even* suffixes, being monotonic increasing and bounded above (by S_1 and all other members of the *odd* sequence), has a limit. Similarly argue that the sequence with *odd* suffixes is monotonic decreasing and is bounded below (by S_2 and all other members of the *even* sequence), and so it also has a limit. Deduce that these two limits are equal, and thus conclude that the sequence converges.

2.3   Napier and Briggs

In 1614 John Napier (1550–1617), of Merchiston Castle, near (now *in*) Edinburgh, published his book *Mirifici Logarithmorum Canonis Descriptio*, in which he gives a table of logarithms and an account of how he computed them. If anyone is entitled to use the word "logarithm" it is Napier, since he coined the word, deriving it from from the two Greek words λόγος (meaning "reckoning," in this context) and ἀριθμός (meaning "number"). Yet, as we will see, Napier's logarithm is not truly a logarithm as it is now defined (see Section 2.2).

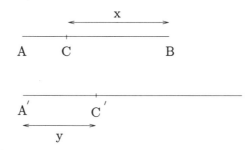

FIGURE 2.2. Napier's kinematical analogy for defining his logarithm. The line segment AB is of length 10^7 units.

Napier based his calculations on a kinematical analogy. He imagined two particles, one moving along a line segment AB, beginning at A at time $t = 0$ and moving with a velocity equal to its distance from B, so that its initial velocity is the distance AB. Thus its velocity decreases with time. The other particle moves along another (infinitely long) line, setting off at time $t = 0$ from a fixed point A' and moving at a constant velocity equal to AB. (See Figure 2.2.) Thus the two particles set off with the same initial velocity. At time t, let the first particle be at a point C, say, at a distance x from B and let the second particle be at a point C' (see Figure 2.2), at a distance y from A'. Then Napier's logarithm is defined as $y = \text{Nap.log } x$. Notice that x is the distance of the first particle from the end point B, while y is the distance of the second particle from the initial point A'. Napier thought of the length of the line segment AB as being a very large number, and he chose the value 10^7. He deduced that as x decreases in geometrical progression, y increases in arithmetical progression. Since Napier was writing this more than two generations before the development of the calculus, this was a notable insight. For with the aid of the calculus, we have a great advantage over Napier. We can deduce from his construction that

$$\frac{dy}{dt} = 10^7 \quad \text{and} \quad \frac{d}{dt}\left(10^7 - x\right) = x.$$

Thus

$$\frac{dy}{dt} = 10^7 \quad \text{and} \quad -\frac{dx}{dt} = x.$$

The differential equation for y gives

$$y = 10^7 t + c,$$

where c is an arbitrary constant. Since $y = 0$ when $t = 0$, we find that $c = 0$, and so

$$y = 10^7 t. \tag{2.32}$$

From the differential equation for x, we see that x must be a constant multiple of a *decreasing* exponential function of t, so that $x = \lambda e^{-t}$, where λ is a constant. When $t = 0$, $x = AB = 10^7$, and so $\lambda = 10^7$. It follows that

$$\frac{x}{10^7} = e^{-t}, \quad \text{or} \quad \frac{10^7}{x} = e^t,$$

and thus

$$t = \log_e\left(\frac{10^7}{x}\right). \tag{2.33}$$

On equating the two values for t obtained from the two solutions (2.32) and (2.33) we find that

$$y = \text{Nap.log } x = 10^7 \log_e\left(\frac{10^7}{x}\right). \tag{2.34}$$

This allows us to compare Napier's logarithm with its descendants, the family of logarithms $\log_a x$, which we discussed in Section 2.2. From (2.34) and (2.10) we can deduce (see Problem 2.3.1) that for all positive x_1 and x_2,

$$\text{Nap.log } x_1 x_2 = \text{Nap.log } x_1 + \text{Nap.log } x_2 - \text{Nap.log } 1, \tag{2.35}$$

and we note that because of the extra term Nap.log 1 on the right of (2.35), Napier's logarithm does not satisfy the fundamental property of logarithms that we saw in (2.10). We will now discuss briefly how Napier constructed his table of logarithms. From his definition, Napier obtained Nap.log $10^7 = 0$. Since the initial velocities of his two hypothetical particles are the same, Napier argued that when x had decreased by 1, y would have increased by approximately 1, so that

$$\text{Nap.log } 10^7 = 0 \qquad \text{and} \qquad \text{Nap.log } (10^7 - 1) \approx 1. \qquad (2.36)$$

But since the first particle is slowing down, during the time when x decreases by 1, y must increase by more than 1. Napier knew that the accuracy of his table would be limited by the accuracy of his starting values, and he found a way of obtaining a more accurate approximation to his logarithm of $10^7 - 1$, as we will now describe. Figure 2.3 shows the positions

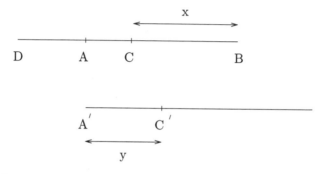

FIGURE 2.3. Diagram that illustrates how Napier obtained his inequalities for Nap.log x, as given by (2.39).

C and C' of the two particles at some given time t. Napier extended the line AB backwards to a point D such that

$$\frac{DA}{DB} = \frac{AC}{AB}, \qquad (2.37)$$

so that D depends on the value of x, and thus on the value of t. Napier then supposed that the first particle, say P, begins its motion again, but starting at D this time, obeying the same law of motion as before, so that its velocity at any point E between D and A is equal to EB. Thus its velocity from A onwards is exactly the same as it was before. Napier deduced that the particle would take the same time to travel from D to A as it does to travel from A to C. This also equals the time that the second particle, say P', takes to travel from A' to C'. Now, as we saw, the velocity of P is monotonic decreasing as it travels from D to C. Also, the velocity of P' is constant and the two particles have the same velocities at A and A', respectively. It follows that

$$AC \leq A'C' \leq DA. \qquad (2.38)$$

Writing $AC = 10^7 - x$, $AB = 10^7$, and $DB = DA + 10^7$, we can solve the equation (2.37) to obtain

$$DA = (10^7 - x) \cdot \frac{10^7}{x}.$$

Thus we obtain from (2.38) Napier's ingenious inequalities

$$10^7 - x \leq \text{Nap.log } x \leq (10^7 - x) \cdot \frac{10^7}{x}. \tag{2.39}$$

It is most interesting to interpret the above inequalities in terms of the natural logarithm. (See Problem 2.3.4.) These inequalities are at their *sharpest* (meaning that they are closest to being equalities) near to $x = 10^7$. For $x = 10^7 - 1$ we obtain from (2.39) that

$$1 \leq \text{Nap.log } (10^7 - 1) \leq \frac{10^7}{10^7 - 1},$$

giving lower and upper bounds for Nap.log $(10^7 - 1)$. Finally, Napier took the arithmetic mean of these lower and upper bounds to give a closer approximation to Nap.log $(10^7 - 1)$ than his first estimate of 1. In practice, he replaced

$$\frac{10^7}{10^7 \quad 1} \qquad \text{by} \qquad \frac{10^7 + 1}{10^7} = 1 + 10^{-7},$$

these two numbers being very close (see Problem 2.3.3), to give the approximation

$$\text{Nap.log } (10^7 - 1) \approx 1 + \frac{1}{2} 10^{-7}.$$

By expressing Napier's logarithm in terms of the natural logarithm we can see (as in Problem 2.3.4) how very accurate this result is. The error is less than 10^{-14}, which testifies to Napier's great mathematical insight in these precalculus days.

Having fixed the values

$$\text{Nap.log } 10^7 = 0 \qquad \text{and} \qquad \text{Nap.log } (10^7 - 1) = 1 + \frac{1}{2} 10^{-7},$$

Napier's idea, *in principle*, was to create a geometric progression with common ratio $1 - 10^{-7}$. This would give him

$$\text{Nap.log } 10^7 = 0,$$
$$\text{Nap.log } 10^7 (1 - 10^{-7}) = 1 + \tfrac{1}{2} 10^{-7},$$
$$\text{Nap.log } 10^7 (1 - 10^{-7})^2 = 2 \left(1 + \tfrac{1}{2} 10^{-7}\right),$$
$$\text{Nap.log } 10^7 (1 - 10^{-7})^3 = 3 \left(1 + \tfrac{1}{2} 10^{-7}\right),$$

and so on, the terms of the arithmetic progression on the right being the Naperian logarithms of members of a geometric progression. Thanks to

Napier's clever choice of common ratio $1 - 10^{-7}$ each multiplication by this factor is attained by taking the number to be multiplied and subtracting from it the same number *shifted* by 7 decimal places. Thus the usually much more taxing operation of multiplication is carried out as easily as a subtraction. Napier computed numbers of the form $(1 - 10^{-7})^r$ to 13 decimal places. Given what we know about the accuracy of his starting values, this again shows Napier's fine numerical sense.

To reduce the vast arithmetical calculations, once he had computed his logarithm for the number $10^7(1 - 10^{-7})^{100}$, he made use of the fact that

$$10^7(1 - 10^{-7})^{100} \approx 10^7(1 - 10^{-5}). \tag{2.40}$$

Making a suitable adjustment to allow for the error of the approximation (2.40), he then had a value for Nap.log $10^7(1 - 10^{-5})$, say a, and he was able to use this new common ratio $1 - 10^{-5}$ to give

$$\text{Nap.log } 10^7 = 0,$$
$$\text{Nap.log } 10^7(1 - 10^{-5}) = a,$$
$$\text{Nap.log } 10^7(1 - 10^5)^2 = 2a,$$
$$\text{Nap.log } 10^7(1 - 10^{-5})^3 = 3a,$$

and so on. The difference between Nap.log $10^7(1 - 10^{-7})^{100}$ and Nap.log $10^7(1 - 10^{-5})$ is quite small. We have

$$\text{Nap.log } 10^7(1 - 10^{-7})^{100} = 100.0000050000003,$$
$$\text{Nap.log } 10^7(1 - 10^{-5}) = 100.0000050000333.$$

The replacement of the common ratio $1 - 10^{-7}$ by the number $1 - 10^{-5}$, which is not so near to 1, meant that he could "travel" through his table faster. He used this device twice more, stepping up another gear to a third common ratio $1 - 5 \cdot 10^{-4}$ and then to a fourth common ratio $1 - 10^{-2}$. This process results in a table of values of Nap.log x, where the values of x are members of four geometric progressions. In Napier's final table the values of x for which Nap.log x is given are equally spaced, that is, they are in arithmetic progression, as in most mathematical tables. Napier achieved this by interpolating to determine Nap.log x for values of x between those in his original table. For more details about Napier's work on logarithms, see Edwards [13] and Goldstine [21].

Henry Briggs (1556–1630) was very excited by Napier's ideas on logarithms. Whereas John Napier, Baron of Merchiston, was a "gentleman scholar" who never held any academic position, Henry Briggs was appointed the first professor of geometry at Gresham College, London in 1596, and later held the Savilian Chair at Oxford, soon after its foundation in 1519. Briggs journeyed to Scotland in the summer of 1617 and again in 1618 to confer with Napier, no mean undertaking in those days. Turnbull (see [52] has published an account of their first meeting, describing how Napier was anxious before Briggs arrived, fearing that Briggs would not come. When Briggs did arrive, he was shown into Napier's presence, "where almost one quarter of an hour was spent, each beholding the other with admiration before one word was spoken. At last Mr. Briggs began: 'My Lord, I have undertaken this long journey purposely to see your person, and to know by what engine of wit or ingenuity you came first to think of this most excellent help unto Astronomy, viz. the Logarithms: but My Lord, being by you found out, I wonder nobody else found it out before, when now being known it appears so easy.' " This seems a rather backhanded compliment, but the two men got on famously. Napier was full of enthusiasm for Briggs's ideas for carrying his logarithms forward and generously encouraged him to pursue work on what would be a true table of logarithms to base 10, which would eclipse Napier's table as a practical aid to calculation. Briggs and Napier agreed that it would be most advantageous to construct such a table of logarithms, for which

$$\log x_1 x_2 = \log x_1 + \log x_2. \tag{2.41}$$

This avoided having to subtract some constant from the right-hand side, as required (recall (2.35)) for Napier's logarithms.

Briggs's process is based on the observation that if we choose any real number $a > 1$ and repeatedly extract the square root, the resulting sequence converges to 1. As we would write it,

$$a^{1/2^n} \to 1 \qquad \text{as} \qquad n \to \infty.$$

We can think of this as a consequence of the function a^x being continuous for all x and of the equality $a^0 = 1$. If we choose $a = 10$ and carry out Briggs's process of extracting repeated square roots, we obtain a partial table of logarithms to base 10. Briggs observed that for small values of x, $\log_{10}(1 + x)$ is roughly proportional to x. The derivation of the constant

$$K = \lim_{x \to 0} \frac{\log_{10}(1 + x)}{x}$$

is illustrated in Table 2.4.

From (2.12) with b replaced by 10, a replaced by e, and x replaced by $1 + x$, we see that

$$\log_{10}(1 + x) = \log_{10} e \cdot \log_e(1 + x), \tag{2.42}$$

and from (2.30) we note that $\log_e(1 + x)$ is close to x for small values of x. More precisely,

$$\lim_{x \to 0} \frac{\log_e(1 + x)}{x} = 1,$$

$1+x$	$\log_{10}(1+x)$	$(\log_{10}(1+x))/x$
10	1	0.111
3.162278	1/2	0.231
1.778279	1/4	0.321
1.333521	1/8	0.375
1.154782	1/16	0.404
1.074608	1/32	0.419
1.036633	1/64	0.427
1.018152	1/128	0.430
1.009035	1/256	0.432
1.004507	1/512	0.433
1.002251	1/1024	0.434

TABLE 2.4. Values of $(\log_{10}(1+x))/x$, leading to Briggs's constant.

and the last two equations yield

$$K = \lim_{x \to 0} \frac{\log_{10}(1+x)}{x} = \log_{10} e.$$

We find that

$$K \approx 0.4342944819032518 \tag{2.43}$$

to 16 decimal places, which, amazingly, is the accuracy to which Briggs estimated this constant. One can only be in awe of the tenacity of Briggs, and indeed also of Napier, when we contemplate the sheer labour involved in their calculations.

The methods that Napier and Briggs used to compute their logarithms are entirely different. As we have seen, Napier's table was essentially computed in one grand calculation where the computation of any one value in his table depended on all the previous results. Of course, this means that just one error at any stage results in a propagation of that error throughout the rest of the table. This is why Napier took such trouble to determine the value of Nap.log $(10^7 - 1)$ with such accuracy. In fact, Napier did make a mistake in his calculations, although the result of this error was not catastrophic. For Briggs, in complete contrast, each logarithm in his initial set of calculations was the result of a self-contained exercise. He was computing a table of logarithms to base 10, and in view of the "multiplication" rule (2.41), he realised that he needed to compute the logarithms of the prime numbers only, in order to find the logarithms of the positive integers. For example

$$\log_{10} 60 = \log_{10}(2^2 \cdot 3 \cdot 5) = 2\log_{10} 2 + \log_{10} 3 + \log_{10} 5.$$

To obtain the logarithm of a given prime number p, Briggs repeatedly extracted square roots to obtain a sequence $(p^{1/2^n})$, for $n = 0, 1$, and so on. As we argued above, this gives a sequence that converges to 1. Briggs computed the members of this sequence until he reached an integer n such that

$$p^{1/2^n} = 1 + x, \qquad \text{where} \qquad x \approx 10^{-16}. \qquad (2.44)$$

He then argued that

$$\log_{10}\left(p^{1/2^n}\right) = \frac{1}{2^n}\log_{10} p = \log_{10}(1+x) \approx Kx \qquad (2.45)$$

and thus

$$\log_{10} p \approx 2^n Kx. \qquad (2.46)$$

Briggs computed $p^{1/2^n}$ in (2.44) to 30 decimal places, so that the number x in (2.44) is a decimal number with 15 zeros after the decimal point followed by a further 15 significant digits.

We have the advantage over Briggs in that we know from (2.42) and (2.30) that

$$\log_{10}(1+x) = K\left(x - \frac{1}{2}x^2 + \frac{1}{3}x^3 - \cdots\right),$$

for $-1 < x \le 1$. Thus from (2.45)

$$\log_{10} p = 2^n K\left(x - \frac{1}{2}x^2 + \frac{1}{3}x^3 - \cdots\right),$$

so that the error in (2.45) is approximately $\frac{1}{2}Kx^2$, which is less than 10^{-30}, and the error in $\log_{10} p$ is approximately $2^{n-1}Kx^2$. For values of p that are of order 10, or a small power of 10, $\log_{10} p$ will be of order 1 and, from (2.46), 2^n will be of order 10^{15}, and so the error in Briggs's estimate of $\log_{10} p$ will be of order 10^{-15}. This shows us that Briggs, like Napier before him, had a sure understanding of what he was doing, since he carried out his calculations to an appropriate precision in order to obtain the accuracy he desired for his table. Note that since $2^{10} = 1024 \approx 10^3$, then $10^{15} \approx 2^{50}$, so that Briggs required the value $n = 50$. Thus, in principle, to compute the logarithm of each prime p Briggs would have to extract the square root repeatedly about *fifty* times, carrying out each calculation to 30 decimal places.

When he was carrying out his repeated square root process, Briggs unravelled a wonderful "pattern" in the numbers. This is a fine example of a mathematical discovery emerging from a numerical experiment. To illustrate this, let us study an example. We will take $p = 3$ and repeatedly extract square roots, obtaining the numbers 3, 1.732050808, and so on, which are displayed in the first column of Table 2.5. We will be content with 9 decimal places rather than the 30 decimal places that Briggs used. As we look at the first column of Table 2.5 we see that the "fractional parts" of the numbers are roughly halved as we go down the column. For example, comparing the entries in lines 4 and 5, we see that 0.071075483,

Square roots	"Differences"
3	
	0.267949192
1.732050808	
	0.049951391
1.316074013	
	0.010834317
1.147202690	
	0.002525862
1.071075483	
	0.000609975
1.034927767	

TABLE 2.5. Repeated square roots of 3 and Briggs's differences.

in the first column, is roughly half of 0.147202690 on the line above. Briggs calculated by how much each fractional part in the first column of Table 2.5 differs from half the fractional part of the number above, and the results of these calculations are displayed in the second column of Table 2.6. For example,

$$\frac{1}{2}(0.147202690) - 0.071075483 = 0.002525862.$$

The first number in the second column is calculated in the same way. For since $3 = 1 + 2$, we compute

$$\frac{1}{2} \cdot 2 - 0.732050808 = 0.267949192.$$

In Table 2.6 we have extended the results in Table 2.5 by computing further repeated square roots in the first column. Column D_1 in Table 2.6 extends the second column of Table 2.5. Note that, following the normal practice adopted in displaying differences in mathematical tables, we have omitted the decimal point in all but the first column of Table 2.6. The entries in columns two to five all represent numbers between 0 and 1 given to nine decimal places, with the decimal point and any zeros after the decimal point omitted. Thus the number 0.000021491 appears as 21491 in column D_2, whose derivation we now describe. Briggs observed that the numbers in column D_1 decrease by a factor of roughly a quarter and the factor grows closer to a quarter as we go down the column. For example, 0.000609975 is roughly a quarter of 0.002525862, and again, Briggs was interested in the discrepancy

$$\frac{1}{4}(0.002525862) - 0.000609975 \approx 0.000021491. \qquad (2.47)$$

Column D_2 records these discrepancies. Briggs then noted that the numbers in column D_2 decrease by a factor of about one-eighth, so again he com-

Square roots	D_1	D_2	D_3	D_4
3				
	267949192			
1.732050808		17035907		
	49951391		475957	
1.316074013		1653531		5773
	10834317		23974	
1.147202690		182717		149
	2525862		1349	
1.071075483		21491		4
	609975		80	
1.034927767		2606		0
	149888		5	
1.017313996		321		*0*
	37151		*0*	
1.008619847		*40*		*0*
	9248		*0*	
1.004300676		5		
	2307			
1.002148031				

TABLE 2.6. Higher-order "differences" in Briggs's table.

puted the discrepancies, and these are given in column D_3. The numbers in column D_3 diminish by a factor of roughly one-sixteenth, and column D_4 displays the discrepancies that arise from these calculations. We have chosen to stop at column D_4. Briggs worked to 30 decimal places and found it necessary to compute more columns of "differences" than the four we have used here.

Now we come to the most important point about Briggs's table: why it was *useful*. The numbers in the upper part of Table 2.6 were calculated, as described above, by taking repeated square roots of 3 and then computing Briggs's differences. We have continued taking square roots in Table 2.6 until the differences in our last column diminish to zero. Then the numbers shown in italics are computed by working from right to left, as follows. Having obtained a zero as the fourth entry in column D_4, we immediately extend column D_4 by inserting further zeros. In Table 2.6 we have added just two zeros (those two displayed in italics), but we could have added more. Then the remaining numbers in italics are computed from right to left, using Briggs's differences. Thus we compute in turn

$$\frac{1}{16} \cdot 5 - 0 = 0,$$

$$\frac{1}{8} \cdot 321 - 0 = 40,$$

$$\frac{1}{4} \cdot 37151 - 40 = 9248,$$

and

$$\frac{1}{2}(0.008619847) - 0.000009248 - 0.004300676,$$

which gives the entry 1.004300676 in the first column. We can thus extend the first column, one number at a time, by repeating a sequence of four calculations like those shown above. In this way, Briggs was able to cut down the labour in his calculations by reducing the number of direct evaluations of square roots.

Let us use our results in Table 2.6 to estimate $\log_{10} 3$ from (2.46). From the last entry in column 1 of the table we have $x = 0.002148031$ and $n = 9$, since we have (effectively) extracted 9 repeated square roots of 3. Then (2.46) gives the estimate $\log_{10} 3 \approx 0.477634$, which compares with the true value of $\log_{10} 3 \approx 0.477121$. Briggs would be ashamed of us for getting such a poor result! Given that we have computed the numbers in Table 2.6 to 9 decimal places, we should have continued our calculation a little further. If we "work back" from right to left seven more times, we find a value of $x = 0.000016764$, corresponding to $n = 16$, and this gives the more accurate estimate $\log_{10} 3 \approx 0.477125$. This result is about as accurate as can be obtained, given that we are working only to 9 decimal places in our table.

As a by-product of his calculations, Briggs obtained the series expansion for $(1 + x)^{1/2}$. Essentially, he began with, say, $(1 + x)^8$, and wrote down its repeated square roots, which are $(1 + x)^4$, $(1 + x)^2$, and $1 + x$, as we did numerically in Table 2.6 above. He then carried out his differencing process *algebraically*. Then by working back through the table, as we did above in computing the italicized numbers in Table 2.6, he could thus estimate the next repeated square root, which is $(1 + x)^{1/2}$. We show this algebraic computation in Table 2.7. The first element in the first column of Table 2.7 is the first 5 terms in the expansion of $(1+x)^8$, and the next three elements in this first column are the full expansions of $(1+x)^4$, $(1+x)^2$ and $1+x$ itself. Then, apart from the last element in each column, all the other elements are obtained by using Briggs's differences. The second element in column D_3 is then computed as one-sixteenth of the first element $\frac{7}{8}x^4$, and the last elements in each of the other columns are then computed by working from right to left, just as we did above. It is very clear by looking at the coefficients of x in the first column of Table 2.7 that the "fractional parts" in the first column are roughly halving, for small values of x. Likewise, from the coefficients of x^2 in column D_1, we see that the numbers in this column are indeed diminishing by a factor that approaches one-quarter, for small values of x. Similarly, the coefficients of x^3 in column D_2 diminish by a factor of about one-eighth for small x, and the second element of column D_3, as we have already said, was *computed* as one-sixteenth of the element above it.

Square roots	D_1	D_2	D_3
$1 + 8x + 28x^2 + 56x^3 + 70x^4$			
	$8x^2 + 24x^3 + 34x^4$		
$1 + 4x + 6x^2 + 4x^3 + x^4$		$4x^3 + 8x^4$	
	$2x^2 + 2x^3 + \frac{1}{2}x^4$		$\frac{7}{8}x^4$
$1 + 2x + x^2$		$\frac{1}{2}x^3 + \frac{1}{8}x^4$	
	$\frac{1}{2}x^2$		$\frac{7}{128}x^4$
$1 + x$		$\frac{1}{16}x^3 - \frac{5}{128}x^4$	
	$\frac{1}{8}x^2 - \frac{1}{16}x^3 + \frac{5}{128}x^4$		
$1 + \frac{1}{2}x - \frac{1}{8}x^2 + \frac{1}{16}x^3 - \frac{5}{128}x^4$			

TABLE 2.7. How Briggs found the series for $(1+x)^{1/2}$.

We have the advantage over Briggs in knowing that for any real number α, the series

$$(1+x)^\alpha = 1 + \binom{\alpha}{1}x + \binom{\alpha}{2}x^2 + \binom{\alpha}{3}x^3 + \cdots \qquad (2.48)$$

is valid for $-1 < x < 1$ and the coefficients, known as *binomial coefficients*, are given by

$$\binom{\alpha}{r} = \frac{\alpha(\alpha-1)\cdots(\alpha-r+1)}{r!},$$

for $r = 1, 2, 3, \ldots$. In particular, for $\alpha = \frac{1}{2}$, we obtain the series that we have already met in (1.75),

$$(1+x)^{1/2} = 1 + \frac{1}{2}x - \frac{1}{8}x^2 + \frac{1}{16}x^3 - \frac{5}{128}x^4 + \frac{7}{256}x^5 + \cdots,$$

and we see that by following Briggs's method in Table 2.7, we have obtained the first five terms of the series for $(1+x)^{1/2}$ correctly. By the same method we could derive more terms of this series. We would need to begin with $(1+x)^{16}$, or take some still higher power of two as the exponent of $1+x$, and thus obtain more elements in the first column of Table 2.7. In fact, Briggs deduced correctly the general term in the series for $(1+x)^{1/2}$, that is, he knew all the terms of this series. Briggs was the first to find a binomial series (2.48) for a value of α that is not an integer.

Briggs obtained the logarithms to base 10 of all the 25 prime numbers between 2 and 97 in the way we have described. He used a lot of ingenuity and developed a mastery of interpolation methods in completing his table of logarithms, *Logarithmorum Chilias Prima*, in 1617. Note how he adopted Napier's term "logarithm," a word that has been part of the language of mathematics to the present day. Briggs's table was extended by Adriaan Vlacq (1600–1660) in his *Arithmetica Logarithmica*, published in 1628. In this massive tome, Vlacq gives the logarithms of all the integers from 1 to

100,000 to 10 decimal places. See Edwards [13] and Goldstine [21] for more details of the work of Briggs.

Problem 2.3.1 Use (2.34) to express Napier's logarithm in terms of the natural logarithm and so verify (2.35).

Problem 2.3.2 Show that for any real number a,

$$\text{Nap.log } x^a = a \cdot \text{Nap.log } x + (1 - a)\text{Nap.log } 1.$$

Problem 2.3.3 Verify that

$$\frac{10^7}{10^7 - 1} - \frac{10^7 + 1}{10^7} = \frac{1}{10^7(10^7 - 1)}.$$

Problem 2.3.4 Make the change of variable $u = 1 - 10^{-7}x$ in Napier's inequalities (2.39), so that $0 < x \leq 10^7$ corresponds to $0 \leq u < 1$, and show that (2.39) is equivalent to

$$u \leq -\log_e(1 - u) \leq \frac{u}{1 - u}.$$

Following Napier, approximate to $-\log_e(1 - u)$ by the arithmetic mean of the above lower and upper bounds and so show that

$$-\log_e(1 - u) \approx \frac{u(1 - \frac{1}{2}u)}{1 - u} = u + \frac{1}{2}u^2 + \frac{1}{2}u^3 + \cdots .$$

Replace u by $-x$ in the line above to give

$$\log_e(1 + x) \approx x - \frac{1}{2}x^2 + \frac{1}{2}x^3 + \cdots$$

and verify that this approximation agrees with the first two terms of the series for $\log_e(1 + x)$.

Problem 2.3.5 Choose a small prime number p other than 3, construct a table similar to Table 2.6, and thus estimate $\log_{10} p$.

2.4   The Logarithm as an Area

The development of the calculus by Isaac Newton (1642–1727), Gottfried Leibniz (1646–1716), and others, including notably James Gregory (1638–1675), not only led to many exciting new results but also shed new light on many earlier mathematical discoveries, including the property of the logarithm as an area that we discuss in this section. The fundamental theorem of the calculus is concerned with the relation between differentiation and integration. Given the importance of this theorem, its proof is surprisingly simple.

Theorem 2.4.1 If f is Riemann integrable on $[a, b]$ and

$$F(x) = \int_a^x f(t)dt$$

for $a \leq x \leq b$, then F is continuous on $[a, b]$. Further, if f is continuous on $[a, b]$, then $F' = f$. ∎

Since every continuous function is Riemann integrable (see for example Haggerty [23]), we could write down a slightly weaker version of the above theorem by *beginning* with the assumption that f is continuous on $[a, b]$ and conclude that F is continuous and that $F' = f$ on $[a, b]$.

We saw in (2.28) that the derivative of $\log_e x$ is $1/x$. Thus we obtain the natural logarithm by *integrating* the function $1/x$, which means that the natural logarithm can be interpreted as an *area* under the curve $y = 1/x$. We will now look at how this discovery was made, and to appreciate its importance, we have to keep in mind that it predates the discovery of the fundamental theorem of the calculus.

Given a function f such that $f(x) > 0$ for $x_0 \leq x \leq x_1$, we write

$$\int_{x_0}^{x_1} f(x)dx$$

to denote the area that is bounded above by the curve $y = f(x)$ and below by the x-axis, and lies between the ordinates $x = x_0$ and $x = x_1$. The work we are about to describe predates this notation, but this will in no way impede our understanding. If the function f is monotonic decreasing over the interval $[x_0, x_1]$, then with x in this interval we have

$$f(x_1) \leq f(x) \leq f(x_0),$$

and so

$$(x_1 - x_0)f(x_1) \leq \int_{x_0}^{x_1} f(x)dx \leq (x_1 - x_0)f(x_0). \qquad (2.49)$$

Given an interval $[a, b]$, let us subdivide it into N equal subintervals of width $(b-a)/N$, for some positive integer N. We will denote the subdividing points by $x_0, x_1, \ldots, x_N$. Thus $x_j = a + j(b - a)/N$, for $j = 0, 1, \ldots, N$, so that $x_0 = a$ and $x_N = b$. If f is monotonic decreasing on the whole interval $[a, b]$, then, since

$$\int_a^b f(x)dx = \sum_{j=1}^N \int_{x_{j-1}}^{x_j} f(x)dx,$$

we can "sum up" N inequalities like (2.49) to give

$$\frac{b-a}{N} \sum_{j=1}^N f(x_j) \leq \int_a^b f(x)dx \leq \frac{b-a}{N} \sum_{j=0}^{N-1} f(x_j), \qquad (2.50)$$

since each subinterval is of width $(b-a)/N$. The inequalities (2.50) apply to any monotonic decreasing function. If f is also *Riemann integrable*, which is always true for a continuous function, then (2.50) can be used to obtain lower and upper bounds for the integral. Further, we can make these bounds as close as we please to the value of the integral by taking N sufficiently large. In particular, for $f(x) = 1/x$ and $0 < a < b$, we obtain from (2.50)

$$\frac{b-a}{N} \sum_{j=1}^{N} \frac{1}{x_j} \leq \int_a^b \frac{dx}{x} \leq \frac{b-a}{N} \sum_{j=0}^{N-1} \frac{1}{x_j}, \tag{2.51}$$

giving lower and upper bounds for the area under the hyperbola $y = 1/x$. Now let us choose any positive number λ and carry out the above process on the function $y = 1/x$ over the interval $[\lambda a, \lambda b]$. This time we obtain

$$\frac{\lambda(b-a)}{N} \sum_{j=1}^{N} \frac{1}{\lambda x_j} \leq \int_{\lambda a}^{\lambda b} \frac{dx}{x} \leq \frac{\lambda(b-a)}{N} \sum_{j=0}^{N-1} \frac{1}{\lambda x_j}. \tag{2.52}$$

A comparison of (2.51) and (2.52) shows that the integrals

$$\int_a^b \frac{dx}{x} \qquad \text{and} \qquad \int_{\lambda a}^{\lambda b} \frac{dx}{x}$$

have the same lower and upper bounds, which we will write as

$$L_N = \frac{b-a}{N} \sum_{j=1}^{N} \frac{1}{x_j} \qquad \text{and} \qquad U_N = \frac{b-a}{N} \sum_{j=0}^{N-1} \frac{1}{x_j},$$

respectively. We observe that

$$0 < U_N - L_N = \frac{b-a}{N} \left(\frac{1}{x_0} - \frac{1}{x_N} \right).$$

Since $x_0 = a > 0$ and $x_N = b > a$, we deduce that

$$0 < U_N - L_N = \frac{1}{N} \frac{(b-a)^2}{ab}, \tag{2.53}$$

which tends to zero as N tends to infinity. Since these common lower and upper bounds can be brought arbitrarily close together by taking N sufficiently large, the above two integrals or areas are equal, that is,

$$\int_a^b \frac{dx}{x} = \int_{\lambda a}^{\lambda b} \frac{dx}{x}, \tag{2.54}$$

for any $\lambda > 0$. This result concerning areas under the curve $y = 1/x$ was first obtained by Gregory of St. Vincent (1584–1667).

Let us now define, for any value of $t \geq 1$,

$$L(t) = \int_1^t \frac{dx}{x}.$$

Then, for $t_1, t_2 \geq 1$,

$$L(t_1 t_2) = \int_1^{t_1} \frac{dx}{x} + \int_{t_1}^{t_1 t_2} \frac{dx}{x} = L(t_1) + \int_{t_1}^{t_1 t_2} \frac{dx}{x}, \qquad (2.55)$$

and on applying (2.54) with $\lambda = t_1$ to the final integral in (2.55), we obtain

$$L(t_1 t_2) = L(t_1) + L(t_2). \qquad (2.56)$$

We can take this further to show that $L(x) = \log_e x$, which explains our choice of notation, in harmony with the use of L in (2.16). With $t_1 = x \geq 1$ and $t_2 = 1 + h/x$, with $h > 0$, in (2.56) we have

$$L(x + h) = L(x) + L(1 + h/x),$$

and so

$$\frac{L(x+h) - L(x)}{h} = \frac{L(1 + \frac{h}{x})}{h}.$$

Hence

$$\lim_{h \to 0} \frac{L(x+h) - L(x)}{h} = \lim_{h \to 0} \frac{L(1 + \frac{h}{x})}{h} = \frac{1}{x} \lim_{x:\, h \to 0} \frac{L(1 + \frac{h}{x})}{\frac{h}{x}},$$

where $h \to 0$ from above. Since for a fixed value of x the ratio h/x tends to zero as h tends to zero, we obtain

$$\lim_{h \to 0} \frac{L(x+h) - L(x)}{h} = \frac{1}{x} \lim_{h \to 0} \frac{L(1 + h)}{h}$$
$$= \frac{1}{x} \lim_{h \to 0} \frac{L(1 + h) - L(1)}{h}, \qquad (2.57)$$

because $L(1) = 0$. The last limit in (2.57) is just $L'(1)$, and we deduce from (2.57) that

$$L'(x) = L'(1) \cdot \frac{1}{x}. \qquad (2.58)$$

Further,

$$L(1 + h) - L(1) = L(1 + h) = \int_1^{1+h} \frac{dx}{x},$$

and we may deduce from the inequalities (2.49) that

$$\frac{h}{1 + h} \leq L(1 + h) - L(1) \leq h,$$

so that

$$\frac{1}{1+h} \leq \frac{L(1+h) - L(1)}{h} \leq 1. \tag{2.59}$$

As $h \to 0$ we have $1/(1+h) \to 1$, and we deduce from (2.59) that $L'(1) = 1$. It then follows from (2.58) that $L'(x) = 1/x$. From this and the relation $L(1) = 0$ we conclude that

$$L(x) = \log_e x,$$

so that the area under the hyperbola is indeed given by the natural logarithm.

Problem 2.4.1 Let f be a function that is positive and monotonic decreasing on the interval $[a, b]$, and let L_N and U_N be the sums defined in the text that give lower and upper bounds for the integral of f over $[a, b]$. Show that for any positive integer N,

$$L_N \leq L_{2N} \leq \int_a^b f(x)dx \leq U_{2N} \leq U_N.$$

Deduce that for any positive integer n,

$$L_1 \leq L_2 \leq \cdots \leq L_{2^n} \leq \int_a^b f(x)dx \leq U_{2^n} \leq \cdots \leq U_2 \leq U_1.$$

Show that the sequence (L_{2^j}) is monotonic increasing and is bounded above, and so has a limit, and, similarly, that the decreasing sequence (U_{2^j}) has a limit. Finally, show that both limits are equal to the above integral. (This argument is similar to that used in Problem 2.2.7.)

2.5   Further Historical Notes

In 1676 Isaac Newton (1642–1727) produced a highly ingenious procedure for the computation of a table of natural logarithms. This was more of an exercise for Newton, although a realistic one, rather than an intention to produce a practical table of logarithms. (See Goldstine [21].) Newton was, of course, aware that natural logarithms could readily be converted to logarithms to base 10 on dividing by the constant

$$\log_e 10 \approx 2.302585092994045, \tag{2.60}$$

the reciprocal of Briggs's constant K, given by (2.43). Newton's scheme was as follows.

1. Find the logarithms of 0.98, 0.99, 1.01, 1.02, using the series for $\log_e(1+x)$. Calculate the logarithm of 100, as twice the logarithm of 10, and use (2.60) to obtain the logarithms of 98, 99,101,102.

2. Subtabulate these by 10 subintervals (that is, *interpolate*) to give the logarithms of all numbers between 98 and 102 in steps of 0.1. By using (2.60) again, he could then find the logarithms of all integers between 980 and 1020.

3. Repeat the subtabulation process used in step 2, this time interpolating in steps of 0.1 between 980 and 1000 only, and thus find the logarithms of all integers between 9800 and 10000.

4. Find the logarithms of all the 25 primes less than 100, as shown below.

5. Hence find the logarithms of all integers not greater than 100.

6. Subtabulate these twice to obtain a table of natural logarithms of all integers between 1 and 10000.

In carrying out step 4, Newton used the formulas

$$\left(\frac{9984 \times 1020}{9945}\right)^{1/10} = 2 \quad \text{and} \quad \left(\frac{8 \times 9963}{984}\right)^{1/4} = 3$$

to compute the logarithms of 2 and 3, respectively. Note how he requires the logarithm of 2 in order to compute the logarithm of 3, using

$$\log 3 = \frac{1}{4}\left(3\log 2 + \log 9963 - \log 984\right).$$

He then used the following formulas to compute the logarithms of the remaining primes less than 100:

$$\frac{10}{2} = 5, \quad \left(\frac{98}{2}\right)^{1/2} = 7, \quad \frac{99}{9} = 11, \quad \frac{1001}{7\times11} = 13, \quad \frac{102}{6} = 17,$$

$$\frac{988}{4\times13} = 19, \quad \frac{9936}{16\times27} = 23, \quad \frac{986}{2\times17} = 29, \quad \frac{992}{32} = 31, \quad \frac{999}{27} = 37,$$

$$\frac{984}{24} = 41, \quad \frac{989}{23} = 43, \quad \frac{987}{21} = 47, \quad \frac{9911}{11\times17} = 53, \quad \frac{9971}{13\times13} = 59,$$

$$\frac{9882}{2\times81} = 61, \quad \frac{9849}{3\times49} = 67, \quad \frac{994}{14} = 71, \quad \frac{9928}{8\times17} = 73, \quad \frac{9954}{7\times18} = 79,$$

$$\frac{996}{12} = 83, \quad \frac{9968}{7\times16} = 89, \quad \frac{9894}{6\times17} = 97.$$

The logarithm tables of Napier, Briggs, and Vlacq mentioned above, and the many other logarithm tables that were to follow, were by no means the earliest mathematical tables. A notable example from the second century BC is the table of *chords* created by the Greek mathematician Hipparchus

(180–125 BC),who worked in Alexandria and Rhodes. If we take a chord AB that subtends an angle 2α at the centre of a circle of radius 1 (so that angle $AOB = 2\alpha$ in Figure 2.4), then

$$AB = \text{chord}(2\alpha) = 2\sin\alpha. \qquad (2.61)$$

So a table of chords is effectively a table of sines. Eves [14] states the following theorem, which is quoted by Abu'l Rainan al-Biruni (973–1048) and attributed to Archimedes. It is called the *broken chord theorem*. (See Figure 2.4.)

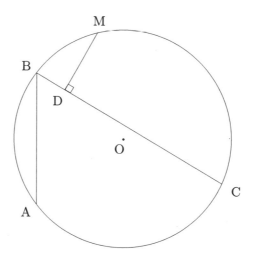

FIGURE 2.4. The broken chord theorem : $AB + BD = DC$, where M is the mid–point of the chord ABC.

Theorem 2.5.1 We begin with a circle and two chords AB and BC, with $BC > AB$. We choose M as the midpoint of the arc ABC and let D be the foot of the perpendicular from M to BC. Then

$$AB + BD = DC. \qquad \blacksquare$$

We will show that this result from antiquity, which is not as well known to present-day mathematicians as it deserves to be, is equivalent to a familiar trigonometrical identity. To verify this we require an even older theorem from the geometry of Euclid: the "angle at the centre" theorem, which states that the angle subtended at the centre of a circle by a given chord is equal to *twice* the angle subtended by the chord at any point on the circumference of the circle on the same side of the chord as the centre. For example, in Figure 2.4 the angle AOB is twice the angle ACB. (See Problem 2.5.1.) As a limiting case of this theorem, where the chord becomes a diameter, the angle at the centre tends to π, and the angle subtended by the diameter at the circumference is $\pi/2$, a right angle.

Since the broken chord theorem is obviously independent of the *size* of the circle, we will choose a circle with radius 1. Let the arcs MC and BM have lengths 2α and 2β, respectively. Recall how an *angle* is defined in radian measure as the ratio of the length of its circular arc divided by the radius. Since the radius here is 1, it follows that angle $MOC = 2\alpha$, where O denotes the centre of the circle, and so $MC = 2\sin\alpha$. Similarly, beginning with the arc BM, with angle 2β, we deduce that $BM = 2\sin\beta$. Thirdly, since M is the midpoint of the arc ABC, angle $AOB = 2(\alpha - \beta)$, and so

$$AB = 2\sin(\alpha - \beta). \tag{2.62}$$

Now we use the "angle at the centre" theorem, which tells us that

$$\text{angle } MBC = \frac{1}{2}\text{ angle } MOC = \alpha$$

and thus, from triangle BDM,

$$BD = BM\cos\alpha = 2\sin\beta\cos\alpha. \tag{2.63}$$

Similarly, we find that angle $MCB = \beta$, and so, from triangle MCD,

$$DC = MC\cos\beta = 2\sin\alpha\cos\beta. \tag{2.64}$$

On combining (2.62),(2.63), and (2.64) we see that $AB + BD = DC$, as stated above, is equivalent to

$$2\sin(\alpha - \beta) + 2\sin\beta\cos\alpha - 2\sin\alpha\cos\beta,$$

which yields the trigonometrical identity

$$\sin(\alpha - \beta) = \sin\alpha\cos\beta - \sin\beta\cos\alpha. \tag{2.65}$$

This, in turn, is equivalent (see Problem 2.5.2) to a relation in terms of chords,

$$\text{chord } \theta \cdot \text{chord }(\pi - \phi) = \text{chord }(\theta + \phi) + \text{chord }(\theta - \phi). \tag{2.66}$$

It is intriguing to realise that (2.66) could be used as an aid to multiplication, as an alternative to a table of logarithms. For to multiply two numbers x and y within the range of the table, we find θ and ϕ such that

$$x = \text{chord } \theta \qquad \text{and} \qquad y = \text{chord }(\pi - \phi).$$

Having found θ and ϕ, we compute $\theta + \phi$ and $\theta - \phi$, and use the table of chords twice to evaluate chord $(\theta + \phi)$ and chord $(\theta - \phi)$. This requires *four* table look-ups, compared with only three when we use a logarithm table, as well as three more additions or subtractions. However, it is interesting that the means of "replacing addition by multiplication" was available such a very long time before the discovery of logarithms.

There is, however, a very much simpler method of replacing multiplication by addition whose origins go back much further still in the history of mathematics. This depends on the identity

$$xy = \left(\frac{x+y}{2}\right)^2 - \left(\frac{x-y}{2}\right)^2, \tag{2.67}$$

which Lanczos [32] attributes to the Babylonians. If we have a table of squares of all positive integers from 1 to 10,000, say, then to multiply any two numbers $x > y$ of up to 4 decimal digits, we need only compute $(x+y)/2$ and $(x-y)/2$, look up their squares in the table, and take the difference of these. If $x + y$ happens to be an odd number, then $x - y$ will also be odd, and then we would need to interpolate in the table of squares.

Problem 2.5.1 To prove the "angle at the centre" theorem, consider a chord AB subtending an angle 2α at the centre O of a given circle and let P be any point on the circumference of the circle on the same side of AB as O. Since $OP = OA = OB$ and an isosceles triangle (one with two equal sides) has two angles equal, we may write

angle OPA = angle $OAP = \beta$ and   angle OAB = angle $OBA = \gamma$,

say. Since the angles in a triangle add up to π, we obtain from triangle OAB that $\gamma = \frac{\pi}{2} - \alpha$. By using the sum of the angles in triangle APB, show that angle $OPB = \alpha + \beta$ and deduce that angle $APB = \alpha$, which is half angle AOB.

Problem 2.5.2 Replace β by $-\beta$ in (2.65) and use the properties

$$\cos(-\beta) = \cos\beta   \text{and}   \sin(-\beta) = -\sin\beta$$

to derive the identity

$$\sin(\alpha + \beta) = \sin\alpha\cos\beta + \sin\beta\cos\alpha.$$

Combine this with (2.65) to give

$$\sin(\alpha + \beta) + \sin(\alpha - \beta) = 2\sin\alpha\cos\beta.$$

Multiply both sides of the last identity by 2, substitute $\theta = 2\alpha$ and $\phi = 2\beta$ with $\alpha > \beta$, and use the definition of chord (2.61) to establish the chord identity (2.66).

3
Interpolation

If I have seen further it is by standing on the shoulders of giants.

Isaac Newton

The problem of estimating the value of a function at a required point, given its values at some points, is called interpolation. One early application of this was prompted by research in astronomy in sixth-century China, where Liú Zhuó used interpolation at three equally spaced points. In the seventeenth century Isaac Newton completely solved the interpolation problem for a function of one variable. The "limiting form" of the interpolating polynomial as the interpolating points "collapse" to the same point gives the first terms of the Taylor series. In this chapter we also consider the interpolation problem for functions of several variables and discuss a method of evaluating the interpolating polynomial by the repeated use of linear (two-point) interpolation.

3.1   The Interpolating Polynomial

Suppose we are given the values of a function $f(x)$ at $n+1$ distinct values of x, say $x_0, x_1, \ldots, x_n$. We can obviously find a linear function of x, say $p_1(x)$, whose graph is a straight line, such that

$$p_1(x_0) = f(x_0) \qquad \text{and} \qquad p_1(x_0) = f(x_0),$$

and it seems plausible that we can find a polynomial $p_2(x)$ such that

$$p_2(x_0) = f(x_0), \qquad p_2(x_1) = f(x_1), \qquad \text{and} \qquad p_2(x_2) = f(x_2).$$

In general, we would expect the graph of $p_2(x)$ to be a parabola, a polynomial of degree two. What about a general value of n? Can we find a polynomial of degree n, say

$$p_n(x) = a_0 + a_1 x + a_2 x^2 + \cdots + a_n x^n,$$

such that $p_n(x_j) = f(x_j)$, for $j = 0, 1, \ldots, n$? This means that we require

$$a_0 + a_1 x_j + a_2 x_j^2 + \cdots + a_n x_j^n = f(x_j), \ j = 0, 1, \ldots, n, \qquad (3.1)$$

giving a system of $n + 1$ linear equations to determine the $n + 1$ unknowns $a_0, a_1, \ldots, a_n$. These will have a unique solution if the matrix

$$\mathbf{V} = \begin{bmatrix} 1 & x_0 & x_0^2 & \cdots & x_0^n \\ 1 & x_1 & x_1^2 & \cdots & x_1^n \\ \vdots & \vdots & \vdots & \vdots & \vdots \\ 1 & x_n & x_n^2 & \cdots & x_n^n \end{bmatrix}, \qquad (3.2)$$

which is called the *Vandermonde* matrix, is nonsingular It is not hard to verify (see Problem 3.1.1) that the determinant of $\mathbf{V}$ is given by

$$\det \mathbf{V} = \prod_{i>j} (x_i - x_j), \qquad (3.3)$$

where the product is taken over all i and j between 0 and n such that $i > j$. For example, when $n = 2$,

$$\det \mathbf{V} = (x_1 - x_0)(x_2 - x_0)(x_2 - x_1).$$

It is then clear that since the abscissas $x_0, x_1, \ldots, x_n$ are distinct, $\det \mathbf{V}$ is nonzero, and so the Vandermonde matrix $\mathbf{V}$ is nonsingular and the system of linear equations (3.1) has a unique solution. We conclude that for a function f defined on a set of distinct points $x_0, x_1, \ldots, x_n$, there is a *unique* polynomial $p_n(x)$ of degree at most n such that $p_n(x_j) = f(x_j)$, for $j = 0, 1, \ldots, n$. This is called the *interpolating polynomial*. Note that the degree may be less than n. For example, if all $n + 1$ points $(x_j, f(x_j))$ lie on a straight line, then the interpolating polynomial will be of degree 1 or 0, the latter case occurring when all the $f(x_j)$ are equal.

Having shown that the existence and uniqueness of the interpolating polynomial follow from the nonsingularity of the Vandermonde matrix, we normally use other lines of attack, associated with the names of Lagrange and Newton, to evaluate the interpolating polynomial. However, before we discuss these ideas, let us say a little more about the direct solution of the system of linear equations (3.1). Given any square matrix $\mathbf{A}$, the $j \times j$ matrix consisting of the first j rows and columns of $\mathbf{A}$ is called its leading submatrix of order j. Thus the leading submatrix of order j of an $(n+1) \times (n+1)$ Vandermonde matrix is simply a $j \times j$ Vandermonde matrix, which is defined by (3.2) with n replaced by $j - 1$. Now let us consider an $n \times n$ matrix $\mathbf{A}$ whose n leading submatrices are all nonsingular. It can be shown by an induction argument that such a matrix can be factorized as a product

$$\mathbf{A} = \mathbf{LU},$$

where $\mathbf{L}$ is a lower triangular matrix with units on the main diagonal and $\mathbf{U}$ is an upper triangular matrix, and that this factorization is unique.

Example 3.1.1 As an example of such a factorization, we have

$$
\begin{bmatrix}
1 & 2 & 3 & -1 \\
2 & -1 & 9 & -7 \\
3 & 4 & -3 & 19 \\
4 & 2 & 6 & -21
\end{bmatrix}
=
\begin{bmatrix}
1 & 0 & 0 & 0 \\
2 & 1 & 0 & 0 \\
-3 & -2 & 1 & 0 \\
4 & 2 & -1 & 1
\end{bmatrix}
\begin{bmatrix}
1 & 2 & 3 & -1 \\
0 & -5 & 3 & -5 \\
0 & 0 & 12 & 6 \\
0 & 0 & 0 & -1
\end{bmatrix},
$$

and it is easily verified that all 4 leading submatrices of the matrix $\mathbf{A}$ on the left side of the last equation are nonsingular. Each leading submatrix of $\mathbf{A}$ is the product of the corresponding leading submatrices of its factors $\mathbf{L}$ and $\mathbf{U}$, and this property holds for all such factorizations.   ∎

If we can factorize a matrix $\mathbf{A}$ in this way, we can more easily solve a system of linear equations of the form

$$\mathbf{Ax} = \mathbf{b}. \tag{3.4}$$

For with $\mathbf{A} - \mathbf{LU}$, we can write

$$\mathbf{LUx} = \mathbf{b},$$

which we can "split" into the two linear systems

$$\mathbf{Ly} = \mathbf{b} \quad \text{and} \quad \mathbf{Ux} - \mathbf{y}. \tag{3.5}$$

We need to solve $\mathbf{Ly} = \mathbf{b}$ first to determine the vector $\mathbf{y}$ and then solve $\mathbf{Ux} = \mathbf{y}$ to determine $\mathbf{x}$. Because of the positions of the zeros in the matrices $\mathbf{L}$ and $\mathbf{U}$, the two linear systems in (3.5) are much more easily solved than the single system (3.4). First let us consider the solution of the system $\mathbf{Ly} = \mathbf{b}$. Since $\mathbf{L}$ is lower triangular, we can find the first element of $\mathbf{y}$ immediately from the first equation, and substitute it into the second equation to find the second element of $\mathbf{y}$. We can thus go down the equations in $\mathbf{Ly} = \mathbf{b}$, finding one element of $\mathbf{y}$ at a time. This process is called *forward substitution*. Having found the vector $\mathbf{y}$, we turn to the system $\mathbf{Ux} = \mathbf{y}$. This time, because $\mathbf{U}$ is upper triangular, we can find the *last* element of the vector

x from the last of these equations, then the second to last element of **x** from the second to last equation, and so on, and this process is called *back substitution*. (The reader may find it helpful to work through a numerical example of the solution of a linear system by matrix factorization. See Problem 3.1.2.) It is quite easy to construct the factors **L** and **U**: we find the ith row of **U** followed by the ith column of **L** in turn, for $i = 0, 1, \ldots, n$. For more details about matrix factorization see Phillips and Taylor [44].

From the foregoing discussion it is clear that since each leading submatrix of a Vandermonde matrix is itself a Vandermonde matrix and so is nonsingular, the Vandermonde matrix has a unique factorization in the form

$$\mathbf{V} = \mathbf{LU},$$

where **L** is a lower triangular matrix with units on the main diagonal and **U** is an upper triangular matrix. Halil Oruç [40] has recently obtained explicit forms for the factors **L** and **U**. (See also Oruç and Phillips [41].) Writing $l_{i,j}$, with $0 \le i, j \le n$ for the elements of the lower triangular matrix **L**, we have $l_{i,j} = 0$ for $j > i$ and $l_{i,i} = 1$ for all i (which is just saying that **L** is a lower triangular matrix with units on the diagonal) and

$$l_{i,j} = \prod_{t=0}^{j-1} \frac{x_i - x_{j-t-1}}{x_j - x_{j-t-1}}, \tag{3.6}$$

for $i > j \ge 1$. Anticipating the definition of Lagrange coefficients, which we give presently, we can interpret $l_{i,j}$ defined by (3.6) as the jth Lagrange coefficient, concerned with interpolation at the abscissas $x_0, x_1, \ldots, x_j$, evaluated at $x = x_i$. The expressions for the elements of the upper triangular matrix **U** involve the *complete symmetric functions* $\tau_r(x_0, x_1, \ldots, x_m)$, defined as the sum of all products of the variables $x_0, x_1, \ldots, x_m$ of degree r, for $r > 0$, with $\tau_0(x_0, x_1, \ldots, x_m) = 1$. For example,

$$\tau_2(x_0, x_1, x_2) = x_0^2 + x_1^2 + x_2^2 + x_0 x_1 + x_0 x_2 + x_1 x_2.$$

The complete symmetric functions satisfy the recurrence relation

$$\tau_r(x_0, \ldots, x_n) = \tau_r(x_0, \ldots, x_{n-1}) + x_n \, \tau_{r-1}(x_0, \ldots, x_n). \tag{3.7}$$

Since **U** is upper triangular, $u_{i,j} = 0$ for $i > j$, and the remaining elements of **U** are defined by

$$u_{i,j} = \tau_{j-i}(x_0, x_1, \ldots, x_i) \, \pi_i(x_i), \tag{3.8}$$

where

$$\pi_i(x) = \begin{cases} 1, & i = 0, \\ (x - x_0)(x - x_1) \cdots (x - x_{i-1}), & 1 \le i \le n. \end{cases} \tag{3.9}$$

For example, with $n = 3$ we obtain

$$
\mathbf{L} = \begin{bmatrix}
1 & 0 & 0 & 0 \\
1 & 1 & 0 & 0 \\
1 & \frac{x_2 - x_0}{x_1 - x_0} & 1 & 0 \\
1 & \frac{x_3 - x_0}{x_1 - x_0} & \frac{(x_3 - x_1)(x_3 - x_0)}{(x_2 - x_1)(x_2 - x_0)} & 1
\end{bmatrix}
\tag{3.10}
$$

and

$$
\mathbf{U} = \begin{bmatrix}
1 & x_0 & x_0^2 & x_0^3 \\
0 & \pi_1(x_1) & (x_0 + x_1)\pi_1(x_1) & (x_0^2 + x_0 x_1 + x_1^2)\pi_1(x_1) \\
0 & 0 & \pi_2(x_2) & (x_0 + x_1 + x_2)\pi_2(x_2) \\
0 & 0 & 0 & \pi_3(x_3)
\end{bmatrix}.
\tag{3.11}
$$

The above discussion shows in a most direct way that the interpolating polynomial exists and is unique amongst all polynomials of degree not greater than n, and the above factorization of the Vandermonde matrix gives a direct method of solving the linear system (3.1) to derive the interpolating polynomial $p_n(x)$.

However, there are ways of *constructing* $p_n(x)$ that are much easier than solving the linear system (3.1). If the abscissas $x_0, x_1, \ldots, x_n$ are distinct, the polynomial

$$
(x - x_1)(x - x_2) \cdots (x - x_n)
$$

is obviously zero at $x = x_1, x_2, \ldots, x_n$ and is nonzero at $x = x_0$. We can scale this polynomial to give

$$
L_0(x) = \frac{(x - x_1)(x - x_2) \cdots (x - x_n)}{(x_0 - x_1)(x_0 - x_2) \cdots (x_0 - x_n)},
$$

which is zero at $x = x_1, x_2, \ldots, x_n$ and takes the value 1 at $x = x_0$. Similarly, we construct

$$
L_i(x) = \prod_{j \neq i} \frac{(x - x_j)}{(x_i - x_j)},
\tag{3.12}
$$

where the product is taken over all j between 0 and n, but excluding $j = i$, and we see that $L_i(x)$ takes the value 1 at $x = x_i$ and is zero at all n other abscissas. Each polynomial $L_i(x)$ is of degree n and is called a Lagrange coefficient, after the French–Italian mathematician J. L. Lagrange (1736–1813). Thus $f(x_i)L_i(x)$ has the value $f(x_i)$ at $x = x_i$ and is zero at the other abscissas. We can express the interpolating polynomial $p_n(x)$ very simply in terms of the Lagrange coefficients as

$$
p_n(x) = \sum_{i=0}^{n} f(x_i)L_i(x),
\tag{3.13}
$$

for the the polynomial on the right of (3.13) is of degree at most n and takes the appropriate value at each abscissa $x_0, x_1, \ldots, x_n$. We call (3.13) the Lagrange form of the interpolating polynomial.

Example 3.1.2 Let us use interpolation in the table

x	0.693	0.916	1.099
$f(x)$	2.0	2.5	3

to estimate the value of $f(1)$. These numbers come from Table 2.3, where the expected value for $f(1)$ is $e \approx 2.718$. With $n = 2$ in (3.13) the Lagrange form of the interpolating polynomial is

$$p_2(x) = \frac{(x - x_1)(x - x_2)}{(x_0 - x_1)(x_0 - x_2)} f(x_0) + \frac{(x - x_0)(x - x_2)}{(x_1 - x_0)(x_1 - x_2)} f(x_1)$$
$$+ \frac{(x - x_0)(x - x_1)}{(x_2 - x_0)(x_2 - x_1)} f(x_2).$$

Substituting the values of x_j and $f(x_j)$ for $j = 0, 1$, and 2 from the table, and putting $x = 1$, we obtain $p_2(1) \approx 2.719$. ∎

In the above example we obtained a value for $p_2(1)$ that is very close to $f(1)$. What can we say, in general, about the accuracy of interpolation? The answer lies in the following theorem.

Theorem 3.1.1 Let the abscissas $x_0, x_1, \ldots, x_n$ be contained in an interval $[a, b]$ on which f and its first n derivatives are continuous, and let $f^{(n+1)}$ exist in the open interval (a, b). Then there exists some number ξ_x, depending on x, in (a, b) such that

$$f(x) - p_n(x) = (x - x_0)(x - x_1) \cdots (x - x_n) \frac{f^{n+1}(\xi_x)}{(n + 1)!}. \tag{3.14}$$

Proof. Consider the function

$$g(x) = f(x) - p_n(x) - \frac{(x - x_0) \cdots (x - x_n)}{(a - x_0) \cdots (a - x_n)} \cdot (f(a) - p_n(a)), \tag{3.15}$$

where $\alpha \in [a, b]$ and α is distinct from all of the abscissas $x_0, x_1, \ldots, x_n$. The function g has been constructed so that it has at least $n + 2$ zeros, at α and all the $n + 1$ interpolating abscissas x_j. We then argue from Rolle's theorem (see Haggerty [23]) that g' must have at least $n + 1$ zeros. (Rolle's theorem simply says that between any two zeros of a differentiable function its derivative must have at least one zero.) By repeatedly applying Rolle's theorem, we argue that g'' has at least n zeros, and finally that $g^{(n+1)}$ has at least one zero, say at $x = \xi_\alpha$. Thus, on differentiating (3.15) $n + 1$ times and putting $x = \xi_\alpha$, we obtain

$$0 = f^{(n+1)}(\xi_\alpha) - \frac{(n + 1)!(f(\alpha) - p_n(\alpha))}{(\alpha - x_0) \cdots (\alpha - x_n)}.$$

Finally we complete the proof by rearranging the last equation to give an expression for $f(\alpha) - p_n(\alpha)$ and replacing α by x. ∎

The above expression for the interpolation error is obviously of limited use, since it requires the evaluation of the $(n+1)$th-order derivative $f^{(n+1)}$ at ξ_x, and in general, we do not even know the value of ξ_x. As if this news were not bad enough, we note that there can also be an error in evaluating $p_n(x)$ due to rounding in the values of $f(x_j)$.

Example 3.1.3 What is the maximum error incurred by using linear interpolation between two consecutive entries in a table of natural logarithms tabulated at intervals of 0.01 between $x = 1$ and $x = 5$? From (3.14) the error of linear interpolation between two points x_0 and x_1 is

$$f(x) - p_1(x) = (x - x_0)(x - x_1)\frac{f''(\xi_x)}{2!}. \tag{3.16}$$

If $|f''(x)| \leq M$ on $[x_0, x_1]$, we can verify (see Problem 3.1.4) that

$$|f(x) - p_1(x)| \leq \frac{1}{8}Mh^2, \tag{3.17}$$

where $h = x_1 - x_0$. For $f(x) = \log x$, we have $f'(x) = 1/x$ and $f''(x) = -1/x^2$. Since $1 \leq x \leq 5$, we can take $M = 1$ in (3.17), and with $h = 0.01$, the error in linear interpolation is not greater than $\frac{1}{8}.10^{-4}$. Thus it would be appropriate for the entries in the table to be given to 4 decimal places. Indeed, one finds in published four-figure tables of the natural logarithm that the entries are tabulated at intervals of 0.01. ■

Problem 3.1.1 Consider the Vandermonde matrix $\mathbf{V}$ in (3.2). One term in the expansion of $\det \mathbf{V}$ is the product of the elements on the main diagonal,

$$x_1 x_2^2 x_3^3 \cdots x_n^n,$$

which has total degree

$$1 + 2 + \cdots + n = \frac{1}{2}n(n + 1).$$

Deduce that $\det \mathbf{V}$ is a polynomial in the variables $x_0, x_1, \ldots, x_n$ of total degree $\frac{1}{2}n(n + 1)$. If $x_i = x_j$ for any i and j, show that $\det \mathbf{V} = 0$ and so deduce that

$$\det \mathbf{V} = C \prod_{i>j}(x_i - x_j),$$

where C is a constant, since the right side of the latter equation is also of total degree $\frac{1}{2}n(n + 1)$. Verify that the choice $C = 1$ gives the correct coefficient for the term $x_1 x_2^2 x_3^3 \cdots x_n^n$ on both sides.

Problem 3.1.2 Solve the linear system

$$
\begin{bmatrix}
1 & 2 & 3 & -1 \\
2 & -1 & 9 & -7 \\
-3 & 4 & -3 & 19 \\
4 & -2 & 6 & -21
\end{bmatrix}
\begin{bmatrix}
x_1 \\
x_2 \\
x_3 \\
x_4
\end{bmatrix}
=
\begin{bmatrix}
7 \\
18 \\
19 \\
-14
\end{bmatrix}
$$

by using the factorization of the above matrix given in Example 3.1.1.

Problem 3.1.3 Construct the interpolating polynomial of degree three for a function f that takes the values 2, -2, 0, and 14 at $x = 0$, 1, 2, and 3, respectively, by writing down the factors **L** and **U** of the 4×4 Vandermonde matrix (see (3.10) and (3.11)) and solving the appropriate linear system (3.1) by the matrix factorization method.

Problem 3.1.4 Show that the function $(x - x_0)(x - x_1)$ has one turning value (where its derivative is zero) and, by finding the value of the function at that point, verify that

$$
\max_{x_0 \leq x \leq x_1} |(x - x_0)(x - x_1)| = \frac{1}{4}(x_1 - x_0)^2
$$

and thus derive the inequality (3.17).

Problem 3.1.5 Verify that

$$
(x - x_0)(x - x_1) = \left(x - \frac{1}{2}(x_0 + x_1) \right)^2 - \frac{1}{4}(x_1 - x_0)^2
$$

and so find the maximum modulus of $(x - x_0)(x - x_1)$ on the interval $[x_0, x_1]$ without using differentiation.

3.2   Newton's Divided Differences

On Christmas day in 1642, the year when Galileo died, the great Isaac Newton was born. Archimedes, Newton, and Gauss are often described as the three greatest mathematicians of all time. Newton tackled the interpolation problem in a most imaginative way, effectively writing the interpolating polynomial in the form

$$
p_n(x) = a_0 \pi_0(x) + a_1 \pi_1(x) + \cdots + a_n \pi_n(x),
\tag{3.18}
$$

where $\pi_i(x)$ is defined above by (3.9). Now, following Newton (a wise choice of guide), let us determine the values of the coefficients a_j by setting $p_n(x_j) = f(x_j)$, for $0 \leq j \leq n$, to give the system of linear equations

$$
a_0 \pi_0(x_j) + a_1 \pi_1(x_j) + \cdots + a_j \pi_j(x_j) = f(x_j),
\tag{3.19}
$$

for $0 \leq j \leq n$. Note that $\pi_i(x_j) = 0$ when $j < i$. The system of equations (3.19) has the matrix

$$
\mathbf{M} = \begin{bmatrix}
\pi_0(x_0) & 0 & 0 & \cdots & 0 \\
\pi_0(x_1) & \pi_1(x_1) & 0 & \cdots & 0 \\
\pi_0(x_2) & \pi_1(x_2) & \pi_2(x_2) & \cdots & 0 \\
\vdots & \vdots & \vdots & \ddots & \vdots \\
\pi_0(x_n) & \pi_1(x_n) & \pi_2(x_n) & \cdots & \pi_n(x_n)
\end{bmatrix},
\tag{3.20}
$$

and we note with some satisfaction that $\mathbf{M}$ is lower triangular. Its determinant is

$$
\det \mathbf{M} = \pi_0(x_0)\,\pi_1(x_1)\cdots\pi_n(x_n).
\tag{3.21}
$$

If the $n+1$ abscissas $x_0, x_1, \ldots, x_n$ are all distinct, it is clear from (3.21) that $\det \mathbf{M} \neq 0$, and so the linear system (3.19) has a unique solution. From (3.19) we can determine a_0 from the first equation, then a_1 from the second equation, and so on, using forward substitution. In general, we determine a_j from the $(j+1)$th equation, and we can see that a_j depends only on the values of x_0 up to x_j and $f(x_0)$ up to $f(x_j)$. In particular, we obtain

$$
a_0 = f(x_0) \qquad \text{and} \qquad a_1 = \frac{f(x_1) - f(x_0)}{x_1 - x_0}
\tag{3.22}
$$

We will write

$$
a_j = f[x_0, x_1, \ldots, x_j], \qquad 0 \leq j \leq n,
\tag{3.23}
$$

to emphasize its dependence on f and $x_0, x_1, \ldots, x_j$, and refer to a_j as a jth divided difference. The form of the expression for a_1 in (3.22) above and the recurrence relation (3.27) below show why the term *divided difference* is appropriate. Thus we may write (3.18) in the form

$$
p_n(x) = f[x_0]\pi_0(x) + f[x_0, x_1]\pi_1(x) + \cdots + f[x_0, x_1, \ldots, x_n]\pi_n(x),
\tag{3.24}
$$

which is Newton's divided difference formula for the interpolating polynomial. Observe that $f[x_0] = f(x_0)$. We write $f[x_0]$ in (3.24) rather than $f(x_0)$ for the sake of harmony of notation. Note also that since we can interpolate on any set of distinct abscissas, we can define a divided difference with respect to any set of distinct abscissas. There is another notation for divided differences, which is to write

$$
[x_0, x_1, \ldots, x_j]f
\tag{3.25}
$$

instead of $f[x_0, x_1, \ldots, x_j]$. In (3.25) we can think of $[x_0, x_1, \ldots, x_j]$ as an *operator* that acts on the function f. We now show that a divided difference is a symmetric function.

$$\begin{array}{llll}
x_0 & f[x_0] \\
& & f[x_0, x_1] \\
x_1 & f[x_1] & & f[x_0, x_1, x_2] \\
& & f[x_1, x_2] & & f[x_0, x_1, x_2, x_3] \\
x_2 & f[x_2] & & f[x_1, x_2, x_3] \\
& & f[x_2, x_3] \\
x_3 & f[x_3]
\end{array}$$

TABLE 3.1. A systematic scheme for calculating divided diffences.

Theorem 3.2.1 A divided difference can be expressed as the following symmetric sum of multiples of $f(x_j)$,

$$f[x_0, x_1, \ldots, x_n] = \sum_{j=0}^{n} \frac{f(x_j)}{\prod_{i \neq j}(x_j - x_i)}. \tag{3.26}$$

Proof. Since the interpolating polynomial is unique, the polynomials $p_n(x)$ in (3.13) and (3.18) are identically equal. We can obtain (3.26) by equating the coefficients of x^n in (3.13) and (3.18). ∎

For example, we have

$$f[x_0, x_1, x_2] = \frac{f(x_0)}{(x_0 - x_1)(x_0 - x_2)} + \frac{f(x_1)}{(x_1 - x_0)(x_1 - x_2)}$$
$$+ \frac{f(x_2)}{(x_2 - x_0)(x_2 - x_1)}.$$

We can use the symmetric form (3.26) to show that

$$f[x_0, x_1, \ldots, x_n] = \frac{f[x_1, x_2, \ldots, x_n] - f[x_0, x_1, \ldots, x_{n-1}]}{x_n - x_0}. \tag{3.27}$$

For we can replace both divided differences on the right of (3.27) by their respective symmetric forms and collect the terms in $f(x_0), f(x_1)$, and so on, showing that this gives the symmetric form for the divided difference $f[x_0, x_1, \ldots, x_n]$. By repeatedly applying the relation (3.27) systematically, we can build up a table of divided differences as depicted in Table 3.1.

Example 3.2.1 Some of the data of Table 2.3 is reproduced in columns 1 and 2 of Table 3.2, the values of x being given to greater accuracy in the latter table. The numbers in columns 3, 4, and 5 of Table 3.2 are the divided differences corresponding to those shown in the same columns of Table 3.1. With $x = 1$ and x_0, x_1, x_2, and x_3 taken from column 1 of Table 3.2, we use the divided difference form (3.24) with $n = 3$ to give $p_3(1) = 2.718210$. This agrees very well with the expected value, which is $e \approx 2.718282$. Note that the values of the divided differences that are used to compute $p_3(1)$ are the first numbers in columns 2 to 5 of Table 3.2. ∎

We can use a relation of the form (3.27) to express the divided difference $f[x, x_0, x_1, \ldots, x_n]$ in terms of $f[x_0, x_1, \ldots, x_n]$ and $f[x, x_0, x_1, \ldots, x_{n-1}]$. On rearranging this, we obtain

$$f[x, x_0, \ldots, x_{n-1}] = f[x_0, \ldots, x_n] + (x - x_n)f[x, x_0, \ldots, x_n]. \qquad (3.28)$$

Similarly, we have

$$f[x] = f[x_0] + (x - x_0)f[x, x_0], \qquad (3.29)$$

where we have again written $f[x]$ and $f[x_0]$ in place of $f(x)$ and $f(x_0)$ for the sake of unity of notation. Now in the right side of (3.29) we can replace $f[x, x_0]$, using (3.28) with $n - 1$, to give

$$f[x] = f[x_0] + (x - x_0)f[x_0, x_1] + (x - x_0)(x - x_1)f[x, x_0, x_1], \qquad (3.30)$$

and we note that (3.30) may be expressed as

$$f(x) - p_1(x) + (x - x_0)(x - x_1)f[x, x_0, x_1],$$

where $p_1(x)$ is the interpolating polynomial for f based on the two abscissas x_0 and x_1. We can continue, replacing $f[x, x_0, x_1]$ in (3.30), using (3.28) with $n = 2$, and so on. Finally, we obtain

$$f(x) = p_n(x) + (x - x_0) \cdots (x - x_n)f[x, x_0, x_1, \ldots, x_n]. \qquad (3.31)$$

On comparing (3.31) and (3.14), we see that if the conditions of Theorem 3.1.1 hold, then there exists a number ξ_x such that

$$f[x, x_0, x_1, \ldots, x_n] = \frac{f^{(n+1)}(\xi_x)}{(n+1)!}.$$

Since this holds for any x belonging to an interval $[a, b]$ that contains all the abscissas x_j, and within which f satisfies the conditions of Theorem 3.1.1, we can replace n by $n - 1$, put $x = x_n$, and obtain

$$f[x_0, x_1, \ldots, x_n] - \frac{f^{(n)}(\xi)}{n!}, \qquad (3.32)$$

x	$f(x)$			
0.693147	2.0			
		2.240706		
0.916291	2.5		1.237369	
		2.742416		0.450446
1.098612	3.0		1.489446	
		3.243573		
1.252763	3.5			

TABLE 3.2. Numerical illustration of Table 3.1.

where $\xi \in (x_0, x_n)$. Thus an nth-order divided difference, which involves $n + 1$ parameters, behaves like a multiple of an nth-order derivative. If we now return to Newton's divided difference formula (3.24) and let every x_j tend to x_0, then, in view of (3.32), we obtain the limiting form

$$p_n(x) = f(x_0) + (x - x_0)\frac{f'(x_0)}{1!} + \cdots + (x - x_0)^n \frac{f^{(n)}(x_0)}{n!}, \qquad (3.33)$$

which is the Taylor polynomial of degree n, the first $n + 1$ terms of the Taylor series for f. As we have seen, the derivation of the interpolating polynomial is purely algebraic. The interpolating polynomial originated in the precalculus era and is essentially a simpler construct than the Taylor polynomial.

We conclude this section by remarking on an interesting connection between divided differences and the complete symmetric functions, which were introduced in Section 3.1. Because these functions are indeed symmetric, they are unchanged if we permute the variables x_j. In particular, we could interchange x_0 and x_n in the recurrence relation (3.7) to give

$$\tau_r(x_0, \ldots, x_n) = \tau_r(x_1, \ldots, x_n) + x_0\,\tau_{r-1}(x_0, \ldots, x_n). \qquad (3.34)$$

If we now subtract (3.7) from (3.34) and divide by $x_n - x_0$, we obtain

$$\tau_{r-1}(x_0, \ldots, x_n) = \frac{\tau_r(x_1, \ldots, x_n) - \tau_r(x_0, \ldots, x_{n-1})}{x_n - x_0}, \qquad (3.35)$$

which reminds us of the recurrence relation for divided differences. It is not hard to show by induction on n that for $0 \leq n \leq m$,

$$\tau_{m-n}(x_0, \ldots, x_n) = f[x_0, \ldots, x_n], \qquad \text{where} \qquad f(x) = x^m. \qquad (3.36)$$

The first step is to check that (3.36) holds when $n = m$, using the fact that $\tau_0(x_0, \ldots, x_m) = 1$ and the result in Problem 3.2.2. We then assume that (3.36) holds for some positive value of $n \leq m$ and use the recurrence relations for the complete symmetric functions and the divided differences to show that (3.36) holds for $n - 1$, and this completes the proof.

Problem 3.2.1 Verify that the matrix $\mathbf{M}$ defined by (3.20) has the same determinant as the Vandermonde matrix $\mathbf{V}$ in (3.2).

Problem 3.2.2 Write down Newton's divided difference formula (3.24) for $f(x) = x^m$ based on the abscissas $x_0, \ldots, x_m$ and deduce from the uniqueness of the interpolating polynomial that $f[x_0, \ldots, x_m] = 1$.

3.3   Finite Differences

When we are computing divided differences, as in Table 3.1, we repeatedly calculate quotients of the form

$$\frac{f[x_{j+1},\ldots,x_{j+k+1}] - f[x_j,\ldots,x_{j+k}]}{x_{j+k+1} - x_j}, \tag{3.37}$$

where k has the same value throughout any one column of the divided difference table. We note that $k = 0$ for first-order divided differences in column 3 of Table 3.1, $k = 1$ in the next column, and so on. Now, if the abscissas x_j are equally spaced, so that $x_j = x_0 + jh$ for $j = 0, 1, \ldots$, where $h > 0$ is a positive constant, then

$$x_{j+k+1} - x_j = (k+1)h,$$

and we observe that the denominators of the divided differences are constant in any one column. In this case, it seems sensible to concentrate on the numerators of the divided differences, which are simply *differences*. We write

$$f(x_{j+1}) - f(x_j) = \Delta f(x_j), \tag{3.38}$$

which is called a first difference. The symbol Δ is the Greek capital delta and denotes "difference" Thus, with equally spaced x_j, we can express a first-order divided difference in terms of a first difference, as

$$f[x_j, x_{j+1}] = \frac{\Delta f(x_j)}{h},$$

where $h = x_{j+1} - x_j$. In order to represent higher-order divided differences, we require differences of differences, and so on. We define higher-order differences recursively from

$$\Delta^{k+1} f(x_j) = \Delta \left(\Delta^k f(x_j) \right) = \Delta^k f(x_{j+1}) - \Delta^k f(x_j), \tag{3.39}$$

for $k = 1, 2, \ldots$, where $\Delta^1 f(x_j)$ means the same as $\Delta f(x_j)$. We refer to each expression of the form $\Delta^k f(x_j)$ as a finite difference, and Δ is called the *forward difference operator*. Continuing our simplification of divided differences when the x_j are equally spaced, we have

$$f[x_j, x_{j+1}, x_{j+2}] = \frac{f[x_{j+1}, x_{j+2}] - f[x_j, x_{j+1}]}{x_{j+2} - x_j} = \frac{\Delta f(x_{j+1}) - \Delta f(x_j)}{2h^2},$$

and, using (3.39), we obtain

$$f[x_j, x_{j+1}, x_{j+2}] = \frac{\Delta^2 f(x_j)}{2h^2}.$$

$$f(x_0)$$
$$\Delta f(x_0)$$
$$f(x_1) \qquad\qquad \Delta^2 f(x_0)$$
$$\Delta f(x_1) \qquad\qquad \Delta^3 f(x_0)$$
$$f(x_2) \qquad\qquad \Delta^2 f(x_1)$$
$$\Delta f(x_2)$$
$$f(x_3)$$

TABLE 3.3. A systematic scheme for calculating finite diffences.

It is easily verified (see Problem 3.3.1) that this generalizes to give

$$f[x_j, x_{j+1}, \ldots, x_{j+k}] = \frac{\Delta^k f(x_j)}{k!\, h^k}, \qquad (3.40)$$

for all $k \geq 1$. We are now almost ready to convert Newton's divided difference formula into a forward difference form. In keeping with the equal spacing of the abscissas x_j, it is helpful to make a change of variable, introducing a new variable s satisfying $x = x_0 + sh$, so that s measures the distance of x from x_0 in units of length h. Then we have $x - x_j = (s - j)h$ and

$$\pi_i(x) = (x - x_0)(x - x_1) \cdots (x - x_{i-1}) = h^i s(s-1) \cdots (s - i + 1).$$

A typical term in Newton's divided difference formula (3.24) is

$$f[x_0, x_1, \ldots, x_i] \cdot \pi_i(x) = \frac{\Delta^i f(x_0)}{i!\, h^i} \cdot h^i s(s-1) \cdots (s - i + 1),$$

and since

$$\frac{s(s-1) \cdots (s - i + 1)}{i!} = \binom{s}{i},$$

we may write

$$f[x_0, x_1, \ldots, x_i] \cdot \pi_i(x) = \binom{s}{i} \Delta^i f(x_0).$$

On summing the results from the last equation over i, we convert Newton's divided difference formula (3.24) into the form

$$p_n(x_0 + sh) = f(x_0) + \binom{s}{1} \Delta f(x_0) + \cdots + \binom{s}{n} \Delta^n f(x_0), \qquad (3.41)$$

where s satisfies $x = x_0 + sh$. This is the *forward difference formula*. We apply it in much the same way as we used the divided difference formula (3.24). We compute a table of forward differences (see Table 3.3), which is laid out in a manner similar to that of the divided difference Table 3.1.

The only entries in Table 3.3 that are required for the evaluation of the interpolating polynomial $p_n(x)$, defined by (3.41), are the first numbers in each column of the forward difference table, namely $f(x_0), \Delta f(x_0)$, and so on. From the uniqueness of the interpolating polynomial, if $f(x)$ is itself a polynomial of degree k, then its interpolating polynomial $p_n(x)$ will be equal to $f(x)$ for $n \geq k$. It then follows from the forward difference formula (3.41) that kth-order differences must be constant and differences of order greater than k must be zero.

Example 3.3.1 As a "fun" illustration of the forward difference formula, which shows that we can have reasonable accuracy with interpolating points that are not very close together, let us take $f(x) = \sin x$, with interpolating abscissas $0, \frac{\pi}{4}, \frac{\pi}{2}, \frac{3\pi}{4}$, and π, so that the corresponding values of $f(x)$ are $0, 1/\sqrt{2}, 1, 1/\sqrt{2}$, and 0, respectively. Let us interpolate at $x = \frac{\pi}{6}$. Here $x_0 = 0$ and $h = \frac{\pi}{4}$, so that $s = \frac{2}{3}$. On computing the difference table we obtain $f(0) = 0$ and

$$\Delta f(0) = \frac{1}{\sqrt{2}}, \qquad \Delta^2 f(0) = 1 - \sqrt{2},$$
$$\Delta^3 f(0) = -3 + 2\sqrt{2}, \qquad \Delta^4 f(0) = 6 - 4\sqrt{2}.$$

Then we obtain from the forward difference formula (3.41) that

$$p_4(\pi/4) = \frac{160}{243} \cdot \sqrt{2} - \frac{35}{81} \approx 0.499,$$

which is close to the value of $\sin \frac{\pi}{6} = \frac{1}{2}$. ∎

Now let us consider the function 2^x evaluated at $x = 0, 1, 2$, and so on. Since $h = 1$, we have

$$\Delta \, 2^x = 2^{x+1} - 2^x = 2^x,$$

and we can apply this relation repeatedly to give

$$\Delta^k \, 2^x = 2^x$$

for $k = 1, 2, \ldots$. Thus, for the function $f(x) = 2^x$, we have $\Delta^k f(0) = 1$ for all $k \geq 1$. In applying the forward difference formula where, as in this case, $x_0 = 0$ and $h = 1$, it follows from $x = x_0 + sh$ that $s = x$. On substituting these results into (3.41) we see that the interpolating polynomial for the function 2^x is given by

$$p_n(x) = 1 + \binom{x}{1} + \binom{x}{2} + \cdots + \binom{x}{n}.$$

It can be shown that as $n \to \infty$, the above series converges to 2^x when $|x| < 1$, so that

$$2^x = 1 + \binom{x}{1} + \binom{x}{2} + \binom{x}{3} + \cdots . \tag{3.42}$$

This is a beautiful series for the exponential function 2^x, which may be compared with the much better known series for the more important exponential function e^x,

$$e^x = 1 + \frac{x}{1!} + \frac{x^2}{2!} + \frac{x^3}{3!} + \cdots, \tag{3.43}$$

which converges for all x. We can think of the series for 2^x as a finite difference analogue of the series for e^x. The latter series is the sum of a sequence of functions $u_j(x) = x^j/j!$, which satisfy

$$\frac{d}{dx} u_j(x) = u_{j-1}(x), \tag{3.44}$$

and the series (3.42) for 2^x may be expressed as the sum of a sequence of functions $v_j(x) = \begin{pmatrix} x \\ j \end{pmatrix}$, which satisfy

$$\Delta v_j(x) = v_{j-1}(x), \tag{3.45}$$

where $\Delta v_j(x) = v_j(x+1) - v_j(x)$. The two relations (3.44) and (3.45) characterize the link between the two exponential series (3.43) and (3.42). However, the series (3.42) is not recommended for evaluating 2^x. For example, putting $x = 0.5$ in (3.42) and using 20 terms, we obtain $\sqrt{2} \approx 1.412$, with an error of approximately 0.002. In contrast, 20 terms of the exponential series for $e^{1/2}$ has an error only a little larger than $(0.5)^{20}/20!$, and so 20 terms of this series will give $e^{1/2}$ correct to 24 decimal places.

On substituting $x = j - 1 + r$, (3.45) yields

$$\begin{pmatrix} j-1+r \\ j-1 \end{pmatrix} = \begin{pmatrix} j+r \\ j \end{pmatrix} - \begin{pmatrix} j-1+r \\ j \end{pmatrix} \tag{3.46}$$

for $r \geq 1$, and when $r = 0$ we need to replace this with the relation

$$\begin{pmatrix} j-1 \\ j-1 \end{pmatrix} = \begin{pmatrix} j \\ j \end{pmatrix}.$$

Then, summing (3.46) over r, we obtain

$$\sum_{r=0}^{n-1} \begin{pmatrix} j-1+r \\ j-1 \end{pmatrix} = \begin{pmatrix} j-1+n \\ j \end{pmatrix}. \tag{3.47}$$

For example, with $j = 2$ in (3.47) we have the well-known expression for the sum of the first n positive integers,

$$1 + 2 + 3 + \cdots + n = \frac{1}{2}n(n+1),$$

and with $j = 3$ and 4 we have respectively

$$1 + 3 + 6 + \cdots + \frac{1}{2}n(n+1) = \frac{1}{6}n(n+1)(n+2)$$

and

$$1 + 4 + 10 + \cdots + \frac{1}{6}n(n+1)(n+2) = \frac{1}{24}n(n+1)(n+2)(n+3).$$

We could use these expressions to find the sum of the kth powers of the first n positive integers, as follows. First, for a fixed positive integer k, we find integers $a_1, a_2, \ldots, a_k$ such that

$$r^k = a_1 \begin{pmatrix} r \\ 1 \end{pmatrix} + a_2 \begin{pmatrix} r+1 \\ 2 \end{pmatrix} + \cdots + a_k \begin{pmatrix} r+k-1 \\ k \end{pmatrix}. \qquad (3.48)$$

If we sum the term involving a_j over r, we obtain

$$\sum_{r=1}^{n} \begin{pmatrix} j-1+r \\ j \end{pmatrix} = \sum_{s=0}^{n-1} \begin{pmatrix} j+s \\ j \end{pmatrix} = \begin{pmatrix} j+n \\ j+1 \end{pmatrix},$$

on using (3.47). Thus, on summing each term in (3.48) over r, from 1 to n, we obtain

$$\sum_{r=1}^{n} r^k = a_1 \begin{pmatrix} n+1 \\ 2 \end{pmatrix} + a_2 \begin{pmatrix} n+2 \\ 3 \end{pmatrix} + \cdots + a_k \begin{pmatrix} n+k \\ k+1 \end{pmatrix}.$$

We can construct (3.48) by beginning with Newton's divided difference formula (3.24) for x^k, based on the interpolating points $0, -1, -2, \ldots, -k$. Another way of finding the sum of kth powers is to express the sum itself in the form of its forward difference formula. (See Problem 3.3.4.)

Example 3.3.2 To find the sum of the squares of the first n positive integers first verify that

$$r^2 = -\begin{pmatrix} r \\ 1 \end{pmatrix} + 2\begin{pmatrix} r+1 \\ 2 \end{pmatrix}$$

and then obtain

$$\sum_{r=0}^{n} r^2 = -\begin{pmatrix} n+1 \\ 2 \end{pmatrix} + 2\begin{pmatrix} n+2 \\ 3 \end{pmatrix}$$

$$= -\frac{1}{2}n(n+1) + \frac{1}{3}n(n+1)(n+2)$$

$$= \frac{1}{6}n(n+1)(2n+1). \qquad \blacksquare$$

Problem 3.3.1 Show that (3.40) holds for $k = 1$ and all $j \geq 0$. Assume that (3.40) holds for some $k \geq 1$ and all j, and deduce that it holds when k is replaced by $k + 1$, and all j. Thus justify by induction that (3.40) holds for all k and j.

Problem 3.3.2 Given that $p(x)$ takes the values 2, -2, 0, and 14 at $x = 0$, 1, 2, and 3, respectively, and that $p(x)$ is a polynomial of degree 3, compute a difference table for $p(x)$ and use the forward difference formula to obtain an explicit polynomial representation of $p(x)$.

Problem 3.3.3 Write down Newton's divided difference formula (3.24) for x^k, based on the interpolating points $0, -1, -2, \ldots, -k$. Deduce that the coefficient a_j in (3.48) is given by

$$a_j = j!\, f[0, -1, -2, \ldots, -j],$$

where $f(x) = x^k$.

Problem 3.3.4 Let

$$S(n) = 1^3 + 2^3 + \cdots + n^3.$$

Compute a difference table and derive the forward difference form of the interpolating polynomial (3.41) for $S(x)$ tabulated at $x = 0, 1, 2, 3, 4$ to show that

$$S(n) = \binom{n}{1} + 7\binom{n}{2} + 12\binom{n}{3} + 6\binom{n}{4}.$$

Simplify this to show that the sum of the first n cubes is given by

$$1^3 + 2^3 + \cdots + n^3 = \frac{1}{4}n^2(n+1)^2.$$

Problem 3.3.5 Show that if $v_j(x) = \binom{x}{j}$, then

$$\Delta v_j(x) = v_{j-1}(x),$$

for $j \geq 1$, where the differences relate to a spacing of $h = 1$. Deduce that

$$\Delta^j v_j(x) = 1.$$

3.4   Other Differences

As we saw in Section 3.2, Newton completely solved the one-dimensional interpolation problem, since his divided difference formula (3.24) is valid for *any* set of distinct abscissas. Yet we saw in Section 3.3 that it was useful to derive a simplified version of Newton's formula for the special case where the points are equally spaced. This resulted in the forward difference formula (3.41). In this section we will explore the form of the interpolating polynomial when the distances between consecutive abscissas form a geometric progression, and obtain another simplification of (3.24). We can always choose the origin, so that $x_0 = 0$, and scale the abscissas so that $x_1 = 1$. Then we will define

$$x_j = 1 + q + q^2 + \cdots + q^{j-1}, \tag{3.49}$$

for $j = 2, 3, \ldots$, where q is some positive number. Since $x_{j+1} - x_j = q^j$, the distances between consecutive abscissas are indeed in geometric progression. In (3.49) we will denote x_j by $[j]$, which we call a q-integer, already introduced in Section 1.2.

We now look at what happens to divided differences for this particular distribution of abscissas. We have

$$f[x_j, x_{j+1}] = \frac{f(x_{j+1}) - f(x_j)}{x_{j+1} - x_j} = \frac{\Delta_q f(x_j)}{q^j}, \tag{3.50}$$

using (3.49), where we have written

$$f(x_{j+1}) - f(x_j) = \Delta_q f(x_j). \tag{3.51}$$

For this first difference, the q-difference operator Δ_q behaves exactly like the forward difference operator Δ. From (3.27) and (3.50) we next obtain

$$f[x_j, x_{j+1}, x_{j+2}] = \left(\frac{\Delta_q f(x_{j+1})}{q^{j+1}} - \frac{\Delta_q f(x_j)}{q^j} \right) / (x_{j+2} - x_j),$$

and since $[2] = 1 + q$, we have

$$x_{j+2} - x_j = q^j + q^{j+1} = q^j(1 + q) = q^j[2],$$

and thus the second-order divided difference may be written as

$$f[x_j, x_{j+1}, x_{j+2}] = \frac{\Delta_q f(x_{j+1}) - q \, \Delta_q f(x_j)}{q^{2j+1}[2]}. \tag{3.52}$$

In view of (3.52) it is useful to *define*

$$\Delta_q^2 f(x_j) = \Delta_q f(x_{j+1}) - q \, \Delta_q f(x_j),$$

so that we may write

$$f[x_j, x_{j+1}, x_{j+2}] = \frac{\Delta_q^2 f(x_j)}{q^{2j+1}[2]}.$$

If we extend our analysis to see what happens to third- and higher-order divided differences when x_j is the q-integer $[j]$, it is expedient to define higher "differences" involving Δ_q recursively from

$$\Delta_q^{k+1} f(x_j) = \Delta_q^k f(x_{j+1}) - q^k \, \Delta_q^k f(x_j). \tag{3.53}$$

Note that when we put $q = 1$ this has precisely the same form as the relation (3.39) concerning higher differences for the "ordinary" difference operator Δ.

   To see what happens when we simplify a divided difference of any order we may need to work through one or two more cases. It is not so hard to spot the general pattern. We find that

$$f[x_j, x_{j+1}, \ldots, x_{j+k}] = \frac{\Delta_q^k f(x_j)}{q^{kj + k(k-1)/2} \, [k]!}, \tag{3.54}$$

where $[k]! = [k][k-1] \cdots [1]$. It is easy to verify that (3.54) holds for any $k \geq 1$ and all $j \geq 0$ by induction on k. First we see from (3.50) that (3.54) holds for $k = 1$ and all j. Assume that it holds for some $k \geq 1$ and all j. Then

$$f[x_j, x_{j+1}, \ldots, x_{j+k+1}] = \frac{f[x_{j+1}, \ldots, x_{j+k+1}] - f[x_j, \ldots, x_{j+k}]}{x_{j+k+1} - x_j},$$

where the denominator on the right is

$$x_{j+k+1} - x_j = q^j + q^{j+1} + \cdots + q^{j+k} = q^j [k+1]$$

and the numerator is

$$\frac{\Delta_q^k f(x_{j+1})}{q^{k(j+1) + k(k-1)/2} \, [k]!} - \frac{\Delta_q^k f(x_j)}{q^{kj + k(k-1)/2} \, [k]!} = \frac{\Delta_q^{k+1} f(x_j)}{q^{k(j+1) + k(k-1)/2} \, [k]!}.$$

It follows that

$$f[x_j, x_{j+1}, \ldots, x_{j+k+1}] = \frac{\Delta_q^{k+1} f(x_j)}{q^{(k+1)j + (k+1)k/2} \, [k+1]!},$$

and this completes the proof by induction.

   Putting $j = 0$ in (3.54), we obtain

$$f[x_0, x_1, \ldots, x_k] = \frac{\Delta_q^k f(x_0)}{q^{k(k-1)/2} \, [k]!}. \tag{3.55}$$

Let us now write $[j] = j$ when $q = 1$ and

$$[j] = \frac{1 - q^j}{1 - q}$$

for $q \neq 1$ and all integers $j \geq 0$. We extend this definition from nonnegative integers j to all nonnegative real numbers t, writing $[t] = t$ when $q = 1$ and

$$[t] = \frac{1 - q^t}{1 - q}$$

otherwise. Since

$$[t] - [j] = q^j [t - j] \tag{3.56}$$

for $t \geq j$, then on putting $x = [t]$ in (3.9), we readily verify that for $k \geq 1$

$$\pi_k(x) = q^{k(k-1)/2} [t][t-1]\cdots[t-k+1] \tag{3.57}$$

for $t \geq k - 1$. We require just one further item of notation, defining

$$\left[\begin{array}{c} t \\ k \end{array} \right] = \frac{[t][t-1]\cdots[t-k+1]}{[k]!} \tag{3.58}$$

for $t \geq k$. Recall from Section 1.2 that we call this a q-binomial coefficient, since it gives the binomial coefficient when $q = 1$. Combining (3.55), (3.57), and (3.58), we see that

$$f[x_0, x_1, \ldots, x_k]\, \pi_k(x) = \left[\begin{array}{c} t \\ k \end{array} \right] \Delta_q^k f(x_0),$$

where $x = [t]$. On summing such terms over k we see that (3.24) becomes

$$p_n(x) = p_n([t]) = f(x_0) + \left[\begin{array}{c} t \\ 1 \end{array} \right] \Delta_q f(x_0) + \cdots + \left[\begin{array}{c} t \\ n \end{array} \right] \Delta_q^n f(x_0), \tag{3.59}$$

where $x = (1 - q^t)/(1 - q)$. Let us take q between 0 and 1. Then the relation between x and t implies that $t = \log_q(1 - (1 - q)x)$, which is defined whenever $1 - (1 - q)x > 0$, that is, for $0 \leq x < 1/(1 - q)$.

If we wish to let $x \to 1/(1 - q)$, then, since $x = (1 - q^t)/(1 - q)$, this corresponds to letting $t \to \infty$. In this case (3.59) is not suitable for evaluating $p_n(x)$, and we can use the divided difference form (3.24), as in the following example, which is similar to one in Schoenberg [48].

Example 3.4.1 It is well known that

$$\lim_{h \to 0} \frac{\sin h}{h} = 1.$$

Let us suppose that we (being very ignorant!) do not know the value of this limit. Since we cannot simply *evaluate* $(\sin h)/h$ at $h = 0$, let us "sneak up" on it by interpolating the function $f(x) = (\sin(2 - x))/(2 - x)$ at $x = [0]$, [1], [2], [3], [4], and [5], with $q = \frac{1}{2}$. Then let us evaluate the interpolating polynomial $p_5(x)$ at $x = 1/(1 - q) = 2$, using the divided difference form (3.24). We obtain the result

$$p_5(2) = 1.00000033,$$

which is so very much closer to 1 than the closest value of $f(x_j)$ used in the interpolation, which is

$$f([5]) = \frac{\sin(1/16)}{1/16} \approx 0.99934909. \qquad \blacksquare$$

If n and r are integers, with $n \geq r \geq 0$, we see from (3.58) that

$$\begin{bmatrix} n \\ r \end{bmatrix} = \frac{[n]!}{[r]![n-r]!}, \tag{3.60}$$

where $[0]! = 1$. It is easily verified that this q-binomial coefficient satisfies the identity

$$\begin{bmatrix} n \\ r \end{bmatrix} = \begin{bmatrix} n-1 \\ r-1 \end{bmatrix} + q^r \begin{bmatrix} n-1 \\ r \end{bmatrix}. \tag{3.61}$$

On putting $q = 1$ we obtain the well-known Pascal identity for the ordinary binomial coefficients. Now, since each q-integer $[j]$ is a polynomial in q, it follows that a q-binomial coefficient must be a *rational function* of q, meaning a polynomial in q divided by a polynomial in q. For example, using (3.60), we find that

$$\begin{bmatrix} 5 \\ 3 \end{bmatrix} = \frac{[5]!}{[3]![2]!} = \frac{[5][4]}{[2][1]},$$

which simplifies to give

$$\begin{bmatrix} 5 \\ 3 \end{bmatrix} = 1 + q + 2q^2 + 2q^3 + 2q^4 + q^5 + q^6, \tag{3.62}$$

which is just a *polynomial* in q. In fact, we can prove by induction on n that for $n \geq r \geq 0$, the q-binomial coefficient $\begin{bmatrix} n \\ r \end{bmatrix}$ is always a polynomial in q. It is called a *Gaussian polynomial*, and is of degree $r(n-r)$. This holds for $n = 1$, since

$$\begin{bmatrix} 1 \\ 0 \end{bmatrix} = \begin{bmatrix} 1 \\ 1 \end{bmatrix} = 1.$$

Let us now assume that the above result holds for some $n - 1 \geq 1$ and all $r \leq n - 1$. Then we see that the q-binomial coefficient on the left side of (3.61) is a polynomial of degree

$$\max\{(r-1)(n-r), \, r + r(n-1-r)\} = r(n-r).$$

The case where $r = n$ is obviously satisfied, and this completes the proof by induction.

We will say that a polynomial

$$p(x) = a_0 + a_1 x + \cdots + a_{m-1} x^{m-1} + a_m x^m$$

is symmetric in its coefficients if $a_0 = a_m$, $a_1 = a_{m-1}$, and so on, as for the polynomial in (3.62). Since

$$x^m p(1/x) = a_m + a_{m-1}x + \cdots + a_1 x^{m-1} + a_0 x^m,$$

the property that a polynomial p of degree m is symmetric in its coefficients is equivalent to saying that

$$x^m p(1/x) = p(x). \tag{3.63}$$

Let us now write

$$[j]' = \frac{1 - q^{-j}}{1 - q^{-1}},$$

so that $[j]'$ is derived from $[j]$ by substituting $1/q$ for q. We note that

$$q^{j-1}[j]' = [j]. \tag{3.64}$$

Similarly, let us write $[r]'!$ and $\begin{bmatrix} n \\ r \end{bmatrix}'$ to denote the expressions we obtain when we substitute $1/q$ for q in $[r]!$ and $\begin{bmatrix} n \\ r \end{bmatrix}$, respectively. We see that

$$q^{r(r-1)/2}[r]'! = [r]!, \tag{3.65}$$

and since

$$\frac{1}{2}n(n-1) - \frac{1}{2}r(r-1) - \frac{1}{2}(n-r)(n-r-1) = r(n-r),$$

it follows from (3.65) and (3.60) that

$$r(n-r)\begin{bmatrix} n \\ r \end{bmatrix}' = \begin{bmatrix} n \\ r \end{bmatrix}.$$

In view of (3.63), this shows that the q-binomial coefficient is a symmetric polynomial in its coefficients, as we found for the particular case given in (3.62).

We now state two identities involving the q-integers,

$$(1+x)(1+qx)\cdots(1+q^{k-1}x) = \sum_{r=0}^{k} q^{r(r-1)/2} \begin{bmatrix} k \\ r \end{bmatrix} x^r, \tag{3.66}$$

which generalizes the binomial expansion, and

$$(1-x)^{-1}(1-qx)^{-1}\cdots(1-q^{k-1}x)^{-1} = \sum_{r=0}^{\infty} \begin{bmatrix} k-1+r \\ r \end{bmatrix} x^r. \tag{3.67}$$

Both identities can be verified by induction on k. Alternatively, to establish (3.67), let us write

$$F_k(x) = (1-x)^{-1}(1-qx)^{-1}\cdots(1-q^{k-1}x)^{-1} = \sum_{r=0}^{\infty} c_r x^r,$$

where the coefficients c_r are to be determined. Now we may write

$$(1-x)F_k(x) = (1-q^k x)F_k(qx),$$

so that

$$(1-x)\sum_{r=0}^{\infty} c_r x^r = (1-q^k x)\sum_{r=0}^{\infty} c_r (qx)^r.$$

On equating coefficients of x^s in the latter equation, for $s \geq 1$ we obtain

$$c_s - c_{s-1} = q^s c_s - q^{k+s-1} c_{s-1},$$

which simplifies to give

$$c_s = \left(\frac{1-q^{k+s-1}}{1-q^s}\right) c_{s-1} = \frac{[k+s-1]}{[s]} c_{s-1}. \tag{3.68}$$

Since $c_0 = 1$, we may apply (3.68) repeatedly to give

$$c_s = \frac{[k+s-1][k+s-2]\cdots[k]}{[s][s-1]\cdots[1]} = \begin{bmatrix} k-1+s \\ s \end{bmatrix},$$

which verifies (3.67). A similar approach (see Problem 3.4.3) may be used to verify (3.66).

To conclude this section, we mention two further results concerning q-differences. We can verify by induction (see Problem 3.4.5) that

$$\Delta_q^k f(x_i) = \sum_{r=0}^{k} (-1)^r q^{r(r-1)/2} \begin{bmatrix} k \\ r \end{bmatrix} f(x_{i+k-r}). \tag{3.69}$$

There is a nice expression for the kth q-difference of a product. Koçak and Phillips [31] have shown that

$$\Delta_q^k (f(x_i)g(x_i)) = \sum_{r=0}^{k} \begin{bmatrix} k \\ r \end{bmatrix} \Delta_q^{k-r} f(x_{i+r}) \Delta_q^r g(x_i). \tag{3.70}$$

This is a q-difference analogue of the Leibniz rule for the kth derivative of a product,

$$\frac{d^k}{dx^k} (f(x)g(x)) = \sum_{r=0}^{k} \binom{k}{r} \frac{d^{k-r}}{dx^{k-r}} f(x) \frac{d^r}{dx^r} g(x).$$

The case of (3.70) where $q = 1$, which involves ordinary forward differences, is well known.

Problem 3.4.1 Show that for any real numbers $x \geq y \geq 0$,

$$[x][y+1] - [x+1][y] = q^y[x-y].$$

Problem 3.4.2 Verify the Pascal-type identity (3.61) and also verify the companion result

$$\left[\begin{array}{c} n \\ r \end{array}\right] = q^{n-r} \left[\begin{array}{c} n-1 \\ r-1 \end{array}\right] + \left[\begin{array}{c} n-1 \\ r \end{array}\right]. \tag{3.71}$$

Problem 3.4.3 Let

$$G_k(x) = (1+x)(1+qx)\cdots(1+q^{k-1}x) = \sum_{r=0}^{k} d_r x^r,$$

and show that

$$(1+q^k x)G_k(x) = (1+x)G_k(qx).$$

Equate coefficients of x^s to show that

$$d_s = q^{s-1}\frac{[k\ \ s+1]}{[s]}d_{s-1},$$

for $s \geq 1$, and hence verify (3.66).

Problem 3.4.4 With $G_k(x)$ as defined in Problem 3.4.3, use the relation

$$(1+q^k x)G_k(x) - G_{k+1}(x)$$

to verify (3.66) by induction on k, making use of the Pascal-type identity (3.71). Similarly verify (3.67).

Problem 3.4.5 Use (3.53) and the second Pascal-type identity (3.71) to verify (3.69) by induction on k.

3.5 Multivariate Interpolation

The title of this section means interpolation of a function of more than one variable. We saw in Section 3.1 that given a function of one variable defined at $n+1$ distinct abscissas, we can choose the $n+1$ monomials $1, x, x^2, \ldots, x^n$ as a *basis* and we can always find a linear combination of these, a *polynomial*, that provides a unique solution to the interpolation problem. In Section 3.2 we also noted Newton's clever use of the polynomials $\pi_i(x)$ as a basis.

Life is not so easy in more than one dimension. Suppose we have a function of two variables, $f(x, y)$, defined on the four points in the plane (x_j, y_j), for $j = 0, 1, 2, 3$. We need to select four functions of x and y to assume the roles that the monomials played in the one-variable case. An obvious choice, which also maintains a symmetry between x and y, is the set of four functions $1, x, y,$ and xy. Then, to determine an interpolating function

$$p(x, y) = a_0 + a_1 x + a_2 y + a_3 xy$$

such that $p(x_j, y_j) = f(x_j, y_j)$, for $j = 0, 1, 2, 3$, we need to solve the linear system of four equations

$$a_0 + a_1 x_j + a_2 y_j + a_3 x_j y_j = f(x_j, y_j), \quad j = 0, 1, 2, 3. \tag{3.72}$$

For the sake of clarity, let us consider the specific case where the four points are $(1, 0), (-1, 0), (0, 1),$ and $(0, -1)$. Then the matrix of the above linear system is

$$\mathbf{M} = \begin{bmatrix} 1 & 1 & 0 & 0 \\ 1 & -1 & 0 & 0 \\ 1 & 0 & 1 & 0 \\ 1 & 0 & -1 & 0 \end{bmatrix}.$$

Since the last column of $\mathbf{M}$ is zero, $\det \mathbf{M} = 0$. Thus the matrix $\mathbf{M}$ is singular and the system of linear equations (3.72) does not always have a solution. (See Problem 3.5.1.)

The above example warns us that interpolation of a function of two variables is not as straightforward as in the one-variable case, although for the above problem we could obtain an interpolation function of the form

$$p(x, y) = a_0 + a_1 x + a_2 y + a_3 x^2,$$

say. However, we can solve the interpolation problem in both a practical and a mathematically pleasing way for some particular arrangements of points, and we will discuss two of these.

The first is to take the *Cartesian product* of the two sets

$$X = \{x_0, x_1, \ldots, x_m\} \quad \text{and} \quad Y = \{y_0, y_1, \ldots, y_n\},$$

namely the set of $(m + 1)(n + 1)$ points (x_i, y_j) where $i = 0, \ldots, m$ and $j = 0, \ldots, n$. We require the x_i to be distinct, and also the y_j to be distinct. These points thus lie on a rectangular grid composed of $m + 1$ lines parallel to the y-axis and $n + 1$ lines parallel to the x-axis. We now define Lagrange coefficients in the variable x, say $L_i(x)$, $i = 0, \ldots, m$, as in Section 3.1. Likewise we similarly define Lagrange coefficients in the variable y, say $M_j(y)$, $j = 0, \ldots, n$. For example,

$$M_0(y) = \prod_{s=1}^{n} \left(\frac{y - y_s}{y_0 - y_s} \right).$$

Then consider the polynomial in x and y defined by

$$p(x, y) = \sum_{i=0}^{m} \sum_{j=0}^{n} f(x_i, y_j) L_i(x) M_j(y). \tag{3.73}$$

Since $L_i(x)M_j(y)$ has the value 1 at the point (x_i, y_j) and is zero at all the other points in the rectangular array, it follows that $p(x, y)$ interpolates $f(x, y)$ at all $(m+1)(n+1)$ points.

Example 3.5.1 Let us take the sets X and Y above to be $X = Y = \{0, 1\}$. The Cartesian product of X and Y is the set of points

$$\{(0,0), (1,0), (0,1), (1,1)\},$$

and the interpolating polynomial for a function f defined on these points is given by

$$p(x, y) = (1-x)(1-y)\, f(0,0) + x(1-y)\, f(1,0)$$
$$+ (1-x)y\, f(0,1) + xy\, f(1,1),$$

so that, for instance, $p(\frac{1}{2}, \frac{1}{2})$ is just the arithmetic mean of the values of f on the four given points. If the four function values are all equal to some constant C, then we may easily verify that $p(x, y)$ is identically equal to C. Let us write $z = p(x, y)$. Then (see Problem 3.5.2) if the coefficient of xy is nonzero, we can shift the origin in xyz-space and scale z so that the surface $z = p(x, y)$ becomes $z = xy$. Shifting the origin and scaling (multiplying by a constant factor) does not change the shape of the original surface, which is a *hyperbolic paraboloid*. Although this is a curved surface, it has straight lines "embedded" in it, which are called *generators*. We can see this by looking at the above expression for $p(x, y)$. For if we replace y by a constant C, we see that $z = p(x, C)$ is the equation of a straight line. This shows that if we look at a "slice" of the surface $z = p(x, y)$, where the plane $y = C$ intersects the surface $z = p(x, y)$, we obtain the straight line $z = p(x, C)$. As we vary C we obtain an infinite system of generators parallel to the zx-plane. Similarly, by putting $x = C$, we obtain $z = p(C, y)$, revealing a second system of generators that are parallel to the yz-plane.

We can express the two-dimensional interpolating polynomial (3.73) in a divided difference form, and we will use the operator form of the divided differences, as in (3.25). We need to use divided differences with respect to x and divided differences with respect to y. Let us write

$$[x_0, \ldots, x_j]_x f$$

to denote the effect of the operator $[x_0, \ldots, x_j]_x$ acting on $f(x, y)$ for a fixed value of y. The suffix x reminds us that we are computing divided differences of f as a function of x, with y fixed. For example,

$$[x_0, x_1]_x f = \frac{f(x_1, y) - f(x_0, y)}{x_1 - x_0}. \tag{3.74}$$

Similarly, $[y_0, y_1]_y f$ denotes the effect of applying the operator $[y_0, y_1]_y$ to $f(x, y)$ with x fixed. Since $[x_0, x_1]_x f$ is a function of y, given by (3.74) above, we may apply the operator $[y_0, y_1]_y$ to it. We write

$$[y_0, y_1]_y ([x_0, x_1]_x f) = [y_0, y_1]_y [x_0, x_1]_x f,$$

and using (3.74) as an intermediate result, we find that

$$[y_0, y_1]_y [x_0, x_1]_x f = \frac{f(x_1, y_1) - f(x_1, y_0)}{(x_1 - x_0)(y_1 - y_0)} - \frac{f(x_0, y_1) - f(x_0, y_0)}{(x_1 - x_0)(y_1 - y_0)}.$$

It is easily verified that we obtain the same result if we apply the operator $[y_0, y_1]_y$ to f and *then* apply the operator $[x_0, x_1]_x$. We say that the operators *commute*, and we have

$$[y_0, y_1]_y [x_0, x_1]_x f = [x_0, x_1]_x [y_0, y_1]_y f.$$

It is also not hard to see that divided difference operators in x and y of any order commute. To express the interpolating polynomial given by (3.73) in a divided difference form we begin by writing down the divided difference form of the interpolating polynomial, based on $y_0, \ldots, y_n$, of the function $f(x, y)$ for a *fixed* value of x,

$$\sum_{k=0}^{n} [y_0, \ldots, y_k]_y f \cdot \pi_k(y) = F(x),$$

say, where we define $\pi_0(y) = 1$ and $\pi_k(y) = (y - y_0) \cdots (y - y_{k-1})$ for $k \geq 1$, as we defined $\pi_k(x)$ in (3.9). Note that the terms $[y_0, \ldots, y_k]_y f$ depend on x, which is why we have written $F(x)$ above. We now find the divided difference form of the interpolating polynomial for $F(x)$ based on $x_0, \ldots, x_m$, giving

$$p(x, y) = \sum_{j=0}^{m} \sum_{k=0}^{n} [x_0, \ldots, x_j]_x [y_0, \ldots, y_k]_y f \cdot \pi_j(x) \pi_k(y). \qquad (3.75)$$

It follows from the uniqueness of the one-dimensional interpolating polynomial that the polynomial $p(x, y)$ in the divided difference form (3.75) is the same as that given in the Lagrange form (3.73).

In the divided difference form (3.75), as in the Lagrange-type formula (3.73), the x_j are arbitrary distinct numbers that can be in any order, and the same holds for the y_k. Now let us consider the special case where both the x_j and the y_k are equally spaced, so that

$$x_j = x_0 + j h_x, \ 0 \leq j \leq m, \qquad \text{and} \qquad y_k = y_0 + k h_y, \ 0 \leq k \leq n,$$

where the values of h_x and h_y need not be the same. Following what we did in the one-dimensional case, we make the changes of variable

$$x = x_0 + s h_x \qquad \text{and} \qquad y = y_0 + t h_y.$$

We also need to use forward differences in the x-direction and forward differences in the y-direction, defining

$$\Delta_x f(x,y) = f(x+h_x) - f(x,y) \quad \text{and} \quad \Delta_y f(x,y) = f(x,y+h_y) - f(x,y).$$

We find that the two difference operators Δ_x and Δ_y commute, as we found above for the divided difference operators. We also define higher-order "mixed" differences in an obvious way. Then, for this "equally spaced" case, we can follow the method used for interpolation of a function of one variable (see Section 3.3) to transmute the divided difference form (3.75) into the forward difference form

$$p(x_0 + s\,h_x, y_0 + t\,h_y) = \sum_{j=0}^{m} \sum_{k=0}^{n} \binom{s}{j} \binom{t}{k} \Delta_x^j \Delta_y^k f(x_0, y_0). \quad (3.76)$$

It is remarkable how easy it is to construct an interpolating polynomial on any higher-dimensional set of points that is defined as a Cartesian product of one-dimensional sets. Although our account above is concerned only with two dimensions, there is no difficulty in extending it to any number of dimensions.

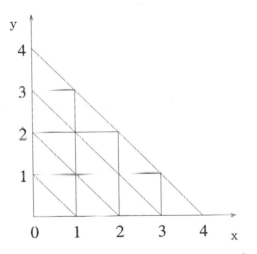

FIGURE 3.1. A triangular interpolation grid.

The other "special" set of interpolating points in two dimensions that we will discuss is a set of points in a triangular, rather than rectangular, array. This arises most naturally. For the simplest functions in two variables are those of the form $x^i y^j$, and we can enumerate these in an obvious way, beginning with

$$1, \quad x, y, \quad x^2, xy, y^2, \quad x^3, x^2 y, xy^2, y^3, \quad x^4, x^3 y, x^2 y^2, xy^3, y^4.$$

The first function is the constant 1, the only function of the form $x^i y^j$ of degree zero, followed by the two functions x and y of degree one, the three functions x^2, xy, and y^2 of degree two, and so on. If we truncate the above list after writing the $n + 1$ functions of degree n, we would have

$$1 + 2 + 3 + \cdots + (n+1) = \frac{1}{2}(n+1)(n+2) = \binom{n+2}{2}$$

functions. These numbers, 1, 3, 6, 10, and so on, of the form

$$N = \frac{1}{2}(n+1)(n+2),$$

are called *triangular numbers*, which makes it natural to interpolate on a triangular number of points N, such as the set of points shown in Figure 3.1.

We generalize the set of points depicted in Figure 3.1 to obtain the set

$$S_n = \{(r, s) \mid r, s \geq 0, \ r + s \leq n\}, \tag{3.77}$$

which consists of $1 + 2 + \cdots + (n+1) = \frac{1}{2}(n+1)(n+2)$ points. Thus, given a function $f(x, y)$ defined on S_n, we seek a polynomial

$$p(x, y) = a_1 + a_2 x + a_3 y + \cdots + a_N y^n$$

such that $p(x, y) = f(x, y)$ on all $N = \frac{1}{2}(n+1)(n+2)$ points defined above. In the one-dimensional case this led us to the Vandermonde linear equations (3.1), and although we could determine the interpolating polynomial by solving this linear system directly, we found it much more convenient to pursue other routes to the solution of the interpolation problem. In the two-dimensional interpolation problem on a triangular set of points, it is also helpful to seek other approaches. First we look for a Lagrange-type solution. Can we find a suitable Lagrange coefficient $L_{i,j}(x, y)$ that takes the value 1 at $(x, y) = (x_i, y_j)$ and the value zero at all the other points? If this is too big a question to answer immediately, let us seek the Lagrange coefficient $L_{4,0}(x, y)$ for the set of interpolating points depicted in Figure 3.1. We see that the polynomial

$$x(x - 1)(x - 2)(x - 3)$$

is zero at all the points except $(4, 0)$, since all of the other points lie on one of the lines with equations

$$x = 0, \quad x - 1 = 0, \quad x - 2 = 0, \quad x - 3 = 0. \tag{3.78}$$

Then we can scale the above polynomial to give

$$L_{4,0}(x, y) = \frac{1}{24} x(x - 1)(x - 2)(x - 3),$$

which indeed takes the value 1 when $(x, y) = (4, 0)$ and the value zero on all the other points. The key to finding all the Lagrange coefficients corresponding to the interpolating points in Figure 3.1 is to note that in addition to the set of lines parallel to the y-axis given in (3.78), there is also a system of lines parallel to the x-axis,

$$y = 0, \quad y - 1 = 0, \quad y - 2 = 0, \quad y - 3 = 0, \qquad (3.79)$$

and a system parallel to the third side of the triangle,

$$x + y - 1 = 0, \quad x + y - 2 = 0, \quad x + y - 3 = 0, \quad x + y - 4 = 0. \quad (3.80)$$

The point $(2, 1)$ has the lines $x = 0$ and $x - 1 = 0$ to the left of it, that is, moving towards the y-axis, and has the line $y = 0$ below it, moving towards the x-axis, and has the line $x + y - 4$ in the direction of the third side of the triangle. Thus the polynomial that is the product of the left sides of these four equations, $x(x - 1)y(x + y - 4)$, is zero on all points in Figure 3.1 except for the point $(2, 1)$. On scaling this polynomial, we find that

$$L_{2,1}(x, y) = -\frac{1}{2}x(x - 1)y(x + y - 4)$$

is the Lagrange coefficient for $(2, 1)$, since it has the value 1 at $(2, 1)$ and is zero on all the other points.

We are now ready to derive the Lagrange coefficients for all the points in the triangular set defined by (3.77). We begin with any point and identify the following sets of lines:

1. The lines like those defined by (3.78), which lie between (i, j) and the y-axis.

2. The lines like those defined by (3.79), which lie between (i, j) and the x-axis.

3. The lines like those defined by (3.80), which lie between (i, j) and the third side of the triangle, defined by the equation $x + y - n = 0$.

There are no lines in the first set if $i = 0$, and if $i > 0$, we have the lines

$$x = 0, \quad x - 1 = 0, \quad \ldots, \quad x - i + 1 = 0.$$

If $j = 0$, there are no lines in the second set, and if $j > 1$, we have the lines

$$y = 0, \quad y - 1 = 0, \quad \ldots, \quad y - j + 1 = 0.$$

If $i + j = n$, the point (i, j) is on the line $x + y - n = 0$ and there are no lines in the third set; otherwise, we have, working towards the third side of the triangle, the lines

$$x + y - i - j - 1 = 0, \quad x + y - i - j - 2 = 0, \quad \ldots, \quad x + y - n = 0.$$

Note that the total number of lines in the three sets enumerated above is

$$i + j + (n - i - j) = n.$$

Now if we draw all these lines on a grid like Figure 3.1, we see that between them they cover all the points on the triangular grid except for the point (i, j). Thus, taking the product of the left sides of all these n equations, we see that

$$\prod_{s=0}^{i-1}(x - s) \cdot \prod_{s=0}^{j-1}(y - s) \cdot \prod_{s=i+j+1}^{n}(x + y - s) \tag{3.81}$$

is zero at all points on the triangular grid except for the point (i, j). If $i = 0$ or $j = 0$ or $i + j = n$, the corresponding product in (3.81) is said to be empty, and its value is defined to be 1. We then just need to scale the polynomial defined by this triple product to give

$$L_{i,j}(x, y) = \prod_{s=0}^{i-1}\left(\frac{x - s}{i - s}\right) \cdot \prod_{s=0}^{j-1}\left(\frac{y - s}{j - s}\right) \cdot \prod_{s=i+j+1}^{n}\left(\frac{x + y - s}{i + j - s}\right), \tag{3.82}$$

which simplifies to give

$$L_{i,j}(x, y) = \binom{x}{i}\binom{y}{j}\binom{n - x - y}{n - i - j}, \tag{3.83}$$

the Lagrange coefficient corresponding to the point (i, j), where it takes the value 1. Thus the interpolating polynomial for a function $f(x, y)$ on the triangular grid defined by (3.77) is given by

$$p_n(x, y) = \sum_{i,j} f(i, j) L_{i,j}(x, y), \tag{3.84}$$

where the summation is over all nonnegative integers i and j such that $i + j \le n$. Note from (3.82) that the numerator of each Lagrange coefficient is a product of n factors, and so the interpolating polynomial $p_n(x, y)$ is a polynomial of total degree at most n in x and y.

Example 3.5.2 When $n = 2$ in (3.84) we have six interpolating points, and the interpolating polynomial is

$$p_2(x, y) = \frac{1}{2}(2 - x - y)(1 - x - y)\, f(0,0) \ + \ x(2 - x - y)\, f(1,0)$$

$$+ y(2 - x - y)\, f(0,1) \ + \ \frac{1}{2}x(x - 1)\, f(2,0)$$

$$+ xy\, f(1,1) \ + \ \frac{1}{2}y(y - 1)\, f(0,2). \quad \blacksquare$$

We obtained the Lagrange form (3.84) for the interpolating polynomial $p_n(x, y)$ for $f(x, y)$ on the triangular grid defined by (3.77). There is also a forward difference form for this polynomial,

$$p_n(x, y) = \sum_{k=0}^{n} \sum_{r=0}^{k} \binom{x}{r} \binom{y}{k-r} \Delta_x^r \Delta_y^{k-r} f(0, 0). \qquad (3.85)$$

See Lee and Phillips [34]. We give an outline of a proof of (3.85) in Section 3.6, following the proof of Theorem 3.6.2.

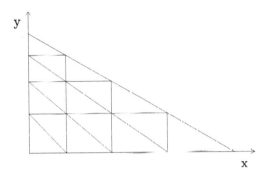

FIGURE 3.2. A triangular interpolation grid based on q integers.

Other triangular interpolation grids were introduced by Lee and Phillips [35]. The simplest of these, illustrated in Figure 3.2 for the case where $n = 4$, is the set of points defined in terms of q-integers by

$$([i], [j]'), \qquad \text{with} \qquad i, j \geq 0 \qquad \text{and} \qquad i + j \leq n, \qquad (3.86)$$

where

$$[i] = 1 + q + q^2 + \cdots + q^{i-1} \qquad \text{and} \qquad [j]' = 1 + q^{-1} + q^{-2} + \cdots + q^{-j+1}$$

for $i > 0$ and $j > 0$, with $[0] = [0]' = 0$. (We discussed q-integers in Section 3.4.) When $q = 1$ we have $[i] = i$ and $[j]' = j$, giving the simple triangular grid defined above in (3.77). The new grid shares with the old one the property that it is created by points of intersection of three systems of straight lines. As we saw in Figure 3.1, the set of points (3.77) consists of three systems of parallel lines, one parallel to each axis and the third parallel to $x + y - n = 0$. The new set of points (3.86) is created by points of intersection of the three systems

$$x - [k] = 0, \quad 0 \leq k \leq n - 1,$$
$$y - [k]' = 0, \quad 0 \leq k \leq n - 1,$$
$$x + q^k y - [k+1] = 0, \quad 0 \leq k \leq n - 1. \qquad (3.87)$$

The first two are systems of lines parallel to the axes. The third system is obviously *not* a parallel system except when $q = 1$. On substituting the values $x = 1/(1 - q)$ and $y = -q/(1 - q)$ into (3.87) with $q \neq 1$, we can see that every line in the third system passes through the *vertex* $(1/(1 - q), -q/(1 - q))$. Thus the x-coordinate of this vertex is negative for $q > 1$, as illustrated in Figure 3.2. We can say that this grid is created by two pencils of lines with vertices at infinity (that is, two systems of parallel lines "meeting at infinity") and a third pencil of lines that meet at a finite vertex. We can now write down a Lagrange form of an interpolating polynomial for a function $f(x, y)$ on this triangular grid as we did for the special case of $q = 1$. The Lagrange coefficient for the point $([i], [j]')$ in this new grid is given by

$$L_{i,j}(x, y) = a_{i,j}(x, y) \cdot b_{i,j}(x, y) \cdot c_{i,j}(x, y), \tag{3.88}$$

where

$$a_{i,j}(x, y) = \prod_{s=0}^{i-1} \left(\frac{x - [s]}{[i] - [s]} \right), \quad b_{i,j}(x, y) = \prod_{s=0}^{j-1} \left(\frac{y - [s]'}{[j]' - [s]'} \right),$$

and

$$c_{i,j}(x, y) = \prod_{s=i+j+1}^{n} \left(\frac{x + q^{s-1}y - [s]}{[i] + q^{s-1}[j]' - [s]} \right).$$

With $q = 1$, this reduces to the expression (3.82) for the Lagrange coefficient corresponding to the point (i, j).

The grid defined by (3.86) is just one of a family of grids based on q-integers that is given in [35]. This includes grids created by one pencil of parallel lines and two pencils with finite vertices, and grids created by three pencils each of which has a finite vertex.

We conclude this section by quoting a remark made by G. G. Lorentz in [38], which we should not forget when we interpolate or approximate a function of more than one variable. *"Even a beginning student may notice that examples of genuine functions of two variables are rare in a course of elementary Calculus. Of course $x + y$ is one such function. But all other functions known to him reduce to this trivial one and to functions of one variable; for example, $xy = e^{\log x + \log y}$."*

Problem 3.5.1 Consider the solution of the system of linear equations (3.72), where (x_j, y_j) takes the values $(1, 0), (-1, 0), (0, 1)$, and $(0, -1)$. Show that a solution exists if and only if the points $(x_j, y_j, f(x_j, y_j))$ lie in the same plane or, equivalently, that

$$f(x_0, y_0) + f(x_1, y_1) = f(x_2, y_2) + f(x_3, y_3).$$

Problem 3.5.2 Consider the surface mentioned above in Example 3.5.1, which is of the form

$$z = a + bx + cy + dxy,$$

where we assume that $d \neq 0$. Write $\xi = x - x_0$, $\eta = y - y_0$ and show that by choosing $x_0 = -c/d$, $y_0 = -b/d$, the above surface is transformed into

$$z = z_0 + d\xi\eta,$$

where $z_0 = a + bx_0 + cy_0 + dx_0y_0$. Finally, by writing $\zeta = (z - z_0)/d$, show that the above surface may be expressed in the form $\zeta = \xi\eta$.

Problem 3.5.3 Write down the interpolating polynomial for a function f defined on the Cartesian product of the sets $X = \{0, 1, 2\}$ and $Y = \{0, 1\}$ in its Lagrange form (3.73) and its divided difference form (3.75).

Problem 3.5.4 Obtain the interpolating polynomial $p_n(x, y)$ for $f(x, y)$ defined on the triangular set defined by (3.77) for the two cases $n = 1$ and $n = 3$.

Problem 3.5.5 Verify the interpolation formula (3.85) for $n = 2$, showing that it agrees with the expression for $p_2(x, y)$ in Example 3.5.2.

Problem 3.5.6 Simplify the denominators in each of the three products in (3.88), using (3.56), (3.64), and (3.65) to give

$$\prod_{s=0}^{i-1}([i] - [s]) = q^{i(i-1)/2}[i]!,$$

$$\prod_{s=0}^{j-1}([j]' - [s]') = q^{-j(j-1)}[j]!,$$

and

$$\prod_{s=i+j+1}^{n}([i] + q^{s-1}[j]' - [s]) = (-q^i)^{n-i-j}[n - i - j]!.$$

3.6   The Neville–Aitken Algorithm

We now describe an algorithm that is named after E. H. Neville (1889–1961) and A. C. Aitken (1895–1967). This allows the one-dimensional interpolating polynomial based on $n + 1$ points, defined by (3.13) or (3.24), to be computed by repeating $\frac{1}{2}n(n + 1)$ times the calculation required to evaluate the linear interpolating polynomial based on two points. Then we will adapt this algorithm to evaluate the two-dimensional interpolating polynomial (3.84).

$$p_0^{[0]}(x) = f(x_0)$$

$$p_1^{[0]}(x)$$

$$p_0^{[1]}(x) - f(x_1) \qquad p_2^{[0]}(x)$$

$$p_1^{[1]}(x) \qquad p_3^{[0]}(x)$$

$$p_0^{[2]}(x) = f(x_2) \qquad p_2^{[1]}(x)$$

$$p_1^{[2]}(x)$$

$$p_0^{[3]}(x) = f(x_3)$$

TABLE 3.4. The quantities computed in the Neville–Aitken algorithm.

We begin with the one-dimensional case. First we need another item of notation. Let $p_k^{[i]}(x)$ denote the interpolating polynomial for the function f based on the arbitrary distinct points $x_i, x_{i+1}, \ldots, x_{i+k}$. Thus $p_k^{[i]}(x)$ is a polynomial of degree at most k, and $p_0^{[i]}(x)$ is the constant $f(x_i)$. We now verify a recursive relation involving the polynomials $p_k^{[i]}(x)$ that is at the heart of the Neville–Aitken algorithm.

Theorem 3.6.1 For $k \geq 0$ and $i \geq 0$,

$$p_{k+1}^{[i]}(x) = \frac{(x - x_i)p_k^{[i+1]}(x) - (x - x_{i+k+1})p_k^{[i]}(x)}{x_{i+k+1} - x_i}. \tag{3.89}$$

Proof. We use induction on k. By definition each $p_0^{[i]}(x)$ is a polynomial of degree zero with the constant value $f(x_i)$. Then, for $k = 0$ and all i, (3.89) gives

$$p_1^{[i]}(x) = \frac{(x - x_i)f(x_{i+1}) - (x - x_{i+1})f(x_i)}{x_{i+1} - x_i},$$

which is the linear interpolating polynomial for the function f based on x_i and x_{i+1}. (Strictly, the previous sentence could be omitted from this proof; it has been included to give us confidence in the algorithm!) We now assume that for some $k \geq 0$, each $p_k^{[i]}(x)$ interpolates $f(x)$ on the appropriate set of abscissas. Now note from (3.89) that if $p_k^{[i]}(x)$ and $p_k^{[i+1]}(x)$ both have the same value C for some choice of x, then $p_{k+1}^{[i]}(x)$ also has the value C. Since, by definition, both $p_k^{[i]}(x)$ and $p_k^{[i+1]}(x)$ take the value $f(x_j)$ for $i + 1 \leq j \leq i + k$, so also does $p_{k+1}^{[i]}(x)$. We complete the proof by putting $x = x_i$ and $x = x_{i+k+1}$ in (3.89) and verifying that $p_{k+1}^{[i]}(x)$ takes the values $f(x_i)$ and $f(x_{i+k+1})$, respectively. ∎

Having proved Theorem 3.6.1 we see that if we carry out a scheme of calculations, illustrated in Table 3.4 for the value $n = 3$, the final number in the table is $p_n^{[0]}(x)$. This coincides with $p_n(x)$ defined by (3.13) or (3.24), the interpolating polynomial for f based on the abscissas $x_0, \ldots, x_n$, and the scheme of calculations is called the Neville–Aitken algorithm. We emphasize that the algorithm must be followed through for each value of x for which we wish to evaluate $p_n(x)$.

It is worth remarking that since the Neville–Aitken algorithm consists in repeatedly constructing the linear interpolating polynomial, it belongs to the class of algorithms that can be carried out using the ancient Greek tools of ruler and compasses, to which we referred in Section 1.2. To carry out the construction related to (3.89), we need to "transfer" the ordinates $p_k^{[i]}(x)$ and $p_k^{[i+1]}(x)$ to the abscissas x_i and x_{i+k+1}, respectively, using the compasses. Then we draw the straight line connecting the two points $(x_i, p_k^{[i]}(x))$ and $(x_{i+k+1}, p_k^{[i+1]}(x))$. The new value $p_{k+1}^{[i]}(x)$ is the ordinate on this straight line at the abscissa with value x. For this given value of x we can thus construct the *length* $p_n(x)$ by drawing $\frac{1}{2}n(n+1)$ straight lines.

We can also derive an iterative process of Neville–Aitken type for evaluating the interpolating polynomial for $f(x,y)$ on the triangular set of points defined above in (3.77). We define $p_k^{[i,j]}(x,y)$ as the interpolating polynomial for $f(x,y)$ on the triangular set of points

$$S_k^{[i,j]} = \{(i+r, j+s) \mid r, s \geq 0, \ r + s \leq k\}. \tag{3.90}$$

The set $S_k^{[i,j]}$ contains $1 + 2 + \cdots + (k+1) = \frac{1}{2}(k+1)(k+2)$ points arranged in a right-angled triangle formation, with (i,j) as the bottom left-hand point. Figure 3.1 illustrates the set $S_4^{[0,0]}$. Thus $p_0^{[i,j]}(x,y)$ has the constant value $f(i,j)$. We can compute the interpolating polynomials $p_k^{[i,j]}(x,y)$ recursively in a Neville–Aitken style, as we will now see.

Theorem 3.6.2 For $k \geq 0$ and $i, j \geq 0$,

$$p_{k+1}^{[i,j]}(x,y) = \left(\frac{k+1+i+j-x-y}{k+1} \right) p_k^{[i,j]}(x,y)$$

$$+ \left(\frac{x-i}{k+1} \right) p_k^{[i+1,j]}(x,y) + \left(\frac{y-j}{k+1} \right) p_k^{[i,j+1]}(x,y). \tag{3.91}$$

Proof. First we note that by definition each $p_0^{[i,j]}(x,y)$ interpolates $f(x,y)$ at the point (i,j). We now use induction. Let us assume that for some $k \geq 0$ and all i and j, the polynomials $p_k^{[i,j]}(x,y)$ interpolate $f(x,y)$ on the appropriate sets of points. Then we observe that if all three polynomials $p_k^{[i,j]}(x,y)$, $p_k^{[i+1,j]}(x,y)$ and $p_k^{[i,j+1]}(x,y)$ on the right of (3.91) have the same value C for some choice of x and y, then the right side of (3.91) has the value

$$\frac{C}{k+1} \left((k+1+i+j-x-y) + (x-i) + (y-j) \right) = C,$$

and so $p_{k+1}^{[i,j]}(x,y)$ also takes the value C. We next see that these three polynomials *all* interpolate $f(x,y)$ on all points $(i+r, j+s)$ for which

$r > 0$, $s > 0$, and $r + s < k + 1$, and so $p_{k+1}^{[i,j]}(x,y)$ also interpolates $f(x,y)$ on all these points. We further show from (3.91) that $p_{k+1}^{[i,j]}(x,y)$ interpolates $f(x,y)$ also on the three "lines" of points, these being subsets of the set $S_{k+1}^{[i,j]}$ corresponding to taking $r = 0$, $s = 0$ and $r + s = k + 1$ in turn. This completes the proof by induction. ∎

The Neville–Aitken scheme (3.91) can be modified to give an analogous process for computing iteratively the interpolating polynomial for a function defined on the triangular grid of points (3.86) based on q-integers.

Finally, we can use (3.91) with $k = n - 1$ and $i = j = 0$, replace each of the three polynomials on the right by its appropriate forward difference representation, as in (3.85), and use induction to verify (3.85). For example,

$$p_{n-1}^{[1,0]}(x,y) = \sum_{k=0}^{n-1} \sum_{r=0}^{k} \binom{x-1}{r} \binom{y}{k-r} \Delta_x^r \Delta_y^{k-r} f(1,0).$$

The expansions for $p_{n-1}^{[0,1]}(x,y)$ and $p_{n-1}^{[1,1]}(x,y)$ involve differences of $f(0,1)$ and $f(1,1)$, respectively. We can then write

$$f(1,0) = f(0,0) + \Delta_x f(0,0),$$

express $f(0,1)$ and $f(1,1)$ similarly in terms of $f(0,0)$ and its differences (see Problem 3.6.4), and so express the right side of (3.91), with $k = n - 1$ and $i = j = 0$, in terms of $f(0,0)$ and its differences. We then simplify the resulting eight summations to obtain $p_n(x,y)$ in the form (3.91). It is not as bad as it may seem. Have a go!

Problem 3.6.1 Verify the last step in the proof of Theorem 3.6.1, that $p_{k+1}^{[i]}(x)$, as defined by (3.89), takes the values $f(x_i)$ and $f(x_{i+k+1})$, respectively, at $x = x_i$ and $x = x_{i+k+1}$.

Problem 3.6.2 Repeat the calculation in Example 3.1.2 using the Neville–Aitken algorithm instead of evaluating the interpolating polynomial from its Lagrange form.

Problem 3.6.3 Verify the last step in the proof of Theorem 3.6.2, that $p_{k+1}^{[i,j]}(x,y)$, as defined by (3.91), interpolates $f(x,y)$ on each of the three subsets of $S_{k+1}^{[i,j]}$ obtained by taking $r = 0$, $s = 0$, and $r + s = k + 1$.

Problem 3.6.4 Show that

$$f(0,1) = f(0,0) + \Delta_y f(0,0)$$

and

$$f(1,1) = f(0,0) + \Delta_x f(0,0) + \Delta_y f(0,0) + \Delta_x \Delta_y f(0,0).$$

$$
\begin{array}{c|c}
k-2,n & C \\
k-1,n & \\
k & \\
\hline
& \\
1,n & \\
2,n & \\
3,n & \\
\end{array}
$$

TABLE 3.5. Notation used by Harriot to denote the fourth term in his forward difference formula.

3.7   Historical Notes

In [21] H. H. Goldstine describes Thomas Harriot (1560–1621) of Oxford as being the "real inventor of the calculus of finite differences." Harriot was tutor in the mathematical sciences, which included astronomy and navigation, in the household of Sir Walter Raleigh. He was also (see Eves [14]) a notable astronomer, who observed sunspots and made the first telescopic map of the moon. The four largest satellites of Jupiter, whose first sighting is generally credited to Galileo (1564–1642) in 1610, were independently observed by Harriot at about the same time. As a young man Harriot was a member of Sir Richard Greville's 1585–86 expedition to the island of Roanoke, off the coast of what was called Virginia but is now part of North Carolina. On his return, he published a personal account of the expedition (see [26]). However, what we would regard as his main achievements have received little general recognition, since none of his scientific work was published in his lifetime. This includes important early work on the solution of equations, and his mastery of the forward difference interpolation formula. Goldstine [21] states that it was Thomas Harriot and Henry Briggs who were mainly responsible for the early development of finite difference methods of interpolation. These methods were put to very good use by Briggs himself in the computation of his table of logarithms. (See Section 2.3.) Since Harriot's work influenced that of other mathematicians, it was not lost, although for much of the time since his death his contribution was overlooked. In particular, the forward difference formula has very often been credited to its independent rediscoverers Isaac Newton and James Gregory, who were not even born until after the deaths of both Harriot and Briggs.

Before leaving Harriot, we comment briefly on the notation he used for his forward difference formula. Table 3.5 shows his notation for the fourth term in his forward difference formula. The symbol C denotes a third difference, which we would denote by $\Delta^3 f(x_0)$, and the symbols to the left of C denote

$$
\frac{(k-2n)(k-n)k}{n \cdot 2n \cdot 3n} = \frac{1}{3!} \frac{k}{n} \left(\frac{k}{n} - 1 \right) \left(\frac{k}{n} - 2 \right),
$$

so that the set of symbols in Table 3.5 indeed denote the fourth term in the forward difference formula (3.41), which we would write as

$$\binom{s}{3} \Delta^3 f(x_0), \qquad \text{with} \qquad s = \frac{k}{n}.$$

Edwards [13] states that James Gregory obtained the binomial series for the function $f(x) = (1+a)^x$ via the forward difference formula, as follows. We tabulate $f(x)$ at $x = 0, 1, \ldots, n$. Then we write

$$\Delta f(j) = (1+a)^{j+1} - (1+a)^j = a(1+a)^j = af(j).$$

Hence $\Delta^k f(j) = a^k f(j)$ and, in particular,

$$\Delta^k f(0) = a^k. \tag{3.92}$$

Since in our notation we are taking $x_0 = 0$ and $h = 1$, it follows from (3.41) and (3.92) that the forward difference formula for $(1+a)^x$ is

$$1 + \binom{x}{1} a + \binom{x}{2} a^2 + \cdots + \binom{x}{n} a^n. \tag{3.93}$$

These are the first $n + 1$ terms of the binomial expansion that Briggs had earlier found for the special case of $x = \frac{1}{2}$, and the above procedure generalizes that used above in deriving the series (3.42) for 2^x.

During the long period of China's cultural isolation from other parts of the world there were (see [36] and [39]) many independent developments in mathematics. The astronomer Liú Zhuó (544–610) obtained a formula for interpolation of a function defined on three equally spaced abscissas. Some two centuries later, the eighth-century astronomer Yì Xíng extended this to interpolate a function defined on three arbitrarily spaced abscissas. Then Guō Shǒujìng (1231–1316) extended the "equally spaced" formula of Liú Zhuó to allow interpolation at four equally spaced abscissas. Lí Yan and Dú Shíràn (see [36]) believe that Guō Shǒujìng was capable of interpolating at *any* number of equally spaced abscissas, and this was some three centuries before Thomas Harriot achieved this in England.

4

Continued Fractions

Problems worthy of attack
Prove their worth by hitting back.

Piet Hein

The basis of this chapter is the Euclidean algorithm, which has been part of mathematics since at least the fourth century BC, predating Archimedes. From the Euclidean algorithm we immediately obtain the expression of any rational number in the form of a finite continued fraction. A study of continued fractions shows us that they provide a more natural method of expressing any real number in terms of integers than the usual decimal expansion. An investigation of the "worst" case in applying the Euclidean algorithm leads to the Fibonacci sequence and so to other sequences generated by a linear recurrence relation.

4.1   The Euclidean Algorithm

We begin with the intuitively obvious statement that every nonempty set of positive integers contains a *least* element. This is called the *well-ordering principle*. When we first encounter it, this statement may seem to be too trivial to be worth writing down. Yet some powerful results can be deduced from it.

The well-ordering principle can be extended from the above statement, concerned only with *positive* integers, to show that any nonempty set of *integers*, none of which is less than some fixed integer m, has a least element. We can justify this simple extension as follows. Let S denote a nonempty set of integers such that

$$s \in S \Rightarrow s \geq m$$

for some fixed integer m. (Recall that the symbol $\in$ means "belongs to," and the symbol $\Rightarrow$ denotes "implies.") If $m > 0$, the set S contains only positive integers and so, by the well-ordering principle, has a least element. If $m \leq 0$, let us define a new set S' as

$$S' = \{s - m + 1 \mid s \in S\},$$

where the vertical bar in the line above means "such that." Since

$$s - m + 1 \geq m - m + 1 = 1,$$

each element of S' is positive. Also, since S is nonempty, S' is nonempty, and the well-ordering principle implies that S' has a least element, say s'. It follows that the least element of S is $s' + m - 1$. You might like to think of the set S as being depicted by a set of integer points on the real line. The correspondence between the points of S and the second set S' is achieved by moving the origin to the point $m - 1$.

We now consider the *division algorithm*. Let a and b be integers, with $b > 0$. We will prove that there exist *unique* integers q and r such that

$$a = qb + r, \quad 0 \leq r < b.$$

We refer to q as the *quotient* and r as the *remainder*. To "pin down" the remainder r, we consider all integers of the form $a - tb$, where t is an integer. Since $r \geq 0$, we restrict our attention to the subset of the numbers $a - tb$ that are nonnegative, defining

$$S = \{s = a - tb \mid t \text{ is an integer and } s \geq 0\}.$$

If we wish to apply the well-ordering principle, we need to show that S is nonempty. If $a \geq 0$, then $s = a - tb$ with $t = 0$ gives $s = a$, and so $a \in S$. If $a < 0$, then $s = a - tb$ with $t = a$ gives

$$s = a - ab = a(1 - b) \in S,$$

since $b \geq 1$, and so $a(1 - b) \geq 0$. Thus, for any choice of a, S is nonempty, and the extension of the well-ordering principle tells us that S has a least element, say r. This means that for some integer $t = q$, say, we have $a - qb = r$, that is,

$$a = qb + r.$$

It remains only to show that $0 \leq r < b$. Since r is an element of S, $r = a - qb \geq 0$ and

$$r - b = (a - qb) - b = a - (1 + q)b.$$

If $r \geq b$, then $r - b = a - (1+q)b$ would be nonnegative and so would belong to S. This would give a member of S *smaller* than its least element, which is impossible. Thus we must have $0 \leq r < b$, which justifies the division algorithm.

Example 4.1.1 If we apply the division algorithm in the case where a is a positive integer and $b = 2$, we obtain unique integers q and r such that

$$a = 2q + r, \quad 0 \leq r < 2.$$

Thus r has the value 0 or 1, giving a formal proof of the intuitively obvious result that every positive integer is either even or odd.   ■

The division algorithm can be applied to obtain the more substantial result that every positive integer can be uniquely represented in any *base b* greater than 1. This means that given any integer $b > 1$, we can write any positive integer a uniquely in the form

$$a = c_k b^k + c_{k-1} b^{k-1} + \cdots + c_1 b + c_0,$$

for some $k \geq 0$, where $0 < c_k < b$ and $0 \leq c_j < b$ for $0 \leq j < k$. This justifies the unique representation of integers in different bases, including the binary (with $b = 2$) and decimal (with $b = 10$) representations.

We now come to our main application of the division algorithm, which is the *Euclidean algorithm*. This is a topic in mathematics with a very long history, going back at least to the fourth-century BC Greek mathematician Euclid, whose *Elements*, although mainly devoted to geometry, also contains material on number theory. Although we may think of both the division algorithm and the Euclidean algorithm as being primarily of a number-theoretical nature, the numbers involved may be interpreted as *lengths*, and so these algorithms both have an obvious geometrical interpretation.

Let r_0 and r_1 be positive integers, with $r_0 > r_1$. On applying the division algorithm we obtain, say,

$$r_0 = m_1 r_1 + r_2, \quad 0 \leq r_2 < r_1,$$

where the quotient m_1 is a positive integer. If the remainder r_2 is positive, we next apply the division algorithm to r_1 and r_2, giving

$$r_1 = m_2 r_2 + r_3, \quad 0 \leq r_3 < r_2,$$

where the quotient m_2 is a positive integer. Clearly, we can keep repeating this process as long as we obtain a positive remainder, and the process will terminate if we obtain a zero remainder. But since the sequence $r_0, r_1, r_2, \ldots$ is a decreasing sequence of nonnegative integers, it must be a *finite* sequence. Thus, for some k, we must have $r_{k+1} = 0$, and the sequence $r_0, r_1, \ldots, r_k$ satisfies the following chain of equations:

$$
\begin{aligned}
r_0 &= m_1 r_1 + r_2, \\
r_1 &= m_2 r_2 + r_3, \\
&\;\;\vdots \\
r_{k-2} &= m_{k-1} r_{k-1} + r_k, \\
r_{k-1} &= m_k r_k.
\end{aligned}
\tag{4.1}
$$

Example 4.1.2 Let us apply the Euclidean algorithm to the positive integers $r_0 = 1899981$ and $r_1 = 703665$. We obtain

$$
\begin{aligned}
1899981 &= 2 \cdot 703665 + 492651, \\
703665 &= 1 \cdot 492651 + 211014, \\
492651 &= 2 \cdot 211014 + 70623, \\
211014 &= 2 \cdot 70623 + 69768, \\
70623 &= 1 \cdot 69768 + 855, \\
69768 &= 81 \cdot 855 + 513, \\
855 &= 1 \cdot 513 + 342, \\
513 &= 1 \cdot 342 + 171, \\
342 &= 2 \cdot 171.
\end{aligned}
$$

If we factorize 1899981 and 703665, we obtain

$$
1899981 = 3^2 \cdot 19 \cdot 41 \cdot 271 \qquad \text{and} \qquad 703665 = 3^2 \cdot 5 \cdot 19 \cdot 823,
$$

and we note that $3^2 \cdot 19 = 171$ is a divisor of both these numbers. ∎

Now let us write (a, b) to denote the *greatest common divisor* (g.c.d.) of the positive integers a and b, meaning the largest integer that divides both a and b. Thus $(18, 12) = 6$, and from the factorizations given in Example 4.1.2, we find that $(1899981, 703665) = 171$. Further, let us write $a \mid b$ to denote "a divides b," meaning that b is an exact multiple of a, where a and b are positive integers. We next prove that the Euclidean algorithm always computes the g.c.d. of the two initial numbers.

We begin with r_0 and r_1, with $r_0 > r_1$. From the first equation generated by the Euclidean algorithm, $r_0 = m_1 r_1 + r_2$, we see that $(r_0, r_1) \mid r_2$, since from (4.1) any positive integer that divides r_0 and r_1 must divide r_2. From the definition of the g.c.d. we also have $(r_0, r_1) \mid r_1$, and we deduce that (r_0, r_1) divides both r_1 and r_2. Since (r_1, r_2) is the largest number that divides r_1 and r_2, it follows that

$$
(r_0, r_1) \mid (r_1, r_2). \tag{4.2}
$$

If we now begin again with the equation $r_0 = m_1 r_1 + r_2$, we can see that (r_1, r_2) divides r_0 and argue similarly that since (r_1, r_2) also divides r_1, we have

$$(r_1, r_2) \mid (r_0, r_1). \tag{4.3}$$

We deduce from (4.2) and (4.3) that

$$(r_0, r_1) = (r_1, r_2).$$

As we work through the equations (4.1) created by the Euclidean algorithm, we find similarly that

$$(r_0, r_1) = (r_1, r_2) = \cdots = (r_{k-2}, r_{k-1}) = (r_{k-1}, r_k),$$

and the final equation of (4.1) shows that $(r_{k-1}, r_k) = r_k$. We have thus proved the following result.

Theorem 4.1.1 Let the Euclidean algorithm be applied to the two positive integers $r_0 > r_1$ to create the sequence of equations (4.1), where all but the last of these equations connect three consecutive members of the decreasing sequence of positive integers

$$r_0 > r_1 > r_2 > \cdots > r_{k-1} > r_k,$$

and the last equation is $r_{k-1} = m_k r_k$. Then the final number r_k is the greatest common divisor of the two initial numbers r_0 and r_1. ■

Let p_j, $j = 1, 2, \ldots$, denote the jth prime number, so that $p_1 = 2$, $p_2 = 3$, and so on. Given any two positive integers a and b, let p_m denote the largest prime occurring in the factorization of a and b into primes. Then we may write

$$a = p_1^{\alpha_1} p_2^{\alpha_2} \cdots p_m^{\alpha_m} \qquad \text{and} \qquad b = p_1^{\beta_1} p_2^{\beta_2} \cdots p_m^{\beta_m},$$

where $\alpha_j, \beta_j \geq 0$ for all j and at least one of α_m and β_m is positive. For example, beginning with 288 and 200 we have

$$288 = 2^5 \cdot 3^2 \cdot 5^0 \qquad \text{and} \qquad 200 = 2^3 \cdot 3^0 \cdot 5^2.$$

It is not hard to see that in the general case,

$$(a, b) = p_1^{\gamma_1} p_2^{\gamma_2} \cdots p_m^{\gamma_m},$$

where $\gamma_j = \min(\alpha_j, \beta_j)$, $1 \leq j \leq m$. Thus

$$(288, 200) = 2^3 \cdot 3^0 \cdot 5^0 = 8.$$

While this is conceptually an easy way to compute the g.c.d. of two numbers, it is far less efficient computationally than the Euclidean algorithm.

Example 4.1.3 Find $d = (245, 161)$ and hence obtain integers x and y such that
$$245x + 161y = d.$$

An equation, such as that above, where solutions are sought in *integers* is called a *Diophantine equation*, after the third-century Greek mathematician Diophantus of Alexandria. On applying the Euclidean algorithm we obtain

$$
\begin{aligned}
245 &= 1 \cdot 161 + 84, \\
161 &= 1 \cdot 84 + 77, \\
84 &= 1 \cdot 77 + 7, \\
77 &= 11 \cdot 7,
\end{aligned}
$$

and thus $d = (245, 161) = 7$. Next we write, using the above equations,

$$
\begin{aligned}
7 &= 84 - 77 = 84 - (161 - 84) = 2 \cdot 84 - 161 \\
  &= 2 \cdot (245 - 161) - 161 = 2 \cdot 245 - 3 \cdot 161.
\end{aligned}
$$

If we equate the first and the last items connected by the above chain of equalities, we obtain $7 = 2 \cdot 245 - 3 \cdot 161$, showing that the Diophantine equation $245x + 161y = 7$ has a solution $x = 2$, $y = -3$. The solution is not unique, since as we can easily verify, $x = 2 - 161t$, $y = -3 + 245t$ is a solution for any choice of integer t. ∎

Given any $r_0 > r_1$, consider the Diophantine equation

$$r_0 x + r_1 y = d. \tag{4.4}$$

Since $(r_0, r_1) \mid (r_0 x + r_1 y)$, this Diophantine equation can have a solution only if $(r_0, r_1) \mid d$. So let us consider the equation

$$r_0 \hat{x} + r_1 \hat{y} = k(r_0, r_1),$$

where k is an integer. This will have solutions of the form $\hat{x} = kx$, $\hat{y} = ky$ if x and y satisfy

$$r_0 x + r_1 y = (r_0, r_1). \tag{4.5}$$

Thus equations of the form (4.4) have solutions in integers only if d is a multiple of (r_0, r_1), and the above argument then reduces the problem to the solution of (4.5). We can solve the latter equation by following the process that we used in Example 4.1.3. We can, equivalently, find a solution of (4.5) by arguing as follows.

Consider the sequence $r_0, r_1, \ldots, r_k$ produced by applying the Euclidean algorithm to r_0 and r_1. A little thought shows that each r_j can be expressed as a sum of integer multiples of r_0 and r_1. Specifically, let us write

$$r_j = s_j r_0 + t_j r_1, \quad 0 \le j \le k.$$

If we can find how to compute all the coefficients s_j and t_j, we can find s_k and t_k and so be able to write down

$$s_k r_0 + t_k r_1 = r_k = (r_0, r_1),$$

thus giving $x = s_k$, $y = t_k$ as a solution of (4.5). How do we find the coefficients s_j and t_j? The answer is given in the statement of the following theorem.

Theorem 4.1.2 Each r_j that occurs in the application of the Euclidean algorithm to $r_0 > r_1$ may be expressed in the form

$$r_j = s_j r_0 + t_j r_1, \quad 0 \leq j \leq k, \tag{4.6}$$

where

$$s_0 = 1, \quad t_0 = 0, \quad s_1 = 0, \quad t_1 = 1, \tag{4.7}$$

and the sequences (s_j) and (t_j) satisfy the same recurrence relation as the sequence (r_j). In particular, (r_0, r_1) can be expressed as a linear combination of r_0 and r_1.

Proof. Let the sequences (s_j) and (t_j) satisfy the initial conditions (4.7) and satisfy the same recurrence relation as the sequence (r_j). Then we see immediately that (4.6) holds for $j = 0$ and $j = 1$. Let us now assume that (4.6) holds for $0 \leq j \leq n$, where $1 \leq n < k$. Thus, in particular,

$$r_{n-1} = s_{n-1} r_0 + t_{n-1} r_1,$$
$$r_n = s_n r_0 + t_n r_1,$$

and from the recurrence relation connecting r_{n-1}, r_n, and r_{n+1} in (4.1), we have

$$\begin{aligned}
r_{n+1} &= -m_n r_n + r_{n-1} \\
&= -m_n(s_n r_0 + t_n r_1) + (s_{n-1} r_0 + t_{n-1} r_1) \\
&= (-m_n s_n + s_{n-1}) r_0 + (-m_n t_n + t_{n-1}) r_1 \\
&= s_{n+1} r_0 + t_{n+1} r_1,
\end{aligned}$$

since (s_j) and (t_j) satisfy the same recurrence relation as (r_j). Thus (4.6) holds for $j = n + 1$, and so by induction, (4.6) holds for $0 \leq j \leq k$. ∎

Table 4.1 is based on Example 4.1.3. We begin with the initial values s_0, t_0, s_1, and t_1, defined in (4.7) above, and the multipliers $m_1 = 1$, $m_2 = 1$, and $m_3 = 1$ from Example 4.1.3. In this case, the multipliers that are used all happen to take the value 1. Note that we do not need the last multiplier, $m_4 = 11$. We compute the values of s_j and t_j for $j = 2, 3$, and 4, using the recurrence relations

$$s_{j+1} = -m_j s_j + s_{j-1}$$

n	m_n	s_n	t_n
0	–	1	0
1	1	0	1
2	1	1	−1
3	1	−1	2
4	–	2	−3

TABLE 4.1. Evaluation of s_j and t_j such that $r_j = s_j r_0 + t_j r_1$.

and
$$t_{j+1} = -m_j t_j + t_{j-1}.$$
We obtain $s_4 = 2$ and $t_4 = -3$, giving
$$2 \cdot 245 - 3 \cdot 161 = 7 = r_4,$$
which agrees with the solution obtained in Example 4.1.3.

Now let us consider the number of steps required in executing the Euclidean algorithm, for given starting values $r_0 > r_1$. In (4.1), how does the number of steps k depend on r_0 and r_1? For an arbitrary choice of r_0 and r_1 we can answer this question only by carrying out the algorithm. But what we can do *without* carrying out the algorithm is find an *upper bound* for k whose value depends on the size of r_0 and r_1. For in (4.1) we know that $m_j \geq 1$ for $1 \leq j \leq k - 1$ and the final multiplier m_k is greater than 1. Let us look at an instructive example.

Example 4.1.4 Beginning with $r_0 = 34$ and $r_1 = 21$, we carry out the Euclidean algorithm and obtain the following equations:

$$34 = 1 \cdot 21 + 13,$$
$$21 = 1 \cdot 13 + 8,$$
$$13 = 1 \cdot 8 + 5,$$
$$8 = 1 \cdot 5 + 3,$$
$$5 = 1 \cdot 3 + 2,$$
$$3 = 1 \cdot 2 + 1,$$
$$2 = 2 \cdot 1. \qquad \blacksquare$$

The above example gives a "worst case," since the multipliers are all as small as they can be. The numbers $r_k, r_{k-1}, \ldots, r_0$ in Example 4.1.4 are

$$1 \quad 2 \quad 3 \quad 5 \quad 8 \quad 13 \quad 21 \quad 34,$$

which are members of the *Fibonacci* sequence. Each number (after 1 and 2 above) is the sum of the two previous numbers. In the usual notation, the Fibonacci numbers form an infinite sequence $(F_n)_{n=1}^{\infty}$ defined by

$$F_1 = F_2 = 1$$

and
$$F_{j+1} = F_j + F_{j-1}, \quad j = 2, 3, \ldots.$$

Thus, if we apply the Euclidean algorithm to any pair of consecutive Fibonacci numbers F_{n+1} and F_n, then, as in the particular case with 34 and 21 discussed in Example 4.1.4, we find that

$$(F_{n+1}, F_n) = 1,$$

showing that the g.c.d. of two consecutive Fibonacci numbers is always 1. If the g.c.d. of two numbers is 1, we say that they are *coprime*, meaning that they have no common factor other than 1. We now ask, If we apply the Euclidean algorithm to a and b, with $a > b$, what is the smallest value of b such that the Euclidean algorithm requires exactly n steps? Working back from the *last* step, we must choose all the numbers as small as they can be. It is clear that the last step must be

$$2 = 2 \cdot 1$$

and the second to last

$$3 = 1 \cdot 2 + 1,$$

as in Example 4.1.4. We deduce that the smallest value of b for which the Euclidean algorithm requires n steps is $b = F_{n+1}$, and to achieve this we also need to choose a of the form $m_1 F_{n+1} + F_n$, where m_1 is a positive integer, so that the first step of the Euclidean algorithm gives

$$a = m_1 b + F_n = m_1 F_{n+1} + F_n$$

and the remaining steps are

$$F_{n+1} = F_n + F_{n-1},$$
$$F_n = F_{n-1} + F_{n-2},$$
$$\vdots$$
$$F_4 = F_3 + F_2,$$
$$F_3 = 2 \cdot F_2.$$

We will now prove that for all $n \geq 3$,

$$F_n > \alpha^{n-2}, \tag{4.8}$$

where $\alpha = \frac{1}{2}(1 + \sqrt{5})$ is called the *golden ratio* or the *golden section*. This famous number was known to the members of the Pythagorean school of mathematics in the sixth century BC. These Greek mathematicians knew, for instance, that this ratio occurs in the "pentagram," or five-pointed star, formed by the the five "diagonals" of a regular pentagon. They knew that any two intersecting sides of the pentagram divide each other in the golden ratio. (See Problem 4.1.8.) They also believed that the rectangle with the most aesthetically pleasing proportions is the one whose sides are in the ratio of $\alpha : 1$. It is easily verified that

$$\alpha^2 = \alpha + 1 \tag{4.9}$$

and that

$$F_3 = 2 > \alpha \approx 1.618 \quad \text{and} \quad F_4 = 3 > \alpha^2 = \alpha + 1 \approx 2.618.$$

Let us now assume that the inequality $F_n > \alpha^{n-2}$ holds for all n from 3 up to some $k \geq 4$. Then

$$F_{k+1} = F_k + F_{k-1} > \alpha^{k-2} + \alpha^{k-3} = \alpha^{k-3}(\alpha + 1) = \alpha^{k-3} \cdot \alpha^2 = \alpha^{k-1},$$

and so by induction the inequality (4.8) holds for all $n \geq 3$. We have thus seen that if we apply the Euclidean algorithm to a and b, with $a > b$, and require n steps in executing the algorithm, then

$$b \geq F_{n+1} > \alpha^{n-1}.$$

Taking logarithms to base 10, we have

$$\log_{10} b > (n-1) \log_{10} \alpha > \frac{1}{5}(n-1),$$

since $\log_{10} \alpha \approx 0.209$. This gives

$$n < 5 \log_{10} b + 1 < 5m + 1$$

if b has m decimal digits, and so $n \leq 5m$. We have thus proved the following.

Theorem 4.1.3 An upper bound (worst case) for n, the number of steps we require in carrying out the Euclidean algorithm on a and b, with $a > b$, is given by

$$n \leq 5m,$$

where m is the number of decimal digits of b.   ■

Problem 4.1.1 Use the Euclidean algorithm to find the g.c.d. of 17711 and 10946 and express it as a linear combination of 17711 and 10946.

Problem 4.1.2 Show that $(12n + 5, 3n + 2) = 1$ for any positive integer n. Hence find integers x and y such that

$$(12n + 5)x + (3n + 2)y = 1.$$

Problem 4.1.3 Show that if a, b, and c are positive integers, then

$$(a + cb, b) = (a, b).$$

Problem 4.1.4 Show that (a, b) is the smallest positive integer that can be written as a linear combination of a and b, that is, the smallest positive integer of the form $ax + by$, where x and y are integers.

Problem 4.1.5 How would you go about finding the g.c.d. of three positive integers a, b, and c?

Problem 4.1.6 Let $(a_1, a_2, \ldots, a_k)$ denote the g.c.d. of the positive integers $a_1, a_2, \ldots, a_k$. Show that for $k \geq 3$,

$$(a_1, a_2, \ldots, a_k) = (a_1, a_2, \ldots, a_{k-2}, (a_{k-1}, a_k)).$$

Problem 4.1.7 Consider a rectangle with adjacent sides of length a and b, with $a > b$. Suppose that a square with side of length b is cut from the rectangle and that the remaining rectangle is found to be *similar* to the original rectangle, meaning that the ratio of the larger and smaller sides of each rectangle is the same. Show that $a/b = \alpha$, where α is the golden ratio, satisfying (4.9).

Problem 4.1.8 Let $A_1 A_2 A_3 A_4 A_5$ denote a regular pentagon. Draw its "diagonals" $A_1 A_3$, $A_3 A_5$, $A_5 A_2$, $A_2 A_4$, and $A_4 A_1$, thus constructing a pentagram, and denote the smaller pentagon in its interior by $B_1 B_2 B_3 B_4 B_5$, where B_j is the vertex furthest from A_j. Show that angle $A_4 A_1 A_3 = \frac{\pi}{5}$. If $A_1 B_4 = x$ and $B_3 B_4 = y$, deduce from triangle $A_1 B_3 B_4$ that

$$\frac{y}{x} = 2 \sin \frac{\pi}{10},$$

and hence, using the result in Problem 1.1.4, verify the Pythagorean relation

$$\frac{x + y}{x} = \frac{1}{2} \left(\sqrt{5} + 1 \right),$$

showing that each pair of intersecting diagonals divide each other in the golden ratio.

4.2   Linear Recurrence Relations

In the previous section we defined the Fibonacci sequence by the recurrence relation

$$F_{n+1} = F_n + F_{n-1}, \quad n \geq 2, \tag{4.10}$$

with $F_1 = F_2 = 1$. In this section we will discuss a family of sequences defined by recurrence relations such as (4.10), and in Section 4.3 we will explore some of the many properties of the Fibonacci sequence.

Consider the sequence $(U_n)_{n=1}^{\infty}$ defined by the recurrence relation

$$U_{n+1} = aU_n + bU_{n-1}, \quad n \geq 2, \tag{4.11}$$

where U_1, U_2 are given real numbers, and a, b are real numbers that do not depend on n. Note that with $U_1 = U_2 = a = b = 1$, we obtain the Fibonacci sequence as a special case. We call (4.11) a second-order recurrence relation with constant coefficients. We can obtain an explicit representation of U_n as follows. Let us begin by assuming that for sequences (U_n) that satisfy (4.11) we can find a value of x such that

$$U_n = x^n.$$

This would imply that $U_1 = x$ and $U_2 = x^2$, and thus $U_2 = U_1^2$, which is not very encouraging. However, at this stage we will *ignore* the initial values U_1 and U_2. We now substitute $U_n = x^n$ into (4.11) to give

$$x^{n+1} = ax^n + bx^{n-1}, \quad n \geq 2. \tag{4.12}$$

A trivial solution of the latter equation is $x = 0$, giving $U_n = 0$ for all n, which will usually not be very helpful. Otherwise, with $x \neq 0$, we can divide (4.12) by x^{n-1} to give

$$x^2 = ax + b \quad \text{or} \quad x^2 - ax - b = 0. \tag{4.13}$$

We call the quadratic expression $x^2 - ax - b$ the *characteristic polynomial* and call (4.13) the *characteristic equation* of the recurrence relation (4.11). The case of greatest interest is that for which this quadratic equation has two distinct real roots, say α and β, that is,

$$x^2 - ax - b = (x - \alpha)(x - \beta)$$

and thus $x = \alpha$ or $x = \beta$. Then $U_n = x^n$ yields $U_n = \alpha^n$ or $U_n = \beta^n$.

What we are saying here is that *if* $U_n = \alpha^n$ or $U_n = \beta^n$, where α and β are the roots (assumed to be distinct) of the quadratic equation $x^2 - ax - b = 0$, then $U_{n+1} = aU_n + bU_{n-1}$. We now argue that any linear combination of α^n and β^n will also satisfy the recurrence relation (4.11). For let us write $U_n = A\alpha^n + B\beta^n$, where A and B are any real numbers. Then

$$U_{n+1} - aU_n - bU_{n-1} = A\alpha^{n+1} + B\beta^{n+1} - a(A\alpha^n + B\beta^n) - b(A\alpha^{n-1} + B\beta^{n-1}),$$

and on rearranging the right side of the above equation, we obtain

$$U_{n+1} - aU_n - bU_{n-1} = A\alpha^{n-1}(\alpha^2 - a\alpha - b) + B\beta^{n-1}(\beta^2 - a\beta - b) = 0,$$

since α and β both satisfy the above quadratic equation. We call

$$U_n = A\alpha^n + B\beta^n \tag{4.14}$$

the *general solution* of the recurrence relation (4.11). Now we are into the "end game." For we can seek values of the parameters A and B such that U_n, given by (4.14), matches the given initial values U_1 and U_2. Putting $n = 1$ and 2 in (4.14), we obtain

$$U_1 = A\alpha + B\beta \qquad \text{and} \qquad U_2 = A\alpha^2 + B\beta^2.$$

We solve these two linear equations to determine the values of A and B,

$$A = \frac{U_2 - \beta U_1}{\alpha(\alpha - \beta)}, \qquad B = \frac{U_2 - \alpha U_1}{\beta(\beta - \alpha)}. \qquad (4.15)$$

Our above assumption, that α and β are distinct, ensures that A and B are defined by (4.15). For the sake of clarity, let us state the result that we have just derived.

Theorem 4.2.1 If the quadratic equation $x^2 - ax - b = 0$ has distinct roots α and β and the sequence (U_n) satisfies the recurrence relation

$$U_{n+1} = aU_n + bU_{n-1}, \quad n \geq 2,$$

where U_1 and U_2 are given initial values, then

$$U_n = A\alpha^n + B\beta^n, \quad n = 1, 2, \ldots,$$

where A and B are given by (4.15). ∎

Example 4.2.1 Let us find the sequence (U_n) that satisfies the recurrence relation

$$U_{n+1} = U_n + 2U_{n-1}, \quad n = 1, 2, \ldots,$$

with initial values $U_1 = -1$ and $U_2 = 7$. In this case the characteristic equation is $x^2 - x - 2 = 0$, with roots 2 and -1. Thus from (4.14) the general solution is

$$U_n = A\,2^n + B(-1)^n.$$

To match the initial conditions, we require that A and B satisfy the equations

$$-1 = 2A - B,$$
$$7 = 4A + B.$$

On adding the above two equations we obtain $6A = 6$, giving $A = 1$, and either equation then gives $B = 3$. Thus

$$U_n = 2^n + 3(-1)^n.$$

It is not worth remembering the expressions for the coefficients A and B in (4.15), which were derived only to show that such a solution always exists. In any particular case it is easier to find the values of A and B afresh, as we did above. ∎

We remark in passing that although hitherto we have been discussing sequences whose first member is U_1, we may wish to discuss sequences of the form $(U_n)_{n=0}^{\infty}$, which begin with U_0, or the doubly infinite sequence $(U_n)_{-\infty}^{\infty}$.

It is interesting to see what happens when the roots of the characteristic equation are *complex*. Then α and β are a complex conjugate pair, having the form $\alpha = x + iy$ and $\beta = x - iy$, where x and y are both real. Alternatively, we can write these in the polar form

$$\alpha = re^{i\theta} \quad \text{and} \quad \beta = re^{-i\theta},$$

where

$$e^{i\theta} = \cos\theta + i\sin\theta \quad \text{and} \quad e^{-i\theta} = \cos\theta - i\sin\theta. \tag{4.16}$$

For example, the characteristic equation of the recurrence relation

$$U_{n+1} = U_n - U_{n-1} \tag{4.17}$$

has roots

$$\alpha = \frac{1}{2}\left(1 + i\sqrt{3}\right), \quad \beta = \frac{1}{2}\left(1 - i\sqrt{3}\right),$$

which we can write in the polar form

$$\alpha = re^{i\theta}, \quad \beta = re^{-i\theta}, \tag{4.18}$$

with $r = 1$ and $\theta = \pi/3$. The parameter r is included in (4.18) because it occurs in the general case when the roots are complex. Then from (4.14) and (4.18) the general solution of (4.17) is of the form

$$U_n = r^n(Ae^{in\theta} + Be^{-in\theta}). \tag{4.19}$$

Now, when we are seeking the solution of a recurrence relation such as (4.11), where a and b are real and the initial values U_1 and U_2 are also real, it follows that all members of the sequence (U_n) are real. How does this square with (4.19)? The answer is to choose A and B as a complex conjugate pair, since then U_n, defined by (4.19), will always be real. For we have

$$e^{in\theta} = \cos n\theta + i\sin n\theta \quad \text{and} \quad e^{-in\theta} = \cos n\theta - i\sin n\theta,$$

which are also a complex conjugate pair. Then we can write

$$Ae^{in\theta} + Be^{-in\theta} = C\cos n\theta + D\sin n\theta, \tag{4.20}$$

where

$$C = A + B \quad \text{and} \quad D = i(A - B)$$

and we see that if $A = c + id$ and $B = c - id$ with c and d real, so that A and B are a complex conjugate pair, then $C = 2c$ and $D = -2d$ are indeed both real.

Example 4.2.2 Let us find the solution of the recurrence relation defined by (4.17) that satisfies the initial conditions $U_1 = 1$ and $U_2 = 3$. We have already seen from (4.19) and (4.20) that the general solution is

$$U_n = r^n(C\cos n\theta + D\sin n\theta),$$

where $r = 1$ and $\theta = \pi/3$. We match this with the initial conditions $U_1 = 1$ and $U_2 = 3$ and obtain the values $C = -2$ and $D = 4/\sqrt{3}$, giving the solution

$$U_n = -2\cos\left(\frac{n\pi}{3}\right) + \frac{4}{\sqrt{3}}\sin\left(\frac{n\pi}{3}\right).$$

The above method can be applied to any second-order recurrence relation whose characteristic equation has complex roots. However, the particular sequence U_n sought here could have been found more easily. This is because the value of θ above is a submultiple of 2π and so the sequence (U_n) is *periodic*, whatever choice we make of the initial values U_1 and U_2. We see from the recurrence relation (4.17) that with $U_1 = 1$ and $U_2 = 3$, the first few members of the sequence (U_n) are

$$1, \quad 3, \quad 2, \quad -1, \quad -3, \quad -2, \quad 1, \quad 3,$$

so that this sequence repeats after the first six terms.   ■

For completeness we now consider the case where $\alpha = \beta$. We will handle this by writing $\beta = \alpha + \delta$ and taking the limit as $\delta \to 0$. Then from (4.15) we have

$$A = \frac{U_2 - (\alpha + \delta)U_1}{-\alpha\delta}, \qquad B = \frac{U_2 - \alpha U_1}{(\alpha + \delta)\delta}, \tag{4.21}$$

and we can easily verify that

$$A + B = \frac{(2\alpha + \delta)U_1 - U_2}{\alpha(\alpha + \delta)}.$$

We now write

$$U_n = A\alpha^n + B\beta^n = (A + B)\alpha^n + B(\beta^n - \alpha^n)$$
$$= (A + B)\alpha^n + B\delta \cdot \frac{(\alpha + \delta)^n - \alpha^n}{\delta}. \tag{4.22}$$

As $\delta \to 0$, we note from (4.21) that

$$\lim_{\delta \to 0} B\delta = \frac{U_2 - \alpha U_1}{\alpha}$$

and, from the definition of a *derivative*,

$$\lim_{\delta \to 0} \frac{(\alpha + \delta)^n - \alpha^n}{\delta} = n\alpha^{n-1}.$$

Thus, in the limit as $\delta \to 0$, we see from (4.22) and the subsequent results that $U_n = A\alpha^n + B\beta^n$ tends to the value

$$U_n = \frac{2\alpha U_1 - U_2}{\alpha^2} \cdot \alpha^n + \frac{U_2 - \alpha U_1}{\alpha} \cdot n\alpha^{n-1},$$

which simplifies to give

$$U_n = -(n-2)\alpha^{n-1}U_1 + (n-1)\alpha^{n-2}U_2, \qquad (4.23)$$

where α is a double root of the characteristic equation. As a check on our result, it may bring comfort to verify that the right side of (4.23) does indeed take the values U_1 and U_2 when $n = 1$ and 2, respectively. We summarize the above analysis as the following theorem.

Theorem 4.2.2 If the sequence (U_n) satisfies a recurrence relation of the form

$$U_{n+1} = 2\alpha U_n - \alpha^2 U_{n-1},$$

then

$$U_n = -(n-2)\alpha^{n-1}U_1 + (n-1)\alpha^{n-2}U_2, \quad n = 1, 2, \ldots. \quad \blacksquare$$

Having derived the solution (4.23) for U_n when the characteristic equation has equal roots, we find it helpful to observe that it is of the form

$$U_n = (C + Dn)\alpha^n, \qquad (4.24)$$

where

$$C = (2\alpha U_1 - U_2)/\alpha^2 \qquad \text{and} \qquad D = (-\alpha U_1 + U_2)/\alpha^2. \qquad (4.25)$$

The important point is that in this "double root" case the solution is of the form (4.24). To determine C and D in a particular example of this kind, it is simpler to use (4.24) and not trouble to remember the formulas for C and D in (4.25), as we now illustrate.

Example 4.2.3 Find the sequence (U_n) that satisfies the recurrence relation

$$U_{n+1} = 2U_n - U_{n-1}, \quad n = 1, 2, \ldots,$$

with initial values $U_1 = -2$ and $U_2 = 1$. Here the characteristic equation is $x^2 - 2x + 1 = 0$, which has the double root $x = 1$. Thus the general solution is

$$U_n = C + Dn,$$

and in order to match the initial conditions, C and D must satisfy

$$-2 = C + D,$$
$$1 = C + 2D.$$

On subtracting we find $D = 3$ and hence obtain $C = -5$, giving the solution

$$U_n = 3n - 5. \quad \blacksquare$$

In this section we have seen how, beginning with a second-order recurrence relation for a sequence (U_n), we can obtain an expression for U_n in the form $A\alpha^n + B\beta^n$, or its variant $r^n(Ce^{in\theta} + De^{-in\theta})$ when α and β are a complex conjugate pair, or in the form $(C + Dn)\alpha^n$ for the "double-root" case. Conversely, if we have an expression for (U_n) in any of these forms, we can immediately say that the sequence (U_n) satisfies a recurrence relation of the appropriate form. Thus, when $U_n = A\alpha^n + B\beta^n$ for α and β distinct, we have the recurrence relation

$$U_{n+1} = (\alpha + \beta)U_n - \alpha\beta U_{n-1},$$

since the characteristic polynomial is

$$(x - \alpha)(x - \beta) = x^2 - (\alpha + \beta)x + \alpha\beta.$$

When $U_n = r^n(Ce^{in\theta} + De^{-in\theta})$ the characteristic polynomial is

$$(x - re^{i\theta})(x - re^{-i\theta}) = x^2 - 2r\cos\theta\, x + r^2,$$

using (4.16), and so U_n satisfies the recurrence relation

$$U_{n+1} = 2r\cos\theta\, U_n - r^2 U_{n-1}.$$

Finally, if $U_n = (C + Dn)\alpha^n$, the characteristic polynomial is

$$(x - \alpha)^2 = x^2 - 2\alpha x + \alpha^2,$$

and so the recurrence relation is

$$U_{n+1} = 2\alpha U_n - \alpha^2 U_{n-1},$$

as in the statement of Theorem 4.2.2.

Example 4.2.4 It follows from the "complex case" of the analysis immediately above that if $U_n = \cos n\theta$, then the roots of the characteristic polynomial are $e^{i\theta}$ and $e^{-i\theta}$ and the sequence (U_n) satisfies the recurrence relation

$$U_{n+1} = 2\cos\theta\, U_n - U_{n-1}. \tag{4.26}$$

Since $U_1 = \cos\theta$ and $U_2 = \cos 2\theta = 2\cos^2\theta - 1$, it follows from (4.26) that U_n is a *polynomial* of degree n in $\cos\theta$. This is called a *Chebyshev* polynomial in honour of its discoverer P. L. Chebyshev (1821–94). ■

Problem 4.2.1 Determine the sequence (U_n) that satisfies the recurrence relation

$$U_{n+1} = 5U_n - 4U_{n-1}, \quad n = 1, 2, \ldots,$$

with initial values $U_1 = 3$ and $U_2 = 15$.

Problem 4.2.2 Find the sequence (U_n) that satisfies the recurrence relation

$$U_{n+1} = 4U_n - 4U_{n-1}, \quad n = 1, 2, \ldots,$$

with initial values $U_1 = 0$ and $U_2 = 4$.

Problem 4.2.3 Show directly that for any sequence (U_n) that satisfies the recurrence relation

$$U_{n+1} = 2\alpha U_n - \alpha^2 U_{n-1},$$

then $U_n = \alpha^n$ and $U_n = n\alpha^n$ are both solutions, and so deduce that $U_n = (C + Dn)\alpha^n$ is also a solution, for any values of C and D.

Problem 4.2.4 Show that the sequence $(U_n)_{n=0}^{\infty}$ that satisfies

$$U_{n+1} = 4U_n + U_{n-1},$$

for $n \geq 1$, with $U_0 = 1$ and $U_1 = 2$, is given by

$$U_n = \frac{1}{2}\left((2 + \sqrt{5})^n + (2 - \sqrt{5})^n\right).$$

Problem 4.2.5 Show that if $U_n = \sin n\theta$, then the sequence (U_n) satisfies the recurrence relation (4.26). Verify by induction that $\sin n\theta / \sin \theta$ is a polynomial in $\cos \theta$ of degree $n - 1$. This is called a Chebyshev polynomial of the second kind.

Problem 4.2.6 Consider the sequence (U_n) defined by the recurrence relation

$$U_{n+1} = 2aU_n + U_{n-1},$$

with $U_0 = 0$ and $U_1 = 1$, where a is any real number. Show that

$$U_n = \frac{\alpha^n - \beta^n}{\alpha - \beta},$$

where α and β are the roots of $x^2 - 2ax - 1 = 0$. Verify that $\alpha\beta = -1$ and that

$$U_{n+1}U_{n-1} - U_n^2 = (-1)^n.$$

4.3 Fibonacci Numbers

The Fibonacci sequence $(F_n)_{n=1}^{\infty}$, as already mentioned in Sections 4.1 and 4.2, satisfies the recurrence relation

$$F_{n+1} = F_n + F_{n-1}, \quad n = 2, 3, \ldots, \tag{4.27}$$

with $F_1 = F_2 = 1$. Since (4.27) is a special case of (4.11) with the particularly simple values of $a = b = 1$, and the initial conditions $F_1 = F_2 = 1$ are also pleasingly simple, it seems inevitable that this sequence should have been discovered at some point in the evolution of mathematics. Indeed, the Fibonacci sequence has a very long pedigree. It is named after the mathematician Leonardo of Pisa (c.1175–1220), who is more usually known as Fibonacci. The latter name is derived from Filius Bonaccii, meaning the son of Bonaccio. He introduced this sequence in *Liber Abaci*, his "book of the abacus", which was published in 1202. The Fibonacci numbers arose in the solution to an interesting problem, discussed by Fibonacci in *Liber Abaci*, concerning the size of a population of rabbits. In the beginning there is a single breeding pair of rabbits. Each pair of rabbits produces another breeding pair every month, and a new pair produces its first breeding pair offspring after two months—such metronomic regularity, each birth being a set of boy–girl twins, and no deaths. Life can sometimes be so wonderful, and what consenting adult rabbits do is none of our business. Fibonacci's question was, How many pairs of rabbits are there after one year?

Let R_j denote the number of pairs of rabbits existing at the beginning of month j. Then R_{j+2} is the sum of the number of pairs alive at the beginning of month $j + 1$ plus the number of pairs born at the beginning of month $j + 2$, which equals the number of pairs alive two months earlier. Thus

$$R_{j+2} = R_{j+1} + R_j, \tag{4.28}$$

with $R_1 = R_2 = 1$, and so $R_j = F_j$ for all $j \geq 1$. Then the number of pairs existing after one year, that is, at the beginning of month 13, is $F_{13} = 233$. If Piero and Piera (*my* choice of names for Fibonacci's very famous first pair of rabbits) were born on 1 January 1200, then their 800th birthday party on 1 January 2000 would be attended by $F_{9601} \approx 1.38 \times 10^{2000}$ pairs of rabbits. The mass of the solar system that we know and love is vanishly small compared with the mass of these hypothetical rabbits. Beware of the power of exponential functions!

The characteristic equation for the Fibonacci numbers is $x^2 - x - 1 = 0$, and we may write

$$x^2 - x - 1 = \left(x - \frac{1}{2}\right)^2 - \frac{5}{4} = 0,$$

so that

$$x - \frac{1}{2} = \frac{\pm\sqrt{5}}{2}.$$

Therefore, the roots of the characteristic polynomial are

$$\alpha = \frac{1 + \sqrt{5}}{2} \quad \text{and} \quad \beta = \frac{1 - \sqrt{5}}{2}. \tag{4.29}$$

We note that

$$x^2 - x - 1 = (x - \alpha)(x - \beta) = x^2 - (\alpha + \beta)x + \alpha\beta,$$

so that

$$\alpha + \beta = 1 \qquad \text{and} \qquad \alpha\beta = -1. \tag{4.30}$$

Thus the Fibonacci numbers have the form

$$F_n = A\alpha^n + B\beta^n,$$

and we seek values of A and B such that this matches the initial values

$$F_1 = F_2 = 1.$$

We obtain from (4.15) that

$$A = \frac{1 - \beta}{\alpha(\alpha - \beta)} = \frac{1}{\alpha - \beta},$$

since $1 - \beta = \alpha$, using (4.30). Similarly, we have

$$B = \frac{1 - \alpha}{\beta(\beta - \alpha)} = \frac{1}{\beta - \alpha},$$

and so we obtain

$$F_n = \frac{\alpha^n - \beta^n}{\alpha - \beta}. \tag{4.31}$$

This explicit representation is called the *Binet* form, named after Jacques Binet (1786–1856).

Since $|\beta| < 1$ and $\alpha - \beta = \sqrt{5}$, F_n is approximated well by $\alpha^n/\sqrt{5}$. For $n \geq 1$ this approximation has an error that satisfies

$$0 < \left|\frac{\beta^n}{\alpha - \beta}\right| \leq \left|\frac{\beta}{\alpha - \beta}\right| = \frac{\sqrt{5} - 1}{2\sqrt{5}} = \frac{1}{2} - \frac{1}{2\sqrt{5}} < \frac{1}{2},$$

and so F_n is the nearest integer to $\alpha^n/\sqrt{5}$. Since the error $\beta^n/(\alpha - \beta)$ alternates in sign with n, this estimate of F_n is alternately too large and too small. For example, we obtain

$$F_{13} \approx 232.99914 \qquad \text{and} \qquad F_{14} \approx 377.00053,$$

and so $F_{13} = 233$ and $F_{14} = 377$.

From our discussion at the end of Section 4.2 it is clear that with the values of α and β defined by (4.29), any sequence of the form

$$U_n = A\alpha^n + B\beta^n$$

satisfies the recurrence relation $U_{n+1} = U_n + U_{n-1}$. In addition to the Fibonacci sequence, there is one other famous sequence belonging to this family, defined by

$$L_n = \alpha^n + \beta^n, \qquad (4.32)$$

which is the nth member of the *Lucas* sequence, in its Binet form. Thus

$$L_1 = \alpha + \beta = 1$$

and

$$L_2 = \alpha^2 + \beta^2 = (\alpha + \beta)^2 - 2\alpha\beta = 1 + 2 = 3,$$

on using the relations (4.30) for $\alpha + \beta$ and $\alpha\beta$. After 1 and 3, the next members of the Lucas sequence are 4, 7, 11, and 18. These numbers are named after François Lucas (1842–91).

Example 4.3.1 From the Binet forms (4.31) and (4.32) for the Fibonacci and Lucas numbers, we have

$$F_n L_n = \frac{\alpha^n - \beta^n}{\alpha - \beta} \cdot (\alpha^n + \beta^n) = \frac{\alpha^{2n} - \beta^{2n}}{\alpha - \beta} = F_{2n}. \quad \blacksquare$$

In Table 4.2, which gives the first few members of the Fibonacci and Lucas sequences, we observe that each Lucas number is the sum of two Fibonacci numbers, the one to the right and the one to the left in the line above, which is saying that

$$L_n = F_{n+1} + F_{n-1}.$$

We leave this result to be verified in Problem 4.3.2.

n	1	2	3	4	5	6	7	8	9	10	11	12
F_n	1	1	2	3	5	8	13	21	34	55	89	144
L_n	1	3	4	7	11	18	29	47	76	123	199	322

TABLE 4.2. The first few members of the Fibonacci and Lucas sequences.

Example 4.3.2 For all $n \geq 2$, we have

$$F_{n+1}^2 - F_n^2 = F_{n+2} F_{n-1}.$$

We can factorize the difference of the two squares to give

$$F_{n+1}^2 - F_n^2 = (F_{n+1} - F_n)(F_{n+1} + F_n)$$
$$= F_{n-1} F_{n+2},$$

on using the recurrence relation (4.27) to simplify each factor. $\blacksquare$

We can easily extend the Fibonacci and Lucas sequences so that F_n and L_n are defined for all integers n and not only for $n \geq 1$. It is implicit in our above discussion of sequences defined by recurrence relations that if we express a member of the sequence (U_n) in the form $U_n = A\alpha^n + B\beta^n$, its members will satisfy its recurrence relation for *all* values of n. Thus the Binet form (4.31) for the Fibonacci numbers yields $F_0 = 0$ and, for $n \geq 1$,

$$F_{-n} = \frac{\alpha^{-n} - \beta^{-n}}{\alpha - \beta} = \frac{\beta^n - \alpha^n}{(\alpha\beta)^n(\alpha - \beta)} = (-1)^{n+1}F_n,$$

since $\alpha\beta = -1$. Similarly, we find from the Binet form (4.32) that $L_0 = 2$ and $L_{-n} = (-1)^n L_n$ for $n \geq 1$. Table 4.3 shows the values of F_n and L_n for small values of $|n|$. Note how the recurrence relation holds throughout the whole table.

n	−5	−4	−3	−2	−1	0	1	2	3	4	5
F_n	5	−3	2	−1	1	0	1	1	2	3	5
L_n	−11	7	−4	3	−1	2	1	3	4	7	11

TABLE 4.3. Values of F_n and L_n for $-5 \leq n \leq 5$.

There is a very large number of interesting identities involving the Fibonacci and Lucas numbers, and a fine selection may be found in Vajda [53]. These can all be proved by replacing each Fibonacci or Lucas number by its Binet form and simplifying the identity algebraically, often using the fact that $\alpha\beta = -1$. Some yield to simple manipulation, using the recurrence relations, as in Example 4.3.2 above or in the following example.

Example 4.3.3 Consider the relation

$$F_{m+n} = F_{m+1}F_n + F_mF_{n-1}. \tag{4.33}$$

Although this may look a little complicated, it can be proved very easily by induction. It clearly holds for $n = 1$ and all m, since this simply gives F_{m+1} on both sides, and also for $n = 2$ and all m, since this merely gives $F_{m+2} = F_{m+1}+F_m$. Now let us assume that the relation holds for $1 \leq n \leq k$ and all m, for some $k \geq 2$. Thus, with $n = k - 1$ and $n = k$ we have

$$F_{m+k-1} = F_{m+1}F_{k-1} + F_mF_{k-2}$$

and

$$F_{m+k} = F_{m+1}F_k + F_mF_{k-1}.$$

On adding the last two equations "by columns," we immediately obtain

$$F_{m+k+1} = F_{m+1}F_{k+1} + F_mF_k.$$

Thus the relation holds for $n = k + 1$ and all m, and so by induction for $n \geq 1$ and all m. We can easily show further that it also holds for $n \leq 0$ and all m. ■

The identity in the last example enables us to prove an interesting number-theoretical result concerning the Fibonacci numbers.

Theorem 4.3.1 If m is divisible by n, then F_m is divisible by F_n.

Proof. Let us write $m = kn$, where k is a positive integer. Then the theorem is obviously true when $k = 1$. Let us assume that it holds for some $k \geq 1$. Then, putting $m = kn$ in (4.33), we have

$$F_{(k+1)n} = F_{kn+1}F_n + F_{kn}F_{n-1}. \tag{4.34}$$

Since by our assumption $F_n \mid F_{kn}$, we see that F_n divides the right side of (4.34), and so divides $F_{(k+1)n}$. Thus, by induction, $F_n \mid F_m$ when m is any multiple of n. ■

As we saw in Section 4.1, if we apply the Euclidean algorithm (4.1) to two consecutive members of the Fibonacci sequence, we find that their g.c.d. is 1. We will require this fact, that consecutive Fibonacci numbers have no common factor, in the proof of the following most beautiful result.

Theorem 4.3.2 For any positive integers m and n,

$$(F_m, F_n) = F_{(m,n)} \tag{4.35}$$

Proof. We will replace m, n by r_0, r_1 with $r_0 > r_1$ and apply the Euclidean algorithm (4.1) to r_0 and r_1, the first step being to write $r_0 = m_1 r_1 + r_2$. Thus we have

$$F_{r_0} = F_{m_1 r_1 + r_2},$$

and we may apply the identity (4.33) with $m = r_2$ and $n = m_1 r_1$ to give

$$F_{r_0} = F_{r_2 + m_1 r_1} = F_{r_2+1}F_{m_1 r_1} + F_{r_2}F_{m_1 r_1 - 1}. \tag{4.36}$$

From Theorem 4.3.1, F_{r_1} divides $F_{m_1 r_1}$, and thus it follows from (4.36) that

$$(F_{r_0}, F_{r_1}) = (F_{r_2}F_{m_1 r_1 - 1}, F_{r_1}).$$

Now, $F_{m_1 r_1 - 1}$ and $F_{m_1 r_1}$, being consecutive Fibonacci numbers, have no common factor, and so $F_{m_1 r_1 - 1}$ and F_{r_1} have no common factor, and we deduce that

$$(F_{r_0}, F_{r_1}) = (F_{r_2}, F_{r_1}).$$

Similarly, from the second step of the Euclidean algorithm (4.1) we can derive the relation

$$(F_{r_1}, F_{r_2}) = (F_{r_2}, F_{r_3}),$$

and finally we obtain

$$(F_{r_0}, F_{r_1}) = F_{r_k}.$$

Since $r_k = (r_0, r_1)$, this completes the proof. ■

Example 4.3.4 We find that $F_{28} = 317811$ and $F_{21} = 10946$. On carrying out the Euclidean algorithm, we obtain

$$317811 = 29 \cdot 10946 + 377,$$
$$10946 = 29 \cdot 377 + 13,$$
$$377 = 29 \cdot 13.$$

Thus

$$(F_{28}, F_{21}) = 13 = F_7 = F_{(28,21)}.$$

Is it just chance that in all three steps of the Euclidean algorithm above the multiplier is 29? Where have you seen the number 29 before? Can you find an identity that will explain the presence of the factor 29 in the above three equations obtained from the Euclidean algorithm? Can you forgive the author for badgering you with so many questions?   ■

We now state and prove a converse of Theorem 4.3.1.

Theorem 4.3.3 If F_m is divisible by F_n, then m is divisible by n.

Proof. If $F_n \mid F_m$, then

$$(F_m, F_n) = F_n,$$

and since by Theorem 4.3.2

$$(F_m, F_n) = F_{(m,n)},$$

we have

$$F_n = F_{(m,n)}.$$

Thus $n = (m, n)$, which implies that $n \mid m$.   ■

From Theorem 4.3.1 and its converse, Theorem 4.3.3, we see that F_m is divisible by F_n if and only if m is divisible by n.

Every positive integer n can be expressed uniquely as a sum of distinct nonconsecutive Fibonacci numbers. This result is called Zeckendorf's theorem and the sequence of Fibonacci numbers that add up to n is called the Zeckendorf representation of n. The theorem and the representation are named after the Belgian amateur mathematician Edouard Zeckendorf (1901–1983). The precise sequence used in the Zeckendorf theorem and representation is the Fibonacci sequence with F_1 deleted, the first few members being

$$1, \ 2, \ 3, \ 5, \ 8, \ 13, \ 21, \ \ldots .$$

Examples of Zeckendorf representations are

$$71 = 55 + 13 + 3,$$
$$100 = 89 + 8 + 3,$$
$$1111 = 987 + 89 + 34 + 1.$$

To construct the Zeckendorf representation of n we choose the largest Fibonacci number not greater than n, say F_{n_1}, and subtract it from n. Unless n is thereby reduced to zero, we then find the largest Fibonacci number not greater than $n - F_{n_1}$, say F_{n_2}, and subtract it, and so on. If n is reduced to zero after k steps, we obtain a Zeckendorf representation of the form

$$n = F_{n_1} + F_{n_2} + \cdots + F_{n_k},$$

where $n_1, n_2, \ldots, n_k$ is a decreasing sequence of positive integers. This representation cannot include two consecutive Fibonacci numbers, say F_m and F_{m-1}, for this would imply that their sum, F_{m+1}, or some larger Fibonacci number should have been chosen in place of F_m. A similar argument shows why the Fibonacci numbers in a Zeckendorf representation must all be different. The smallest integer whose Zeckendorf representation is the sum of k Fibonacci numbers is

$$F_2 + F_4 + \cdots + F_{2k} = F_{2k+1} - 1. \tag{4.37}$$

The latter result is analogous to a relation concerning binary representations: The smallest integer whose binary representation is the sum of k powers of 2 is $2^k - 1$. Given that Fibonacci numbers have been known to mathematics for some 800 years, it seems rather surprising that this property of them did not receive attention until relatively recently. Indeed, nothing appeared in print concerning the Zeckendorf representation until the middle of the twentieth century, with the publication of a paper of C. G. Lekkerkerker in 1952, although (see Kimberling [29]) Zeckendorf had a proof of his theorem by 1939. For $m \geq n \geq 2$, the Zeckendorf representation of $F_m F_n$ is (see Freitag and Phillips [18])

$$F_m F_n = \sum_{r=1}^{[n/2]} F_{m+n+2-4r} \tag{4.38}$$

for n even. When n is odd, we need to add one further term to the sum in (4.38). We add the term F_{m-n+1} when $m > n$ and the term F_2 when $m = n$. In the upper limit of the summation $[n/2]$ denotes the greatest integer not greater than $n/2$.

An amusing trivial "application" of the Zeckendorf representation is a method of converting miles into kilometres and vice versa without having to perform a multiplication. It relies on the coincidence that the number of kilometres in a mile (approximately 1.609) is close to the golden section,

$$\alpha = \frac{1}{2} \left(\sqrt{5} + 1 \right) \approx 1.618$$

and, from (4.31),

$$\lim_{n \to \infty} \frac{F_{n+1}}{F_n} = \alpha.$$

Thus to convert miles into kilometres we write down the (integer) number of miles in Zeckendorf form and replace each of the Fibonacci numbers by its successor. This will give the Zeckendorf form of the corresponding approximate number of kilometres. For example,

$$50 = 34 + 13 + 3 \text{ miles}$$

is approximately

$$55 + 21 + 5 = 81 \text{ kilometres,}$$

and 50 kilometres is approximately

$$21 + 8 + 2 = 31 \text{ miles.}$$

Problem 4.3.1 Use the Binet form (4.31) to show that

$$F_{n+1}F_{n-1} - F_n^2 = (-1)^n,$$

for $n \geq 2$, remembering that $\alpha\beta = -1$. Generalize this to give

$$F_{n+k}F_{n-k} - F_n^2 = (-1)^{n+k-1}F_k^2,$$

for $n \geq k + 1$. Find an identity analogous to the second of those above for the sequence (U_n) defined in Problem 4.2.6.

Problem 4.3.2 Verify that the identity $L_n = F_{n+1} + F_{n-1}$ holds for $n = 2$ and $n = 3$. Assume that it holds for all $n \leq k$, for some $k \geq 3$, and use the recurrence relations for the Fibonacci and Lucas numbers to deduce that the identity holds for $n = k + 1$ and so, by induction, holds for all $n \geq 2$. Next show that the identity holds for all integer values of n.

Problem 4.3.3 Show that the harmonic mean of F_n and L_n is F_{2n}/F_{n+1}.

Problem 4.3.4 $F_{n+1}^2 + F_n^2$ is always a Fibonacci number. Guess which Fibonacci number it is by checking the first few values of n, and verify your conjecture by using the Binet form (4.31).

Problem 4.3.5 Use induction to verify that each of the following identities holds for all $n \geq 1$:

$$F_1 + F_2 + \cdots + F_n = F_{n+2} - 1,$$
$$F_1 + F_3 + \cdots + F_{2n-1} = F_{2n},$$
$$F_2 + F_4 + \cdots + F_{2n} = F_{2n+1} - 1.$$

Problem 4.3.6 Verify by induction that

$$\sum_{r=0}^{n} F_r^2 = F_n F_{n+1}.$$

Problem 4.3.7 Show by induction that

$$L_{n+1} + L_{n-1} = 5F_n$$

for all $n \geq 2$ and use the relations $F_{-n} = (-1)^{n+1}F_n$ and $L_{-n} = (-1)^n L_n$ with $F_0 = 0$ and $L_0 = 2$ to show that the above identity holds for all integers n.

Problem 4.3.8 Show that $(L_{n+1}, L_n) = 1$.

Problem 4.3.9 Are there results analogous to Theorems 4.3.1 and 4.3.2 for the Lucas numbers?

Problem 4.3.10 Use the Binet form (4.32) to verify that

$$L_{2n} = L_n^2 + 2(-1)^{n-1} \quad \text{and} \quad L_{3n} = L_n^3 + 3(-1)^{n-1}L_n,$$

and hence show that

$$L_{3n} = L_n(L_{2n} + (-1)^{n-1}).$$

Problem 4.3.11 Use the Binet forms (4.31) and (4.32) to show that

$$F_{(n+1)k} = L_k F_{nk} + (-1)^{k+1}F_{(n-1)k}.$$

Problem 4.3.12 Verify, using the Binet form (4.32), that

$$L_{(n+1)k} = L_k L_{nk} + (-1)^{k+1}L_{(n-1)k}.$$

Problem 4.3.13 Show that the Fibonacci number F_n is divisible by 7 if and only if n is divisible by 8.

Problem 4.3.14 Which Fibonacci numbers are divisible by 47?

Problem 4.3.15 Observe that $L_1, L_2,$ and L_3 are respectively odd, odd, and even. Deduce from the recurrence relation for (L_n) that this pattern repeats and hence L_{3n-2} and L_{3n-1} are odd and L_{3n} is even, for all n.

4.4 Continued Fractions

Let us look again at the system of equations (4.1) that connects the sequence of positive integers $(r_j)_{j=0}^k$ generated by the Euclidean algorithm. The jth equation,

$$r_{j-1} = m_j r_j + r_{j+1},$$

may be recast in the form

$$\frac{r_{j-1}}{r_j} = m_j + 1 / \frac{r_j}{r_{j+1}}, \tag{4.39}$$

which holds for $1 \le j \le k - 1$, and the kth equation may be expressed as

$$\frac{r_{k-1}}{r_k} = m_k. \qquad (4.40)$$

Thus we have

$$\frac{r_0}{r_1} = m_1 + 1/\frac{r_1}{r_2} = m_1 + \frac{1}{m_2 + 1/\frac{r_2}{r_3}},$$

and so on. The full expansion of r_0/r_1 is usually written in the condensed form

$$\frac{r_0}{r_1} = m_1 + \frac{1}{m_2+} \frac{1}{m_3+} \cdots \frac{1}{m_k}, \qquad (4.41)$$

and is called a *continued fraction*. For instance, with $r_0 = 245$ and $r_1 = 161$ as in Example 4.1.3, we have

$$\frac{245}{161} = 1 + \frac{1}{1+} \frac{1}{1+} \frac{1}{11}.$$

Example 4.4.1 From the identity in Problem 4.3.11 we see that for k *odd*,

$$F_{(n+1)k} = L_k F_{nk} + F_{(n-1)k}$$

and thus

$$\frac{F_{(n+1)k}}{F_{nk}} = L_k + 1/\frac{F_{nk}}{F_{(n-1)k}},$$

for $n \ge 2$, and from Example 4.3.1 we have

$$\frac{F_{2k}}{F_k} = L_k.$$

Thus, for k odd, $F_{(n+1)k}/F_{nk}$ may be expressed as the continued fraction

$$\frac{F_{(n+1)k}}{F_{nk}} = L_k + \frac{1}{L_k+} \frac{1}{L_k+} \cdots \frac{1}{L_k}, \qquad (4.42)$$

where L_k occurs n times. For instance, with $n = 4$, $k = 3$ and $n = 3$, $k = 5$, we have

$$\frac{610}{144} = 4 + \frac{1}{4+} \frac{1}{4+} \frac{1}{4} \quad \text{and} \quad \frac{6765}{610} = 11 + \frac{1}{11+} \frac{1}{11},$$

respectively. With $k = 1$ in (4.42) we have the continued fraction

$$\frac{F_{n+1}}{F_n} = 1 + \frac{1}{1+} \frac{1}{1+} \cdots \frac{1}{1}, \qquad (4.43)$$

where there are $n - 1$ divisions.   ∎

Following Hardy and Wright [25], we will express a continued fraction using the notation

$$a_0 + \frac{1}{a_1+} \frac{1}{a_2+} \cdots \frac{1}{a_n}, \tag{4.44}$$

and we will sometimes write this continued fraction in the alternative form

$$[a_0, a_1, a_2, \ldots, a_n]. \tag{4.45}$$

Although there are other types of continued fractions, where the 1's in (4.44) may be replaced by some other quantities, we will be mainly concerned with those defined by (4.44). In order to develop the theory of continued fractions it is helpful to think of (4.44) and the equivalent form (4.45) as a *function* of the $n + 1$ real variables $a_0, a_1, \ldots, a_n$, although we initially chose these as positive integers. We have, for the first few values of n,

$$[a_0] = a_0, \qquad [a_0, a_1] = a_0 + \frac{1}{a_1} = \frac{a_1 a_0 + 1}{a_1},$$

and

$$[a_0, a_1, a_2] = a_0 + \frac{1}{a_1 + 1/a_2} = \frac{a_2 a_1 a_0 + a_2 + a_0}{a_2 a_1 + 1}.$$

In general, $[a_0, a_1, a_2, \ldots, a_k]$ is a rational function of $a_0, a_1, a_2, \ldots, a_k$, for $0 \le k \le n$. For $k = 1$ we have

$$[a_0, a_1, \ldots, a_k] = [a_0, a_1] = a_0 + \frac{1}{a_1}$$

and, for $k > 1$,

$$[a_0, a_1, \ldots, a_k] = [a_0, a_1, \ldots, a_{k-2}, a_{k-1} + 1/a_k]. \tag{4.46}$$

Note that we have $k + 1$ variables within the square brackets on the left of (4.46), and k variables within the brackets on the right, the kth variable being $a_{k-1} + 1/a_k$. When the a_j are positive integers, $a_{k-1} + 1/a_k$ is not a positive integer, except when $a_k = 1$. This is a sufficient reason for wishing not to restrict the definition of (4.44) and (4.45) to positive integer values of $a_0, a_1, \ldots, a_n$. We also have

$$[a_0, a_1, \ldots, a_k] = a_0 + \frac{1}{[a_1, a_2, \ldots, a_k]} = [a_0, [a_1, a_2, \ldots, a_k]]$$

for $1 \le k \le n$, and

$$[a_0, a_1, \ldots, a_k] = [a_0, a_1, \ldots, a_{j-1}, [a_j, a_{j+1}, \ldots, a_k]], \tag{4.47}$$

for $1 \le j < k \le n$.

We say that $[a_0, a_1, \ldots, a_k]$ is the kth *convergent* to the continued fraction $[a_0, a_1, \ldots, a_n]$. If the a_j are all real numbers, the most obvious way of computing these convergents is "from the bottom up," via a sequence of calculations that begins

$$[a_0, a_1, \ldots, a_k] = [a_0, \ldots, a_{k-2}, [a_{k-1}, a_k]] = [a_0, \ldots, a_{k-3}, [a_{k-2}, a_{k-1}, a_k]],$$

using (4.47) at each stage. Each step of the calculation reduces the number of parameters in the continued fraction by 1 until, after $k - 1$ steps, we obtain

$$[a_0, a_1, \ldots, a_k] = [a_0, [a_1, a_2, \ldots, a_k]].$$

Example 4.4.2 Let us evaluate the continued fraction $[1, 2, 1, 2, 1]$, using the "bottom up" process described above. We have

$$
\begin{aligned}
[1, 2, 1, 2, 1] &= [1, 2, 1, [2, 1]] = [1, 2, 1, 3] \\
&= [1, 2, [1, 3]] = [1, 2, 4/3] \\
&= [1, [2, 4/3]] = [1, 11/4]
\end{aligned}
$$

and thus

$$[1, 2, 1, 2, 1] = \frac{15}{11}. \quad \blacksquare$$

Although the "bottom up" process is easy to understand and easy to use, there is a much more subtle and more useful method that starts at the "top" of the continued fraction and works its way down, in the following way. Let us write

$$[a_0, a_1, \ldots, a_k] = \frac{p_k}{q_k},$$

for $0 \le k \le n$. We now show that the sequences (p_k) and (q_k) both satisfy the same second-order recurrence relation, but with different initial conditions, thus allowing us to compute $[a_0, a_1, \ldots, a_k]$ for $k = 0, 1, \ldots, n$ in turn.

Theorem 4.4.1 If p_k and q_k satisfy the same recurrence relation, defined by

$$p_k = a_k p_{k-1} + p_{k-2} \quad \text{and} \quad q_k = a_k q_{k-1} + q_{k-2}, \tag{4.48}$$

for $2 \le k \le n$, but with the different initial conditions

$$p_0 = a_0, \; p_1 = a_1 a_0 + 1 \quad \text{and} \quad q_0 = 1, \; q_1 = a_1,$$

then

$$[a_0, a_1, \ldots, a_k] = \frac{p_k}{q_k} \tag{4.49}$$

for $0 \le k \le n$.

Proof. It is clear that (4.49) holds for $k = 0$ and $k = 1$, since

$$[a_0] = \frac{a_0}{1} = \frac{p_0}{q_0}$$

and
$$[a_0, a_1] = \frac{a_1 a_0 + 1}{a_1} = \frac{p_1}{q_1}.$$

Now let us assume that (4.49) holds for all $k \leq m$ for some m, where $1 \leq m < n$. Thus (4.49) applies to continued fractions that have no more than $m + 1$ parameters. Let us write

$$[a_0, a_1, \ldots, a_m, a_{m+1}] = [a_0, \ldots, a_{m-1}, a_m + 1/a_{m+1}], \qquad (4.50)$$

on using (4.46). Since the continued fraction on the right of (4.50) has $m+1$ parameters, then by our above assumption, it is expressible as a quotient of the form P/Q, where, using (4.48),

$$\frac{P}{Q} = \frac{(a_m + 1/a_{m+1})p_{m-1} + p_{m-2}}{(a_m + 1/a_{m+1})q_{m-1} + q_{m-2}}.$$

The latter equation is perhaps the cleverest line not only in this proof, but in any of the proofs in this book. Thus

$$\begin{aligned}[a_0, a_1, \ldots, a_m, a_{m+1}] &= \frac{(a_m + 1/a_{m+1})p_{m-1} + p_{m-2}}{(a_m + 1/a_{m+1})q_{m-1} + q_{m-2}} \\ &= \frac{(a_{m+1}a_m + 1)p_{m-1} + a_{m+1}p_{m-2}}{(a_{m+1}a_m + 1)q_{m-1} + a_{m+1}q_{m-2}} \\ &= \frac{a_{m+1}(a_m p_{m-1} + p_{m-2}) + p_{m-1}}{a_{m+1}(a_m q_{m-1} + q_{m-2}) + q_{m-1}}.\end{aligned}$$

We now use the recurrence relations (4.48) and obtain

$$[a_0, a_1, \ldots, a_m, a_{m+1}] = \frac{a_{m+1}p_m + p_{m-1}}{a_{m+1}q_m + q_{m-1}} = \frac{p_{m+1}}{q_{m+1}},$$

and this completes the proof by induction.   ■

It is worth making a minor change to the above algorithm for computing the convergents to a continued fraction. We simplify the initial values by introducing two "artificial" variables p_{-1} and q_{-1}, defined by

$$p_{-1} = 1 \quad \text{and} \quad q_{-1} = 0, \quad \text{with} \quad p_0 = a_0 \quad \text{and} \quad q_0 = 1 \qquad (4.51)$$

as before, and then compute p_k and q_k for $k = 1$ to n, using (4.48).

Example 4.4.3 Let us evaluate the continued fraction $[1, 2, 1, 2, 1, 2, 1]$. We use the recurrence relations (4.48), with the initial conditions given by (4.51). The calculations are set out in Table 4.4, where we find that

$$[1, 2, 1, 2, 1, 2, 1] = \frac{56}{41}.   ■$$

n	-1	0	1	2	3	4	5	6
a_n	–	1	2	1	2	1	2	1
p_n	1	1	3	4	11	15	41	56
q_n	0	1	2	3	8	11	30	41
p_n/q_n	–	1	1.5	1.3333	1.3750	1.3636	1.3667	1.3659

TABLE 4.4. Convergents to the continued fraction $[1, 2, 1, 2, 1, 2, 1]$.

In Table 4.4 the quotients p_n/q_n are given in decimal form, rounded to four figures, so that we can compare them easily. There is a pattern in the convergents that, as we will see, holds for all continued fractions defined by (4.44) in which a_j is positive for $j \geq 1$. The even-order convergents, beginning with p_0/q_0, are all less than or equal to the value of the continued fraction and are increasing. The odd-order convergents, beginning with p_1/q_1, are all greater than or equal to the value of the continued fraction and are decreasing. Example 4.4.3 suggests another line of enquiry. Table 4.4 shows that there is very little difference in the values of the final convergent $[1, 2, 1, 2, 1, 2, 1]$ and the second to last one $[1, 2, 1, 2, 1, 2]$. What happens if we keep adding more parameters to a continued fraction? Does the limit

$$\lim_{n \to \infty} [a_0, a_1, \ldots, a_n]$$

exist for any choice of positive a_j? We will show presently that this limit always exists. Meanwhile, let us assume that the infinite continued fraction $[1, 2, 1, 2, \ldots]$ does have a limit, and that the limit is x. Then

$$[1, 2, 1, 2, \ldots] = x = [1, 2, x] = [1, 2 + 1/x] = 1 + \frac{x}{2x + 1}.$$

Thus x satisfies the quadratic equation $2x^2 - 2x - 1 = 0$, whose sole *positive* solution gives

$$[1, 2, 1, 2, \ldots] = \frac{1}{2}\left(1 + \sqrt{3}\right) \approx 1.366025,$$

and if we extend Table 4.4 to compute further convergents of the infinite continued fraction $[1, 2, 1, 2, \ldots]$, we find that

$$\frac{p_{10}}{q_{10}} = \frac{780}{571} \approx 1.366025,$$

which certainly supports the case for the existence of this particular infinite continued fraction.

Let us now return to our investigation of the general case, writing

$$p_k q_{k-1} - p_{k-1} q_k = (a_k p_{k-1} + p_{k-2}) q_{k-1} - p_{k-1}(a_k q_{k-1} + q_{k-2})$$
$$= -(p_{k-1} q_{k-2} - p_{k-2} q_{k-1}).$$

We can use this equation repeatedly with k replaced in turn by $k-1$, $k-2$, and so on, giving

$$\begin{aligned}
p_k q_{k-1} - p_{k-1} q_k &= (-1)(p_{k-1} q_{k-2} - p_{k-2} q_{k-1}) \\
&= (-1)^2 (p_{k-2} q_{k-3} - p_{k-3} q_{k-2}) \\
&= \cdots = (-1)^k (p_0 q_{-1} - p_{-1} q_0).
\end{aligned}$$

Since from (4.51) we have $p_{-1} = 1$, $q_{-1} = 0$, $p_0 = a_0$, and $q_0 = 1$, we find that $p_0 q_{-1} - p_{-1} q_0 = -1$, and thus we obtain

$$p_k q_{k-1} - p_{k-1} q_k = (-1)^{k+1}, \tag{4.52}$$

for $k \geq 0$. Another inspection of Table 4.4 is called for, to verify that its entries are consistent with the beautiful relation (4.52). Then, on dividing (4.52) throughout by $q_k q_{k-1}$, we obtain the following result.

Theorem 4.4.2 The difference of consecutive convergents to a continued fraction satisfies

$$\frac{p_k}{q_k} - \frac{p_{k-1}}{q_{k-1}} = \frac{(-1)^{k+1}}{q_k q_{k-1}}, \quad k \geq 1. \quad \blacksquare \tag{4.53}$$

Our observations about even and odd convergents in Table 4.4 prompt us to look at

$$\begin{aligned}
p_k q_{k-2} - p_{k-2} q_k &= (a_k p_{k-1} + p_{k-2}) q_{k-2} - p_{k-2}(a_k q_{k-1} + q_{k-2}) \\
&= a_k(p_{k-1} q_{k-2} - p_{k-2} q_{k-1}),
\end{aligned}$$

and combining this with (4.52), we derive its companion formula

$$p_k q_{k-2} - p_{k-2} q_k = (-1)^k a_k. \tag{4.54}$$

From (4.54) we easily derive (4.55) below, and if $a_j > 0$ for $j \geq 1$, then $q_k > 0$ for all $k \geq 0$, and we have the following theorem.

Theorem 4.4.3 For a given continued fraction $[a_0, a_1, \ldots, a_n]$, where the a_j are positive for $j \geq 1$, the difference between consecutive *even* convergents, or consecutive *odd* convergents, satisfies

$$\frac{p_k}{q_k} - \frac{p_{k-2}}{q_{k-2}} = \frac{(-1)^k a_k}{q_k q_{k-2}}, \quad k \geq 2. \tag{4.55}$$

The sequence of even-order convergents is monotonic increasing, and the sequence of odd-order convergents is monotonic decreasing. $\quad \blacksquare$

For the remainder of this section we will take the a_j to be positive *integers*, for $j \geq 1$. In this case, a continued fraction of the form (4.44), and also the limiting form of (4.44) as $n \to \infty$, is called *simple*. We note from Theorem 4.4.2 that in order to find out how close the kth and $(k-1)$th convergents are to each other, we need to be able to estimate the sizes of their denominators q_k and q_{k-1}. We can easily obtain lower bounds for these, which we now state and justify.

Theorem 4.4.4 The denominators in the convergents to a continued fraction $[a_0, a_1, \ldots, a_n]$, where the a_j are positive integers, satisfy

$$q_k \geq F_{k+1} \tag{4.56}$$

for all $k \geq 0$ and

$$q_k > \alpha^{k-1} \tag{4.57}$$

for $k \geq 2$, where $\alpha = \frac{1}{2}(1 + \sqrt{5})$.

Proof. Since $q_0 = 1 = F_1$ and $q_1 = a_1 \geq 1 = F_2$, (4.56) holds for $k = 0$ and $k = 1$. Assume that it holds for all $j \leq k$, for some $k \geq 1$. Then from the recurrence relation for (q_n) in (4.48) we may write

$$q_{k+1} = a_{k+1}q_k + q_{k-1} \geq q_k + q_{k-1} \geq F_{k+1} + F_k = F_{k+2},$$

and so (4.56) holds when k is replaced by $k + 1$ and hence, by induction, holds for all $k \geq 0$. Finally, (4.57) follows from (4.8). $\blacksquare$

One obvious consequence of this theorem is that the differences of consecutive convergents of an infinite continued fraction tend to zero. For from (4.53) and (4.57),

$$\left| \frac{p_k}{q_k} - \frac{p_{k-1}}{q_{k-1}} \right| = \frac{1}{q_k q_{k-1}} < \frac{1}{\alpha^{k-1} \cdot \alpha^{k-2}} = \frac{1}{\alpha^{2k-3}}$$

for $k \geq 3$, where $\alpha = (1 + \sqrt{5})/2$. Since $\alpha > 1$, $1/\alpha^{2k-3} \to 0$ as $k \to \infty$, and so

$$\left| \frac{p_k}{q_k} - \frac{p_{k-1}}{q_{k-1}} \right| \to 0 \qquad \text{as} \qquad k \to \infty. \tag{4.58}$$

Having proved that the sequence of even-order convergents and the sequence of odd-order convergents are both monotonic, we can "connect" these two sequences via Theorem 4.4.2: if we replace k by $2k + 1$ in (4.53), we see that

$$\frac{p_{2k+1}}{q_{2k+1}} - \frac{p_{2k}}{q_{2k}} > 0.$$

On combining this with the monotonicity of the "even" and "odd" sequences, we obtain the chain of inequalities

$$\frac{p_0}{q_0} < \frac{p_2}{q_2} < \cdots < \frac{p_{2k}}{q_{2k}} < \frac{p_{2k+1}}{q_{2k+1}} < \cdots < \frac{p_3}{q_3} < \frac{p_1}{q_1}, \tag{4.59}$$

and we note that all members of the "even" sequence are to the left of all members of the "odd" sequence. Thus, for an infinite continued fraction, the "even" sequence, being monotonic increasing and bounded above (by p_1/q_1, for example), has a limit L_E. Likewise, the "odd" sequence, being monotonic decreasing and bounded below (by p_0/q_0, for example), has a limit L_O. It is not hard to see that the two limits must be equal. For

$$L_O - L_E = \left(L_O - \frac{p_{2k+1}}{q_{2k+1}} \right) + \left(\frac{p_{2k}}{q_{2k}} - L_E \right) + \left(\frac{p_{2k+1}}{q_{2k+1}} - \frac{p_{2k}}{q_{2k}} \right). \tag{4.60}$$

The modulus of each of the three terms on the right of (4.60) may be made as small as we please by taking k sufficiently large; for the first and second terms, this follows from the definitions of L_O and L_E, and (4.58) justifies this statement for the third term. Thus $L_O - L_E$ must be zero. Let us therefore write

$$L_O = L_E = L,$$

and we have

$$\frac{p_{2k}}{q_{2k}} \le L \le \frac{p_{2k+1}}{q_{2k+1}} \tag{4.61}$$

for all $k \ge 0$. We also note that each convergent p_k/q_k is in its lowest terms, meaning that p_k and q_k have no common factor. For if $d \mid p_k$ and $d \mid q_k$, then

$$d \mid (p_k q_{k-1} - p_{k-1} q_k),$$

and in view of (4.52), this implies that $d = 1$.

Since from (4.61) the value of a continued fraction lies between any two consecutive convergents, we have

$$\left| L - \frac{p_k}{q_k} \right| < \left| \frac{p_{k+1}}{q_{k+1}} - \frac{p_k}{q_k} \right| = \frac{1}{q_{k+1} q_k}. \tag{4.62}$$

This is called an a posteriori error bound, meaning that it is obtained *after* the calculations have been carried out.

Example 4.4.4 Let us apply the inequality (4.62) to the data in Example 4.4.3, with $k = 6$. We need to extend Table 4.4, since we require the value of q_7, which is

$$q_7 = 2 \cdot 41 + 30 = 112.$$

Thus we see from (4.62) that the limit L of the infinite continued fraction $[1, 2, 1, 2, \dots]$ satisfies the inequalities

$$\left| L - \frac{56}{41} \right| < \frac{1}{112 \cdot 41} < 0.000218.$$

Since $L = (1 + \sqrt{3})/2$ in this case, we can compare the above upper bound with the actual error, which is

$$\left| L - \frac{56}{41} \right| \approx 0.000172. \quad \blacksquare$$

As we remarked earlier, there are other types of continued fractions, for example the continued fraction in (1.74), where the 1's in (4.44) are replaced by some other quantities. We now meander from the main path in this section to give another example of a continued fraction that is not of the form (4.44), and will give further such examples in the next section.

Example 4.4.5 Let us express $\sqrt{13}$ as a continued fraction. Since $\sqrt{13}$ lies between 3 and 4, we write

$$\sqrt{13} = 3 + (\sqrt{13} - 3) = 3 + \frac{(\sqrt{13} + 3)(\sqrt{13} - 3)}{(\sqrt{13} + 3)},$$

and so

$$\sqrt{13} = 3 + \frac{4}{\sqrt{13} + 3} = 3 + \frac{4}{6 + (\sqrt{13} - 3)}.$$

Since

$$6 + (\sqrt{13} - 3) = 6 + \frac{4}{\sqrt{13} + 3},$$

we have

$$\sqrt{13} = 3 + \frac{4}{6+} \frac{4}{6+} \cdots .$$

This continued fraction was first derived by Rafaello Bombelli (1526–73), who is best known for his work on the solution of the cubic equation. ∎

We will now resume our discussion of *simple* continued fractions, those with 1's in the numerators. The infinite continued fraction $[1, 2, 1, 2, \ldots]$ discussed in Example 4.4.3 is called a *periodic continued fraction*. In general, this is an infinite continued fraction $[a_0, a_1, a_2, \ldots]$ in which

$$a_j = a_{j+k} \tag{4.63}$$

for some fixed integer $k > 1$ and all $j \geq N$, for some fixed integer $N \geq 0$. This implies that from a_N onwards, the parameters a_j repeat in blocks of k. We write such a continued fraction in the succinct form

$$[a_0, a_1, \ldots, a_{N-1}, \overline{a_N, a_{N+1}, \ldots, a_{N+k-1}}],$$

where the bar indicates the part to be repeated indefinitely. For example,

$$[1, 2, 1, 2, 1, 2, \ldots] = [\overline{1, 2}]$$

and

$$[3, 1, 4, 1, 5, 9, 1, 2, 1, 2, 1, 2, \ldots] = [3, 1, 4, 1, 5, 9, \overline{1, 2}].$$

In our analysis following Example 4.4.3 we evaluated $[\overline{1, 2}]$ by solving a quadratic equation. Let us now explore how to evaluate a general periodic continued fraction. We begin with

$$x = [a_0, a_1, \ldots, a_{N-1}, \overline{a_N, a_{N+1}, \ldots, a_{N+k-1}}], \tag{4.64}$$

and write

$$b_N = [\overline{a_N, a_{N+1}, \ldots, a_{N+k-1}}] \tag{4.65}$$

to denote the "periodic part" of x. Thus we have

$$b_N = [a_N, a_{N+1}, \ldots, a_{N+k-1}, b_N]. \tag{4.66}$$

Now we make use of the convergents to a continued fraction and express

$$[a_N, a_{N+1}, \ldots, a_{N+k-1}] = \frac{P_1}{Q_1}$$

and

$$[a_N, a_{N+1}, \ldots, a_{N+k-2}] = \frac{P_0}{Q_0},$$

assuming that $k \geq 2$. Then, since the continued fractions in the last three equations are three consecutive convergents, it follows from the recurrence relations (4.48) that

$$b_N = \frac{P_1 b_N + P_0}{Q_1 b_N + Q_0}. \tag{4.67}$$

Thus b_N satisfies the quadratic equation

$$Q_1 b_N^2 + (Q_0 - P_1)b_N - P_0 = 0, \tag{4.68}$$

which has the two roots

$$b_N = \frac{P_1 - Q_0 \pm ((P_1 - Q_0)^2 + 4P_0 Q_1)^{1/2}}{2Q_1}.$$

Since P_0 and Q_1 are both positive and

$$(P_1 - Q_0)^2 + 4P_0 Q_1 > (P_1 - Q_0)^2,$$

we observe that one root is positive and one is negative. Clearly, we need to choose the positive root. Finally, we have from (4.64) and (4.65) that

$$x = [a_0, a_1, \ldots, a_{N-1}, b_N],$$

and we use the recurrence relations (4.48) once more to give

$$x = \frac{p_{N-1} b_N + p_{N-2}}{q_{N-1} b_N + q_{N-2}}, \tag{4.69}$$

provided that $N \geq 2$. We now summarize the process described above in the following theorem.

Theorem 4.4.5 Let p_{N-2}/q_{N-2} and p_{N-1}/q_{N-1} denote the last two convergents of the continued fraction $[a_0, a_1, \ldots, a_{N-1}]$, where $N \geq 2$. Then

$$[a_0, a_1, \ldots, a_{N-1}, \overline{a_N, a_{N+1}, \ldots, a_{N+k-1}}] = \frac{p_{N-1} b_N + p_{N-2}}{q_{N-1} b_N + q_{N-2}},$$

where b_N is the positive root of the quadratic equation

$$b_N = \frac{P_1 b_N + P_0}{Q_1 b_N + Q_0} \tag{4.70}$$

and P_0/Q_0, P_1/Q_1 are the last two convergents of the continued fraction $[a_N, a_{N+1}, \ldots, a_{N+k-1}]$. ∎

Thus we have a simple procedure for evaluating any periodic continued fraction. It is not worth remembering equation (4.70) for evaluating b_N, since we can derive it when we need it, as in Example 4.4.6 below. But before leaving Theorem 4.4.5, we deduce from it the following algebraic property of periodic continued fractions.

Theorem 4.4.6 A periodic continued fraction is a root of a quadratic equation with integer coefficients.

Proof. We can rearrange (4.69) to express b_N in terms of x:

$$b_N = \frac{p_{N-2} - q_{N-2}x}{q_{N-1}x - p_{N-1}}.$$

If we now substitute this value for b_N into (4.68) and multiply throughout by $(q_{N-1}x - p_{N-1})^2$ to clear the denominators, we obtain a quadratic equation in x with integer coefficients. ∎

Example 4.4.6 Let us evaluate the periodic continued fraction

$$x = [2, \overline{1, 1, 1, 4}].$$

First we compute the convergents to the continued fraction $[1, 1, 1, 4]$, which are $1/1$, $2/1$, $3/2$ and $14/9$, the latter two being required for our next step. For we now obtain

$$y = [\overline{1, 1, 1, 4}] = [1, 1, 1, 4, y] = \frac{14y + 3}{9y + 2}$$

in the same way we obtained (4.67), by using the recurrence relations (4.48). This gives a quadratic equation for y, and we need to choose the positive solution, $y = (2 + \sqrt{7})/3$. Finally, we write

$$x = [2, y] = 2 + \frac{1}{y} = 2 + \frac{3}{\sqrt{7} + 2},$$

from which we obtain

$$x = 2 + \frac{3(\sqrt{7} - 2)}{(\sqrt{7} - 2)(\sqrt{7} + 2)} = 2 + (\sqrt{7} - 2),$$

and so

$$[2, \overline{1, 1, 1, 4}] = \sqrt{7}. \quad ∎$$

There is a converse to Theorem 4.4.6, that an infinite continued fraction that represents a root of a quadratic equation must be periodic. Hardy and Wright [25] give a proof of this result, which they attribute to J. L. Lagrange. Thus, unless n is a square, $\sqrt{n}$ can be expressed as a periodic continued fraction.

Example 4.4.7 Let us obtain the continued fraction for $\sqrt{3}$. We begin by writing $\sqrt{3}$ as a positive integer plus a fractional part,

$$\sqrt{3} = 1 + (\sqrt{3} - 1) = 1 + \frac{(\sqrt{3}+1)(\sqrt{3}-1)}{(\sqrt{3}+1)}.$$

Thus

$$\sqrt{3} = 1 + \frac{2}{\sqrt{3}+1} = 1 + \frac{1}{\frac{1}{2}(\sqrt{3}+1)}, \qquad (4.71)$$

and so

$$\sqrt{3} + 1 = 2 + \frac{2}{\sqrt{3}+1}$$

and, on dividing by 2,

$$\frac{1}{2}(\sqrt{3}+1) = 1 + \frac{1}{\sqrt{3}+1}. \qquad (4.72)$$

We see from (4.71) and (4.72) that

$$\sqrt{3} = [1, 1, \sqrt{3}+1],$$

from which we deduce that

$$\sqrt{3} + 1 = [2, 1, \sqrt{3}+1] = [\overline{2,1}],$$

and we see from the last two equations that

$$\sqrt{3} = [1, \overline{1,2}]. \quad \blacksquare$$

Problem 4.4.1 Find the continued fraction for $41/29$.

Problem 4.4.2 Use the results in Problems 4.3.12 and 4.3.15 and the first equation in Problem 4.3.10 to show that if k is an odd multiple of 3, then L_k is even and

$$\frac{L_{(n+1)k}}{L_{nk}} = \left[L_k, L_k, \ldots, L_k, \frac{1}{2}L_k \right],$$

where the above simple continued fraction has $n+1$ parameters. How must the above continued fraction be modified so that it remains simple (that is, with all parameters positive integers) when k is odd and is not a multiple of 3?

Problem 4.4.3 Evaluate the continued fraction $[1, 2, 3, 4, 5, 6]$ by using the recurrence relations (4.48), with initial values given by (4.51). As a check on your result, evaluate the same continued fraction by the "bottom up" method that was used in Example 4.4.2.

Problem 4.4.4 Find the periodic continued fraction for $\sqrt{2}$.

Problem 4.4.5 In Example 4.4.5 we found a continued fraction for $\sqrt{13}$. Show that the "standard" simple continued fraction for $\sqrt{13}$, where the numerators are all 1's, is

$$\sqrt{13} = [3, \overline{1, 1, 1, 1, 6}].$$

Problem 4.4.6 Evaluate the periodic continued fraction $[1, \overline{2, 3}]$.

Problem 4.4.7 Show that $[n, \overline{n, 2n}] = (n^2 + 2)^{1/2}$ and so write down a continued fraction for $\sqrt{11}$.

Problem 4.4.8 Deduce from the result in Problem 4.3.10 that

$$L_{4n+2} = L_{2n+1}^2 + 2$$

and use the result in Problem 4.4.7 to show that

$$\sqrt{L_{4n+2}} = [L_{2n+1}, \overline{L_{2n+1}, 2L_{2n+1}}].$$

Problem 4.4.9 If $x = [\overline{a, b}]$, show that

$$x = \frac{1}{2}\left(a + \sqrt{a^2 + \frac{4a}{b}}\right).$$

Problem 4.4.10 The continued fraction for $\sqrt{19}$ has the form $[4, \overline{a}]$, where a has six parameters. Find this continued fraction.

Problem 4.4.11 Obtain a periodic continued fraction for $\sqrt{n^2 + 1}$.

Problem 4.4.12 Show that $\sqrt{n(n + 2)} = [n, \overline{1, 2n}]$.

Problem 4.4.13 Verify that for $n \geq 2$,

$$\sqrt{n^2 + 2n - 1} = [n, \overline{1, n - 1, 1, 2n}].$$

Problem 4.4.14 Show that if $a^2 + b > 0$, then

$$\sqrt{a^2 + b} = a + \frac{b}{2a+} \frac{b}{2a+} \cdots .$$

Problem 4.4.15 Verify that the fractions $\frac{265}{153}$ and $\frac{1351}{780}$, which (see (1.6)) were used by Archimedes as his lower and upper bounds for $\sqrt{3}$, are even- and odd-order convergents to $[1, \overline{1, 2}]$, the simple continued fraction for $\sqrt{3}$. Given his choice of lower bound, which convergent might we have expected Archimedes to use for his upper bound?

4.5   Historical Notes

In the last section we quoted the continued fraction for $\sqrt{13}$, which was obtained by Bombelli. We conclude this chapter by citing some other noteworthy continued fractions, making one further comment and quoting a relatively more recent result. William, Viscount Brouncker (1620–84), the first President of the Royal Society, derived the following continued fraction involving π,

$$\frac{4}{\pi} = 1 + \frac{1^2}{2+} \frac{3^2}{2+} \frac{5^2}{2+} \frac{7^2}{2+} \cdots ,$$

taking as his starting point the infinite product

$$\frac{\pi}{2} = \frac{2 \cdot 2 \cdot 4 \cdot 4 \cdot 6 \cdot 6 \cdot 8 \cdot 8}{1 \cdot 3 \cdot 3 \cdot 5 \cdot 5 \cdot 7 \cdot 7 \cdot 9} \cdots , \tag{4.73}$$

which is due to John Wallis (1616–1703).

Leonhard Euler derived a continued fraction for e,

$$e = 1 + [1, 1, 2, 1, 1, 4, 1, 1, 6, 1, 1, 8, \ldots],$$

which we quoted in Chapter 2, and also the following continued fractions related to e,

$$\frac{e - 1}{e + 1} = [0, 2, 6, 10, 14, 18, \ldots] \tag{4.74}$$

and

$$\frac{1}{2}(e - 1) = [0, 1, 6, 10, 14, 18, \cdots].$$

Example 4.5.1 In (4.74), using the values $a_0 = 0$, $a_1 = 2$, up to $a_8 = 30$ and the recurrence relations in (4.48), we find from the eighth convergent to the continued fraction in (4.74) that

$$\frac{e - 1}{e + 1} \approx \frac{p_8}{q_8} = \frac{268163352}{580293001},$$

so that

$$e \approx \frac{q_8 + p_8}{q_8 - p_8} = \frac{848456353}{312129649}.$$

For comparison, we have

$$e = 2.71828\ 18284\ 59045\ 23536 \ldots ,$$

$$\frac{q_8 + p_8}{q_8 - p_8} = 2.71828\ 18284\ 59045\ 23475 \ldots ,$$

so that the error is less than 10^{-18}.   ∎

J. H. Lambert generalized Euler's formula (4.74) to give

$$\frac{e^x - 1}{e^x + 1} = [0, 2/x, 6/x, 10/x, 14/x, 18/x, \ldots].$$

Lambert also found the first few coefficients a_j for the simple continued fraction for π,

$$\pi = [3, 7, 15, 1, 292, 1, 1, 1, 2, 1, 3, 1, 14, 2, 1, 1, 2, 2, 2, 2, 1, \ldots], \qquad (4.75)$$

the first few convergents being

$$\frac{3}{1}, \quad \frac{22}{7}, \quad \frac{333}{106}, \quad \frac{355}{113}, \quad \frac{103993}{33102}, \quad \frac{104348}{33215}, \ldots$$

The convergent $355/113$ is the approximation to π obtained by Zǔ Chōngzhī (429–500), with an error in the seventh decimal place. This is one of the highlights of early Chinese mathematics. Comparing the last of the convergents given above with π, we have

$$\frac{104348}{33215} \approx 3.14159\ 26539,$$

$$\pi \approx 3.14159\ 26535.$$

This continued fraction for π has no regular pattern, unlike the continued fraction for e given above. Lambert found some other notable continued fractions, including

$$\log(1 + x) = \frac{x}{1+} \ \frac{1^2 x}{2+} \ \frac{1^2 x}{3+} \ \frac{2^2 x}{4+} \ \frac{2^2 x}{5+} \ \frac{3^2 x}{6+} \ \frac{3^2 x}{7+} \cdots, \qquad |x| < 1,$$

and

$$\tan^{-1} x = \frac{x}{1+} \ \frac{x^2}{3+} \ \frac{4x^2}{5+} \ \frac{9x^2}{7+} \ \frac{16x^2}{9+} \cdots, \qquad |x| < 1,$$

which were both also obtained by J. L. Lagrange, and

$$\tan x = \frac{x}{1-} \ \frac{x^2}{3-} \ \frac{x^2}{5-} \ \frac{x^2}{7-} \cdots.$$

The above continued fraction for $\tan x$ is complemented by the following one due to C. F. Gauss for the hyperbolic tangent,

$$\tanh x = \frac{x}{1+} \ \frac{x^2}{3+} \ \frac{x^2}{5+} \ \frac{x^2}{7+} \cdots.$$

Finally, we quote an amazing continued fraction discovered independently by P. S. Laplace (1749–1827) and A. M. Legendre (1752–1833),

$$\int_0^x e^{-t^2} dt = \frac{\sqrt{\pi}}{2} - \frac{\frac{1}{2} e^{-x^2}}{x+} \ \frac{1}{2x+} \ \frac{2}{x+} \ \frac{3}{2x+} \ \frac{4}{x+} \cdots, \qquad x > 0.$$

In the continued fraction (4.75) for π, there are 9 occurrences of 1 amongst the 20 numbers $a_1 = 7, a_2 = 15, \ldots, a_{20} = 1$. This statistic is worth pursuing. Let us begin with a positive real number x_0 and compute $x_1, x_2, \ldots$ from

$$x_0 = a_0 + \frac{1}{x_1},$$

$$x_1 = a_1 + \frac{1}{x_2},$$

and so on, where a_j is the *integer part* of x_j. Thus, if x_0 has an *infinite* continued fraction, it follows that $0 < 1/x_j < 1$ for all j and

$$x_0 = [a_0, a_1, a_2, \ldots].$$

The parameter a_j will have the value k if and only if

$$\frac{1}{k+1} < \frac{1}{x_j} < \frac{1}{k}. \tag{4.76}$$

We cannot have an *equality* in (4.76), for this would imply that the continued fraction for x_0 is finite. Now, if x_0 is irrational and is not the root of a quadratic equation with integer coefficients, it follows from Theorem 4.4.6 that its simple continued fraction is not periodic. Thus we might expect that the fractions $1/x_j$ are randomly distributed in the interval $[0, 1]$, and so the probability that a given x_j satisfies the inequalities (4.76) is just the size of the interval $[1/(k+1), 1/k]$, which is

$$\frac{1}{k} - \frac{1}{k+1} = \frac{1}{k(k+1)} \tag{4.77}$$

Note that the word "expect" used in the last sentence is, like "hope" and "pray," not part of the formal language of mathematics, and so this is not a *proof*. However, the application of this nonrigorous argument to (4.77) strongly suggests that the probability of a given a_j having the value 1 is $\frac{1}{2}$, with probabilities of $\frac{1}{6}$ and $\frac{1}{12}$ that it has the values 2 and 3, respectively, and in general a probability of $\frac{1}{k(k+1)}$ that it has the value k.

We conclude this section by quoting a further result concerning the growth of the denominators of the convergents of continued fractions. Let us recall Theorem 4.4.4, where we showed that given an infinite continued fraction $[a_0, a_1, \ldots]$, where the a_j are all positive integers, the sequence of denominators (q_n) of its convergents grows exponentially, at least as fast as the Fibonacci sequence. The denominator of the nth convergent of the continued fraction $[1, 1, \ldots]$ is $q_n = F_{n+1}$, and we have in this case

$$\lim_{n \to \infty} q_n^{1/n} = \lim_{n \to \infty} (F_{n+1})^{1/n} = \frac{1}{2}\left(1 + \sqrt{5}\right),$$

the golden section, whose value is approximately 1.618. A. Ya. Khinchin (1894–1959) derived a much deeper and rather surprising result on the growth of (q_n). He showed (see Rockett and Szüsz [47]) that for *almost all* continued fractions $[a_0, a_1, \ldots]$, where the a_j are all positive integers,

$$\lim_{n \to \infty} q_n^{1/n} = e^{\gamma},$$

with

$$\gamma = \frac{\pi^2}{12 \log 2}.$$

We note that $e^{\gamma} \approx 3.276$, which is about twice as large as the golden section, the limit obtained for the "Fibonacci" case.

Problem 4.5.1 Let

$$I_j = \frac{2}{\pi} \int_0^{\pi/2} \sin^j \theta \, d\theta.$$

Deduce from

$$\sin^{2j+1} x \le \sin^{2j} x \le \sin^{2j-1} x, \quad 0 \le x \le \frac{1}{2}\pi,$$

that

$$I_{2j+1} \le I_{2j} \le I_{2j-1} = \frac{2j+1}{2j} I_{2j+1}$$

for $j \ge 1$, the last step following from the result in Problem 1.4.3. Hence derive the inequalities

$$1 \le \frac{I_{2j}}{I_{2j+1}} \le 1 + \frac{1}{2j}$$

and thus obtain the limit

$$\lim_{j \to \infty} \frac{I_{2j}}{I_{2j+1}} = 1.$$

Problem 4.5.2 With the notation of Problem 4.5.1, show that

$$I_{2j+1} = \left(\frac{2j}{2j+1} \right) \left(\frac{2j-2}{2j-1} \right) \cdots \left(\frac{2}{3} \right) \frac{2}{\pi}$$

and combine this with the expression for I_{2j} given in Problem 1.4.3 and the result of Problem 4.5.1 to justify Wallis's infinite product (4.73).

Problem 4.5.3 It is argued above that for an infinite continued fraction that is not periodic, the probability that a given a_j has the value k is the reciprocal of $k(k+1)$. On summing these probabilities for $k = 1, 2, \ldots$, this implies that

$$\sum_{k=1}^{\infty} \frac{1}{k(k+1)} = 1.$$

Verify that the above infinite series does indeed have the sum 1.

5
More Number Theory

Mathematics is the queen of the sciences, and the theory of numbers is the queen of mathematics.

C. F. Gauss

We have already discussed some concepts in the theory of numbers in Chapter 4, in our study of the Euclidean algorithm, continued fractions, and Fibonacci numbers. Gauss's stirring quotation above encourages us to pursue this topic further. In this chapter we begin with the glorious theorem from ancient Greek mathematics that so elegantly demonstrates that the number of primes is infinite. We will discuss other properties of prime numbers, including how irregular they are "in the small," yet how orderly they are "in the large." The concept of congruences, developed by Gauss, will be used to obtain results concerning divisibility. The theory of quadratic residues leads us on to Wilson's theorem, Gauss's lemma, and Gauss's law of quadratic reciprocity. Much of this chapter is devoted to the study of Diophantine equations, of which solutions are sought in integers. This is the area in which the notorious Fermat's last theorem lies, that there are no solutions in positive integers x, y, and z of the equation $x^n + y^n = z^n$ if n is an integer greater than 2. A study of Andrew Wiles's proof of this, published in 1995, is very much beyond the scope of this book. However, we give proofs for the special cases where $n = 3$ and $n = 4$. As a prelude to the proof of the case where $n = 3$, we first discuss properties of *algebraic integers*, which is a fascinating topic in its own right. The reader may agree that the successful ascent of the subproblem of Fermat's last theorem when $n = 3$ is sufficient cause for celebration.

5.1   The Prime Numbers

A *prime* number is an integer greater than 1 that has no divisor except for 1 and itself. If a number greater than 1 is not a prime, it is called *composite*, the first composite number being $4 = 2 \times 2$. The number 1 is neither prime nor composite. The first few primes are

2, 3, 5, 7, 11, 13, 17, 19, 23, 29, 31, 37, 41, 43, 47, 53, 59, 61, 67.

In principle, the prime numbers can be identified by an elementary process called the *sieve of Eratosthenes*, in which we choose a positive integer $n > 2$ and write down the sequence of integers from 2 up to n. We keep 2 and cross out every second number after 2, that is $4, 6, 8$, and so on. We next keep the first surviving number, which is 3, and cross out every third number after 3 on the original list, that is, $6, 9, 12$, and so on. Note that we have crossed out some numbers twice, the first being 6. Next we keep the first surviving number, which is 5, and cross out every fifth number, namely $10, 15, 20$, and so on. We continue this process until, after identifying the prime number p and cancelling $2p, 3p, 4p, \ldots$, the first surviving number is greater than $\sqrt{n}$. Then all the numbers that are not crossed out in the list of numbers from 1 to n are primes. Thus if for some value of n we have a table of all the primes up to $\sqrt{n}$, this process will allow us to extend our table up to n. As n is increased, more cancellations are made, and we see intuitively that the proportion of primes in the first n integers decreases with n. This is illustrated in Table 5.1, where p_n denotes the nth prime number. One of

n	200	400	600	800	1000
p_n	1223	2741	4409	6133	7919
n/p_n	0.164	0.146	0.136	0.130	0.126

TABLE 5.1. Distribution of primes.

the great gems of Greek mathematics is the following theorem and proof given in Euclid's *Elements*, which was written circa 300 BC.

Theorem 5.1.1 The number of primes is infinite.

Proof. We begin by assuming that the number of primes is finite. Let us denote them by $p_1, p_2, \ldots, p_n$. Now consider the number

$$q = p_1 p_2 \cdots p_n + 1, \tag{5.1}$$

where we have multiplied together all the primes, and added 1. This integer q cannot be a prime, since it is larger than all the primes. Thus q must have a prime factor, say p, which must be one of the primes $p_1, p_2, \ldots, p_n$. But it is clear from (5.1) that none of these primes divides q. This contradicts our initial assumption that the number of primes is finite.   ∎

The above theorem gives a profound result, which is complemented by an extraordinarily simple proof. It is an early example of the style of proof known as *reductio ad absurdum*, in which we assume that the statement of a theorem is false and show that this leads to an untenable conclusion.

If $n = ab$, we say that the positive integers a and b are *divisors* or *factors* of n. Every integer $n > 1$ has a unique factorization into primes,

$$n = p_1^{m_1} p_2^{m_2} \cdots p_k^{m_k},$$

where each m_j is greater than or equal to zero and $m_k > 0$. Although this may seem intuitively obvious, it requires proof! However, rather than go through the same type of argument twice, we will defer the proof to Section 5.5, where we discuss unique factorization in $\mathbb{Z}[\omega]$, a set that includes the positive integers as a subset.

Apart from 2, all primes are odd. We can divide the odd primes into two classes, those of the form $4n + 1$ and those of the form $4n + 3$. There is an infinite number of primes in each class, the first few being respectively

$$5,\ 13,\ 17,\ 29,\ 37,\ 41,\ 53,\ 61,\ 73,\ 89,\ 97,\ 101,\ 109,\ 113$$

and

$$3,\ 7,\ 11,\ 19,\ 23,\ 31,\ 43,\ 47,\ 59,\ 67,\ 71,\ 79,\ 83,\ 103,\ 107.$$

We now give a simple proof, which resembles the proof of Theorem 5.1.1 above, to show that the second class is infinite.

Theorem 5.1.2 There is an infinite number of primes of the form $4n + 3$.

Proof. We use *reductio ad absurdum*, as in the proof of Theorem 5.1.1. Suppose there is only a finite number of primes of the form $4n + 3$, say $q_1, q_2, \ldots, q_k$, with $q_1 = 3$, $q_2 = 7$, and so on, and consider the positive integer

$$q = 4q_1 q_2 \cdots q_k - 1.$$

Then q is of the form $4n + 3$. It cannot be a prime, since it is greater than all the primes of this form. All factors of q must be odd and (see Problem 5.1.1) all factors of q cannot be of the form $4n + 1$, since otherwise q itself would be of that form. It follows that q must be divisible by one of the q_j, which is impossible. ∎

As mentioned above, it is also true that there is an infinite number of primes of the form $4n + 1$. Moreover, it is known that for large N the numbers of primes of the form $4n + 1$ and of the form $4n + 3$ that are less than N are asymptotically the same. The obvious adaption of the above proof of Theorem 5.1.2 to show that there is an infinite number of primes of the form $4n + 1$ fails. (See Problem 5.1.3.) However, a simple proof of the infinitude of primes of the form $4n + 1$ can be deduced from a result (Theorem 5.2.4) that we will prove in Section 5.2, that if an odd prime p is a factor of an integer of the form $a^2 + 1$, then p is of the form $4n + 1$.

Theorem 5.1.3 There is an infinite number of primes of the form $4n + 1$.

Proof. Assume that there is only a finite number of primes of the form $4n + 1$, say $r_1, r_2, \ldots, r_k$, with $r_1 = 5$, $r_2 = 13$, and so on. Let us write

$$q = 4(r_1 r_2 \cdots r_k)^2 + 1. \qquad (5.2)$$

Then either q is prime, which is impossible, since q is a number of the form $4n + 1$ and is larger than all primes of this form, or q has a prime factor. But since q is odd and is of the form $a^2 + 1$, by Theorem 5.2.4 any prime factor must be of the form $4n + 1$ and so must be one of the primes r_j, which is also impossible. ∎

Theorems 5.1.1, 5.1.2, and 5.1.3 are all special cases of the following much deeper result due to P. G. L. Dirichlet (1805–59).

Theorem 5.1.4 Any sequence of the form $(a + bn)_{n=0}^{\infty}$ contains an infinite number of primes, where a and $b > 0$ are integers with greatest common divisor 1. ∎

Pierre de Fermat (1601–65) conjectured that

$$f_n = 2^{2^n} + 1$$

is a prime for every choice of positive integer n. These are called *Fermat numbers*. In fact, f_n is a prime for $1 \le n \le 4$, when we obtain

$$f_1 = 5, \quad f_2 = 17, \quad f_3 = 257, \quad f_4 = 65537.$$

Leonhard Euler showed in 1732 that f_5 is not a prime, since

$$f_5 = 641 \cdot 6700417,$$

and the following ingenious argument, quoted in Hardy and Wright [25], shows that 641 is a factor of f_5 without explicitly dividing 641 into f_5. Let us write

$$641 = 5^4 + 2^4 = 5.2^7 + 1 = x + 1,$$

say, and observe that 641 divides

$$a = 2^{28}(5^4 + 2^4) \qquad \text{and} \qquad (x + 1)(x - 1)(x^2 + 1) = 5^4 \cdot 2^{28} - 1 = b,$$

and so divides

$$a - b = 2^{32} + 1 = f_5.$$

Theorem 5.2.5 (see Section 5.2) shows how we can narrow down the search for a prime factor of a Fermat number.

The Fermat numbers can be used to give an upper bound for the nth prime p_n, by building on the following property of Fermat numbers.

Theorem 5.1.5 The g.c.d. of any two Fermat numbers is 1.

Proof. For any $m, k > 0$, let $(f_m, f_{m+k}) = d$. Then, with $a = 2^{2^m}$, we have

$$\frac{f_{m+k} - 2}{f_m} = \frac{a^{2^k} - 1}{a + 1} = a^{s-1} - a^{s-2} + \cdots + a - 1,$$

where $s = 2^k$. Thus

$$f_m \mid f_{m+k} - 2,$$

and so $d \mid 2$. Since f_m and f_{m+k} are odd, we deduce that $d = 1$, and this completes the proof. ∎

Since no two Fermat numbers have a common divisor greater than 1, each must be divisible by an odd prime that does not divide any of the others. This gives, as a bonus, a different proof of Theorem 5.1.1 and also shows that

$$p_{n+1} < f_n = 2^{2^n} + 1.$$

This bound for p_{n+1}, although it is very far indeed from being sharp, at least has the merit of being easily obtained.

Marin Mersenne (1588–1648) stated that the number $2^n - 1$ is prime for

$$n = 2, \ 3, \ 5, \ 7, \ 13, \ 17, \ 19, \ 31, \ 67, \ 127, \ 257$$

and for no other values of $n \leq 257$. It is clear that $2^n - 1$ cannot be a prime unless n is prime, since $2^{mk} - 1$ is divisible by $2^m - 1$ and $2^k - 1$. The number $2^n - 1$ is called the nth Mersenne number. There are five errors in Mersenne's assertion. Two on his list, M_{67} and M_{257}, are *not* primes, and he omitted M_{61}, M_{89}, and M_{107}, which *are* primes. For example,

$$M_{67} = 2^{67} - 1 = 1 \ 47573 \ 95258 \ 96764 \ 12927,$$

which is the product of the two prime factors

$$193707721 \qquad \text{and} \qquad 76 \ 18382 \ 57287 \ .$$

E. T. Bell [3] describes how F. N. Cole multiplied these two numbers on a blackboard at a meeting of the American Mathematical Society in 1903, without speaking a word, and showed that their product indeed equals $2^{67} - 1$. The factorization of a number of the size of M_{67} is now a very simple calculation. Indeed, the rapid growth of computing power has been matched by a growth in the size of n for which M_n is known to be prime. For example, the Mersenne number M_n where $n = 6972593$ is a prime number with 2098960 decimal digits.

Within number theory in general, and in the study of primes in particular, it seems so easy to pose questions that can be easy to answer (if we can spot the right approach) or extremely difficult. For example, from 3 onwards, there is a gap of at least two between consecutive primes. For the primes from 3 to 97, a gap of 2 (such as that between 3 and 5) occurs eight times, a gap of 4 occurs seven times, a gap of 6 seven times and a gap of 8 occurs once. Consider the following questions:

Question 1   In the infinite sequence of primes, is there an infinite number of occurrences of a gap of two?

Question 2   Given any positive integer n, do there exist consecutive primes which differ by at least n?

It is believed that the answer is Yes to the first question, but at the time of writing there is no proof. This is the famous "twin primes" conjecture, that there is an infinite number of pairs of primes that differ by 2, for example 3 and 5, 59 and 61, 821 and 823. The answer to the second question is also Yes, and the proof is very easy. The sequence

$$n! + 2, n! + 3, \ldots, n! + n$$

gives $n - 1$ consecutive positive integers that are all composite, since 2 divides the first, 3 divides the second, and so on. This ensures that for some value of k, there is a gap of at least n between the largest of the primes that are not greater than $n! + 1$, say p_k, and the next prime p_{k+1}, which is clearly not less than $n! + n + 1$.

It is not possible to find a prime number p, apart from $p = 3$, such that $p + 2$ and $p + 4$ are also primes, since one of the three numbers p, $p + 2$, and $p + 4$ must be divisible by 3. However, Hardy and Wright [25] conjecture that there is an infinite number of prime triples of the forms $p, p + 2, p + 6$ and $p, p + 4, p + 6$. Many other simply posed questions concerning primes remain unanswered. The most famous is the conjecture of C. Goldbach (1690–1764) that every even number greater than 4 is the sum of two (odd) primes. The following are a few of the many other unsolved problems.

There is an infinite number of primes of the form $n^2 + 1$.
There is always a prime between n^2 and $(n + 1)^2$.
There is an infinite number of primes of the form $p_1 p_2 \cdots p_n + 1$.
There is an infinite number of primes of the form $n! + 1$.

To conclude this section, we return to the topic of the distribution of the primes. Let $\pi(n)$ denote the number of primes not greater than n. Gauss conjectured that

$$\pi(n) \sim \int_2^n \frac{dt}{\log t} = g_n,$$

say, but did not give a proof. This is equivalent to saying that

$$\pi(n) \sim \frac{n}{\log n},$$

meaning that

$$\text{if} \quad \rho_n = \frac{\pi(n)}{n/\log n} \quad \text{then} \quad \lim_{n \to \infty} \rho_n = 1. \tag{5.3}$$

n	10^3	10^6	10^9
π_n	168	78498	50847478
$n/\log n$	145	724×10^2	48255×10^3
g_n	177	786×10^2	50849×10^3

TABLE 5.2. Distribution of primes.

P. L. Chebyshev made considerable progress towards this result, and J. Hadamard (1865–1963) and C. J. de la Vallée Poussin (1866–1962) proved it independently in 1896. (This also seems to demonstrate that proving the *prime number theorem* is very good for one's health.) An "elementary" proof of the prime number theorem was published in 1949 by Paul Erdős (1913–1996) and Atle Selberg (born 1917). In his delightful book [28] about Paul Erdős, Paul Hoffman alludes in rhyme to a simpler theorem proved by Chebyshev, which settled an earlier conjecture of Joseph Bertrand (1822–1900):

> Chebyshev said it, and I say it again
> There is always a prime between n and $2n$.

In the prime number theorem, the convergence of ρ_n to 1 (see (5.3)) is very slow. For example, with $n = 10^3, 10^6$, and 10^9, we have $\rho_n \approx 1.159, 1.084$, and 1.053, respectively. Table 5.2 gives a comparison of $\pi(n)$, $n/\log n$, and g_n for $n = 10^3, 10^6$, and 10^9, the entries in the last two rows being given only approximately. Note that Gauss's integral g_n gives a very much closer approximation to $\pi(n)$ than that given by $n/\log n$. The astounding relative accuracy of Gauss's estimate of $\pi(n)$ for large n strongly suggests that he had a very deep intuitive feel for the nature of the distribution of the prime numbers.

Problem 5.1.1 Verify that

$$(4n_1 + 1)(4n_2 + 1) = 4N + 1,$$

where $N = 4n_1 n_2 + n_1 + n_2$, and that $(4n_1 + 3)(4n_2 + 3)$ can also be written in the form $4N + 1$, but $(4n_1 + 1)(4n_2 + 3)$ is of the form $4N + 3$.

Problem 5.1.2 As a variant of the proof of Theorem 5.1.2, replace the number q defined in that proof by $q_1 q_2 \cdots q_k + 3 + (-1)^{k+1}$. Show that this always has the form $4n + 3$, and that the proof can be completed similarly.

Problem 5.1.3 Assume that there is only a finite number of primes of the form $4n + 1$, say $r_1, r_2, \ldots, r_k$, and consider the positive integer $q = 4r_1 r_2 \cdots r_k + 1$. Why cannot we infer that q always has a prime factor of the form $4n + 1$?

Problem 5.1.4 Using Theorem 5.2.5, verify that 641 is only the fifth prime one needs to test as a possible factor of the Fermat number f_5.

Problem 5.1.5 Verify that $f_{m+1} - 2 = f_m(f_m - 2)$ and deduce that

$$f_{m+1} = 3f_1f_2 \cdots f_m + 2.$$

Problem 5.1.6 Show that if $a^m - 1$ is a prime, then $a = 2$ and m is prime.

Problem 5.1.7 If p and p' are twin primes that are both greater than 3, show that $p + p'$ is divisible by 12 and that $pp' + 1$ is a perfect square.

Problem 5.1.8 Chebyshev showed that for n sufficiently large, there is always a prime between n and $6n/5$, an improvement on Bertrand's conjecture. Compose a suitable verse to celebrate this, of comparable literary merit to the couplet quoted in the text.

5.2   Congruences

In Section 4.1 we used the notation $n \mid x - u$ to denote n divides $x - u$. An alternative way of expressing this relation between n and $x - u$ is to write

$$x \equiv u \,(\text{mod } n), \qquad\qquad (5.4)$$

and we say that x is *congruent* to u *modulo* n. This concept is due to Gauss, who appreciated its algebraic advantages. The word "modulo" is a legacy to mathematics from Gauss's devotion to Latin, which was mentioned in Section 1.4. Congruences satisfy the three basic properties

$$x \equiv x \,(\text{mod } n),$$
$$x \equiv y \,(\text{mod } n) \quad \Rightarrow \quad y \equiv x \,(\text{mod } n),$$
$$x \equiv y \,(\text{mod } n) \quad \text{and} \quad y \equiv z \,(\text{mod } n) \quad \Rightarrow \quad x \equiv z \,(\text{mod } n),$$

which are called respectively the reflexive, symmetric, and transitive properties. More generally in mathematics, any relation between two members of a given set that satisfies these three properties is called an *equivalence relation*. For the congruence equivalence relation we may further verify that if

$$x \equiv u \,(\text{mod } n) \qquad \text{and} \qquad y \equiv v \,(\text{mod } n),$$

then

$$x + y \equiv u + v \,(\text{mod } n) \qquad \text{and} \qquad xy \equiv uv \,(\text{mod } n).$$

If $x \equiv a \,(\text{mod } n)$, we say that a is a *residue* of x modulo n. The set of all residues of a given number, modulo n, is called a *residue class*. Clearly, there are n residue classes modulo n, namely those that are congruent to $0, 1, \ldots, n-1$.

Recall the definition already given in Section 4.1 that if the g.c.d. of two positive integers a and b is 1, we say that a and b are *coprime*. Alternatively, we say that one of the numbers is *prime* to the other. We will need this concept in our discussion of some results concerning divisibility, leading up to the congruence relation known as Fermat's little theorem. The first of these results states that the product of n consecutive positive integers is divisible by $n!$

Theorem 5.2.1 For any positive integer n and any integer $m \geq 0$,

$$n! \quad \text{divides} \quad \prod_{j=1}^{n}(m+j). \tag{5.5}$$

Proof. We use a "double induction" argument on n and m. First we see that (5.5) holds for $n = 1$ and all $m \geq 0$, and it also holds for any positive integer n and $m = 0$. Let us assume that it holds for some $n = k \geq 1$ and all $m \geq 0$. We know that (5.5) holds for $n = k+1$ and $m = 0$. Let us assume that it holds for $n = k+1$ and some $m \geq 0$. Then

$$\prod_{j=1}^{k+1}(m+1+j) \quad \prod_{j=1}^{k+1}(m+j) + (k+1)\prod_{j=1}^{k}(m+1+j), \tag{5.6}$$

where we have expressed the last factor on the left of (5.6) as the sum of $m+1$ and $k+1$. From the assumptions made above, it follows that $(k+1)!$ divides both terms on the right of (5.6), showing that (5.5) holds for $n = k+1$ and $m+1$. By induction on m, we deduce that (5.5) holds for $n = k+1$ and all m. Finally, using induction on n, we find that (5.5) holds for all $n \geq 1$ and all $m \geq 0$. ∎

One application of this theorem is the well-known result that the binomial coefficient

$$\binom{m}{n} = \frac{m(m-1)\cdots(m-n+1)}{n!}$$

is an integer, for $m \geq n \geq 0$. Alternatively, this can be proved by an induction argument based on the recurrence relation

$$\binom{m}{n} = \binom{m-1}{n} + \binom{m-1}{n-1},$$

but a little thought shows that this argument is equivalent to the proof of Theorem 5.2.1 that we have given above. We now state the following theorem:

Theorem 5.2.2 For any prime p, the binomial coefficients

$$\binom{p}{1}, \binom{p}{2}, \ldots, \binom{p}{p-1}$$

are all divisible by p.

Proof. For $1 \leq n \leq p-1$,

$$\binom{p}{n} = \frac{p(p-1)\cdots(p-n+1)}{n!}$$

is an integer, and thus

$$n! \mid p(p-1)\cdots(p-n+1).$$

Since $n!$ and p are coprime, it follows that

$$n! \mid (p-1)(p-2)\cdots(p-n+1),$$

which completes the proof. ■

We can now state and prove Fermat's little theorem.

Theorem 5.2.3 For any prime p and any positive integer a not divisible by p,

$$a^{p-1} \equiv 1 \pmod{p}. \tag{5.7}$$

Proof. In view of Problem 5.2.5 it suffices to establish (5.7) for values of a such that $1 \leq a \leq p-1$. We will show by induction that

$$a^p \equiv a \pmod{p} \tag{5.8}$$

for all integers a such that $1 \leq a \leq p-1$. Clearly, (5.8) holds for $a = 1$. Let us assume that it holds for some integer a such that $1 \leq a < p-1$. Then, from the binomial expansion and the application of Theorem 5.2.2, we obtain

$$(1+a)^p = \sum_{n=0}^{p} \binom{p}{n} a^n \equiv 1 + a^p \equiv 1 + a \pmod{p},$$

showing that (5.8) holds for $a+1$ and hence, by induction, for all integers a such that $1 \leq a \leq p-1$. Thus $p \mid (a^p - a)$ and hence $p \mid (a^{p-1} - 1)$, since p does not divide a. ■

We now use Fermat's little theorem to prove the following theorem:

Theorem 5.2.4 Let p denote a prime for which there exists a number a such that $a^2 \equiv -1 \pmod{p}$. Then $p = 2$ or $p \equiv 1 \pmod{4}$.

Proof. First we note that the relation $a^2 \equiv -1 \,(\mathrm{mod}\ 2)$ is satisfied by any odd integer a. Now suppose, contrary to the statement of the theorem, that there exists a number a such that

$$a^2 \equiv -1 \,(\mathrm{mod}\ p) \qquad (5.9)$$

for some prime p of the form $4n + 3$. It is clear that if a satisfies (5.9), it is not divisible by p. Then from Theorem 5.2.3 we have, for this value of p,

$$a^{p-1} = a^{4n+2} \equiv 1 \,(\mathrm{mod}\ p).$$

However, we deduce from (5.9) that

$$a^{4n+2} = (a^2)^{2n+1} \equiv (-1)^{2n+1} \equiv -1 \,(\mathrm{mod}\ p),$$

which gives a contradiction. In Example 5.3.2 we will show that the congruence $a^2 \equiv -1 \,(\mathrm{mod}\ p)$ always has a solution when $p \equiv 1 \,(\mathrm{mod}\ 4)$. ∎

We now make use of the last two theorems in our proof of the following theorem concerning the form of a prime factor of a Fermat number (see Section 5.1):

Theorem 5.2.5 Any prime factor of $f_n = 2^{2^n} + 1$ must be of the form $2^{n+1}m + 1$, where m is a positive integer.

Proof. Let p denote a prime that divides $2^{2^n} + 1$. Then

$$2^{2^n} \equiv -1 \,(\mathrm{mod}\ p), \qquad (5.10)$$

and thus

$$2^{2^{n+1}} = \left(2^{2^n}\right)^2 = 1 \,(\mathrm{mod}\ p) \qquad (5.11)$$

If we define

$$d = (2^{n+1}, p - 1),$$

we may deduce from Theorem 4.1.2 that

$$d = 2^{n+1}a + (p - 1)b$$

for some choice of integers a and b, and so

$$2^d = (2^{2^{n+1}})^a \cdot (2^{p-1})^b. \qquad (5.12)$$

We now use (5.11) and, from Fermat's little theorem (Theorem 5.2.3), we also have

$$2^{p-1} \equiv 1 \,(\mathrm{mod}\ p).$$

Thus we can greatly simplify (5.12) to give

$$2^d \equiv 1 \,(\mathrm{mod}\ p). \qquad (5.13)$$

Since $d \mid 2^{n+1}$, we may write $d = 2^k$, where $0 \le k \le n + 1$. We now show that in fact, $k = n + 1$. For it follows from (5.13) that

$$2^{2^k} - 2^d \equiv 1 \,(\mathrm{mod}\ p).$$

However, in view of (5.10) and the fact that $2^{2^{j+1}} = (2^{2^j})^2$ for any integer $j \ge 0$, it follows that $k > n$ and thus $k = n + 1$. Finally, since $d = 2^{n+1}$ and $d \mid p - 1$, we have

$$p - 1 = 2^{n+1}m,$$

for some positive integer m, and this completes the proof. ∎

Euler introduced the function $\phi(n)$ to denote the number of integers m, with $1 \le m \le n$, such that $(m, n) = 1$. Thus $\phi(n)$ is the number of positive integers not greater than n that are prime to n. The following theorem shows the *multiplicative* nature of Euler's ϕ-function.

Theorem 5.2.6 If $(m_1, m_2) = 1$, we have

$$\phi(m_1 m_2) = \phi(m_1)\phi(m_2). \tag{5.14}$$

Proof. Let $(m_1, m_2) = 1$, and let a_1, a_2, a_1', and a_2' satisfy

$$a_2 m_1 + a_1 m_2 \equiv a_2' m_1 + a_1' m_2 \,(\mathrm{mod}\ m_1 m_2).$$

It follows that

$$a_1 m_2 \equiv a_1' m_2 \,(\mathrm{mod}\ m_1),$$

and since $(m_1, m_2) = 1$, we conclude that $a_1 \equiv a_1' \,(\mathrm{mod}\ m_1)$. We similarly deduce that $a_2 \equiv a_2' \,(\mathrm{mod}\ m_2)$. This shows that as a_1 takes the values of all m_1 residues modulo m_1, and a_2 takes the values of all m_2 residues modulo m_2, then the $m_1 m_2$ incongruent values $a_2 m_1 + a_1 m_2$ must give *all* the residues of $m_1 m_2$. We can further show that

$$(a_2 m_1 + a_1 m_2, m_1 m_2) = 1 \quad \Leftrightarrow \quad (a_1 m_2, m_1) = 1 \quad \text{and} \quad (a_2 m_1, m_2) = 1$$
$$\Leftrightarrow \quad (a_1, m_1) = 1 \quad \text{and} \quad (a_2, m_2) = 1.$$

Thus the $\phi(m_1 m_2)$ numbers that are less than and prime to $m_1 m_2$ are simply the smallest positive values of $a_2 m_1 + a_1 m_2$ such that $(a_1, m_1) = 1$ and $(a_2, m_2) = 1$, so that $\phi(m_1 m_2) = \phi(m_1)\phi(m_2)$. ∎

If p is a prime, the numbers $1, 2, \ldots, p - 1$ are all prime to p, and so $\phi(p) = p - 1$. Now consider the positive integer p^n, where $n \ge 1$ and p is a prime. Then the only numbers not greater than p^n that are *not* prime to p^n are of the form

$$\lambda p, \quad \text{where} \quad 1 \le \lambda \le p^{n-1},$$

and there are p^{n-1} such numbers. Thus

$$\phi(p^n) = p^n - p^{n-1} = p^{n-1}(p - 1) = p^n \left(1 - \frac{1}{p}\right). \tag{5.15}$$

If N has the prime factorization

$$N = p_1^{n_1} p_2^{n_2} \cdots p_k^{n_k},$$

it follows from (5.14) and (5.15) that

$$\phi(N) = \prod_{j=1}^{k} p_j^{n_j} \left(1 - \frac{1}{p_j}\right) = N \prod_{j=1}^{k} \left(1 - \frac{1}{p_j}\right). \qquad (5.16)$$

Let

$$a_1, a_2, \ldots, a_{\phi(n)} \qquad (5.17)$$

denote a complete set of residues that are prime to n, and let λ be prime to n. Then

$$\lambda a_1, \lambda a_2, \ldots, \lambda a_{\phi(n)} \qquad (5.18)$$

is also a complete set of residues that are prime to n. For it is clear that each λa_j is prime to n. Also, no two can be congruent modulo n, for otherwise n would divide $\lambda a_r - \lambda a_s$ for some $r \neq s$. Since λ and n are coprime, this would imply that n divides $a_r - a_s$, and this is impossible because the a_j are all distinct residues modulo n.

Example 5.2.1 We have from (5.16) that

$$\phi(60) = 60 \left(1 - \frac{1}{2}\right)\left(1 - \frac{1}{3}\right)\left(1 - \frac{1}{5}\right) = 16,$$

$$\phi(100) = 100 \left(1 - \frac{1}{2}\right)\left(1 - \frac{1}{5}\right) = 40,$$

and we can check these results directly from the definition of $\phi(n)$. ∎

We now present a theorem, due to Euler, which generalizes Fermat's little theorem (Theorem 5.2.3) from primes to all positive integers.

Theorem 5.2.7 For any positive integer n and any a coprime to n,

$$a^{\phi(n)} \equiv 1 \pmod{n}.$$

Proof. Let $b_1, b_2, \ldots, b_{\phi(n)}$ denote a complete set of residues prime to n. Then, as we saw above, if we multiply each of these residues by a that is prime to n, we still have a complete set of residues prime to n. Thus

$$\prod_{j=1}^{\phi(n)} b_j \equiv \prod_{j=1}^{\phi(n)} a b_j \equiv a^{\phi(n)} \prod_{j=1}^{\phi(n)} b_j \pmod{n}.$$

Since each b_j is prime to n, we deduce that

$$a^{\phi(n)} \equiv 1 \pmod{n}. \qquad ∎$$

It is well known that a polynomial equation of degree n with real coefficients has n roots in the complex plane, counting multiple zeros. Thus, for example, we say that $x^2(x - 1)^{n-2} = 0$ has n roots, namely 1 with multiplicity $n - 2$ and 0 with multiplicity two. We now consider polynomial *congruences*, leading up to a theorem named after J. L. Lagrange. Consider the polynomials

$$f(x) = a_0 x^n + a_1 x^{n-1} + \cdots + a_{n-1} x + a_n,$$
$$g(x) = b_0 x^n + b_1 x^{n-1} + \cdots + b_{n-1} x + b_n,$$

where the coefficients a_j and b_j are integers. If each pair of corresponding coefficients a_j and b_j are congruent modulo m, we will write

$$f(x) \equiv g(x) \pmod{m}.$$

In particular, if the coefficients of $f(x)$ are all congruent to zero modulo m, we can replace $g(x)$ by the zero function in the latter equation. Suppose that m does not divide a_0 and that there exists an integer x_1 such that $f(x_1) \equiv 0 \pmod{m}$. Then there exists a polynomial $h(x)$ of degree $n - 1$ with leading coefficient a_0 such that

$$f(x) \equiv (x - x_1)\, h(x) \pmod{m}. \tag{5.19}$$

For we have

$$f(x) - f(x_1) = \sum_{j=0}^{n} a_j (x^{n-j} - x_1^{n-j}),$$

and we note that the last term in the above sum is a_n multiplied by zero. Thus $x - x_1$ divides each term in the above sum, and so (5.19) follows. We can build on (5.19) to obtain the following more substantial result.

Theorem 5.2.8 Let $f(x) = a_0 x^n + a_1 x^{n-1} + \cdots + a_{n-1} x + a_n$ and let p denote a prime that does not divide a_0. Then if $f(x_j) \equiv 0 \pmod{p}$, for $1 \leq j \leq s$, where $s \leq n$ and the x_j are distinct residues modulo p, then

$$f(x) \equiv (x - x_1)(x - x_2) \cdots (x - x_s)\, h_{n-s}(x) \pmod{p}, \tag{5.20}$$

where $h_{n-s}(x)$ is a polynomial of degree $n - s$ with leading coefficient a_0.

Proof. We will use induction on s. We have already seen that (5.20) holds for $s = 1$. Let us assume that for some value of k such that $1 \leq k < s$, we have

$$f(x) \equiv (x - x_1)(x - x_2) \cdots (x - x_k)\, h_{n-k}(x) \pmod{p},$$

where $h_{n-k}(x)$ is a polynomial of degree $n - k$ with leading coefficient a_0. Then, since $f(x_{k+1}) \equiv 0 \pmod{p}$, we have

$$0 \equiv f(x_{k+1}) \equiv (x_{k+1} - x_1)(x_{k+1} - x_2) \cdots (x_{k+1} - x_k)\, h_{n-k}(x_{k+1}) \pmod{p}.$$

The x_j are distinct residues modulo p, which means that the prime p cannot divide any of the factors $(x_{k+1} - x_j)$. Thus p must divide $h_{n-k}(x_{k+1})$. Since $h_{n-k}(x_{k+1}) \equiv 0 \pmod{p}$, we may write

$$h_{n-k}(x) \equiv (x - x_{k+1}) \, h_{n-k-1}(x) \pmod{p},$$

where $h_{n-k-1}(x)$ is a polynomial of degree $n - k - 1$ with leading coefficient a_0. Thus (5.20) follows with $s = k + 1$, and this completes the proof by induction. ■

This brings us to Lagrange's theorem.

Theorem 5.2.9 Given any prime p and a polynomial

$$f(x) = a_0 x^n + a_1 x^{n-1} + \cdots + a_{n-1} x + a_n, \tag{5.21}$$

where p does not divide a_0, then $f(x) \equiv 0 \pmod{p}$ is satisfied by at most n distinct residues modulo p.

Proof. We will assume that the congruence is satisfied by more than n distinct residues and obtain a contradiction. Let us suppose that $f(x) \equiv 0$ is satisfied by the distinct residues $x_1, x_2, \ldots, x_n, x_{n+1}$. Then, using the first n of these residues, we may deduce from Theorem 5.2.8 that

$$f(x) = (x - x_1)(x - x_2) \cdots (x - x_n) \, h_0(x) \pmod{p}, \tag{5.22}$$

where $h_0(x)$ is a polynomial of degree $n - n = 0$ with leading coefficient a_0, and so $h_0(x) = a_0$. Thus we have

$$f(x) \equiv (x - x_1)(x - x_2) \cdots (x - x_n) \, a_0 \pmod{p}. \tag{5.23}$$

Since by our above assumption $f(x_{n+1}) \equiv 0 \pmod{p}$, we obtain

$$(x_{n+1} - x_1)(x_{n+1} - x_2) \cdots (x_{n+1} - x_n) \, a_0 \equiv 0 \pmod{p}. \tag{5.24}$$

This is impossible, and thus we cannot have more than n distinct residues x satisfying $f(x) \equiv 0 \pmod{p}$. For in (5.24), p divides neither a_0 nor any of the factors $(x_{n+1} - x_j)$, since the x_j are distinct residues modulo p. This completes the proof. ■

Example 5.2.2 If p is any prime, the congruence $x^p - x \equiv 0 \pmod{p}$ is satisfied by all p distinct residues modulo p, the maximum number allowable by Lagrange's theorem. For it is satisfied by $x = 0$ and, from Fermat's little theorem, it is satisfied by $x = 1, 2, \ldots, p - 1$. ■

Pursuing the theme of the above example, we can derive the following interesting result from Lagrange's theorem.

Theorem 5.2.10 If p is a prime of the form $4n + 1$, then each of the congruences

$$x^{\frac{1}{2}(p-1)} \equiv -1 \pmod{p} \qquad \text{and} \qquad x^{\frac{1}{2}(p-1)} \equiv 1 \pmod{p}$$

is satisfied by one-half of the residues congruent to $1, 2, \ldots, p - 1$ modulo p.

Proof. With $p = 4n + 1$ we have

$$x^{p-1} - 1 = (x^{2n} - 1)(x^{2n} + 1) \equiv 0 \pmod{p}. \tag{5.25}$$

From Fermat's little theorem this congruence is satisfied by the $p - 1 = 4n$ residues congruent to $1, 2, \ldots, p - 1$ modulo p, and by Lagrange's theorem half of these must be associated with each of the factors in (5.25), since each of the congruences

$$x^{2n} \equiv 1 \pmod{p} \qquad \text{and} \qquad x^{2n} \equiv -1 \pmod{p}$$

has at most $2n$ distinct residue solutions modulo p.   ■

Problem 5.2.1 Show that if $x \equiv u \pmod{n}$ and $y \equiv v \pmod{n}$, then we also have $x + y \equiv u + v \pmod{n}$ and $xy \equiv uv \pmod{n}$.

Problem 5.2.2 Express the results obtained in Problem 5.1.1 in the language of congruences.

Problem 5.2.3 Show that

$$2^{1,000,000} \equiv 61 \pmod{97}.$$

Problem 5.2.4 Let $\gamma_0 = 10^{100}$, and define $\gamma_{n+1} = 10^{\gamma_n}$, for all $n \geq 0$. Show that $17 \mid (4\gamma_n + 1)$ only for $n = 0$, and that $13 \mid (4\gamma_n + 1)$ for all $n \geq 0$. (The numbers γ_0 and γ_1 are called a *googol* and a *googolplex*, respectively.)

Problem 5.2.5 If $x \equiv y \pmod{n}$, show that $x^k \equiv y^k \pmod{n}$ for any positive integer k.

Problem 5.2.6 Show that $x^2 \equiv 0 \pmod{4}$ if x is even and $x^2 \equiv 1 \pmod{4}$ if x is odd.

Problem 5.2.7 Let

$$f(x) = a_0 x^n + a_1 x^{n-1} + \cdots + a_{n-1} x + a_n,$$

where $a_0, a_1, \ldots, a_n$ are integers. Show that

$$x \equiv x' \Rightarrow f(x) \equiv f(x') \pmod{p},$$

where p is any prime.

Problem 5.2.8 Find the six residues that satisfy each of the congruences

$$x^6 \equiv -1 \,(\text{mod } 13) \qquad \text{and} \qquad x^6 \equiv 1 \,(\text{mod } 13)$$

in accordance with Theorem 5.2.10.

5.3   Quadratic Residues

Let p be an odd prime and let a be any integer such that $1 \leq a \leq p-1$. Consider again our argument above that (5.17) and (5.18) are equivalent complete sets of residues. As a special case of this, given a positive integer λ that is prime to p, the set of numbers $\{\lambda, 2\lambda, 3\lambda, \ldots, (p-1)\lambda\}$ is a complete set of residues modulo p, and thus exactly one of them is congruent to a modulo p. Thus there is some positive integer, say λ', such that

$$\lambda\lambda' \equiv a \,(\text{mod } p). \tag{5.26}$$

If for some λ we find that $\lambda' = \lambda$ then

$$\lambda^2 \equiv a \,(\text{mod } p), \tag{5.27}$$

and we say that a is a *quadratic residue* of p. If there is no such λ, we say that a is a quadratic nonresidue of p. We observe that

$$(p-\lambda)^2 - p^2 - 2p\lambda + \lambda^2 \equiv \lambda^2 \,(\text{mod } p),$$

and so to find all the different residues of the form λ^2 modulo p, it suffices to consider values of λ between 1 and $\frac{1}{2}(p-1)$. We also note that if

$$1 \leq \lambda, \, \mu \leq \frac{1}{2}(p-1),$$

then

$$\lambda^2 \equiv \mu^2 \,(\text{mod } p) \Leftrightarrow (\lambda - \mu)(\lambda + \mu) \equiv 0 \,(\text{mod } p).$$

This means that $p \mid \lambda - \mu$ or $p \mid \lambda + \mu$, and since $\lambda + \mu$ lies between 2 and $p-1$, the only possibility is that $\lambda = \mu$. Thus, if λ and μ are distinct positive integers less than $\frac{1}{2}(p-1)$, λ^2 is not congruent to μ^2 modulo p. We conclude that there are $\frac{1}{2}(p-1)$ distinct quadratic residues of the odd prime p, and so there are also $\frac{1}{2}(p-1)$ distinct quadratic nonresidues of p. Half of the $p-1$ integers $1, 2, \ldots, p-1$ are quadratic residues and half are nonresidues.

Example 5.3.1 For $p = 11$, we have

$$1^2 \equiv 10^2 \equiv 1 \,(\text{mod } 11),$$
$$2^2 \equiv 9^2 \ \equiv 4 \,(\text{mod } 11),$$
$$3^2 = 8^2 \ = 9 \,(\text{mod } 11),$$
$$4^2 \equiv 7^2 \ \equiv 5 \,(\text{mod } 11),$$
$$5^2 \equiv 6^2 \ \equiv 3 \,(\text{mod } 11),$$

and so 1, 3, 4, 5, 9 are quadratic residues of 11, and 2, 6, 7, 8, 10 are quadratic nonresidues.   ∎

If a is not a quadratic residue of p, the argument used above in deriving (5.26) shows that the numbers 1 to $p-1$ can be arranged in pairs λ, λ' that satisfy (5.26), and there are $\frac{1}{2}(p-1)$ such pairs. In this case,

$$(p-1)! \equiv a^{\frac{1}{2}(p-1)} \pmod{p}. \tag{5.28}$$

However, if a *is* a quadratic residue of p, there are two numbers, say μ and $p - \mu$, such that

$$\mu^2 \equiv (p-\mu)^2 \equiv a \pmod{p}, \tag{5.29}$$

and the remaining $p - 3$ numbers between 1 and $p - 1$ can be arranged in pairs λ, λ' that satisfy (5.26). Thus, if a is a quadratic residue of p, we have

$$(p-1)! \equiv \mu(p-\mu) \cdot a^{\frac{1}{2}(p-3)} \pmod{p}, \tag{5.30}$$

and since $\mu(p-\mu) \equiv -\mu^2 \pmod{p}$, it follows from (5.30) and (5.29) that

$$(p-1)! \equiv -a^{\frac{1}{2}(p-1)} \pmod{p}. \tag{5.31}$$

Although we have taken a to be any integer between 1 and $p-1$, it is clear that we may take a to be any integer such that $(a, p) = 1$, and then either (5.31) or (5.28) will hold, depending on whether a is or is not a quadratic residue of p. Now, for any a such that $(a, p) = 1$, let us now write

$$(a/p) = \begin{cases} +1 & \text{if } a \text{ is a quadratic residue of } p, \\ -1 & \text{if } a \text{ is not a quadratic residue of } p, \end{cases}$$

where (a/p) is called the *Legendre symbol*. Using this notation, we may combine (5.28) and (5.31) to give the following result.

Theorem 5.3.1 Let p denote any odd prime. Then for any integer a not divisible by p, we have

$$(p-1)! \equiv -(a/p) \cdot a^{\frac{1}{2}(p-1)} \pmod{p}. \qquad \blacksquare \tag{5.32}$$

Since $1^2 \equiv (p-1)^2 \equiv 1 \pmod{p}$, it is obvious that $(1/p) = 1$ for all odd p. We can then substitute $a = 1$ into (5.32) to give the following result, which is called Wilson's theorem.

Theorem 5.3.2 For any prime p,

$$(p-1)! \equiv -1 \pmod{p}. \tag{5.33}$$

Proof. The above verification of (5.32), and the consequent verification of (5.33), is valid for all odd primes p. It is easily verified directly that (5.33) also holds for $p = 2$ and thus holds for *all* primes.   ∎

As an application of Wilson's theorem, the following example shows that $a^2 \equiv -1 \pmod{p}$ (see Theorem 5.2.4) always has a solution when $p \equiv 1 \pmod{4}$.

Example 5.3.2 Let $p = 4n + 1$ and let us write

$$(p-1)! = (2n)! \, (2n+1)(2n+2) \cdots (4n). \qquad (5.34)$$

Then, since

$$2n + j \equiv -(2n - j + 1) \,(\text{mod } p)$$

for $1 \leq j \leq 2n$, we can write

$$(2n+1)(2n+2) \cdots (4n) \equiv (-1)^{2n}(2n)! \,(\text{mod } p),$$

and it then follows from (5.34) and Wilson's theorem (Theorem 5.3.2) that

$$-1 \equiv (p-1)! \equiv a^2 \,(\text{mod } p),$$

where $a = (2n)! = ((p-1)/2)!$ ∎

For any odd prime p and any a such that $(a, p) = 1$, we deduce from Theorems 5.3.1 and 5.3.2 that

$$1 \equiv (a/p) \cdot a^{\frac{1}{2}(p-1)} \,(\text{mod } p)$$

and thus

$$(a/p) \equiv a^{\frac{1}{2}(p-1)} \,(\text{mod } p). \qquad (5.35)$$

It is rather amusing that we are able to learn something apparently new, in (5.35), by combining the result of Theorem 5.3.1 with its special case Theorem 5.3.2. On putting $a = -1$ in (5.35), we derive the following result.

Theorem 5.3.3 For any odd prime p, we have

$$(-1/p) = (-1)^{\frac{1}{2}(p-1)},$$

and thus -1 is a quadratic residue of all primes of the form $4n + 1$ and is not a quadratic residue of any prime of the form $4n + 3$. ∎

It is not hard to verify (see Problem 5.3.3) that

$$(a/p) \cdot (b/p) = (ab/p) \qquad \text{if} \qquad (a, p) = (b, p) = 1, \qquad (5.36)$$

and thus the product of two quadratic residues is a quadratic residue, the product of two nonresidues is a residue, and the product of a quadratic residue and a nonresidue is a nonresidue.

Given any odd prime p we define the *minimal* residue of n modulo p to be a number a such that

$$n \equiv a \,(\text{mod } p) \qquad \text{and} \qquad -\frac{1}{2}(p-1) \leq a \leq \frac{1}{2}(p-1).$$

For example, the minimal residue of 8 modulo 5 is -2. Now let m be any integer that is prime to p and let the minimal residues of the $\frac{1}{2}(p-1)$ numbers

$$m, 2m, \ldots, \frac{1}{2}(p-1)m \qquad (5.37)$$

be written as

$$-r_1, -r_2, \ldots, -r_\nu, s_{\nu+1}, s_{\nu+2}, \ldots, s_{\frac{1}{2}(p-1)}, \tag{5.38}$$

where the r_j and s_j are all positive. We have written these $\frac{1}{2}(p-1)$ minimal residues in this way to emphasize that ν of them are negative. Gauss, as we will see, showed how this number ν determines whether or not m is a quadratic residue of p. We note that in (5.38) no two of the r_j can be equal, nor any two s_j, since the numbers in (5.37) from which they are derived are all incongruent. Moreover, we cannot have any $r_j = s_k$, for then

$$am \equiv -r_j \pmod{p} \qquad \text{and} \qquad bm \equiv s_k \pmod{p}$$

and thus

$$(a+b)m \equiv 0 \pmod{p} \tag{5.39}$$

for some a and b, with $1 \le a, b \le \frac{1}{2}(p-1)$. Since

$$0 < a + b < p - 1 \qquad \text{and} \qquad (m, p) = 1,$$

we see that (5.39) cannot hold. Since the r_j and s_j are all distinct, they are simply a permutation of the numbers $1, 2, \ldots, \frac{1}{2}(p-1)$.

We can now state and prove the following theorem, named after Gauss, which gives a direct method for evaluating the Legendre symbol (m/p).

Theorem 5.3.4 (Gauss's Lemma) If p is an odd prime and $(m, p) = 1$, we have

$$(m/p) = (-1)^\nu, \tag{5.40}$$

where ν is the number of the minimal residues of

$$m, 2m, \ldots, \frac{1}{2}(p-1)m$$

that are negative.

Proof. Since the r_j and s_j defined above are a permutation of the numbers $1, 2, \ldots, \frac{1}{2}(p-1)$, we have

$$m \cdot 2m \cdots \frac{1}{2}(p-1)m \equiv (-1)^\nu 1 \cdot 2 \cdots \frac{1}{2}(p-1) \pmod{p}.$$

We deduce that

$$m^{\frac{1}{2}(p-1)} \equiv (-1)^\nu \pmod{p},$$

and so (5.40) follows from (5.35).   ∎

Example 5.3.3 To illustrate Theorem 5.3.4 let us take $m = 5$ and $p = 17$. We need to compute the minimal residues of

$$5, 10, 15, 20, 25, 30, 35, 40$$

modulo 17, and we find that three are negative (those corresponding to 10, 15, and 30), so that $\nu = 3$, and we see from (5.40) that 5 is not a quadratic residue of 17. If we take $m = 13$ and seek the minimal residues of

$$13, 26, 39, 52, 65, 78, 91, 104$$

modulo 17, we find that four are negative (those corresponding to 13, 26, 65, and 78). Thus $\nu = 4$, and so 13 is a quadratic residue of 17. As a check, we find that $8^2 \equiv 13 \pmod{17}$. ■

In the above use of Gauss's lemma, we determined the value of (m/p) by evaluating $\frac{1}{2}(p-1)$ residues. This is really not so very impressive when we consider that we can determine *all* the quadratic residues and nonresidues of p by carrying out a similar number of calculations, as we did in Example 5.3.1. A much more significant application of Gauss's lemma is to determine those odd primes for which 2 is a quadratic residue. In view of (5.37), we need to determine ν, the number of minimal residues of members of the set

$$2, 4, 6, \ldots, p - 1 \tag{5.41}$$

that are negative. Thus ν is just the number of members in the set (5.41) that are greater that $\frac{1}{2}(p-1)$ It is convenient to treat primes of the forms $4n + 1$ and $4n - 1$ separately. If $p = 4n + 1$, we see that ν is the number in the set

$$2(n + 1), 2(n + 2), \ldots, 2(2n),$$

so that $\nu = n$. Then ν is even if n is even, so that p has the form $8q + 1$, and ν is odd if n is odd, when p has the form $8q - 3$. If $p = 4n - 1$, we find that ν is the number in the set

$$2n, 2(n + 1), \ldots, 2(2n - 1),$$

so that again $\nu = n$. In this case ν is even if p has the form $8q - 1$ and ν is odd if p has the form $8q + 3$. We may summarize these results as follows.

Theorem 5.3.5 The number 2 is a quadratic residue of all primes of the form $8q + 1$ or $8q - 1$ and is a nonresidue of all primes of the form $8q + 3$ or $8q - 3$. ■

We conclude this section with the following result, known as Gauss's *law of quadratic reciprocity*, which connects (p/q) and (q/p). The proof given here is modelled on that given by Long [37].

Theorem 5.3.6 If p and q are distinct odd primes, then

$$(p/q) \cdot (q/p) = (-1)^{\frac{1}{4}(p-1)(q-1)}, \tag{5.42}$$

and thus $(p/q) = (q/p)$ unless p and q are both of the form $4n + 3$, in which case $(p/q) = -(q/p)$. ■

Proof. For $1 \le k \le \frac{1}{2}(p-1)$, write

$$kq = p\left[\frac{kq}{p}\right] + t_k, \tag{5.43}$$

where $[x]$ denotes the integer part of x, and consequently $1 \le t_k \le p-1$. With the notation used in our proof of Gauss's lemma, let $p - r_1, \ldots, p - r_\nu$ denote the values of t_k that are greater than $\frac{1}{2}p$ and let $s_{\nu+1}, \ldots, s_{\frac{1}{2}(p-1)}$ denote the values of t_k that are less than $\frac{1}{2}p$. We have from Gauss's lemma that $(q/p) = (-1)^\nu$. Now let $r = \sum r_j$ and $s = \sum s_j$. Since, as we have already noted, the numbers r_j and s_j are a permutation of the numbers $1, 2, \ldots, \frac{1}{2}(p-1)$, we have

$$r + s = \sum_{k=1}^{(p-1)/2} k = \frac{1}{8}(p^2 - 1). \tag{5.44}$$

We also have

$$\sum t_k = \sum(p - r_j) + \sum s_j = \nu p - r + s, \tag{5.45}$$

since there are ν terms in the first summation on the right side of equation (5.45). On summing (5.43) over k and using (5.45), we obtain

$$\frac{1}{8}(p^2 - 1)q = p\sum_{k=1}^{(p-1)/2}\left[\frac{kq}{p}\right] + \nu p - r + s. \tag{5.46}$$

If we subtract (5.44) from (5.46), we find that

$$\frac{1}{8}(p^2 - 1)(q - 1) = p\sum_{k=1}^{(p-1)/2}\left[\frac{kq}{p}\right] - 2r + \nu p. \tag{5.47}$$

At this stage it is helpful to be aware that to evaluate $(-1)^\nu$ in Gauss's lemma we need to know only whether ν is congruent to 0 or 1 modulo p. It is thus useful to deduce from (5.47) that since $\frac{1}{8}(p^2 - 1)$ is an integer, q is odd and p is an odd prime,

$$\sum_{k=1}^{(p-1)/2}\left[\frac{kq}{p}\right] \equiv \nu \,(\mathrm{mod}\ 2). \tag{5.48}$$

Hence

$$(q/p) = (-1)^u, \qquad \text{where} \qquad u = \sum_{k=1}^{(p-1)/2}\left[\frac{kq}{p}\right]. \tag{5.49}$$

If we interchange the roles of p and q, we similarly obtain

$$(p/q) = (-1)^v, \qquad \text{where} \qquad v = \sum_{k=1}^{(q-1)/2}\left[\frac{kp}{q}\right]. \tag{5.50}$$

The remainder of the proof is devoted to finding simpler expressions for the sums in (5.49) and (5.50). Let S denote the set of all numbers of the form $jp - kq$, where $1 \le j \le \frac{1}{2}(q-1)$ and $1 \le k \le \frac{1}{2}(p-1)$. The number of elements in S is thus $\frac{1}{2}(p-1) \cdot \frac{1}{2}(q-1)$. If for any element of S, $jp = kq$, then $p \mid kq$, which is impossible, since the prime p obviously does not divide either k or q. It follows that the elements of S are either positive or negative. For any fixed j, we note that $jp > kq$ for all values of k from 1 to $[jp/q]$. On summing over j, we find that the number of positive elements of S is

$$v = \sum_{j=1}^{(q-1)/2} \left[\frac{jp}{q} \right],$$

and similarly we find that the number of negative elements of S is

$$u = \sum_{k=1}^{(p-1)/2} \left[\frac{kq}{p} \right],$$

where u and v are already defined in (5.49) and (5.50), respectively. Thus the total number of elements of S is

$$u + v = \frac{1}{2}(p-1) \cdot \frac{1}{2}(q-1),$$

and this completes the proof. ■

Problem 5.3.1 Show that modulo 11,

$$4! \equiv 2, \quad 5! \equiv -1, \quad 7! \equiv 2, \quad 9! \equiv 1,$$

and so verify Wilson's theorem directly for $p = 11$.

Problem 5.3.2 Show that for any odd prime p,

$$(p-2)! \equiv 1 \,(\text{mod } p).$$

Problem 5.3.3 Deduce from (5.35) that if $(a, p) = (b, p) = 1$, then

$$(a/p) \cdot (b/p) = (ab/p).$$

Problem 5.3.4 Use Theorem 5.3.4 to determine whether or not 5 is a quadratic residue of 13.

Problem 5.3.5 Deduce from Theorem 5.3.5 that for any odd prime p,

$$(2/p) = (-1)^{(p^2-1)/8}.$$

Problem 5.3.6 Use Gauss's lemma to give an alternative proof of Theorem 5.3.3.

5.4   Diophantine Equations

In Section 4.1 (see (4.4)) we considered an equation of the form

$$ax + by = c, \tag{5.51}$$

where a, b, and c are given positive integers, and sought integer values of x and y that satisfy (5.51). Any algebraic equation for which integer solutions are sought is called a Diophantine equation. We saw that (5.51) has solutions in integers if and only if $(a, b) \mid c$, and discussed how to find solutions when this condition is satisfied. It is easy to write down a large number of Diophantine equations, perhaps by generalizing a particular arithmetical oddity or by generalizing another equation. For example, with the relation $25 + 2 = 27$ in mind, we might seek solutions of the Diophantine equation

$$x^2 + 2 = y^3.$$

Pierre de Fermat found that this equation has only the one solution, and that the similar equation

$$x^2 + 4 = y^3,$$

which is satisfied by $x = y = 2$, has only one other solution. Can you find it? The equation $x^2 + y^2 = z^2$, which we discuss below, suggests that we consider its extension involving higher powers, such as $x^3 + y^3 = z^3$, and so on. Fermat conjectured that

$$x^n + y^n = z^n \tag{5.52}$$

has no solutions in positive integers for $n > 2$, and even claimed he had a proof. Due to lack of a proof for more than 350 years, this conjecture was always called "Fermat's last theorem." This famous conjecture was finally shown to be correct by Andrew Wiles, whose proof appeared in his paper "Modular elliptic curves and Fermat's last theorem," published in *Annals of Mathematics* in 1995. (See Simon Singh's very readable and interesting account [50] of Wiles's epic struggle with this problem.) You may think it very strange that mathematicians sometimes expend considerable effort on proving that something cannot be done!

Although no cube is the sum of two cubes, the relation

$$3^3 + 4^3 + 5^3 = 6^3 \tag{5.53}$$

prompts us to ask what can be said about solutions of the equation

$$x^3 + y^3 + z^3 = t^3, \tag{5.54}$$

and we will pursue this in Section 5.7. We remark in passing that the simplest special case of $x^2 + y^2 = z^2$, which is $3^2 + 4^2 = 5^2$, followed by (5.53), looks like the beginning of a most interesting sequence of equations! But alas, as the reader will easily verify, the expected third equation involving the sum of four consecutive fourth powers does not hold, and indeed *no* sum of four consecutive fourth powers is a fourth power. (See Problem 5.4.2.)

Let us now consider the Diophantine equation

$$x^2 + y^2 = z^2. \tag{5.55}$$

We know from the converse of Pythagoras's theorem that a triangle with sides of lengths x, y, and z satisfying (5.55) has a right angle opposite the longest side z. Any solution (x, y, z) of (5.55) in positive integers is called a *Pythagorean triple*, the simplest being $(3, 4, 5)$, and although this is named after the mathematicians of the Pythagorean school, which flourished in Greece in the sixth century BC, such triples were studied much earlier. Eves [14] quotes a number of "Pythagorean" triples found on a Babylonian mathematical tablet, now known as Plimpton 322, that is thought to date from around 1900 to 1600 BC. The Babylonian mathematicians were seriously interested in the equation (5.55): one of the triples on the Plimpton tablet is $(13500, 12709, 18541)$. In (5.55), if $p \mid x$ and $p \mid y$, for some prime p, then from (5.55) we have $p \mid z^2$ and hence $p \mid z$. We could then divide the equation (5.55) throughout by p^2. We can therefore assume that all such common factors have been removed and that $(x, y) = 1$. (Recall from Section 4.1 that (x, y) denotes the g.c.d. of x and y.) It is not possible (see Problem 5.2.6) for both x and y to be odd. The only possibility is that on the left side of (5.55) one of x and y is even and the other is odd, and therefore z is odd. Since it does not matter which is which between x and y, we will take x even and thus y odd. Then $z + y$ and $z - y$ are both even and

$$\left(\frac{1}{2}(z + y), \frac{1}{2}(z - y) \right) = 1,$$

for otherwise y and z would have a common factor, and so x, y, and z would have a common factor. If some $p \mid x$, we see that $p^2 \mid x^2$, and so $p^2 \mid \frac{1}{2}(z + y)$ or $\frac{1}{2}(z - y)$. Thus $\frac{1}{2}(z + y)$ and $\frac{1}{2}(z - y)$ must both be squares, say

$$\frac{1}{2}(z + y) = u^2 \quad \text{and} \quad \frac{1}{2}(z - y) = v^2$$

for some positive integers u and v. This determines the values of y and z, and hence the value of x, in terms of u and v, and we have the following result.

Theorem 5.4.1 All solutions of the Diophantine equation

$$x^2 + y^2 = z^2$$

in positive integers are of the form

$$x = 2\lambda uv, \quad y = \lambda(u^2 - v^2), \quad z = \lambda(u^2 + v^2), \tag{5.56}$$

where λ, u, and v are positive integers, with

$$v < u, \qquad (u, v) = 1, \qquad \text{and} \qquad u + v \equiv 1 \,(\text{mod } 2). \qquad \blacksquare \qquad (5.57)$$

u	2	3	4	4	5	5	6	6	7	7	7
v	1	2	1	3	2	4	1	5	2	4	6
x	4	12	8	24	20	40	12	60	28	56	84
y	3	5	15	7	21	9	35	11	45	33	13
z	5	13	17	25	29	41	37	61	53	65	85

TABLE 5.3. The first few primitive Pythagorean triples (x, y, z).

Since one of u and v is even and one is odd, we note from (5.56) that x is always a multiple of 4. Table 5.3 lists the first few *primitive* Pythagorean triples, meaning those where x, y, and z have no common factor. These are enumerated in Table 5.3 according to increasing values of u where, for a given value of u, we run through all values of v such that (5.57) holds. Given positive integers x, y, and z satisfying $x^2 + y^2 = z^2$, we can determine the value of λ in (5.56) by computing the g.c.d. of x, y, and z. It suffices to consider the case where $\lambda = 1$, and thus the triple is primitive, consisting of one even and two odd numbers. Then x is the even number, and y and z are respectively the smaller and larger odd numbers, and

$$u^2 = \frac{1}{2}(z + y), \qquad v^2 = \frac{1}{2}(z - y). \qquad (5.58)$$

Problem 5.4.4 shows that $x^2 + y^2 = z^2$ has an infinite number of solutions for which $z = x + 1$, and Table 5.3 shows that $3^2 + 4^2 = 5^2$ is not the only example of the sum of two consecutive squares being a square. Another example is $20^2 + 21^2 = 29^2$. Indeed, there is an infinite number of solutions of $x^2 + y^2 = z^2$ for which x and y are consecutive integers. (See Problem 5.4.5.)

Let us consider sums of more than two consecutive squares that give a square, described by the Diophantine equation

$$(x + 1)^2 + (x + 2)^2 + \cdots + (x + k)^2 = z^2. \qquad (5.59)$$

We can recover $3^2 + 4^2 = 5^2$ from (5.59) by putting $x = 2$, $k = 2$, and $z = 5$. We can recast (5.59) in the form

$$kx^2 + k(k + 1)x + \frac{1}{6}k(k + 1)(2k + 1) = z^2.$$

When $k = 3$, the left side is $3x^2 + 12x + 14$. Since this is congruent to 2 modulo 3, it cannot be a square, since z^2 can be congruent only to 0 or 1 modulo 3. Thus (5.59) has no solutions for $k = 3$, and by similar arguments one can show that there are no solutions for $3 \leq k \leq 10$. The smallest value of $k > 2$ that yields a solution is $k = 11$. For example we have

$$18^2 + 19^2 + \cdots + 27^2 + 28^2 = 77^2$$

and

$$38^2 + 39^2 + \cdots + 47^2 + 48^2 = 143^2.$$

The only solution with $x = 0$ and $k > 1$ is

$$1^2 + 2^2 + \cdots + 24^2 = 70^2.$$

The determination of which values of k yield solutions of (5.59) is rather complicated. (For more details, see Freitag and Phillips [17].) An infinite class of solutions is given by the following parametric form, for every choice of positive integer r:

$$s = \frac{1}{2}r(3r \pm 1),$$
$$x = 12s^2 - 11s - 2,$$
$$k = 24s + 1,$$
$$z = (6r \pm 1)(12s^2 + s + 1).$$

As we stated above, the equation $x^4 + y^4 = z^4$ has no solution in positive integers. This is a consequence of the following theorem, where we show that $x^4 + y^4$ cannot even be a square.

Theorem 5.4.2 The equation

$$x^4 + y^4 = z^2 \tag{5.60}$$

has no solution in positive integers.

Proof. We will assume that there is a solution of (5.60) in positive integers and obtain a contradiction. Let S be the set of all positive integers z for which (5.60) has a solution in positive integers. By the well-ordering principle (see Section 4.1) there exists a smallest member of S, which we will denote by m, and there exist positive integers x and y for which

$$x^4 + y^4 = m^2. \tag{5.61}$$

Then we must have $(x, y) = 1$; otherwise, we could divide (5.61) throughout by the fourth power of (x, y) and obtain a solution of (5.60) with a value of z smaller than m. We next argue that at least one of x and y is odd, and thus

$$m^2 = x^4 + y^4 \equiv 1 \text{ or } 2 \pmod{4}.$$

From Problem 5.2.6 we see that $m^2 \equiv 2 \,(\mathrm{mod}\ 4)$ is impossible. We deduce that we cannot have both values odd, and so we may take x even and y odd. We can then apply Theorem 5.4.1 to the equation

$$(x^2)^2 + (y^2)^2 = m^2$$

and deduce that there exist positive integers u and v such that

$$x^2 = 2uv, \quad y^2 = u^2 - v^2, \quad m = u^2 + v^2,$$

where $u > v$, $(u, v) = 1$, and $u + v \equiv 1 \,(\mathrm{mod}\ 2)$. If u were even and v odd, we would have

$$y^2 \equiv -1 \,(\mathrm{mod}\ 4),$$

which is impossible. Thus u is odd and $v = 2w$, say, is even. Then

$$\left(\frac{x}{2}\right)^2 = uw, \quad \text{with} \quad (u, w) = 1,$$

and so u and w are both squares, say

$$u = s^2, \quad w = t^2,$$

where s and t are positive integers with $(s, t) = 1$. It follows that

$$y^2 = u^2 - v^2 = s^4 - 4t^4,$$

so that

$$(2t^2)^2 + y^2 = (s^2)^2 \tag{5.62}$$

and no two of $2t^2$, y, and s^2 have a common factor. We can now apply Theorem 5.4.1 to (5.62) to give

$$2t^2 = 2ab, \quad y = a^2 - b^2, \quad s^2 = a^2 + b^2, \tag{5.63}$$

where $a > b > 0$, $(a, b) = 1$, and $a + b \equiv 1 \,(\mathrm{mod}\ 2)$. Since $t^2 = ab$ and $(a, b) = 1$, a and b must both be squares, say

$$a = c^2 \quad \text{and} \quad b = d^2, \quad \text{with} \quad (c, d) = 1. \tag{5.64}$$

Then it follows from (5.63) and (5.64) that

$$c^4 + d^4 = s^2, \tag{5.65}$$

where

$$s \le s^2 = u \le u^2 < u^2 + v^2 = m,$$

showing that (5.65) is an equation of the form $x^4 + y^4 = z^2$ with a value of z smaller than m. This contradicts our above assumption about m, thus completing the proof.   ∎

In the above most ingenious proof, the assumption that the given equation had a solution in positive integers led us to another solution involving smaller positive integers, giving a contradiction. This technique, called the *method of infinite descent*, was pioneered by Fermat.

Problem 5.4.1 Show that the Diophantine equation

$$(x - 1)^3 + x^3 + (x + 1)^3 = (x + 2)^3$$

has only one solution, when $x = 4$, giving (5.53).

Problem 5.4.2 Consider the Diophantine equation

$$(x - 1)^4 + x^4 + (x + 1)^4 + (x + 2)^4 = y^4.$$

Show that the left side is congruent to 2 modulo 4 and deduce that the equation has no solutions in integers.

Problem 5.4.3 Given the Pythagorean triple

$$(x, y, z) = (13500, 12709, 18541)$$

referred to in the text, find values of the parameters u and v such that x, y, and z are given by (5.56).

Problem 5.4.4 Verify that

$$(2n + 1)^2 + (2n^2 + 2n)^2 = (2n^2 + 2n + 1)^2$$

for all positive integers n and express the Pythagorean triple that satisfies the above equation in the form (5.56).

Problem 5.4.5 Verify from Theorem 5.4.1 that if the Diophantine equation $x^2 + y^2 = z^2$ has a primitive solution satisfying $|x - y| - 1$, then we may write

$$y - x = u^2 - v^2 - 2uv = \pm 1.$$

Deduce from the result of Problem 4.2.6 that $u = U_{n+1}$ and $v = U_n$ for any $n \geq 1$ gives such solutions, where the sequence (U_n) is defined by

$$U_{n+1} = 2U_n + U_{n-1},$$

with $U_0 = 0$ and $U_1 = 1$. As part of your proof, you will need to verify that $(U_{n+1}, U_n) = 1$ and that $U_{n+1} + U_n \equiv 1 \pmod 2$.

Problem 5.4.6 Begin with the parametric form (5.56) and choose $\lambda = 1$, and write down the residue classes of x, y, and z corresponding to all possible residue classes of u and v modulo 3. Thus show that in every

Pythagorean triple, one member is divisible by 3. Similarly, show that one member of every Pythagorean triple is divisible by 5. Since, as we saw above, x is always divisible by 4, all Pythagorean triples share these three properties with the simplest triple $(3, 4, 5)$. What is the smallest solution (x, y, z) after $(3, 4, 5)$ such that one of x, y, and z is divisible by 3, one by 4, and one by 5?

Problem 5.4.7 Show that

$$x = 2uv, \quad y = |2u^2 - v^2|, \quad z = 2u^2 + v^2,$$

where u and v are any positive integers, is a solution of the Diophantine equation $2x^2 + y^2 = z^2$.

Problem 5.4.8 Find solutions of the Diophantine equation $3x^2 + y^2 = z^2$.

5.5   Algebraic Integers

The integers, namely the set $\mathbb{Z} = \{0, \pm 1, \pm 2, \ldots\}$, may be regarded as a special case of a set of *algebraic integers*, which we now define. An algebraic integer is a number x that satisfies a polynomial equation of the form

$$x^n + a_1 x^{n-1} + \cdots + a_n = 0, \tag{5.66}$$

where $a_1, a_2, \ldots, a_n$ all belong to $\mathbb{Z}$. Thus the elements of $\mathbb{Z}$ are the only algebraic integers that satisfy an equation of the form (5.66) with $n = 1$. Obviously, we require a different such equation for each element of $\mathbb{Z}$. Two other systems of algebraic integers will be introduced in this section, and these are denoted by $\mathbb{Z}[\omega]$ and $\mathbb{Z}[i]$. Since these two systems share many common properties, it will suffice to work through the details for only one of them. We will begin with a study of $\mathbb{Z}[\omega]$, since it is essential to our understanding of Section 5.6.

We begin with the factorization of $x^3 - 1$,

$$x^3 - 1 = (x - 1)(x - \omega)(x - \omega^2), \tag{5.67}$$

where

$$\omega = \frac{1}{2}(-1 + i\sqrt{3})$$

and so

$$\omega^2 + \omega + 1 = 0. \tag{5.68}$$

Then we consider numbers of the form

$$a + b\omega,$$

where a and b are rational numbers. We denote the set of all such numbers by $\mathbb{Q}[\omega]$. It is easy to verify that if α and β belong to $\mathbb{Q}[\omega]$, then so does $c\alpha + d\beta$, where c and d are rational numbers, and $\alpha\beta$ also belongs to $\mathbb{Q}[\omega]$. Further, multiplication and addition in $\mathbb{Q}[\omega]$ is *commutative*, meaning that $\alpha\beta = \beta\alpha$, and $\alpha + \beta = \beta + \alpha$. In fact (see, for example, [1]) $\mathbb{Q}[\omega]$ is a *field*. We also note that

$$(a + b\omega)(a + b\omega^2) = a^2 - ab + b^2, \tag{5.69}$$

in view of (5.68), and that

$$a^2 - ab + b^2 = (a - \tfrac{1}{2}b)^2 + \tfrac{3}{4}b^2 \geq 0. \tag{5.70}$$

We define $N(\alpha)$, called the *norm* of α, as

$$N(\alpha) = a^2 - ab + b^2, \qquad \text{where} \qquad \alpha = a + b\omega. \tag{5.71}$$

We observe from (5.70) that $N(\alpha) > 0$ unless $a = b = 0$, so that $\alpha = 0$, and we note that $N(0) = 0$. It is easily verified that $a + b\omega^2$ is the complex conjugate of $a + b\omega$, and thus, in view of (5.69), $N(\alpha)$ has the same meaning as $|\alpha|^2$ in the language of complex numbers. It follows that

$$N(\alpha)N(\beta) = N(\alpha\beta). \tag{5.72}$$

One might expect to define $N(\alpha)$ as $|\alpha|$, rather than $|\alpha|^2$. In some situations this would be a more natural definition of a norm, since we would then have $N(c\alpha) = |c| \cdot N(\alpha)$ for all rational values of c. However, the advantage of the definition chosen here is that $N(a + b\omega)$ is a nonnegative integer when $a, b \in \mathbb{Z}$. For $\alpha \neq 0$, if we divide (5.69) throughout by $a^2 - ab + b^2$, we see that the *inverse* of α, which we will denote by α^{-1}, is given by

$$\alpha^{-1} = (a^2 - ab + b^2)^{-1}(a + b\omega^2) = (a^2 - ab + b^2)^{-1}((a - b) - b\omega).$$

This shows that given any $\alpha \neq 0 \in \mathbb{Q}[\omega]$, there is a unique $\alpha^{-1} \in \mathbb{Q}[\omega]$ such that $\alpha\alpha^{-1} = 1$. We call any element α for which $N(\alpha) = 1$ a *unit* of $\mathbb{Q}[\omega]$. From (5.70) and (5.71), we see that $N(\alpha) = 1$ implies that

$$(2a - b)^2 + 3b^2 = 4,$$

whose only solutions in integers are

$$a = \pm 1, b = 0, \qquad a = 0, b = \pm 1, \qquad a = b = \pm 1.$$

Since $1 + \omega = -\omega^2$, we see that there are six units,

$$\alpha = \pm 1, \ \pm\omega, \ \pm\omega^2.$$

Following our use of $\mathbb{Z}$ to denote the integers, we define

$$\mathbb{Z}[\omega] = \{a + b\omega \mid a, b \in \mathbb{Z}\},$$

and we call the elements of $\mathbb{Z}[\omega] \subset \mathbb{Q}[\omega]$ the *integers* of $\mathbb{Q}[\omega]$, or simply the integers when there is no danger of confusion with the elements of $\mathbb{Z}$. We note that $\mathbb{Z}[\omega]$ is (see, for example, [1]) a *ring*. It is not necessary to be familiar with the theory of rings to understand what follows, but the reader who wishes to know more about this may consult Allenby [1], for example. If $x = a + b\omega$, where $a, b \in \mathbb{Z}$, it is easily verified that

$$x^2 - (2a - b)x + (a^2 - ab + b^2) = 0. \tag{5.73}$$

In view of the definition given at the beginning of this section, (5.73) shows that $\mathbb{Z}[\omega]$ is a set of algebraic integers.

If $\alpha = \beta\gamma$ in $\mathbb{Z}[\omega]$, we say that β and γ are divisors of α and write

$$\beta \mid \alpha \qquad \text{and} \qquad \gamma \mid \alpha.$$

We say that an element α in $\mathbb{Z}[\omega]$ that is not a unit is *prime* unless we can write $\alpha = \beta\gamma$, for some integers β and γ that are not units. We need to be careful here. To avoid confusion, for the remainder of this section (and also in the next section) we will write "prime," as just defined, to denote an integer in $\mathbb{Z}[\omega]$ that has no divisor other than a unit or itself, and write "prime number in $\mathbb{Z}$" to denote one of the numbers $2, 3, 5, 7$, and so on. Later in this section we will also discuss primes in the system $\mathbb{Z}[i]$. If $\alpha = \beta\gamma$, where neither β nor γ is a unit, then $N(\beta), N(\gamma) > 1$, and it follows from

$$N(\alpha) = N(\beta)N(\gamma)$$

that $N(\alpha)$ is not a prime number in $\mathbb{Z}$. We conclude that if $N(\alpha)$ *is* a prime number in $\mathbb{Z}$, then α is a prime in $\mathbb{Z}[\omega]$. For example, $1 - \omega$ is prime, since $N(1 - \omega) = 3$ is a prime number in $\mathbb{Z}$. The converse does not hold, since we can have a prime α whose norm is not a prime number in $\mathbb{Z}$. For example $N(2) = 4$, which is not a prime number in $\mathbb{Z}$, whereas 2 *is* a prime in $\mathbb{Z}[\omega]$, as we will now prove. If $\alpha = 2$ were not a prime, we could write $\alpha = (a + b\omega)(c + d\omega)$ and thus obtain

$$N(\alpha) = 4 = (a^2 - ab + b^2)(c^2 - cd + d^2),$$

where neither $a + b\omega$ nor $c + d\omega$ is a unit and so

$$a^2 - ab + b^2 = 2.$$

From (5.70) this is equivalent to

$$(2a - b)^2 + 3b^2 = 8.$$

We may readily verify that the Diophantine equation $x^2 + 3y^2 = 8$ has no solution (in integers), and thus 2 is a prime in $\mathbb{Z}[\omega]$.

If ϵ is any unit, then $\epsilon\alpha$ is said to be an *associate* of α. Therefore, the associates of α are

$$\pm\alpha, \quad \pm\omega\alpha, \quad \pm\omega^2\alpha,$$

and if $\alpha = a + b\omega$, these are

$$\pm(a + b\omega), \quad \pm(-b + (a-b)\omega), \quad \pm((a-b) + a\omega).$$

Since multiplication in $\mathbb{Z}[\omega]$ is commutative, then for $\beta \neq 0$ we have $\alpha\beta^{-1} = \beta^{-1}\alpha$, and we will write

$$\alpha\beta^{-1} = \beta^{-1}\alpha = \frac{\alpha}{\beta}.$$

The above remarks about primes in $\mathbb{Z}[\omega]$ prompts the question, Can we find a prime number p in $\mathbb{Z}$ that is not a prime in $\mathbb{Z}[\omega]$? For such a p we would require $p = \alpha\beta$, where α, $\beta \in \mathbb{Z}$ are not units, and we have

$$p^2 = N(p) = N(\alpha)N(\beta) \Rightarrow N(\alpha) = N(\beta) = p. \tag{5.74}$$

Thus if $\alpha = a + b\omega$, we must have $\beta = a + b\omega^2$, the complex conjugate of α. We have already proved that 2 is a prime in $\mathbb{Z}[\omega]$. Pursuing (5.74) with $p = 3$ we seek $\alpha = a + b\omega$ such that

$$3 = N(a + b\omega) = a^2 - ab + b^2 = (a - \frac{1}{2}b)^2 + \frac{3}{4}b^2, \tag{5.75}$$

on using (5.70). An obvious solution is $a = 1$, $b = -1$, and we have

$$3 = (1 - \omega)(1 - \omega^2).$$

Thus 3 is not a prime in $\mathbb{Z}[\omega]$, since $1 - \omega$ and $1 - \omega^2$ are not units. If a general prime number $p \neq 3$ in $\mathbb{Z}$ is not to be prime in $\mathbb{Z}[\omega]$, the condition $N(\alpha) = p$ obtained in (5.74) implies, in view of (5.70), that

$$4p = (2a - b)^2 + 3b^2 \equiv (2a - b)^2 \equiv 1 \,(\text{mod } 3),$$

since p is not congruent to zero modulo 3. The above condition cannot hold if $p \equiv 2 \,(\text{mod } 3)$, and we conclude that a prime number p in $\mathbb{Z}$ such that $p \equiv 2 \,(\text{mod } 3)$ is a prime in $\mathbb{Z}[\omega]$. It may seem surprising that $p = 2$ and odd prime numbers p in $\mathbb{Z}$ such that $p \equiv 2 \,(\text{mod } 3)$ are the only prime numbers in $\mathbb{Z}$ that are also primes in $\mathbb{Z}[\omega]$. For Hardy and Wright [25] show that no prime number p in $\mathbb{Z}$ such that $p \equiv 1 \,(\text{mod } 3)$ is a prime in $\mathbb{Z}[\omega]$.

We now state and prove a result concerning the elements of $\mathbb{Z}[\omega]$ that is like the division algorithm for $\mathbb{Z}$, considered in Section 4.1.

Theorem 5.5.1 Given $\gamma_0 = a_0 + b_0\omega$, $\gamma_1 = a_1 + b_1\omega \in \mathbb{Z}[\omega]$, with $\gamma_1 \neq 0$, there exist integers μ_1 and γ_2 in $\mathbb{Z}[\omega]$ such that

$$\gamma_0 = \mu_1\gamma_1 + \gamma_2, \quad \text{with} \quad N(\gamma_2) < N(\gamma_1).$$

Proof. We have

$$\frac{\gamma_0}{\gamma_1} = \frac{a_0 + b_0\omega}{a_1 + b_1\omega} = \frac{(a_0 + b_0\omega)(a_1 + b_1\omega^2)}{(a_1 + b_1\omega)(a_1 + b_1\omega^2)},$$

which gives

$$\frac{\gamma_0}{\gamma_1} = \frac{(a_0a_1 + b_0b_1 - a_0b_1) + (a_1b_0 - a_0b_1)\omega}{a_1^2 - a_1b_1 + b_1^2} = c + d\omega, \tag{5.76}$$

say. In general, c and d are rational numbers. We can find nearest elements in $\mathbb{Z}$ to c and d, say m and n, such that

$$|c - m| \leq \frac{1}{2} \quad \text{and} \quad |d - n| \leq \frac{1}{2}$$

and hence

$$\left|\frac{\gamma_0}{\gamma_1} - (m + n\omega)\right|^2 = (c - m)^2 - (c - m)(d - n) + (d - n)^2 \leq \frac{3}{4}. \tag{5.77}$$

Thus with $\mu_1 = m + n\omega$ and $\gamma_2 = \gamma_0 - \mu_1\gamma_1$ we have

$$\gamma_2 = \gamma_1\left(\frac{\gamma_0}{\gamma_1} - \mu_1\right),$$

so that

$$N(\gamma_0 - \mu_1\gamma_1) = N(\gamma_2) = N(\gamma_1)N(\gamma_0/\gamma_1 - \mu_1)$$

and hence

$$N(\gamma_2) = N(\gamma_1) \cdot \left|\frac{\gamma_0}{\gamma_1} - \mu_1\right|^2. \tag{5.78}$$

It then follows from (5.78) and (5.77) that

$$N(\gamma_2) \leq \frac{3}{4}N(\gamma_1) < N(\gamma_1),$$

which completes the proof. ∎

Note that we do not have always have a unique choice of μ_1 and γ_2 above, as we do for their counterparts in the division algorithm for $\mathbb{Z}$. For example, with $b_0 = 3$, $a_1 = b_1 = 2$, and a_0 arbitrary, we see from (5.76) that

$$c = \frac{a_0a_1 + b_0b_1 - a_0b_1}{a_1^2 - a_1b_1 + b_1^2} = \frac{6}{4} = \frac{3}{2},$$

and so we could take $m = 1$ or 2. From the above division algorithm for $\mathbb{Z}[\omega]$ we can derive a Euclidean algorithm for $\mathbb{Z}[\omega]$ that includes the classical Euclidean algorithm for $\mathbb{Z}$ (see Section 4.1) as a special case.

Theorem 5.5.2 Given any $\gamma_0 = a_0 + b_0\omega$, $\gamma_1 = a_1 + b_1\omega \in \mathbb{Z}[\omega]$ such that $\gamma_1 \neq 0$, then there exists a positive integer n and the following integers in $\mathbb{Z}[\omega]$,

$$\mu_j, \; 1 \leq j \leq n, \quad \text{and} \quad \gamma_j, \; 2 \leq j \leq n,$$

such that

$$
\begin{aligned}
\gamma_0 &= \mu_1\gamma_1 + \gamma_2, \\
\gamma_1 &= \mu_2\gamma_2 + \gamma_3, \\
&\;\;\vdots \\
\gamma_{n-2} &= \mu_{n-1}\gamma_{n-1} + \gamma_n, \\
\gamma_{n-1} &= \mu_n\gamma_n.
\end{aligned}
\tag{5.79}
$$

Moreover, we have

$$N(\gamma_n) < N(\gamma_{n-1}) < \cdots < N(\gamma_2) < N(\gamma_1). \tag{5.80}$$

Proof. We may apply the above division algorithm for $\mathbb{Z}[\omega]$ repeatedly. Since at each stage we have $N(\gamma_{j+1}) < N(\gamma_j)$, the process must terminate after a finite number of steps, and this completes the proof. ∎

Note that if we take $a_0 > a_1 > 0$ and $b_0 = b_1 = 0$, then the process described above in Theorem 5.5.2 reduces to the classical Euclidean algorithm, described by (4.1).

We can talk about a *greatest* common divisor of two positive integers in $\mathbb{Z}$, because these integers are *ordered*, that is, given any two integers m and n in $\mathbb{Z}$, then either $m < n$ or $n < m$ or $m = n$. There is not such an ordering in $\mathbb{Z}[\omega]$. Nevertheless, let us consider the divisors of a given integer in $\mathbb{Z}[\omega]$. First we observe that for each unit ϵ of $\mathbb{Z}[\omega]$ there is an inverse unit, say ϵ^{-1}, such that $\epsilon\epsilon^{-1} = 1$. Since there are only six units, we can easily verify this. For example, $(-\omega)^{-1} = -\omega^2$. Then, if β is a divisor of α, so is $\epsilon\beta$, where ϵ is any unit. This follows from the statement

$$\alpha = \beta\gamma \quad \Leftrightarrow \quad \alpha = (\epsilon\beta)(\epsilon^{-1}\gamma).$$

Thus the divisors of a given integer α can be arranged in equivalence classes, each class consisting of six associates, meaning that these six integers can be generated by multiplying any one of them by each of the six units. We define a *highest common divisor* of two integers α and β in $\mathbb{Z}[\omega]$ to be an integer ξ in $\mathbb{Z}[\omega]$ that divides α and β, and that is divided by every common divisor of α and β. We write $\xi = (\alpha, \beta)$. It follows from the definition of highest common divisor that if $\xi = (\alpha, \beta)$, then $\epsilon\xi = (\alpha, \beta)$, where ϵ is any unit. Notice that if $\alpha, \beta \in \mathbb{Z}[\omega]$ are both in the subset of positive integers in $\mathbb{Z}$, their highest common divisor is simply their g.c.d. and its associates.

Using the same arguments that we applied in Section 4.1, we see that the Euclidean algorithm for $\mathbb{Z}[\omega]$ given above computes a highest common divisor of two integers in $\mathbb{Z}[\omega]$. Thus the integer γ_n determined by (5.79) is a highest common divisor of γ_0 and γ_1. Any integer ξ in $\mathbb{Z}[\omega]$ that is a highest common divisor of γ_0 and γ_1 must satisfy

$$\xi \mid \gamma_n \quad \text{and} \quad \gamma_n \mid \xi,$$

and so ξ must be an associate of γ_n. The highest common divisors of γ_0 and γ_1 are therefore

$$\pm\gamma_n, \quad \pm\omega\gamma_n, \quad \pm\omega^2\gamma_n.$$

Example 5.5.1 Let us apply the Euclidean algorithm in $\mathbb{Z}[\omega]$ to the two integers $\gamma_0 = 3 - 27\omega$ and $\gamma_1 = 2 - 23\omega$. We obtain

$$3 - 27\omega = 1 \cdot (2 - 23\omega) + (1 - 4\omega),$$
$$2 - 23\omega = (5 - \omega) \cdot (1 - 4\omega) + (1 + 2\omega),$$
$$1 - 4\omega = (-3 - 2\omega) \cdot (1 + 2\omega),$$

and thus $1 + 2\omega$ is a highest common divisor of $3 - 27\omega$ and $2 - 23\omega$. The associates of $1 + 2\omega$,

$$\pm(1 + 2\omega), \quad \pm(2 + \omega), \quad \pm(1 - \omega),$$

are the only highest common divisors of $3 - 27\omega$ and $2 - 23\omega$. ∎

Let π be any prime in $\mathbb{Z}[\omega]$ and let us apply the Euclidean algorithm to π and any integer α. Then either $\pi \mid \alpha$ or $(\pi, \alpha) = 1$. If $(\pi, \alpha) = 1$ and we apply the Euclidean algorithm (see (5.79)) to π and α, we will obtain $\gamma_n = \epsilon$, where ϵ is a unit. If we then multiply each equation in (5.79) throughout by β, we will obtain a new value of γ_n equal to $\epsilon\beta$, showing that

$$(\pi\beta, \alpha\beta) = \beta. \tag{5.81}$$

So if $\pi \mid \alpha\beta$ and $(\pi, \alpha) = 1$, it follows that (5.81) holds, and since π divides both $\pi\beta$ and $\alpha\beta$, then π must also divide their highest common divisor β. We have thus proved the following key result concerning $\mathbb{Z}[\omega]$.

Theorem 5.5.3 For any integers α and β and any prime π in $\mathbb{Z}[\omega]$,

$$\pi \mid \alpha\beta \quad \Rightarrow \quad \pi \mid \alpha \quad \text{or} \quad \pi \mid \beta. \quad \blacksquare$$

If a prime π divides $\alpha_1\alpha_2\cdots\alpha_n$, it follows from Theorem 5.5.3 that π is a divisor of one of $\alpha_1, \alpha_2, \ldots, \alpha_n$. We can deduce that each integer in $\mathbb{Z}[\omega]$ has a unique factorization into primes in $\mathbb{Z}[\omega]$, if we count a prime and its associates as being equivalent. For suppose we have two representations of a given integer α,

$$\alpha = \sigma_1^{m_1}\sigma_2^{m_2}\cdots\sigma_r^{m_r} = \tau_1^{n_1}\tau_2^{n_2}\cdots\tau_s^{n_s},$$

where the σ_j and τ_j are primes in $\mathbb{Z}[\omega]$. Since each σ is a prime divisor of α, it must be a divisor of one of the τ's and so must be an associate of one of the τ's. Similarly, each τ must be an associate of a σ, and so $r = s$. For any given $\sigma_j = \sigma$, we must have $\sigma = \epsilon\tau$ for some $\tau_k = \tau$, where ϵ is a unit. Suppose that

$$\alpha = \sigma^m\gamma = \epsilon^m\tau^m\gamma = \tau^n\delta, \tag{5.82}$$

where γ denotes the rest of the σ-factorization and δ denotes the rest of the τ-factorization, so that τ does not divide γ or δ. We can assume that $m \geq n$. If $m > n$, we can divide (5.82) throughout by τ^n to give

$$\epsilon^m\tau^{m-n}\gamma = \delta,$$

where γ and δ involve primes other than τ and its associates. But the last equation shows that $\tau \mid \delta$, which gives a contradiction. Thus the prime factorization in $\mathbb{Z}[\omega]$ is unique, counting a prime and its associates as being equivalent. Since $\mathbb{Z} \subset \mathbb{Z}[\omega]$, this justifies the uniqueness of factorization of the ordinary positive integers. Although, as was remarked earlier, the latter result may seem intuitively obvious, most of us ordinary mortals do *not* have such an intuitive feeling for the arithmetic of $\mathbb{Z}[\omega]$ as we have for the positive integers, and so very much need the reassurance of the above *proof* of the uniqueness of factorization in $\mathbb{Z}[\omega]$.

As Hardy and Wright say, "Gauss   was the first mathematician to use complex numbers in a really confident and scientific way." Indeed, when Gauss was only twenty he gave the first satisfactory proof of the *fundamental theorem of algebra*, that a polynomial equation with complex coefficients has at least one complex root.

Gauss considered the set of complex numbers whose real and imaginary parts are both integers. We will denote this by

$$\mathbb{Z}[i] = \{a + bi \mid a, b \in \mathbb{Z}\}, \tag{5.83}$$

and call $\mathbb{Z}[i]$ the set of *Gaussian integers*. If $\alpha = a + bi$ and $\bar{\alpha} = a - bi$, then

$$(x - \alpha)(x - \bar{\alpha}) = x^2 - 2ax + a^2 + b^2,$$

showing that $\alpha = a + bi$ satisfies an equation like (5.66) and so is an algebraic integer. For $\alpha \in \mathbb{Z}[i]$, we define $N(\alpha)$, called the *norm* of α, as

$$N(\alpha) = a^2 + b^2, \qquad \text{where} \qquad \alpha = a + bi. \tag{5.84}$$

This norm satisfies

$$N(\alpha\beta) = N(\alpha)N(\beta), \tag{5.85}$$

as we found in (5.72) for the norm in $\mathbb{Z}[\omega]$. Using the above account of the ring of algebraic integers $\mathbb{Z}[\omega]$ as our guide, we can write down a parallel account for the ring of Gaussian integers $\mathbb{Z}[i]$. First we define the *units* of $\mathbb{Z}[i]$ to be the elements $\alpha = a + bi$ for which

$$N(\alpha) = a^2 + b^2 = 1.$$

It is clear that there are just four units in $\mathbb{Z}[i]$, namely

$$\alpha = \pm 1, \ \pm i.$$

If ϵ is any unit, then $\epsilon\alpha$ is said to be an *associate* of α. The associates of α are thus

$$\pm \alpha, \quad \pm i\alpha.$$

We define "divisor" and "prime" in $\mathbb{Z}[i]$ exactly as we did above for $\mathbb{Z}[\omega]$, and we can show that if $N(\alpha)$ is a prime number in $\mathbb{Z}$, then α is a prime in $\mathbb{Z}[i]$. Again, as we did for $\mathbb{Z}[\omega]$, we can write down a division algorithm and a Euclidean algorithm for $\mathbb{Z}[i]$. Similarly we can show that for any elements α and β in $\mathbb{Z}[i]$ and any prime π in $\mathbb{Z}[i]$,

$$\pi \mid \alpha\beta \quad \Rightarrow \quad \pi \mid \alpha \quad \text{or} \quad \pi \mid \beta,$$

and deduce that each element of $\mathbb{Z}[i]$ has a unique prime factorization, apart from associates.

We now use the Gaussian integers to prove one of the most beautiful results in number theory. As an encouragement to the reader let me say that a successful understanding of the proof of Theorem 5.5.4 will earn you an implicit commendation from G. H. Hardy (1877–1947), who wrote the following (see [24]) about this important result: "Unfortunately there is no proof within the comprehension of anybody but a fairly expert mathematician."

Theorem 5.5.4 Every prime p of the form $4n + 1$ can be written in the form $p = x^2 + y^2$, where x and y are positive integers.

Proof. We saw in Example 5.3.2 that

$$p \mid a^2 + 1 = (a + i)(a - i), \qquad \text{where} \qquad a = ((p - 1)/2)!.$$

If p were a prime in $\mathbb{Z}[i]$, this would imply that p divides $a + i$ or $a - i$, which is impossible, since neither of the elements $a/p \pm i/p$ belongs to $\mathbb{Z}[i]$. Since p is not a prime in $\mathbb{Z}[i]$, we can express it as

$$p = (x + yi)(u + vi),$$

and it follows from (5.85), the multiplicative property of the norm in $\mathbb{Z}[i]$, that

$$p^2 = (x^2 + y^2)(u^2 + v^2),$$

where each of the two factors on the right of the latter equation is greater than 1. We conclude that $p = x^2 + y^2$. We can show that this representation of p is unique. For suppose that

$$p = x^2 + y^2 = u^2 + v^2.$$

Then

$$(x + yi)(x - yi) = (u + vi)(u - vi),$$

and since the norm of each of the factors $x \pm yi$ and $u \pm vi$ is the prime number p, each factor is a prime in $\mathbb{Z}[i]$. From the uniqueness of factorization in $\mathbb{Z}[i]$, apart from associates, we may deduce that

$$x + yi = \pm(u \pm vi) \qquad \text{or} \qquad x + yi = \pm i(u \pm vi)$$

and thus $x = \pm u$ or $x = \pm v$, showing that p has a unique representation as the sum of two squares. ∎

It is clear that $2 = (1 + i)(1 - i)$ is not a prime in $\mathbb{Z}[i]$, and Theorem 5.5.4 shows that for any prime number p in $\mathbb{Z}$ of the form $4n + 1$, we may write

$$p = x^2 + y^2 = (x + yi)(x - yi),$$

and so such a p is not a prime in $\mathbb{Z}[i]$. We can also show (see Problem 5.5.8) that all prime numbers in $\mathbb{Z}$ of the form $4n + 3$ are also primes in $\mathbb{Z}[i]$.

It follows from Theorems 5.5.4 and 5.1.3 that there is an infinite number of primes of the form $x^2 + y^2$. In their recent paper [19], which runs to nearly a hundred pages of highly technical mathematics, Friedlander and Iwaniec prove that there is also an infinite number of primes of the form $x^2 + y^4$, and they derive an asymptotic estimate of how many primes there are of this form, just as the prime number theorem does for all primes.

Problem 5.5.1 Verify the relation $N(\alpha)N(\beta) = N(\alpha\beta)$ for both $\mathbb{Z}[\omega]$ and $\mathbb{Z}[i]$.

Problem 5.5.2 Let $\alpha = a + b\omega$ and $\bar{\alpha} = a + b\omega^2$. Show that the quadratic equation

$$(x - \alpha)(x - \bar{\alpha}) = 0$$

is equivalent to (5.73), so justifying that the elements of $\mathbb{Z}[\omega]$ are algebraic integers.

Problem 5.5.3 Show that there is no $\alpha \in \mathbb{Z}[\omega]$ whose norm $N(\alpha)$ takes the value $2(2m - 1)$, where m is any positive integer.

Problem 5.5.4 Verify that

$$a^2 - ab + b^2 = \frac{1}{4}(a + b)^2 + \frac{3}{4}(a - b)^2 = \frac{1}{2}(a^2 + (a - b)^2 + b^2).$$

Problem 5.5.5 Verify that 3 is an associate of $(1 - \omega)^2$.

Problem 5.5.6 Show that the associates of $1 - \omega$ are

$$\pm(1 - \omega), \quad \pm(1 - \omega^2), \quad \pm\omega(1 - \omega).$$

Problem 5.5.7 Obtain the factorizations of 7 and 13 in $\mathbb{Z}[\omega]$, remembering that a factorization is unique, apart from associates.

Problem 5.5.8 Make use of (5.74) in $\mathbb{Z}[i]$ to show that every prime number in $\mathbb{Z}$ of the form $4n + 3$ is also a prime in $\mathbb{Z}[i]$.

5.6   The equation $x^3 + y^3 = z^3$

In this section we show that the equation $x^3 + y^3 = z^3$ has no solution in positive integers. We follow the proof given in Hardy and Wright [25], which, as they state, is modelled on the account given by Edmund Landau (1877–1938). The method of attack is to prove the stronger result that this equation has no solution in the ring $\mathbb{Z}[\omega]$, defined in the previous section, which includes the integers $\mathbb{Z}$ as a subset.

We saw above that $1 - \omega$ is a prime in $\mathbb{Z}[\omega]$. We now state and prove some results concerning $1 - \omega$ that we will require to obtain the main result of this section. In what follows, we need to extend Gauss's concept of congruences from $\mathbb{Z}$ to $\mathbb{Z}[\omega]$ in an obvious way, writing

$$\alpha \equiv \beta \,(\mathrm{mod}\ \gamma)$$

to mean $\gamma \mid \alpha - \beta$, where $\alpha, \beta, \gamma \in \mathbb{Z}[\omega]$.

Theorem 5.6.1 For any integer $a + b\omega$ in $\mathbb{Z}[\omega]$, we may write

$$a + b\omega \equiv 0,\ 1,\ \mathrm{or}\ -1 \,(\mathrm{mod}\ \sigma),$$

where $\sigma = 1 - \omega$.

Proof. We have

$$a + b\omega = a + b - b(1 - \omega) \equiv a + b \,(\mathrm{mod}\ \sigma).$$

Now, since $(1 - \omega)(1 - \omega^2) = 3$, we have $1 - \omega = \sigma \mid 3$. Then, since for any $a, b \in \mathbb{Z}$ we have

$$3 \mid a + b,\ a + b - 1,\ \mathrm{or}\ a + b + 1,$$

it follows that

$$\sigma \mid a + b,\ a + b - 1,\ \mathrm{or}\ a + b + 1,$$

which completes the proof.   ∎

Theorem 5.6.2 If $\mu \in \mathbb{Z}[\omega]$ is not divisible by $\sigma = 1 - \omega$, then

$$\mu^3 \equiv \pm 1 \pmod{\sigma^4}.$$

Proof. From Theorem 5.6.1,

$$\mu \equiv 0, \; 1, \; \text{or} \; -1 \pmod{\sigma},$$

and if σ does not divide μ, we can choose $\nu = \pm \mu$ such that

$$\nu \equiv 1 \pmod{\sigma}, \qquad \text{so that} \qquad \nu = 1 + \alpha \sigma,$$

for some α in $\mathbb{Z}[\omega]$. Therefore,

$$\pm(\mu^3 \mp 1) = \nu^3 - 1 = (\nu - 1)(\nu - \omega)(\nu - \omega^2)$$
$$= \alpha\sigma(\alpha\sigma + 1 - \omega)(\alpha\sigma + 1 - \omega^2),$$

and since

$$1 - \omega^2 = \sigma(1 + \omega) = -\sigma\omega^2,$$

we obtain

$$\pm(\mu^3 \mp 1) = \sigma^3 \alpha(\alpha + 1)(\alpha - \omega^2). \tag{5.86}$$

Now it follows from the factorization of $1 - \omega^2$ that $\omega^2 \equiv 1 \pmod{\sigma}$ and thus

$$\alpha(\alpha + 1)(\alpha - \omega^2) \equiv \alpha(\alpha + 1)(\alpha - 1) \equiv 0 \pmod{\sigma}, \tag{5.87}$$

the last step following from Theorem 5.6.1. Finally, we see from (5.86) and (5.87) that

$$\sigma^4 \mid \pm(\mu^3 \mp 1),$$

so that $\mu^3 \equiv \pm 1 \pmod{\sigma^4}$. ∎

Having prepared the groundwork with the above discussion of properties of the ring $\mathbb{Z}[\omega]$, we are now ready for our assault on the equation $x^3 + y^3 = z^3$.

Theorem 5.6.3 If $\xi^3 + \eta^3 + \zeta^3 = 0$, then $\sigma = 1 - \omega$ is a divisor of at least one of ξ, η, and ζ.

Proof. If σ is not a divisor of ξ, η, or ζ, then by Theorem 5.6.2,

$$0 = \xi^3 + \eta^3 + \zeta^3 \equiv \pm 1 \pm 1 \pm 1 \pmod{\sigma^4}.$$

In the line above, either all three signs are the same or there are two of one sign and one of the opposite sign. Thus we have

$$0 = \xi^3 + \eta^3 + \zeta^3 \equiv \pm 1 \; \text{or} \; \pm 3 \pmod{\sigma^4},$$

and so

$$\sigma^4 \mid 1 \quad \text{or} \quad \sigma^4 \mid 3.$$

We cannot have $\sigma^4 \mid 1$, because $\sigma = 1 - \omega$ is not a unit. From Problem 5.5.5 we see that 3 is an associate of σ^2, and thus we cannot have $\sigma^4 \mid 3$. This completes the proof. ∎

Now let us seek a solution of

$$\xi^3 + \eta^3 + \zeta^3 = 0 \tag{5.88}$$

in $\mathbb{Z}[\omega]$. If some α is a divisor of any two of ξ, η, and ζ, it must also be a divisor of the third. Thus we can assume that we have divided out by any such common divisors and seek a solution of (5.88) such that

$$(\eta, \zeta) = (\zeta, \xi) = (\xi, \eta) = 1.$$

From this and Theorem 5.6.3 we see that σ is a divisor of precisely one of ξ, η, and ζ. Let us assume that $\sigma \mid \zeta$ and thus σ is not a divisor of ξ or η. Further, let us write

$$\zeta = \sigma^m \phi$$

where $m \geq 1$ is chosen such that σ is not a divisor of ϕ. Thus (5.88) becomes

$$\xi^3 + \eta^3 + \sigma^{3m} \phi^3 = 0,$$

where $(\xi, \eta) = 1$ and σ is not a divisor of $\xi\eta\phi$. For notational reasons we will replace ϕ above by ζ and we will show that there is no such solution by proving a stronger result, that there is no solution of

$$\xi^3 + \eta^3 + \epsilon \sigma^{3m} \zeta^3 = 0, \tag{5.89}$$

where ϵ is any unit, with

$$(\xi, \eta) = 1 \quad \text{and} \quad \sigma \quad \text{does not divide} \quad \xi\eta\zeta. \tag{5.90}$$

We next show that m must be at least 2.

Theorem 5.6.4 For any solution of (5.89) satisfying the conditions in (5.90) we must have $m \geq 2$.

Proof. On applying Theorem 5.6.2, we deduce from (5.89) that

$$-\epsilon \sigma^{3m} \zeta^3 = \xi^3 + \eta^3 \equiv \pm 1 \pm 1 \pmod{\sigma^4}.$$

If the plus and minus signs are the same, we have

$$-\epsilon \sigma^{3m} \zeta^3 \equiv \pm 2 \pmod{\sigma^4},$$

and since σ is not a divisor of the prime 2, this is impossible. So the signs must be opposite, giving

$$-\epsilon \sigma^{3m} \zeta^3 \equiv 0 \pmod{\sigma^4},$$

and since σ is not a divisor of ϵ or ζ, we must have $m \geq 2$.   ∎

Beginning with (5.89), we now write (see Problem 5.6.1)

$$-\epsilon \sigma^{3m} \zeta^3 = \xi^3 + \eta^3 = (\xi + \eta)(\xi + \omega\eta)(\xi + \omega^2\eta). \tag{5.91}$$

The differences of the three factors $\xi + \eta$, $\xi + \omega\eta$, and $\xi + \omega^2\eta$ above are (see Problem 5.6.2) all associates of $\eta\sigma$. Thus each difference is divisible by σ but not by any higher power of σ, since σ does not divide η. Now, from (5.91), since $m \geq 2$, one of the factors on the right of (5.91) must be divisible by σ^2, and since the differences of the factors are divisible by σ, the other two factors must be divisible by σ. However, the other two factors cannot be divisible by σ^2, since the differences are not. We can suppose that σ^2 divides $\xi + \eta$, for if it were one of the other two we could replace η by its appropriate associate. Thus we obtain from (5.91) that

$$\xi + \eta = \sigma^{3m-2}\lambda_1, \quad \xi + \omega\eta = \sigma\lambda_2, \quad \xi + \omega^2\eta = \sigma\lambda_3, \tag{5.92}$$

where none of λ_1, λ_2, and λ_3 is divisible by σ. Let us write $\lambda = (\lambda_2, \lambda_3)$, and then λ divides both

$$\lambda_2 - \lambda_3 = \omega\eta$$

and

$$\omega\lambda_3 - \omega^2\lambda_2 = \omega\xi.$$

Thus λ divides both ζ and η and so divides $(\xi, \eta) - 1$. This shows that λ is a unit and $(\lambda_2, \lambda_3) = 1$. We can show similarly that

$$(\lambda_3, \lambda_1) = (\lambda_1, \lambda_2) = 1.$$

From (5.91) and (5.92) we have

$$-\epsilon\zeta^3 = \lambda_1\lambda_2\lambda_3,$$

and so, from the uniqueness (apart from associates) of prime factorization in $\mathbb{Z}[\omega]$, it follows that each λ_j is an associate of a cube, so that

$$\xi + \eta = \epsilon_1 \sigma^{3m-2}\zeta_1^3, \quad \xi + \omega\eta = \epsilon_2 \sigma\xi_1^3, \quad \xi + \omega^2\eta = \epsilon_3 \sigma\eta_1^3, \tag{5.93}$$

say, where ϵ_1, ϵ_2, and ϵ_3 are units and ξ_1, η_1, and ζ_1 have no common factor and are not divisible by σ. Since $1 + \omega + \omega^2 = 0$, we may write

$$0 = (1 + \omega + \omega^2)(\xi + \eta) - (\xi + \eta) + \omega(\xi + \omega\eta) + \omega^2(\xi + \omega^2\eta), \tag{5.94}$$

so that from (5.93) and (5.94) we have

$$\epsilon_2 \omega\sigma\xi_1^3 + \epsilon_3 \omega^2\sigma\eta_1^3 + \epsilon_1 \sigma^{3m-2}\zeta_1^3 = 0.$$

On multiplying the above equation throughout by $\epsilon_2^{-1}\omega^2\sigma^{-1}$, we obtain

$$\xi_1^3 + \delta_1\eta_1^3 + \delta_2 \sigma^{3m-3}\zeta_1^3 = 0, \tag{5.95}$$

where $\delta_1 = \epsilon_2^{-1}\epsilon_3\omega$ and $\delta_2 = \epsilon_1\epsilon_2^{-1}\omega^2$ are units. Since $m \geq 2$, we see that σ^3 divides $\xi_1^3 + \delta_1\eta_1^3$, and so certainly

$$\xi_1^3 + \delta_1\eta_1^3 \equiv 0 \,(\mathrm{mod}\ \sigma^2). \tag{5.96}$$

Since σ is not a divisor of ξ_1 or η_1, it follows immediately from Theorem 5.6.2 that

$$\xi_1^3 \equiv \pm 1 \,(\mathrm{mod}\ \sigma^2) \quad \text{and} \quad \eta_1^3 \equiv \pm 1 \,(\mathrm{mod}\ \sigma^2). \tag{5.97}$$

We could have written σ^4 instead of σ^2 both times in (5.97), but σ^2 will suffice. Then from (5.96) and (5.97) we have

$$1 \pm \delta_1 \equiv 0 \,(\mathrm{mod}\ \sigma^2). \tag{5.98}$$

Now, δ_1 is a unit, and it is easily verified (see Problem 5.6.3) that (5.98) is not satisfied when $\delta_1 = \pm\omega$ or $\pm\omega^2$. So we must choose $\delta_1 = \pm 1$. If $\delta_1 = -1$, we may replace η_1 by $-\eta_1$ in (5.95), and so in either case of $\delta_1 = \pm 1$ we have a solution of

$$\xi_1^3 + \eta_1^3 + \delta_2\,\sigma^{3m-3}\zeta_1^3 = 0. \tag{5.99}$$

We have thus established the following result.

Theorem 5.6.5 If there exists a solution in $\mathbb{Z}[\omega]$ of the equation

$$\xi^3 + \eta^3 + \epsilon\sigma^{3m}\zeta^3 = 0,$$

where ϵ is any unit, $(\xi, \eta) = 1$, and σ does not divide $\xi\eta\zeta$, then the discussion from (5.89) leading up to (5.99) shows that if $m > 1$, there also exists such a solution with m replaced by $m - 1$. ∎

After this very clever use of the method of descent, we are in sight of the promised land.

Theorem 5.6.6 The equation

$$\xi^3 + \eta^3 + \zeta^3 = 0 \tag{5.100}$$

has no solution in $\mathbb{Z}[\omega]$, and so the equation

$$x^3 + y^3 = z^3 \tag{5.101}$$

has no solution in positive integers.

Proof. We saw from Theorem 5.6.4 that for any solution in $\mathbb{Z}[\omega]$ of

$$\xi^3 + \eta^3 + \epsilon\sigma^{3m}\zeta^3 = 0, \tag{5.102}$$

where ϵ is a unit, $(\xi, \eta) = 1$, and where $\sigma = 1 - \omega$ does not divide $\xi\eta\zeta$, we must have $m > 1$. On the other hand, Theorem 5.6.5 shows that if there exists such a solution of (5.102), there must exist such a solution with m replaced by $m-1$. These two theorems provide a contradiction. Thus there is no solution of (5.100) in $\mathbb{Z}[\omega]$, and hence there is no solution of (5.101) in integers.   ∎

Problem 5.6.1 Replace x by $-\xi/\eta$ in (5.67) and deduce that

$$\xi^3 + \eta^3 = (\xi + \eta)(\xi + \omega\eta)(\xi + \omega^2\eta).$$

Problem 5.6.2 Show that the differences of the three factors of

$$(\xi + \eta)(\xi + \omega\eta)(\xi + \omega^2\eta),$$

namely

$$\pm\eta(1 - \omega), \quad \pm\eta\omega(1 - \omega), \quad \pm\eta(1 - \omega^2),$$

are all associates of $\eta\sigma$, where $\sigma = 1 - \omega$.

Problem 5.6.3 If $\delta_1 = +\omega$ or $\pm\omega^2$, verify that $1 \pm \delta_1$ assumes one of the values $-\omega$, $-\omega^2$, σ, or $-\omega^2\sigma$, and so prove that $1 \pm \delta_1$ cannot be congruent to zero modulo σ^2, where $\sigma = 1 - \omega$.

5.7   Euler and Sums of Cubes

The set of all solutions in integers of the equation $x^3 + y^3 + z^3 - t^3$, already mentioned in Section 5.4, is the same as the set of all solutions of

$$x^3 + y^3 - z^3 + t^3 \tag{5.103}$$

in integers, the simplest solution of the latter equation being $x = 3$, $y = 4$, $z = -5$, $t = 6$. Euler found all solutions of (5.103) in *rational* numbers, which therefore includes all integer solutions. Here we follow an analysis given by Hardy and Wright [25], who describe the resulting solution as being that of Euler, with a simplification due to Binet. We begin by making the change of variables

$$x = \xi + \eta, \quad y = \xi - \eta, \quad z = \zeta + \tau, \quad t = \zeta - \tau, \tag{5.104}$$

and then (5.103) becomes

$$\xi(\xi^2 + 3\eta^2) = \zeta(\zeta^2 + 3\tau^2). \tag{5.105}$$

We now pursue the latter equation in the complex plane, factorizing both sides to give

$$\xi(\xi + i\sqrt{3}\eta)(\xi - i\sqrt{3}\eta) = \zeta(\zeta + i\sqrt{3}\tau)(\zeta - i\sqrt{3}\tau).$$

Suppose that ξ and η are not both zero, which merely excludes the trivial solution for (5.103) given by $x = y = 0$ and $z = -t$. Then we write

$$\frac{\zeta + i\sqrt{3}\tau}{\xi + i\sqrt{3}\eta} = u + i\sqrt{3}v, \tag{5.106}$$

and by carrying out the above division, we have taken the first step down a road that leads us to solutions of (5.103) in rational numbers rather than in integers. If we take the complex conjugate of each side of (5.106), we obtain

$$\frac{\zeta - i\sqrt{3}\tau}{\xi - i\sqrt{3}\eta} = u - i\sqrt{3}v. \tag{5.107}$$

We will also require

$$\frac{\zeta^2 + 3\tau^2}{\xi^2 + 3\eta^2} = u^2 + 3v^2, \tag{5.108}$$

which follows by equating the product of the left sides of equations (5.106) and (5.107) with the product of their right sides. This is equivalent to taking the squares of the moduli of both sides of either (5.106) or (5.107). Then, on cross multiplying in (5.106), we obtain

$$\zeta + i\sqrt{3}\tau = (u + i\sqrt{3}v)(\xi + i\sqrt{3}\eta),$$

and equating real and imaginary parts yields

$$\zeta = u\xi - 3v\eta \tag{5.109}$$

and

$$\tau = v\xi + u\eta. \tag{5.110}$$

Next we obtain from (5.105) and (5.108) that

$$\xi = \zeta(u^2 + 3v^2), \tag{5.111}$$

and then combining (5.109) and (5.111) gives

$$\xi = (u\xi - 3v\eta)(u^2 + 3v^2),$$

which may be rearranged to give

$$\xi \cdot \left(u(u^2 + 3v^2) - 1\right) = \eta \cdot 3v(u^2 + 3v^2). \tag{5.112}$$

If

$$u(u^2 + 3v^2) - 1 = 0 \qquad \text{and} \qquad 3v(u^2 + 3v^2) = 0, \tag{5.113}$$

then the second equation in (5.113) implies that $v = 0$, and hence the first equation gives $u = 1$, so that (5.111) implies that $\xi = \zeta$ and (5.110) implies $\tau = \eta$. This, as we see from (5.104), yields the trivial solution for (5.103) given by $x = z$ and $y = t$. Unless both equations in (5.113) hold, (5.112) shows that we can write

$$\xi = 3\lambda v(u^2 + 3v^2), \qquad \eta = \lambda\left(u(u^2 + 3v^2) - 1\right), \qquad (5.114)$$

and then (5.109) and (5.110) give

$$\zeta = 3\lambda v, \qquad \tau = \lambda\left((u^2 + 3v^2)^2 - u\right). \qquad (5.115)$$

If u, v, and λ are any rational numbers, and if ξ, η, ζ, and τ are defined by (5.114) and (5.115), then we may verify that (5.109) and (5.110) hold and hence

$$\begin{aligned}
\zeta(\zeta^2 + 3\tau^2) &= 3\lambda v\left((u\xi - 3v\eta)^2 + 3(v\xi + u\eta)^2\right) \\
&= 3\lambda v(u^2 + 3v^2)(\xi^2 + 3\eta^2) \\
&= \xi(\xi^2 + 3\eta^2),
\end{aligned}$$

so that (5.105) and hence (5.103) holds. From (5.104) the parametric form for ξ, η, ζ, and τ given by (5.114) and (5.115) determines values for x, y, z, and t in terms of the three parameters u, v, and λ. These are cited in the statement of the following theorem, in which we summarize our findings above.

Theorem 5.7.1 Apart from the trivial solutions

$$x = y = 0, \; z = -t \qquad \text{and} \qquad x = z, \; y = t$$

all solutions of the equation $x^3 + y^3 = z^3 + t^3$ in rational numbers are given by the parametric equations

$$\begin{aligned}
\tau &= \lambda\left((u + 3v)(u^2 + 3v^2) - 1\right), \\
y &= \lambda\left(1 - (u - 3v)(u^2 + 3v^2)\right), \\
z &= \lambda\left((u^2 + 3v^2)^2 - (u - 3v)\right), \\
t &= \lambda\left((u + 3v) - (u^2 + 3v^2)^2\right),
\end{aligned}$$

where u, v, and λ are any rational numbers, with $\lambda \neq 0$. ∎

Given any rational numbers u and v, we can obviously choose an appropriate value of λ (unique apart from its sign) to obtain *integer* values of x, y, z, and t that have no common factor. Conversely, given any nontrivial solution x, y, z, and t of (5.103) we obtain from (5.104) that

$$\xi = \frac{1}{2}(x + y), \quad \eta = \frac{1}{2}(x - y), \quad \zeta = \frac{1}{2}(z + t), \quad \tau = \frac{1}{2}(z - t). \quad (5.116)$$

We then solve the simultaneous equations (5.109) and (5.110) to determine u and v, and hence find λ from (5.115), giving

$$u = \frac{\xi\zeta + 3\eta\tau}{\xi^2 + 3\eta^2}, \quad v = \frac{\xi\tau - \eta\zeta}{\xi^2 + 3\eta^2}, \quad \lambda = \frac{\zeta}{3v}. \qquad (5.117)$$

Let us consider when the denominators in (5.117) can be zero. If $\xi^2 + 3\eta^2 = 0$, we have $\xi = \eta = 0$, which gives the trivial solution $x = y = 0$ and $z = -t$. If $v = 0$, we see from (5.117) that $\xi\tau = \eta\zeta$, so that

$$\xi = \mu\zeta \qquad \text{and} \qquad \eta = \mu\tau,$$

for some value of μ. From (5.104) this implies that $x = \mu z$ and $y = \mu t$, and on substituting into (5.103), we obtain only $\mu = 1$, giving the trivial solution $x = z$ and $y = t$. Thus, to any nontrivial solution of (5.103), there corresponds a unique triple of rational numbers u, $v \neq 0$ and $\lambda \neq 0$ that provides the parametric representation defined in Theorem 5.7.1. Note that the effect of replacing v by $-v$ is just to replace x, y, z, and t by $-y$, $-x$, $-t$, and $-z$, respectively, which does not give any essentially new solution.

u	v	λ	x	y	z	t
1	1	$1/3$	5	3	6	-4
-1	1	1	7	17	20	-14
1	$1/2$	$16/3$	18	10	19	-3
-1	$1/2$	16	-2	86	89	-41
$-1/2$	1	$16/3$	38	66	75	-43
1	$1/3$	9	15	9	16	2
-1	$1/3$	9	-9	33	34	-16

TABLE 5.4. Some solutions of the equation $x^3 + y^3 = z^3 + t^3$.

There is a major difference between the above parametric solution for (5.103) and the parametric solution (5.56) that we derived for the equation $x^2 + y^2 = z^2$. In the latter case, we find all solutions of the equation by taking integer values of the parameters u, v, and λ, whereas we need to use rational values of u, v, and λ to find all integer solutions of the cubic equation. An obvious strategy for obtaining at least some solutions involving small integers is to choose rational values of u and v with small denominators. Table 5.4 lists a few solutions of (5.103) together with the values of the parameters u, v, and $\lambda \neq 0$ that generate them. It is pleasing that the simple choice of $u = v = 1$ and the value $\lambda = \frac{1}{3}$, chosen to remove the common factor in the resulting values of x, y, z, and t, yields $5^3 + 3^3 = 6^3 + (-4)^3$, giving the simple equation $3^3 + 4^3 + 5^3 = 6^3$.

Example 5.7.1 The last two lines in Table 5.4 correspond to the solutions

$$15^3 + 9^3 = 16^3 + 2^3 \qquad \text{and} \qquad 34^3 + 9^3 = 33^3 + 16^3,$$

and noting the presence of 16 and 9 in each equation, we can add them together to produce the "new" solution

$$34^3 + 2^3 = 33^3 + 15^3.$$

It is interesting to compute the values of u, v, and λ associated with the values $x = 34$, $y = 2$, $z = 33$, and $t = 15$ in the latter solution. From (5.116) and (5.117) we obtain

$$u = \frac{72}{91}, \quad v = -\frac{37}{182}, \quad \lambda = -\frac{1456}{37}. \quad \blacksquare$$

The above example illustrates the difficulties in using the above parametric form to generate solutions of (5.103) in integers. For finding solutions in small integers it is easier to use brute force, running through small values of x, y, and z and seeking values of t such that (5.103) holds. If we do this, it is easier to treat the equations

$$x^3 + y^3 = z^3 + t^3 \qquad \text{and} \qquad x^3 + y^3 + z^3 = t^3$$

separately and search for solutions in positive integers. The smallest solution of $x^3 + y^3 = z^3 + t^3$ in positive integers is

$$12^3 + 1^3 = 10^3 + 9^3.$$

This equation is the subject of an anecdote of G. H. Hardy, concerning his association with the famous Indian mathematician S. Ramanujan, to whom we have already referred in Section 1.2. This is recounted by C. P. Snow in his foreword to Hardy's *A Mathematician's Apology* [24]. Everyone, not only mathematicians, should read this beautifully written book, in which Hardy magically succeeds in showing something of the power, the elegance, and the attraction of mathematics, with scarcely an equation in sight. Snow's foreword, which runs to some fifty pages, gives a fascinating view of the great man, including an account of his passion for cricket. It was Hardy who had been instrumental in bringing Ramanujan from India to England. By a happy chance E. H. Neville, whom we have already mentioned in Section 3.6, went out to India in 1914 as a visiting lecturer and, at Hardy's request, sought out Ramanujan. He was able to persuade Ramanujan to accompany him home to Cambridge in the summer of 1914, just in time before the outbreak of war. As T. A. A. Broadbent [10] wrote, "This was a notable service to mathematics, and Neville was justly proud of his part." There followed an all too brief but brilliant collaboration in mathematics between Hardy and Ramanujan at the University of Cambridge. Later, when Hardy visited Ramanujan in hospital in Putney, London, he remarked that 1729, the number of the taxi in which he arrived, seemed a rather dull number. Ramanujan is reported as replying, "No, Hardy! No, Hardy! It is a very interesting number. It is the smallest number expressible as the sum of two cubes in two different ways."

Problem 5.7.1 Find the values of u, v, and λ associated with the equation

$$12^3 + 1^3 = 10^3 + 9^3.$$

Problem 5.7.2 In Theorem 5.7.1 replace u by a/b, v by c/d, and λ by $b^4 d^4$, where a, b, c, and d are integers, to give a four-parameter family of integer solutions of (5.103).

Problem 5.7.3 Verify that the two-parameter representation

$$x = 3u^2 + 5uv - 5v^2, \quad y = 4u^2 - 4uv + 6v^2,$$
$$z = 5u^2 - 5uv - 3v^2, \quad t = 6u^2 - 4uv + 4v^2$$

gives solutions of $x^3 + y^3 + z^3 = t^3$. This family of solutions was obtained by Ramanujan.

Problem 5.7.4 Show that every solution given by Ramanujan's parametric form (see Problem 5.7.3) satisfies

$$x + z = 4(t - y).$$

Find a solution of $x^3 + y^3 + z^3 = t^3$ that is not expressible in Ramanujan's form.

References

[1] R. B. J. T. Allenby. *Rings, Fields and Groups: An Introduction to Abstract Algebra, 2nd Edition*, Edward Arnold, 1991.

[2] R. B. J. T. Allenby and E. J. Redfern. *Introduction to Number Theory with Computing*, Edward Arnold, 1989.

[3] E. T. Bell. *Mathematics, Queen and Servant of Science*, G. Bell and Sons, London, 1952.

[4] Lennart Berggren, Jonathan Borwein, and Peter Borwein (eds.) *Pi: A Source Book*, Springer-Verlag, New York, 1997.

[5] David Blatner *The Joy of π*, Penguin, 1997.

[6] J. M. Borwein and P. B. Borwein. *Pi and the AGM*, John Wiley & Sons, New York, 1987.

[7] J. M. Borwein and P. B. Borwein. A cubic counterpart of Jacobi's identity and the AGM, *Transactions of the American Mathematical Society* **323**, 691–701, 1991.

[8] J. M. Borwein and P. B. Borwein. Ramanujan, Modular Equations, and Approximations to Pi or How to Compute One Billion Digits of Pi, *American Mathematical Monthly* **96**, 201–219, 1989.

[9] C. Brezinski. Convergence acceleration during the 20th century, *JCAM* (in press).

[10] T. A. A. Broadbent. Eric Harold Neville, *Journal of the London Mathematical Society* **37**, 479–482, 1962.

[11] B. C. Carlson. Algorithms involving arithmetic and geometric means, *American Mathematical Monthly* **78**, 496–505, 1971.

[12] D. P. Dalzell. On $\frac{22}{7}$, *Journal of the London Mathematical Society* **19**, 133–134, 1944.

[13] C. H. Edwards, Jr. *The Historical Development of the Calculus*, Springer-Verlag, New York, 1979.

[14] H. Eves. *An Introduction to the History of Mathematics, 5th Edition*, Saunders, Philadelphia, 1983.

[15] D. M. E. Foster and G. M. Phillips. A Generalization of the Archimedean Double Sequence, *Journal of Mathematical Analysis and Applications* **101**, 575–581, 1984.

[16] D. M. E. Foster and G. M. Phillips. The Arithmetic–Harmonic Mean, *Mathematics of Computation* **42**, 183–191, 1984.

[17] H. T. Freitag and G. M. Phillips. On the sum of consecutive squares, *Applications of Fibonacci Numbers* **6**, G. E. Bergum, A. N. Philippou, and A. F. Horadam (eds.), 137–142, Kluwer, Dordrecht, 1996.

[18] H. T. Freitag and G. M. Phillips. Elements of Zeckendorf Arithmetic, *Applications of Fibonacci Numbers* **7**, G. E. Bergum, A. N. Philippou, and A. F. Horadam (eds.), 129–132, Kluwer, Dordrecht, 1998.

[19] John Friedlander and Henryk Iwaniec. The polynomial $X^2 + Y^4$ captures its primes, *Annals of Mathematics* **148**, 945–1040, 1998.

[20] C. F. Gauss. *Werke Vol. 3*, Königlichen Gesellschaft der Wissenschaften, Göttingen, 1966.

[21] H. H. Goldstine. *A History of Numerical Analysis from the 16th through the 19th Century*, Springer-Verlag, New York, 1977.

[22] Ralph P. Grimaldi. *Discrete and Combinatorial Mathematics: An Applied Introduction, 3rd Edition*, Addison–Wesley, Reading, Massachusetts, 1994.

[23] Rod Haggerty. *Fundamentals of Mathematical Analysis, 2nd Edition*, Addison–Wesley, Wokingham, 1993.

[24] G. H. Hardy. *A Mathematician's Apology*, Cambridge University Press, 1940. Reprinted with Foreword by C. P. Snow, 1967.

[25] G. H. Hardy and E. M. Wright. *An Introduction to the Theory of Numbers, 5th Edition*, Clarendon Press, Oxford, 1979.

[26] Thomas Harriot. *A Briefe and True Report of the New Found Land of Virginia*, 1588. *2nd Edition* 1590, republished by Dover, New York, 1972.

[27] T. L. Heath. *A History of Greek Mathematics Vols. 1 and 2*, Dover, New York, 1981.

[28] Paul Hoffman. *The Man Who Loved Only Numbers: The Story of Paul Erdős and the Search for Mathematical Truth*, Fourth Estate, London, 1998.

[29] Clark Kimberling. Edouard Zeckendorf, *Fibonacci Quarterly* **36**, 416–418, 1998.

[30] W. R. Knorr. Archimedes and the measurement of the circle: A new interpretation, *Archive for History of Exact Sciences* **15**, 115–140, 1975–6.

[31] Zeynep F. Koçak and George M. Phillips. B-splines with geometric knot spacings, *BIT* **34**, 388–399, 1994.

[32] C. Lanczos. Computing Through the Ages. In *Proceedings of the Royal Irish Academy Conference in Numerical Analysis, 1972*, John J. H. Miller (ed.), Academic Press, London, 1973.

[33] D. H. Lehmer. On the compounding of certain means, *Journal of Mathematical Analysis and Applications* **36**, 183–200, 1971.

[34] S. L. Lee and G. M. Phillips. Interpolation on the Triangle, *Communications in Applied Numerical Methods* **3**, 271–276, 1987.

[35] S. L. Lee and G. M. Phillips. Polynomial interpolation at points of a geometric mesh on a triangle, *Proceedings of the Royal Society of Edinburgh* **108A**, 75–87, 1988.

[36] Lí Yan and Dú Shíràn. *Chinese Mathematics: A Concise History*, translated by John N. Crossley and Anthony W.-C. Lun, Oxford University Press, Oxford, 1987.

[37] Calvin T. Long. *Elementary Introduction to Number Theory*, D. C. Heath, Boston, 1965.

[38] G. G. Lorentz. *Approximation of Functions*, Holt, Rinehart and Winston, New York, 1966.

[39] J. Needham. *Science and Civilisation in China Vol. 3 Part I*, Cambridge University Press, Cambridge, 1959.

[40] Halil Oruç. *Generalized Bernstein Polynomials and Total Positivity*, Ph.D thesis, University of St Andrews, 1998.

[41] Halil Oruç and George M. Phillips. Explicit factorization of the Vandermonde matrix, *Linear Algebra and Its Applications* (in press).

[42] G. M. Phillips. Archimedes the Numerical Analyst, *American Mathematical Monthly* **88**, 165–169, 1981.

[43] G. M. Phillips. Archimedes and the Complex Plane, *American Mathematical Monthly* **91**, 108–114, 1984.

[44] G. M. Phillips and P. J. Taylor. *Theory and Applications of Numerical Analysis, 2nd Edition*, Academic Press, London, 1996.

[45] S. Ramanujan. Squaring the circle, *Journal of the Indian Mathematical Society* **5**, 132, 1913.

[46] S. Ramanujan. Modular Equations and Approximations to π, *Quarterly Journal of Mathematics* **45**, 350–372, 1914.

[47] Andrew M. Rockett and Peter Szüsz. *Continued Fractions*, World Scientific, Singapore, 1992.

[48] I. J. Schoenberg. On polynomial interpolation at the points of a geometric progression, *Proceedings of the Royal Society of Edinburgh* **90A**, 195–207, 1981.

[49] I. J. Schoenberg. *Mathematical Time Exposures*, The Mathematical Association of America, 1982.

[50] Simon Singh. *Fermat's Last Theorem: The Story of a Riddle that Confounded the World's Greatest Minds for 358 Years*, Fourth Estate, London, 1997.

[51] John Todd. *Basic Numerical Mathematics Vol. 1: Numerical Analysis*, Birkhäuser Verlag, Basel and Stuttgart, 1979.

[52] H. W. Turnbull. *The Great Mathematicians*, Methuen & Co. Ltd., London, 1929.

[53] S. Vajda. *Fibonacci & Lucas Numbers, and the Golden Section: Theory and Applications*, Ellis Horwood, Chichester, 1989.

[54] N. N. Vorob'ev. *Fibonacci Numbers*, Pergamon Press, Oxford, 1961.

[55] Andrew Wiles. Modular elliptic curves and Fermat's last theorem, *Annals of Mathematics (2)* **141**, 443–551, 1995.

Index